THE TIBETAN EMPIRE
IN CENTRAL ASIA

The Tibetan Empire in Central Asia: A History of the Struggle for Great Power among Tibetans, Turks, Arabs, and Chinese during the Early Middle Ages

CHRISTOPHER I. BECKWITH

Princeton University Press
PRINCETON, NEW JERSEY

Published by Princeton University Press,
41 William Street, Princeton, New Jersey 08540
In the United Kingdom: Princeton University Press,
Chichester, West Sussex

Library of Congress Cataloging-in-Publication Data

Beckwith, Christopher I., 1945–
    The Tibetan empire in central Asia: a history of the struggle for great
power among Tibetans, Turks, Arabs, and Chinese during the early Middle
Ages / Christopher I. Beckwith.
        p.   cm.
    "Fourth printing, and first paperback edition, with a new afterword,
1993"—Colophon.
    Includes bibliographical references and index.
    ISBN 0-691-02469-3 (pbk.: alk. paper)
    1. Tibet (China)—History.   2. Asia, Central—History.   I. Title.
DS786.B38   1993   92-36307
951'.5—dc20

Fourth printing, and first paperback edition, with a new afterword, 1993

Publication of this book has been aided by a grant from the Publications
Program of the National Endowment for the Humanities, an independent
Federal agency

10   9   8   7   6   5   4

Printed in the United States of America

CONTENTS

Appendices

Maps

PREFACE

This book is, to my knowledge, the first detailed narrative history of the Tibetan Empire in Central Asia written in any language. If this is so, it may not be necessary to provide excuses for having written it. However, Eurasia is vast, and has many historians. Not a few of them have written synthetic accounts of some aspect of Eurasian history, oftentimes touching upon Tibet. It is more for their sake than for the Tibetologists among them that I have written this preface.

Tibetan historiography is still in its infancy. The few studies of early Tibetan history that do exist are sketchy at best, or are full of unusual interpretations. For this reason, and also because I prefer to derive my opinions from the original source materials—not from long-outdated or unscientific works—I have decided to provide references to the primary sources (so far as they are known to me) to the fullest extent possible. Several relatively recent scholarly studies of early Tibetan history exist, and I have consulted them, as will appear from the footnotes and bibliography. But running references to many previous scholars' discussions of the events are not provided, even when my interpretations differ radically from theirs. No doubt some readers will find this inconvenient, but I felt that this was a necessary evil to be borne if the work were ever to be completed.

A rough draft of this book was completed by the end of the summer of 1983. It was my intention at that time to ignore any publications which might appear during revising and rewriting, and any older ones that I had overlooked. In the fall of that year, however, my colleague Elliot Sperling graciously presented me with a copy of the invaluable compilation of references to Tibet in the *Ts'e fu yüan kuei* by Su Chin-jen and Hsiao Lien-tzu, which was published in Chengtu in 1982. In the following spring, Takao Moriyasu very kindly sent me a copy of his important 1984 article on the Tibetan Empire in Central Asia. During the summer of that year, while revising the manuscript, I took into account these two works whenever possible. Since several other works published in 1983 or earlier had not yet become available (or known) to me by the end of the spring of 1984, of necessity I limited my updating (with few exceptions) to the above two works.

As I mentioned before, in the early stages of writing this book I decided to approach the subject from the primary sources. In early medieval Oriental history, however, these are not technically primary sources at all: they are mainly the surviving narrative accounts, written long after the fact, in Old Tibetan, Arabic, Old Turkic, and Chinese. Indeed, almost all of the Arabic and Chinese material is known solely from late manuscripts and prints and is available only in published typeset editions of uncertain reliability. Thus, I have based my interpretations on my own reading of these sources in all cases except those for which I was unable to see the original-language text, or at least an editor's transcription of it. However much I may have criticized or ignored their productions, I am nevertheless indebted both to the generations of earlier scholars who have worked on these materials, and to the authors of earlier synthetic histories who have attempted to interpret them.

A few specific words are in order on the methods used in writing this book. The narrative is based first of all on a reading of the monumental history of Ssu-ma Kuang, the *Tzu chih t'ung chien*, and the anonymous annalistic chronicle from Tun-huang known as the *Old Tibetan Annals*. My method of using the former work was to scan for proper names, stopping at those related directly to Inner Asia; I read and took extensive notes on all such passages. Later, I compared these notes with the basic annals (*pen chi*) sections of the two official T'ang histories known as the *Chiu T'ang shu* and *Hsin T'ang shu*, and with other Chinese sources. To this material I added information taken from the *Old Tibetan Annals* and *Old Tibetan Chronicle*, from the Old Turkic inscriptions, and from the Arabic histories of Ṭabarî, Balâdhurî, Ibn Aʿtham al-Kûfî, and Azraqî, among others. From these notes, which I modified to reflect the studies of Chavannes, Gibb, Shaban, Mackerras, Satô, and others, I composed my basic text.

With respect to the non-Chinese sources, I have read the whole of the *Old Tibetan Annals* and most of the *Old Tibetan Chronicle*. Thanks are due to Professor Helmut Hoffmann, with whom I had the great pleasure of reading parts of these fascinating texts. His kind loan of photographs made from his microfilm copy enabled me to examine these sources. (The microfilm was in turn procured for him from the Bibliothèque Nationale in Paris through the gratefully acknowledged assistance of Professor R. A. Stein.) I have read all sections of the Old Turkic inscriptions which appeared to be relevant. In doing so, I read the Toñuquq inscription in the original, the others in translation, and then checked them all against the transcribed originals and translations published by Tekin. I have read all the relevant passages in Arabic which I could discover through the use of, on the one hand, the indices, and on the other, the studies by Barthold, Gibb, Shaban, and others. It is probable that I have overlooked important material in the Arabic histories—especially those of Tabarî and Ibn Aʿtham al-Kûfî—because I find it impossible to scan Arabic texts for proper names, and had no time to read several thousand pages of Arabic text on the chance that some piece of useful but previously unnoticed information might be found.

The Epilogue represents my attempt to relate the narrative to better-known areas of medieval history. It is a critical evaluation of the currently accepted view of early medieval Eurasian history;

in it, the Tibetan Empire is placed within the broader context of early medieval world history.

While the present book might seem to be a comprehensive account of the history of early medieval Central Asia, such is not the case. There is a popular misconception that few sources exist for such a history. Actually, for just the history of the Pamirs in the fifth decade of the eighth century, there is enough primary and secondary material (in many languages) to fill a hefty tome. Moreover, except for Uyghur history, nearly everything remains to be done, especially for the period between 750 and 850. I hope that this book will be a stimulus and a starting point for further research and historical writing by those who might seek to correct the mistakes I may have committed. At the very least, they will increase understanding of the great role of Tibet and Central Asia in world history.

ACKNOWLEDGMENTS

I would like to thank all those who in some way helped me to finish this book. Most important are my teachers and friends, especially Helmut Hoffmann, Thubten Jigme Norbu, and Elliot Sperling. Also very generous and helpful have been several overseas colleagues, in particular Takao Moriyasu, Géza Uray, and my student and friend Tsuguhito Takeuchi. For my academic position and frequent summer financial assistance, I am indebted to Gustav Bayerle and Denis Sinor.

In addition, I wish to thank Mr. Roger Purcell and Mr. John M. Hollingsworth, cartographers at Indiana University, for preparing the beautiful maps which accompany the text. I am also indebted to the Indiana University Office of Research and Graduate Development for a summer faculty fellowship in 1982, and for a grant-in-aid. For his meticulous copyediting of the manuscript I would like to thank Andrew Mytelka of Princeton University Press. This is a much better book because of him.

Finally, I thank my wife Connie, my daughter Ming, and my son Lee for giving me the time to work on the book at home.

NOTE ON
TRANSCRIPTION AND
TRANSLATION OF
ORIENTAL
LANGUAGES

For proper names that have well-established English spelling, for place names that have continued in use and thus have modern spellings, and for well-known foreign terms (such as "khan") I have generally retained the traditional forms. In some cases, I have followed convention and used modern rather than medieval place names, for example Aksu (i.e., Aqsu) for Po-huan. I have transcribed other terms according to the following systems.

Tibetan: k, kh, g, ṅ, c, ch, j, ń, t, th, d, n, p, ph, b, m, ts, tsh, dz, w, ź, z, ʿ, y, r, l, ś, s, h, ʾ. (The last letter, the glottal stop, is left unmarked except for cases of possible ambiguity.) Final ʿa *chuṅ* is transcribed "á." I follow in general the commonly used values for consonants and vowels; however, I believe in transcribing Tibetan as a language rather than as an unconnected string of alien syllables haunted by strange practices such as capitalization in the middle of words. Thus, I write Tibetan words as words. This astonishing practice may require a certain amount of adjustment on the part of Tibetologist readers, but then so does all the "strict transliteration" (which is neither strict nor transliteration) of Tibetan that I have ever seen. (Even Greek is not reconvertible from the usual transliteration unless one knows a little of the language.) The two rules I use in transcribing Tibetan words are:

1. When a preceding syllable ends in a vowel, it is connected to the following syllable without a hyphen. If it ends in a consonant, a hyphen is provided to avoid the ambiguity which could result in some cases.
2. All suffixes or dependent morphemes (case suffixes, nominal suffixes, etc.) are connected without hyphens to the syllables preceding them, whether or not the latter end in vowels.

Perhaps the use of this system of transcription will help rid the world of the nonsensical idea, still current, that the Tibetan language—which is, like Japanese, *written* in monosyllables—could possibly be even remotely similar to the "monosyllabic language" that Classical Chinese is commonly supposed to be.

Arabic: ', b, t, th, ǵ, ḥ, kh, d, dh, r, z, s, ś, ṣ, ḍ, ṭ, ẓ, ', gh, q, k, l, m, n, h, w, y. *Alif maqṣûra* is transcribed "á." When giving "strict" transliteration, *alif* is transcribed "â," and an undotted tooth (the base for "b," "t," etc.) is transcribed as a period (".").

Chinese: The modified Wade-Giles system, as used in modern Sinology, is retained. Note that it is the only English-language transcription system that correctly represents the phonetic values of the initial stop consonants in modern Mandarin Chinese (which lacks voiced stops).

Turkic: a, b, c, d, ä, e, i, ï, gh, g, q, k, l, m, n, ń, ng, o, ö, p, r, s, ś, t, u, ü, y, z. When deciding whether to transcribe a Turkic word with "s" or "ś," I have followed the Chinese evidence, where it exists. Some readers may find surprising the large number of Turkic names, taken from Chinese sources, that appear in Turkic form rather than in twentieth-century Mandarin Chinese disguise. While a few of the reconstructions may be incorrect, I decided that it was much better to make an effort to give the original forms of these names when it seemed possible to do so. I encourage those who disagree with my reconstructions to examine them and propose their own. All reconstructions from the Chinese are prefixed with an asterisk. Where the equation is more obvious—as in Chinese I-nan-ju = Turkic Inancu—or has already become widely adopted, no asterisk is provided or further explanation given. More problematic cases are left in their Chinese guise.

All translations from Oriental-language sources are by me, with a few exceptions that are noted in each case. Other translations have been used when my own translation would differ from them only on minor points, although there are undoubtedly many cases where my translations are very close to those of previous writers. As a rule, I have not given references to the numerous existing translations of standard works such as the *T'ang shu* accounts of Tibet and the Turks. Anyone who wishes may consult them easily and compare the translations therein with mine.

NOTE ON
CHRONOLOGY

In order to understand some of the problems of chronology faced
in this book, it is important to remember that in the Middle Ages
writers did not have the same interests as we do. In fact, the per-
spectives and goals of medieval historians are so radically different from our own as to be occasionally incomprehensible. Due to
these differences, as well as to the major differences in methodology, it is quite frequently the case that the medieval historian
omits information just where the modern reader would consider
it most important. More seriously, a great deal of important primary material had already disappeared in the Middle Ages. The
result is that, for example, there is simply no information in any
source on the outcome of a military campaign, who led it, or—to
return to the subject at hand—when exactly it took place. Under
the circumstances, I have attempted to give the most precise dates
possible, but have simply left them off when unavailable.

In addition to the problem of the lack of dates, there is the further problem that the Oriental sources on which this book is
based use lunar calendars, all of them incompatible with each
other and with the Western calendar. The Old Tibetan and Old

Turkic animal years, however, do correspond to the Chinese animal years. In general, Chinese and Muslim dates have been converted according to the tables in Y. Ch'en's *Chung hsi hui shih jih li* (1972). There are still numerous problematic cases, however, which defy simple conversion, and for Tibetan and Old Turkic dating the situation is much more complex.

Although the accepted wisdom on the dates in Chinese records is that they merely indicate the dates on which the given information was received or recorded at court, there is little if any evidence to support such a view with respect to sources on the T'ang. The date of a rendezvous in the Pamirs, for example, could hardly have been recorded as the date the completion of the expedition was reported in Ch'ang-an. Significantly, it is well known that T'ang armies were accompanied by imperial officials whose duties seem to have included record keeping. It would seem much more appropriate to assume—as did medieval Chinese historians such as Ssu-ma Kuang—that the date of an event as recorded in the T'ang chronicles is the date on which the event was supposed to have occurred, unless the source leads one to believe otherwise.

Another characteristic of the Chinese sources, which further complicates their use, is the frequent use of retrospective entries. These entries, which sum up the events preceding the time being described at that place in the chronicle, begin with the most recent event (but this is sometimes omitted!) and then, often without warning, give the background history in chronological order, but usually without precise dates.

The Old Tibetan calendar is still a subject of muted debate. It is clear that it differed radically from the Chinese calendar and from later Tibetan calendars. One Chinese source reports that "they take the ripening of the wheat as the beginning of the year."[1] This is of course not unusual as medieval calendars go, but the lack of precise dates hinders the interpretation of the major Old Tibetan source for political history, the *Annals*, which only begins to indicate the season of the year with the Sheep year 671-

[1] *HTS*, 216a:6063.

672. In this book it is usually assumed that "summer" in the *Annals* refers approximately to the second half of a Western-style year and that "winter" refers approximately to the first half. (Unfortunately, if this interpretation is followed too strictly, a number of events appear to be misdated; and therefore, I have followed a somewhat looser interpretation in practice.) There is very little in the *Annals* that can help in determining exactly how one is to interpret the entries chronologically. To compound these problems, the fragmentary continuation of the *Annals* is missing most of the year names and is out of chronological order as well. Dating problems in this source are noted individually in the text.

The chronology of the Arabic sources presents few technical problems. More serious is the general sparsity of precise dates. Normally, the only date given for an event is the Muslim lunar year, which usually corresponds to parts of two Western years. Obviously there is often a great deal of imprecision in the dates from these works.

As historical sources, the Old Turkic inscriptions have yet to be thoroughly investigated. Until they are, the chronology that may be determined from their contents will remain uncertain. Briefly, the inscriptions date events according to the age of the person in whose honor the text was written; occasionally, it is according to the animal cycle. As a result, dates (when actually given) are usually determined by calculating backward from the year the given individual died. Since the accounts do not give the age of the subject for every event, it is frequently necessary to interpolate, and thus a certain amount of imprecision is unavoidable.

ABBREVIATIONS

AEMA: *Archivum Eurasiae Medii Aevi.*

AHR: *American Historical Review.*

AOH: *Acta Orientalia Academiae Scientiarum Hungaricae.*

Azraqî: Abû al-Walîd Muḥammad b. ʿAbd Allâh al-Azraqî. *Akhbâr Makka*. Mecca, 1965.

Balâdhurî: Abû al-ʿAbbâs Aḥmad b. Yaḥyá b. Ġâbir al-Balâdhurî. *Kitâb futûḥ al-buldân*. Leiden, 1866; repr. Leiden, 1968.

BSO(A)S: *Bulletin of the School of Oriental (and African) Studies.*

CCTC: Li Tsung-t'ung, ed. *Ch'un ch'iu tso chuan chin chu chin i*. 3 vols. Taipei, 1971.

CDT: Ariane Spanien and Yoshiro Imaeda, eds. *Choix de documents Tibétains*. Vol. 2. Paris, 1979.

CHC: *The Cambridge History of China*. Vol. 3. Cambridge, 1979; repr. Taipei, 1979.

CHI: *The Cambridge History of Iran*. Vol. 4. Cambridge, 1975.

CKKCTMTTT: *Chung-kuo ku chin ti-ming ta tz'u-tien*. Shanghai, 1930; repr. Taipei, 1979.

CS: Ling-hu Te-fen. *Chou shu.* 3 vols. Peking, 1971; repr. Taipei, 1974.

CTS: Liu Hsü. *Chiu T'ang shu.* 16 vols. Peking, 1975.

CTW: *Ch'in ting ch'üan T'ang wen.* 21 vols. Kyoto, 1976.

Dhahabî: Muḥammad b. Aḥmad al-Dhahabî. *Ta'rîkh al-Islâm wa ṭabaqât al-maśâhir wa al-aʿlâm.* Cairo, 1947–.

E.I.1:   *Encyclopaedia of Islam.* 1st ed. Leiden, 1913-1934.

E.I.2:   *Encyclopaedia of Islam.* 2d ed. Leiden, 1960–.

EW: *East and West.*

FHG: Carolus Müllerus, ed. *Fragmenta Historicorum Graecorum.* Vol. 4. Paris, 1868.

HHS: Fan Yeh, *Hou Han shu chu.* 5 vols. Peking, 1965; repr. Taipei, 1973.

HTS: Sung Ch'i and Ou-yang Hsiu. *Hsin T'ang shu.* 20 vols. Peking, 1975.

Ibn al-Athîr: ʿIzz al-Dîn Abû al-Ḥasan ʿAlî b. al-Athîr. *Al-kâmil fî al-ta'rîkh.* 13 vols. Beirut, 1965-1967.

Ibn Aʿtham al-Kûfî: Abû Muḥammad Aḥmad b. Aʿtham al-Kûfî. *Kitâb al-futûḥ.* 8 vols. Hyderabad, 1968-1975.

Ibn Khurdâdhbih: ʿUbayd Allâh b. ʿAbd Allâh b. Khurdâdhbih, *Kitâb al-masâlik wa al-mamâlik.* Leiden, 1889; repr. 1967.

JA: *Journal Asiatique.*

JAOS: *Journal of the American Oriental Society.*

JESHO: *Journal of the Economic and Social History of the Orient.*

KDG: Wolfgang Braunfels, ed. *Karl der Grosse: Lebenswerk und Nachleben.* 5 vols. Düsseldorf, 1965-1968.

MD: Dpábo Gtsug-lag ʿphreṅba. *Chos-byuṅ Mkhaspaʿi dgáston.* 2 vols. Delhi, n.d. [1980].

Morohashi: Tetsuji Morohashi. *Dai Kan-Wa jiten.* 13 vols. Tokyo, 1955-1968.

OTA: *The Old Tibetan Annals.* MS Pelliot tibétain 1288 and India Office 750. Reprod. in *CDT,* pls. 579-591.

OTAC: *The Old Tibetan Annals, Continuation.* MS British Museum Or. 8212 (187). Reprod. in *CDT,* pls. 592-595.

OTC: *The Old Tibetan Chronicle.* MS Pelliot tibétain 1287. Reprod. in *CDT,* pls. 557-577.

PS: Li Yen-shou. *Pei shih.* 10 vols. Peking, 1974.

Ptolemaios: Klaudios Ptolemaios. *Geographie 6, 9-12: Ostiran und Zentralasien*. Part 1. Ed. and trans. Italo Ronca. Rome, 1971.

Saṁghavardhana: *Dgra bcompa Dgeʿdun ʿphelgyi luṅ-bstanpa*. In Daisetz T. Suzuki, ed. *The Tibetan Tripitaka: Peking Edition*. Vol. 129 (Tokyo, 1957), 296b-299e [Bstan-hgyur mdo-hgrel skyes-rabs II gtam-yig ṅe: 435r-444r].

SPAW: *Sitzungsberichte der Preussischen Akademie der Wissenschaften* (philologisch-historische Klasse).

SS: Wei Cheng. *Sui shu*. 3 vols. Peking, 1973; repr. Taipei, 1974.

Tabarî: Abû Ġaʿfar Muḥammad b. Ġarîr al-Ṭabarî. *Taʾrîkh al-rusul wa al-mulûk*. 15 vols. Leiden, 1879-1901; repr. Leiden, 1964-1965.

Taishô: *Taishô shinshû daizôkyô*. 85 vols. Tokyo, 1924-1932; repr. Tokyo, 1960-1978.

TCTC: Ssu-ma Kuang. *Tzu chih t'ung chien*. 10 vols. Peking, 1956; repr. Taipei, 1979.

TFYK: Wang Ch'in-jo. *Ts'e fu yüan kuei*. 20 vols. Hong Kong, 1960.

TG: *Tôyô Gakuhô*.

Thaʿâlibî: ʿAbd al-Malik b. Muḥammad al-Thaʿâlibî. *Thimâr al-qulûb*. Cairo, 1965.

TKPSC: Tu Fu. *Tu Kung-pu shih chi*. 2 vols. Taipei, 1966.

TP: *T'oung Pao*.

TSHHR: Michael Aris and Aung San Suu Kyi, eds. *Tibetan Studies in Honour of Hugh Richardson*. Warminster, 1980.

TT: Tu Yu. *T'ung tien*. Shanghai, 1935.

TTHYC: Hsüan Tsang. *Ta T'ang hsi yü chi*. In *Taishô*, Vol. 51 (No. 2087), 867-947.

WC: Chang Chiu-ling. *Ch'ü chiang Chang hsien sheng wen chi*. 4 vols. [Ssu-pu ts'ung-k'an, chi-pu, Vols. 616-623.] Shanghai, n.d.

WKJCC: Yüan Chao. *Wu K'ung ju Chu chi*. In *Taishô*, Vol. 51 (No. 2089), 979-981.

WSTB: *Wiener Studien zur Tibetologie und Buddhismuskunde*. Nos. 10-11. [Ernst Steinkellner and Helmut Tauscher, eds.

Proceedings of the Csoma de Kőrös Symposium Held at Velm-Vienna, Austria, 13-19 September 1981. Vols. 1-2.] Vienna, 1983.

WWTCKC: Hui Ch'ao. *Wang wu T'ien-chu kuo chuan*. In *Taishô*, Vol. 51 (No. 2089), 975-979.

Yaʿqûbî: Aḥmad b. Abî Yaʿqûb al-Yaʿqûbî. *Taʾrîkh al-Yaʿqûbî*. 2 vols. Beirut, 1960.

YHCHTC: Li Chi-fu. *Yüan ho chün hsien t'u chih*. Taipei, 1973; repr. Taipei, 1979.

ZAS: *Zentralasiatische Studien*.

ZDMG: *Zeitschrift der Deutschen Morgenländischen Gesellschaft*.

The reader is directed to the Bibliography for complete citations of the sources not included in this list.

THE TIBETAN EMPIRE
IN CENTRAL ASIA

TIBET AND CENTRAL ASIA BEFORE THE EMPIRE

The mystery of the origins of peoples has fascinated scholars for generations. It is now generally accepted, however, that it is difficult, if not impossible, to identify preliterate archeological remains with specific linguistic groups of today.[1] So it is with the Tibetans. Recent archeological discoveries have shown that the land of Tibet has been occupied by humans from remote prehistoric times, at the least since the microlithic and megalithic periods. To which ethnic group these early Tibetans belonged is unknown. Theories of Tibetan ethnic affinity, as with those of most other peoples, are back-projections derived from conjecture about the linguistic relationship of Tibetan with other languages of Asia.[2]

[1] For more information on the background to the rise of the Tibet Empire, see my dissertation, "A Study of the Early Medieval Chinese, Latin, and Tibetan Historical Sources on Pre-Imperial Tibet" (1977). There is as yet no convenient book or survey-article on the recent archeological discoveries in Tibet.

[2] Theories about the linguistic affinities of Tibetan are not as numerous as one might expect, considering the location of Tibet and the unusual charac-

3

Tibet is surrounded by Indo-European speakers on the south and west; by Turkic and Mongolic (in ancient times, by Indo-European) speakers on the north and northeast; by Chinese on the east; and by Burmese speakers (in ancient times, also Thai, Malayo-Polynesian, and others) on the southeast. By its very location, therefore, it would seem that whatever language group (if any) Tibetan is to be connected with, the choices are not limited to Chinese. Even a brief acquaintance with the language itself would lead one to suspect some sort of relationship with Indo-European and Mongolic, although neither of these language families has received much attention in this regard.[3] Although it is of

---

teristics of the language. The dominant "Sino-Tibetan" theory—one that has never been articulated in a professional work of comparative-historical linguistic scholarship—attempts to force Tibetan into a "family" along with Chinese, Thai, and Burmese, Although numerous revisionists have eliminated Thai from their systems, contemporary political-racial considerations (rather than linguistic ones) seem to be keeping Tibetan bound to Chinese. (It is worth pointing out, incidentally, that no one seems to have disputed the probable relationship with Burmese, despite the fact that the latter affinity has also never been scientifically demonstrated.) One could perhaps consider the work of A. Conrady (*Eine indo-chinesische Causativ-Denominativ-Bildung und ihr Zusammenhang mit den Tonaccenten* [1896]) to be an attempt at a serious comparative-historical theory of relationship among the above four language groups. Unfortunately, when compared to work done in the field of Indo-European linguistics, even with that of his contemporaries, Conrady's book falls short. It has, moreover, been almost a full century since Conrady's work was published; yet nothing has been written to improve upon it.

[3] The Tibetan verbal system is strongly reminiscent of Germanic tongues, but the language exhibits systemically entrenched proto-Indo-Iranian vocabulary. Together, these features indicate a relationship with the *divergent* "Indo-European" group, but the agglutinative grammatical structure, among other features (especially of modern spoken Tibetan), indicates a relationship with languages of the *convergent* "Altaic" group. (On the terminology used here, see the following note.) Vocabulary and some other features do indicate a probable relationship of some sort with Burmese (and Tangut, if it was in fact a language of the "Burmic" type). Any divergent relationship with Chinese is unlikely—although still conceivable for the remotest prehistoric times—for just about every possible reason. (That modern Central Tibetan dialects have phonemic "tones" is only indicative of Tibet's physical location in an area of the world—Eastern Eurasia—where nearly all languages that have been there very long [beside Chinese, also

course possible that Tibetan is divergently related to Chinese, it is rather unlikely, and in any case probably unprovable. As the most perceptive linguist writing on the subject has shown, the most strenuous recent efforts expended in demonstrating a relationship have been quite unsuccessful. The fact is, even if the Tibetan and Chinese language families were ultimately divergently related, they would have had to have split into two distinct groups many thousands of years ago, long before the creation of any linguistic remains that could help prove or disprove such affinity.[4]

The first historical references to people later identified—rightly or wrongly—as Tibetans are to be found in much later literary records. The earliest of these are the references in the Shang Chinese oracle-bone inscriptions, from around four thousand years ago, to a people called Ch'iang.[5] They are supposed to have been nomadic—the name Ch'iang is a Chinese word that combines the signs for Sheep and Man—but extremely little is known about them. Their successors in the Chinese records are known as the Chiang, who lived in and around the area of present-day northwest China, but were considered to be non-Chinese. They spoke foreign languages and dressed differently from the

---

Thai, Burmese, Vietnamese, and Japanese, among others] have tonal systems.) The whole subject of comparative-historical linguistics of non-Indo-European languages is very much underdeveloped, especially with respect to methodology. In short, it is uncertain what languages Tibetan *is* related to, but anyone with a knowledge of both comparative-historical linguistics and the Tibetan and Chinese languages (the pillars of the "Sino-Tibetan" theory) has great difficulty imagining that two such radically different tongues could be genetically related.

[4] See R. Miller's review of R. Shafer, *Introduction to Sino-Tibetan* (1968). I use the term "divergently" instead of "genetically" for two reasons. Firstly, the latter term has racial (and today, political) overtones that have nothing to do with linguistics. Secondly, the former term refers to one of the two types of linguistic relationship, namely, divergent and convergent. It is clear that in some cases convergence is a more active factor in linguistic change than divergence. Of course, any two languages that are in contact are constantly diverging and converging at different rates.

[5] See, among other works, S. Shirakawa, *Kōkotsubun no seikai* (1972) 171-185.

Chinese.[6] Then, in classical antiquity, the Ch'iang reappear under their earlier name, and are firmly established on the eastern marches of Tibet.

What may have been a crucial formative influence on the proto-Tibetans was the migration of the people known in Chinese sources as the *Hsiao-* (or "Little"-) Yüeh-chih, a branch of the *Ta-* (or "Great"-) Yüeh-chih. After defeat by the Hsiung-nu in the second century B.C., the Ta-Yüeh-chih migrated to Bactria, and are generally identified with the Tokharians, who according to Greek sources invaded and conquered Bactria at just that time. Those among them who were unable to make the trip moved instead into the Nan Shan area, where they mixed with the Ch'iang tribes, and became like them in customs and language.[7] Unfortunately, we know nothing substantial about the customs of the early Tokharians, and cannot guess what sorts of practices and beliefs they may have introduced.

The Ch'iang of classical times eventually became a military power along the edge of the early Silk Road. Especially during the Later Han dynasty, the Chinese were continually worried about a possible linkup between the Ch'iang and the nomadic Hsiung-nu of the northern side of the trade routes. But in the

---

[6] *CCTC*, II:842-844. The character Chiang, undoubtedly the result of ta-boo-avoidance of the name Ch'iang, is composed of the signs for Sheep and Woman.

[7] *HHS*, 87:2899. See B. Watson, *Records of the Grand Historian of China, Translated from the Shih Chi of Ssu-ma Ch'ien* (1961) 2:163, 264, 267-268, for a translation of the famous account of the fall of the Ta-Yüeh-chih. It is my opinion that the Chinese name Ta-Yüeh-chih was etymologized by the ancient Chinese to give a convenient name to those who had settled in the Nan Shan. If the Greek transcription Thagouroi (i.e., T'a-gur if converted to a Chinese-style notation)—for a people thought to be in the area of the Nan Shan—is indeed a reflection of the name of these "Lesser" Tokharians, one could not object to the vowel of the initial *Ta-*. A form *gar* lies behind the T'ang-period *Yüeh* according to the earliest phonetic transcriptions of Chinese, the T'ang-period Tibetan-script works. The final *-chih* may be either a Central Asian ending, as thought by some scholars, or the Chinese word (the same character, pronounced in all other cases *shih*) meaning "clan" or "family."

long run neither Ch'iang nor Hsiung-nu were able to seriously endanger the Han state.[8]

The one notable occurrence during this period was the first mention in either Western or Eastern historical sources of the native ethnonym of Tibet. Klaudios Ptolemaios, the Hellenistic father of the science of mathematically precise geography, mentioned a people called Baitai, or (more correctly) Bautai—i.e., the "Bauts." The same people are described by the later Greco-Roman writer Ammianus Marcellinus as having lived "on the slopes of high mountains to the south" of another people in the area of Serica (East Asia).[9] At the same time, Chinese sources recorded that certain Ch'iang tribesmen, after their defeat by the Chinese, escaped deep into the Tibetan interior, where they took refuge with a Ch'iang group whose name is today pronounced Fa, but was in classical times pronounced something like Puat.[10] The latter was undoubtedly intended to represent Baut, the name that became pronounced by seventh-century Tibetans as Bod (and now, in the modern Lhasa dialect, rather like the French *peu*).[11] Unfortunately, several centuries were to pass before anyone was to record the name again.

During the Great Migration of Peoples, which affected the classical East as well as the West, Ch'iang leaders were among those who established more or less ephemeral states on Chinese territory.[12] It seems fairly clear that these Ch'iang were ethnically

[8] See the recent studies by T. Kuan, "Han-tai ch'u-li Ch'iang-tsu wen-t'i ti pan-fa ti chien-t'ao" (1971-1972).

[9] Ptolemaios, 56. For an extensive discussion of the classical material see Beckwith, 1977:22 et seq.

[10] *HHS*, 87:2884-2885; cf. *HHS*, 87-2898: "The Fa Ch'iang, T'ang-mao, and so forth are very distant (from China); there has never been any communication (between the two nations)." B. Karlgren, *Grammata Serica Recensa* (1957) 86, reconstructs the ancient pronunciation of the character Fa as *$p\underset{\smile}{i}w\hat{a}t$. Note that the "$\underset{\smile}{i}$" of Karlgren's reconstructions is a conventional symbol and does not necessarily indicate an articulated phone.

[11] An important consideration here is the Indic form of the name, Bhauṭṭa, which is phonetically comparable to the classical Western and Eastern transcriptions of the name Bod.

[12] An unpublished (and to me, at least, unavailable) dissertation by Mar-

unrelated to the Tibetan-speaking people who founded the Tibetan Empire in the seventh century of our era. In any event, Tibetans and "Ch'iang" from the early seventh century onward
were and are without question linguistically—and, apparently,
culturally—unrelated peoples. Since the traditional Chinese theory of the Tibetans' relationship to the ancient Ch'iang is explicitly based on precisely this seventh-century identification, it must
be concluded that the Tibetan ethnos has no certain connection
with the Ch'iang as a group, but only—perhaps—with the people
who were called Fa Ch'iang in late classical Chinese sources.

More to the point, it is stated in the *Old Tibetan Chronicle* that
Sroṅ btsan sgampo's father, Gnam ri slon mtshan, and his people
conquered the region of "Rtsaṅ-Bod." This is generally believed
to be the equivalent of modern Ü-tsang,[13] the south-central
heartland of Tibet. In other words, the Tibetans of Gnam ri slon
mtshan—who never call him "king of Bod" in the *Chronicle* but
always "king of Spu," and refer to themselves as poor southern
farmers who conquered the rich northern herders—did not originally have the ethnonym Bod, but acquired it by conquest.[14] In
sum, the Tibetan people are probably as autochthonous as any
other people of Eurasia. But knowledge of where they originally
came from, and to which other peoples they are related, is now
lost in the mists of time.

The early medieval Tibetan armies, like their contemporaries
in Arabia, marched northward to conquer first the contiguous
lands which were similar to their homeland. Only afterwards did
they march further north into the lands of Central Asia and beyond. There they met two cultures: a sedentary one of highly civ-

---

garet Inver Scott ("A Study of the Ch'iang with Special Reference to Their
Settlements in China from the Second to the Fifth Century A.D. [University
of Cambridge, 1953]) presumably has dealt with the subject in great detail.
In addition, the excellent book of E. Zürcher, *The Buddhist Conquest of China*
(1972), despite mistakenly lumping Ti and Ch'iang together and calling them
all Tibetans, may be consulted with great profit.

[13] Now written Dbus-gtsaṅ. The second syllable was regularly written
rtsaṅ in Old Tibetan.

[14] See Beckwith, 1977:208, 232, 260.

ilized Buddhist Indo-Europeans, and a nomadic one of Buddhist-influenced Turkic and Mongolic steppe-warriors. Central Asia was in those days fast becoming the focus of economic, intellectual, and political activity in Eurasia. Although its location had made it important for international trade since antiquity, it was only with the economic resurgence of the sixth and seventh centuries that Central Asia became of fundamental importance for the history of Eurasia.

Since classical times, Ptolemy's geographical division of Central Asia into two parts—"the two Skythias"—has been recognized by Western writers. For centuries, the geographical division was not reflected by any sharp differences among the common Indian-, Persian-, and Chinese-influenced Buddhist cultures. But by the time the Tibetans surfaced as a unified people, geography once again had come to play a significant role. In the early seventh century, Central Asia was divided into several fairly distinct regions. The major division of classical times—into an Eastern and a Western half—was still culturally relevant with respect to Eastern Skythia (or the Tarim Basin countries) and one part of ancient Western Skythia, namely Ṭukhâristân (in ancient times, Bactria), a country which was in large part coterminous with modern Afghanistan and the southernmost part of Soviet Central Asia. These two regions, connected directly by the lofty Wakhan Corridor, maintained their Buddhist traditions. But the economic heartland of Central Asia, Sogdiana, had replaced Buddhism with a local creed which included many Buddhist elements, although it seems clear that Buddhism continued to be active there for several centuries. A fourth region, the lands between Ṭukhâristân and Persia, was at the time under the rule of the Persian Sassanid dynasty, and thus under pressure to adopt the official Zoroastrian religion.

The conquest of most of western Central Asia by the Turks in the late sixth century was of fundamental economic importance because it linked Central Asia to the major peripheral civilizations of Eurasia—Europe, Persia, India, and China.[15] But this conquest

[15] See the Epilogue to this book.

actually had very little effect on the ethnicity of the region, although it may have affected some other aspects of the indigenous culture. By the early seventh century, for example, Turkic political influence in Sogdiana and eastern Central Asia, originally reinforced by intermarriage with the local ruling houses, had practically disappeared. When the nomadic Turks again intervened in Central Asia (in the seventh century and later), either on their own behalf or in the employ of the Arabs or Chinese, they were viewed culturally as foreigners.[16] Nonetheless, prosperity followed in the wake of their partly successful attempt to unify the lands of the silk routes. And the prosperity of these Central Asian lands drew the attention of the Greeks, the Arabs, the Chinese, and the Tibetans.

[16] The best survey of the history of the Turks in Central Asia during the sixth and seventh centuries is still that in É. Chavannes, *Documents sur les Toukiue (Turcs) occidentaux* (1903) 217-303.

Chapter 1

ENTRANCE INTO CENTRAL ASIA

The origin of the Yarlung dynasty, the family which was to end up ruling the vast dominions of the Tibetan Empire, is still quite unknown. The *Old Tibetan Chronicle* does not say when the kings of this family began to rule a significant part of Tibet, nor does it hint about any possible foreign ancestry.[1] According to all early

[1] Despite its accepted location deep in the heart of the agricultural south, it has long been believed that the Tibetan state was founded by the descendants of alien or partly alien nomadic steppe-warriors. See for example H. Hoffmann, *Tibet: A Handbook* (1975) 39-40. While there may have been some ultimately foreign influence on the early Tibetans—the Hsiao-Yüeh-chih, for example, moved into the area of northeastern Amdo in mid-classical antiquity (see Watson, 1961, 2:268)—there are absolutely no indications of this hypothetical nomadic structure in south-central Tibet during the time of Gnam ri slon mtshan and his successors. The contemporary Tibetan sources are silent on nomads, nomadism, and steppe-warriors. Moreover, everything in the Chinese sources (with the exception of the *topos* applied to nearly every foreign people—partially true for Tibetans, to be sure—that they wandered in search of grass and water) indicates that the Chinese were well aware that the Tibetans were not primarily a nomadic people. Both Tibetan and Chinese sources remark on the castles built by various Tibetan emperors—surely evidence of their nonmobile lifestyle. These sources further

11

I. Early Medieval Central Asia

reports, the first king came down from the sky;[2] therefore, the sacral character of the dynasty[3] as well as its autochthony may be considered well established. In fact, of the long list of kings who are supposed to have lived and ruled on earth, the earliest who can be considered even partly historical is Dri gum btsanpo, because he inadvertently cut the "sky-rope" which had allowed his predecessors to return to heaven upon the end of their respective reigns. So he died indeed, and was buried in a tomb.[4] There follows in all of the sources another long list of shadowy kings before ascertainably historical personages emerge, and true Tibetan history begins.

In the Phyiṅba district of ʿPhyoṅs-rgyas, a small side-valley of the Yarlung River, which is itself a tributary of the great Gtsaṅpo or Brahmaputra, the feudal lord Stagbu sña gzigs[5] had his castle, named Stag rtse ("Tiger Peak").[6] He was probably no more than a *primus inter pares* in that deeply cloven southern part of the Tibetan Plateau. His subjects were not at all wealthy—they were farmers,[7] and Tibet is a hard land for agriculture—but the account in the *Old Tibetan Chronicle* reveals that this prince had extensive contacts with nobles of distant clans.[8] These clan chiefs—

---

state that early Tibetan methods of warfare were totally non-nomadic: warriors wore full suits of heavy iron chain mail, and dismounted to do battle. (See *TT*, 190:1023; *HTS*, 216a:6073; and below, Chapter Five.)

[2] In addition to *OTC* and other Old Tibetan sources, see Gardîzî's *Zayn al-Akhbâr*. The section dealing with Tibet has been newly translated by P. Martinez in "Gardîzî's Two Chapters on the Turks" (1982) 128-131. Gardîzî says (p. 130): "the Xāqān of Tibet (*Töböt Xāqān*) pretends that he has come from heaven and has a cuirass [made] of light."

[3] On sacral knigship in early Tibet, see G. Tucci, "La regalità sacra nell'antico Tibet" (1959).

[4] See H. Hoffmann, "Die Gräber der tibetischen Könige im Distrikt 'Pʿyoṅs-rgyas" (1950), and G. Tucci, *The Tombs of the Tibetan Kings* (1950).

[5] His name is given as Stag ri gñan gzigs in *MD*, ja:11v (p. 172).

[6] The full name of the castle is Phyiṅba stag rtse.

[7] In a song in *OTC*, iv, the minister Zu tse sings "In the beginning, Pyiṅ [i.e., Phyiṅba] had (only) wheat; now [lit., 'finally'] it has been surrounded with yaks." In Inner Asia, nomads have traditionally been considered wealthier than farmers; for example, most of the words for "wealth" in Tibetan are words for "cattle" (typically, yaks) as well.

[8] For example, the Khyuṅpo and Myaṅ clans. (*OTC*, iv).

referred to in the Old Tibetan sources and later histories as "ministers"—held positions of trust with, or were vassals of, another powerful feudal lord known as Dgu gri Ziṅporje. According to the *Chronicle*, he was the overlord of Ṅaspo, the region between present-day ʿPhanpo and Rkoṅpo north of the Brahmaputra, and was apparently the vassal in turn of the Lig-myi dynasty, whose shadowy Źaṅ-źuṅ confederation ruled most of Tibet at the time. It so happened that several of the Ziṅporje's noblemen became disenchanted with his rule due to his preference for evil ministers and his highhanded and unfair treatment of virtuous vassals. A group of conspirators managed to convince Stagbu sña gzigs that he would benefit from joining with them to overthrow the Ziṅporje. At this point, however, he died,[9] and negotiations had to begin again with his son and successor, Gnam ri slon mtshan.

Gnam ri needed no convincing, but he and his brother asked for and got sworn oaths of allegiance from all of the conspirators. According to the text of this oath, as represented in the *Chronicle*, they swore that ". . . from now on, they would renounce the Ziṅporje forever, they would always cherish Spurgyal, they would never be disloyal to Emperor[10] Spurgyal, they would

---

[9] On these events see *OTC*, iii.

[10] The term "emperor" translates the Tibetan title *btsanpo*. The equivalence of this term with the Chinese term for "emperor" has been well known since the publication of P. Pelliot's study of a short Old Tibetan text from Tun-huang, in his posthumous *Histoire ancienne du Tibet* (1961) 143. Unfortunately, several writers have continued to translate *btsanpo* as "king" or in any case have not yet begun to use the precise terminology that reflects the early medieval meaning of this word. The English word "king" (and its equivalents in other modern languages) is translated by the Tibetan *rgyalpo*. Although in postimperial Tibetan writings, after the title *btsanpo* had fallen out of use, the Tibetan emperors were often called *rgyalpo*, this is an inaccuracy on the part of later Tibetan writers and should not cause confusion today. As reported by Pelliot, the title *btsanpo* is translated in a contemporary Old Tibetan-Chinese glossary as "Son of Heaven," i.e., "Emperor." To quote the glossary: "*Bodkyi btsanpo* [:] *Tʼu-fan tʼien tzu*." Literally, this means: "[Tibetan:] The Emperor (*btsanpo*) of Tibet = [Chinese:] The Emperor (Tʼien tzu, 'Son of Heaven') of Tibet." "Son of Heaven" was, of course, the Chinese title for *Chinese* emperors. The same translation occurs in a Tʼang-period biography of a Chinese who had been a prisoner of the Tibetans for

never consider power, they would always wish to cope with his directions, they would never want to conspire, they would never doubt, they would always be brave, they would never want to abandon the life (of the Emperor), whatever Emperor Slon btsan [Gnam ri slon mtshan] ordered they would always listen, and although someone else enticed them they would never listen."[11]

The seriousness of such an oath cannot be underestimated. According to Chinese reports, these men became the sworn companions of the *btsanpo*, the sacred ruler, in life and in death. The account in the *Hsin T'ang shu* describes this: "Their lord and his ministers—five or six persons, called 'common-fated ones'—make friends with each other. When the lord dies, they all commit suicide to be buried with him; and the things he wore, baubles he enjoyed, and horses he rode, all are buried with him."[12]

---

several years, but had served the Tibetan emperor in some capacity. The prisoner's title was translated into Chinese as *T'ien tzu chia ch'en*, which may be rendered into English as "Chamberlain to the Son of Heaven." On this, see L. Chao's *Yin hua lu* (1958) 97, and the interesting study of this biography by E. Sperling, "A Captivity in Ninth Century Tibet" (1979). It may be noted that H. Satô and T. Moriyasu regularly translate *btsanpo* into Japanese with the word *ô* (in Chinese, read *wang*). For example Satô, in his recent work *Chibetto rekishi chiri kenkyû* (1978) 420, equates the word *ô* with *btsanpo*: ". . . *kono ôkoku no ô* (= *tsenpo*)," which would normally be understood as "this kingdom's king (= *tsenpo*)." (Note that *tsenpo* is his transcription of *btsanpo*.) Moriyasu, in "Toban no Chûô Ajia shinshutsu" (1984) passim, also translates it with *ô*. However, in a personal communication, Professor Moriyasu has informed me that this practice, common among Japanese scholars, *does* recognize the correct understanding of the word *btsanpo*. He says, ". . . we Japanese scholars . . . use *ô* . . . as a *Japanese* word, which has [a] much broader meaning than the Chinese counterpart; we use *ô* to mean not only 'king; prince', but also 'ruler, sovereign'. In Japanese-Japanese dictionaries, *ô* is equated to *ôkimi* . . . which means Japanese Emperor *tennô*. . . . Thus, when we translate *btsanpo* [as] *ô*, we do not exclude the meaning of 'emperor'. . . . We are quite conscious of this aspect but we prefer to avoid [using] the word *tennô* . . . because of its connotation." Finally, the Arabs usually say the title of the ruler of Tibet is Khâqân, i.e., Qaghan, and explain that he had the imperial dignity over the Turks.

[11] *OTC*, iv.

[12] *HTS*, 216a:6073; cf. Pelliot, 1961:81-82, and *CTS*, 196a:5220: "When the btsanpo dies, they bury people with him; things like the clothing, pre-

Having thus sworn fealty in true medieval Central Eurasian fashion,[13] it only remained for the conspirators to carry out their plan. With the aid of surprise, they overthrew the Ziṅporje and frightened his son into fleeing to Turkistan. If, as seems quite possible, this last event actually took place, it represents the earliest Tibetan contact with a Central or Inner Asian people known from Tibetan historical sources. Thanks to the initial victories against the Ziṅporje, and subsequently in Dwagspo, Gnam ri slon mtshan gained great personal prestige. He was soon able to push his conquests into the region immediately to the west, called Rtsaṅ-Bod, by defeating its lord Mar-mun, another vassal of Źaṅ-źuṅ.[14]

This first mention of the name Bod, the usual name for Tibet in the later Tibetan historical sources, is significant in that it is used to refer to a conquered region.[15] In other words, the ancient name Bod originally referred to only a part of the Tibetan Plateau, a part which, together with Rtsaṅ (Tsang, in Tibetan now spelled Gtsaṅ), has come to be called Dbus-gtsaṅ (Central Tibet).[16] The early kings of Yarlung were, as they themselves say, southerners.[17] They conquered first Central Tibet and then the

---

cious trinkets, and horses and swords used by him, they bury them all." (Cf. Pelliot, 1961:3.) Apparently early on in the Tibetan imperial period the influence of Buddhism altered this practice so that the ones slated to die did not actually die. Instead, they were considered to be ritually dead, and were confined to the burial precinct to live out their days on donations. (See D. Snellgrove and H. Richardson, *A Cultural History of Tibet* [1968] 52-53.) In spite of both of these ritual practices, one must note that Sroṅ btsan sgampo was not killed upon his son's accession; he reappeared after the death of Guṅ sroṅ guṅ brtsan, who ruled only five years. See note 31, below.

[13] See my article, "Aspects of the Early History of the Central Asian Guard Corps in Islam" (1984a).

[14] *OTC*, iv. In *OTC*, ii, Gnam ri's minister, Moṅ Khri do re maṅ tshab, is given credit for this deed.

[15] Note that the territory of the Ziṅporje centered on the Skyi Chu and 'Phanpo, according to *OTC*, ii.

[16] Bod was often used even in modern times to refer to "Central Tibet." (See also the discussion in the Introduction.)

[17] Minister Źaṅ snaṅ even sings about the "southern bamboo" defeating the yak, the symbol of the nomadic north (*OTC*, iv).

rest of the Tibetan Plateau, except for those regions already allied to them by marriage or personal oaths of fealty. Much of the success of these campaigns, particularly those in the west and northeast, must be credited to a political-military genius, the minister Khyuṅpo Spuṅ-sad Zutse. He was no doubt self-serving, ruthless, and quick to commit murder (especially by deceit), as the Tibetan histories claim. But he did help build for the *btsanpo* the foundations of empire.

The newly united and vigorous state, still referred to as the realm of "the Spurgyal, the Btsanpo Gnam ri slon mtshan," was now only separated from China in the east by minor tribes. In the northeast around the Koko Nor, however, stood the powerful empire of the nomadic Mongolic-speaking people of northern origin known as the Togon or ʿAźa in Tibetan,[18] and as the T'u-yü-hun, T'ui-hun, or A-ch'ai in Chinese.[19] Some of the predominantly nomadic tribal peoples in between were subjects of the ʿAźa; others were vassals of the new Tibetan state.[20]

The first contacts of Tibetans with the outside world, so far as can be determined from foreign sources, were two embassies sent to China in 608 and 609. These embassies must ultimately be connected with the outcome of a war between the Chinese and the ʿAźa. To summarize the events very briefly, the emperor Yang-ti of the Sui dynasty wanted control of the routes to the West. But dominion over the three existing routes was then divided between the Turks and the ʿAźa.[21] In the mid-fifth century, the T'u-yü-hun had conquered at least the southeastern portion of the

[18] See G. Uray, "The Annals of the ʿA-ža Principality" (1978). On their language, see L. Ligeti, "Le Tabghatch" (1970) and the manuscript Fonds Pelliot tibétain 1283, published in J. Bacot, "Reconnaissance en haute Asie septentrionale par cinq envoyés ouigours au VIIIᵉ siècle" (1957) lines 28-29, where the languages (and cultural features that are mentioned) of the Khitan and T'u-yü-hun are said to be more or less the same. Cf. the study of this valuable text by Moriyasu in "Chibetto-go shiryô chû ni arawareru Hoppô minzoku——Dru-gu to Hor——" (1977a) 21, 34.

[19] Cf. G. Molè, *The T'u-yü-hun from the Northern Wei to the Time of the Five Dynasties* (1970).

[20] *SS*, 83:1859; cf. *PS*, 96:3194.

[21] Molè, 1970:150 (n. 378).

Tarim Basin, and had even extended their influence as far as Kho-tan.[22] Some of that control yet remained at the beginning of the seventh century. Yang-ti therefore had his minister P'ei Chü persuade a neighboring group of T'ieh-le Turks to attack the ʿAźa. Since the ʿAźa were their enemies, the Turks were more than happy to oblige: in the seventh month (August 17 to September 14) of 608, the Turks inflicted a severe defeat on them.[23] In the following year, the Chinese armies, under the personal direction of Yang-ti, pressed into T'u-yü-hun territory. On July 5, 609, the Chinese crushed the ʿAźa forces and captured two of their cities.[24] The great majority of the people surrendered to the Chinese, bringing with them their livestock. The ʿAźa ruler (the qaghan) and a small band of his supporters fled to the Great Snow Mountains and sought refuge among the Tanguts.[25] With this overwhelming triumph, the Chinese had conquered all the territory up to the tribes that then separated the Tibetan state from the ʿAźa.

It is thus no coincidence that the Tibetans chose the year 608 to send their first embassy to the Chinese court. The Chinese sources record only that: "In the fourth year of the Ta-yeh period, their king sent a total of eight persons—the envoy Su fu and others—to go to court. The next year, he again sent his servant I-lin to lead sixty Chia-liang *i* [foreigners] to give tribute. They wanted to present their fine horses, but because the roads were dangerous and blocked, they requested that a mountain road be opened in order to improve the giving of tribute. Yang-ti . . . did not give his consent."[26] Since the second embassy proceeded to the Chinese court through the Chia-liang, or Rgyaroṅ,[27] country

[22] Molè, 1970:xv, has mistakenly enlarged their conquest.

[23] *TCTC*, 181:5641. Cf. Molè, 1970:44, 146 (n. 370).

[24] *TCTC*, 181:5644; Molè, 1970:148-149 (n. 378). These "cities" (Ch'ih-shui *ch'eng* and Wan-t'ou *ch'eng*—cf. Molè, 1970:102 [n. 125], 133 [n. 281]) seem to have been real cities, and not merely fortresses.

[25] Molè 1970:44-45, 48. The ethnonym "Tangut" is used herein to refer to the people usually called Tang-hsiang by the T'ang Chinese.

[26] *SS*, 83:1859.

[27] On the identification of Chia-liang *i* with Rgya-roṅ, see Beckwith, 1977:128 et seq.

and the then southwesternmost Chinese province of Shu[28] (the Szechuan Basin)—a substantial detour—it is quite obvious that a struggle between the Tibetans and the ʿAźa was already underway. The veiled reference to an intermediate enemy who prevented the Tibetans from gaining easy access to Chinese markets (the "giving of tribute" of the source[29]) hints perhaps at the real purpose of the embassy. Subsequently the Sui established at the edge of their expanding territory the office of *chu tao tsung kuan* in order, the *Sui shu* says, "to watch over (the Tibetans) from afar."[30]

It was not long after that the deaths of both Sui Yang-ti (in 618) and Gnam ri slon mtshan (probably in the same year)[31] forced the matter of Sino-Tibetan relations into the background. While Tibet and China were thus undergoing a period of internal political turmoil, the ʿAźa freed themselves from the Chinese yoke and regained much of their lost power.[32] The reign of Khri sroṅ brtsan, who succeeded to the throne upon the death of his father Gnam ri slon mtshan, marked the rise of the young kingdom to the status of an empire, which was now known to the world as "Tibet."[33] Henceforth, neighboring states—even haughty

[28] *SS*, 83:1858-1859.

[29] See for example *CHC*, 3:500, and C. Suzuki, "China's Relations with Inner Asia" (1968).

[30] *SS*, 83:1859; *PS*, 96:3194.

[31] Assuming that Tibetan emperors were normally at least thirteen years old at the time of their accession. Since according to Tibetan historians, the heir apparent ascended the throne upon reaching the age of thirteen—when the father "died" or was killed (see Hoffmann, 1975:40-41)—this age can be taken as an absolute minimum. Thus, assuming he was at least thirteen years old when he sent his first embassy to China, Sroṅ btsan sgampo could not have been born any later than 621. Since *his* son, Guṅ sroṅ guṅ brtsan, ascended at age thirteen (as the sources relate) and reigned five years—see W. Shakabpa, *Tibet: A Political History* (1967) 27—the son must have been born no later than 628. Because Sroṅ btsan sgampo took the throne upon the death of his father, it would appear that Gnam ri slon mtshan could have died no later than 618. Shakabpa, relying upon several Tibetan sources, arrives at the date A.D. 617 for Gnam ri's death (Shakabpa, 1967:25). This discrepancy may be due to the fact that the Tibetan year does not correspond exactly to the Western year. See above, note 12.

[32] G. Molè, 1970:48.

[33] The Chinese name now pronounced T'u-fan transcribes the same for-

China—were to deal with Tibet on an equal level, and actually refer to the *btsanpo* either by his Tibetan title or, in unofficial writings, with Chinese terms meaning "emperor."[34] The spread of Tibetan power soon left them little choice.

The young ruler, popularly known as Sroṅ btsan sgampo in Tibetan histories, quickly put down the rebellion that accompanied his father's death by poisoning.[35] He then began the systematic reduction of all opposition to his rule on the Tibetan Plateau. Myaṅ Maṅporje Źaṅ snaṅ, the prime minister he had inherited from his father, assisted greatly in this work by subjugating the Sumpas, former allies from the northeast who had revolted.[36] Marriage alliances, such as that with still-powerful Źaṅ-źuṅ, and murders of convenience, including probably that of his much-too-powerful minister Zutse, complemented the military campaigns. Soon after Sroṅ btsan sgampo's sister, Sad mar kar, was married to Lig-myi rhya, the king of Źaṅ-źuṅ,[37] an opportunity for intrigue presented itself; she led her unsuspecting husband into an ambush in which he was killed and his army defeated.[38] With this victory, Sroṅ btsan sgampo became the master of the high Tibetan Plateau.

During this period, while the tumultuous transition from the Sui to the T'ang dynasties was taking place in China, the once-again independent ʿAźa apparently left the Chinese alone.[39] When the militaristic T'ang emperor T'ai-tsung finally took the

---

eign name "Tibet," but has nothing whatsoever to do with the country's native name, Bod, as was proven conclusively half a century ago by Pelliot. One may add to that the corollary that the word Bon (the name of one of the two types of Tibetan Buddhism) is equally unrelated to the name "Tibet" (especially in its Chinese transcription, T'u-fan), and probably to Bod as well. See Pelliot, "Quelques transcriptions chinoises de noms tibétains" (1915) 18-20, and Beckwith, 1977:118-126.

[34] Beckwith, 1977:161-163 (n. 77).

[35] *OTC*, vi.

[36] *OTC*, v.

[37] *OTC* viii. See G. Uray, "Queen Sad-mar-kar's Songs in the Old Tibetan Chronicle" (1972).

[38] *OTC*, viii.

[39] Very little is said about the ʿAźa during this period in Chinese sources.

throne, however, he cast his eyes westward. The ʿAźa sent embassies to the T'ang court offering nominal submission. But after a few of their raids on Chinese border towns—so we are told by the Chinese sources—T'ai-tsung organized a punitive expedition composed of Chinese border troops and levies of Ch'i-pi Turks[40] and Tanguts in July 634.[41] On October 29th of that year, the army, under the command of Tuan Chih-hsüan, Grand General of the Courageous Guard of the Left and Commander-in-Chief of the Hsi Hai *tao* Expeditionary Army,[42] attacked and defeated the ʿAźa and pursued them for over 800 *li*.[43] Much booty, in the form of livestock, was captured.[44]

Immediately after the attack, the Tibetan emperor sent an embassy to the Chinese court. It arrived on December 11, 634.[45] The sources unfortunately say nothing about this embassy of the Tibetans to the T'ang, so whatever its message there is no way to tell if it affected Chinese policy towards the ʿAźa at this time. A Chinese ambassador, Feng Te-hsia, was, however, sent to Tibet in reply. A few days later, on December 16, the Chinese ordered a major attack on the T'u-yü-hun. By the 28th of December, an expeditionary force for attacking them was organized, with Li Ching as Commander-in-Chief.[46] In early 635, perhaps in response to the Chinese threat, the Tanguts, who had previously submitted to China, went over to the ʿAźa. Simultaneously, the Ch'iang tribes of T'ao *chou* rebelled, but the Chinese quickly sup-

[40] The Ch'i-pi were a T'ieh-le Turkic tribe in Chinese service. See Molè, 1970:157 (n. 407).

[41] *TCTC*, 194:6106; Molè, 1970:50, 156.

[42] Hsi Hai, "the Western Sea," here refers to the Koko Nor. Since in this case, as in other later ones, the area had not been conquered by the Chinese, the term *tao* is not meant in the sense of a T'ang administrative "circuit." In connection with T'ang expeditionary armies, it indicates the direction of attack and could perhaps be translated as "road."

[43] *TCTC*, 194:6107. There are approximately three *li* to a mile, so the pursuit lasted over 250 miles.

[44] Molè, 1970:50.

[45] *TCTC*, 194:6107.

[46] Ibid.

pressed them.[47] Finally, on May 29, 635,[48] the T'ang army defeated the T'u-yü-hun at K'u Shan. They quickly followed this
success with victory after victory until the ʿAźa were totally
crushed that summer.[49] The campaign covered the length and
breadth of T'u-yü-hun territory, and brought Chinese armies
(and ʿAźa refugees, no doubt) into the Tibetan borderlands. The
status of the ʿAźa country as a buffer state, insofar as it had indeed
functioned as one, was now effectively destroyed.

Following the defeat of the ʿAźa, Sroṅ btsan sgampo sent another embassy, which accompanied the Chinese ambassador
Feng on his return home[50] and proposed a marriage alliance between Tibet and China. The proposal was rejected by T'ai-tsung
and, according to all sources, the circumstances of that rejection
were the cause of the war that ensued.[51] In brief, it appears that
Sroṅ btsan sgampo had learned from Feng Te-hsia that both the
Turks and the T'u-yü-hun had received Chinese princesses in
marriage alliances. He therefore resolved to obtain such an alliance for Tibet, and so sent an official carrying gold and other
presents for T'ai-tsung—no doubt on the advice of Feng—with
the returning Chinese envoy. But the Tibetan ambassador was
angered by what he considered to be a slight against the Tibetan
legation. He claimed that when he first arrived, he was well received at court, but when an ʿAźa mission arrived, he was treated
with scant respect, and the marriage proposal was turned down.
Upon his return to Tibet, he reported this to the emperor and
Sroṅ btsan sgampo was duly offended. He strengthened his army
with Źaṅ-źuṅ troops and attacked and easily defeated the T'u-yü-
hun, probably in 637 or 638.[52] He followed up this success by subjugating two powerful tribes: the Tanguts, who lived in the area
between the ʿAźa and the Sumpa of Rgyaroṅ (the vassal-state
through which the Tibetans had probably entered the ʿAźa

[47] TCTC, 194:6110; Molè, 1970:51-52 (n. C), 163 (n. 427).

[48] TCTC, 194:6110; Molè, 1970:52 (n. C).

[49] TCTC, 194:6110-6113; Molè, 1970:52-54. On the route followed by Li
Ching, see Satô, 1978:227-247.

[50] TCTC, 195:6139.

[51] TCTC, 195:6138 et seq.

[52] The date is not given in the sources.

lands), and the Po-lan, who were located in the area between the
ʿAźa and Central Tibet.[53] It is notable that the Tibetans definitely
did not attack the ʿAźa from the west or the north (i.e., from
Central Asia) or even from the southwest. The Tibetan state orig-
inated in the agricultural south, and, at the time of this war, its
strength still lay largely in southerly and easterly lands.[54]

Having established himself as an enemy to be feared, Sroṅ
btsan sgampo raided the Chinese border town of Sung chou[55] on
September 12, 638.[56] The Tibetan emperor let it be known that if
he did not receive a princess forthwith, he would lead his army
deep into China. He easily defeated a Chinese force sent against
him by the commander in Sung chou, and he incited the local
Ch'iang tribes to revolt against their Chinese masters. On October 18, 638, after the Tibetan army had camped near Sung chou
for ten days, a Chinese force attacked by surprise, and inflicted a
minor defeat on them. According to the Chinese sources, Sroṅ
btsan sgampo withdrew, and sent an ambassador to T'ai-tsung to
"beg forgiveness for his crimes" and to renew his request for a
marriage alliance. This time, with face saved, the Chinese emperor agreed to the proposal.[57]

[53] This story, which is practically identical in both Chinese and Classical
Tibetan sources, is curious in more ways than one. The Chinese historians
seem to think that the story of ʿAźa interference at court is a fabrication. It
may very well be that T'ai-tsung made a private agreement with the Tibetans
to conclude a marriage alliance if they would finish off the still-troublesome
ʿAźa. Cf. TCTC, 194:6117.

[54] Although the purpose of the war was ostensibly to secure peaceful relations with China through a political marriage, it seems that before the
Chinese princess finally arrived in 641, Sroṅ btsan sgampo had subjugated
Tibet's southern neighbor, Nepal, and had received a Nepalese princess to
cement the relationship. This is the conclusion to be drawn from the Tibetan
sources. One must observe, however, that the Chinese princess (and thus
probably the Nepalese one as well) was obtained not for Sroṅ btsan sgampo
himself, but for his son Guṅ sroṅ guṅ brtsan, who ruled only five years (641-
646). Upon the death of his son, the old emperor took to wife the Chinese
princess. Cf. Shakabpa, 1967:27.

[55] Note its southerly location on Map I.

[56] TCTC, 195:6139.

[57] HTS, 2:38; cf. TCTC, 195: 6139-6140, where the number of Tibetans

On December 11, 640,[58] the great minister Mgar Stoṅ rtsan "the Conqueror"[59] arrived at the T'ang court with 5,000 ounces of gold and several hundred "precious baubles." Agreement was soon reached on the marital question: the Chinese would give Princess Wen-ch'eng to the Tibetan ruler. And so, on February 20 of the following year, Mgar returned to the Chinese court with the purpose of escorting the princess back to Tibet.[60] A week later, Mgar had an audience with T'ai-tsung during which he gave such clever replies that the Chinese emperor said that he wished to give him a princess as well. Mgar declined, and instead was granted the honorary title of "Great Protecting General of the Right."[61] On March 2, 641, Princess Wen-ch'eng left for Tibet; she was escorted by Tao-tsung (the Prince of Chiang-hsia) and Mgar Stoṅ rtsan.[62]

The peace so secured by Tibetan efforts was honored quite well by both sides, and lasted until the death of T'ai-tsung in 649[63] and of Sroṅ btsan sgampo a few months later.[64] Contacts between the two powers were friendly, and a lively cultural exchange took

---

killed is given as "over 1000 heads." This statement is taken at face value in *CHC*, 3:230, where it says "a T'ang army drove them off with heavy casualties." Even if the number were reliable, by early medieval standards it was not a major battle.

[58] *CTS*, 3:52; *TCTC*, 195:6157.

[59] The *TCTC* (195:6157) specifies Mgar, whereas the *CTS* (3:52) only says "an envoy." Despite the opinion expressed by Uray in his article, "The Annals of the ʿA-ža Principality" (1978) 561-562, there is no reason to doubt that Mgar was the envoy. He may not have gone far from Ch'ang-an, or even have left it at all, but in any case he did have two and a half months in which to do any necessary traveling back and forth. There is a common misconception that the trip from Central Tibet to Ch'ang-an took a year or more. In fact, if the Princess Chin-ch'eng in 710 could travel all the way from Ch'ang-an to Rasa (Lhasa) in Central Tibet—with stops for ceremonies in ʿAža and elsewhere along the way—in only five or six months, a general such as Mgar obviously could make it from the Tibetan border to Ch'ang-an and back several times in the period available.

[60] *CTS*, 3:52.

[61] *TCTC*, 196:6164.

[62] Ibid.

[63] On June 15, 649 (*CTS*, 3:62, 4:66).

[64] See below.

place throughout the period. With the exception of the defeat and subjugation of the Indian kingdom of Tîrabhukti in 648 (in support of the T'ang ambassador Wang Hsüan-ts'e[65]), Sroṅ btsan sgampo concerned himself largely with the consolidation of his considerable conquests.[66] He seems to have spent his final years principally in the work of completely assimilating the former Žaṅ-žuṅ state into his empire.[67] In a similar manner, T'ai-tsung occupied himself in his last years with the subjugation of the T'ieh-le Turks[68] and of the kingdom of Kucha.[69] In 649, the new Chinese emperor, Kao-tsung,[70] who was a fervent Buddhist, bestowed upon Sroṅ btsan sgampo the title of Pao-wang.[71] In

[65] See S. Lévi, "Les missions de Wang Hiuen-ts'e dans l'Inde" (1900); cf. TCTC, 199:6257-6258.

[66] TCTC, 198:6251, includes Tibet in a list of countries ordered on January 26, 648, to assist in the "chastising" of the Kingdom of Kucha; see TFYK, 985:16v-18v (pp. 11571-11572), for the edict containing this information. Cf. Moriyasu, 1984:6-7. (It should be noted that Moriyasu, like many Japanese scholars, regularly gives the *approximate* Western year equivalent of the Chinese year. In this case, for example, he has 647.)

[67] Satô, Kodai Chibetto shi kenkyû (1959) 2:11. CTS, 3:60, includes Žaṅ-žuṅ (Chinese, Yang-t'ung) among the countries listed as having come to court in 648.

[68] TCTC, 198:6238 et seq.

[69] TCTC, 198:6251.

[70] Installed on July 15, 649 (TCTC, 199:6268).

[71] TFYK, 974:13v (p. 11443). TT, 190:1023, CTS, 196a:5222, and HTS, 216a:6074, have Tsung-wang, "Cloth-tribute King," while TFYK, 964:7r (p. 11340), has Pin-wang, "Guest King" (as does the Po-na edition of CTS, 196a:3r). These characters are all very similar and easily confused; the only one that makes any sense to me is Pao-wang. The Chinese sources also record that Kao-tsung had previously given two other titles to the Tibetan emperor: Fu-ma tu-wei ("military commander/imperial son-in-law") and Hsi-hai chün-wang ("Sovereign of the Western Sea"). Upon the bestowal of the latter, these Sources report, Sroṅ btsan sgampo wrote a letter to the Chinese minister Chang-sun Wu-chi. In it, he stated that if the T'ang had any problems, the Tibetan ruler would promptly send an army to help straighten them out. He then was given the title presently in question (TCTC, 199:6269-6270). I would tend to accept the later title, but not the earlier ones, as having been given to Sroṅ btsan sgampo. It would seem that, in this case, the Chinese historians have confused the Tibetans (Chinese, T'u-fan) with the ʿAźa (T'u-yü-hun) because of their similar locations, their involvement

Chinese Buddhism, *pao-wang* ("Precious King" or "King of Jewels") is an epithet of the ruler of the West; it also appears to be a title of the Buddha Amitâbha, whose realm was thought to be in the West (as seen from China).[72] Significantly, it is known that Sroṅ btsan sgampo was identified with Amitâbha from very early times. It seems probable that Tibetan Buddhism began as a court religion that was fostered by the Chinese and Nepalese princesses along with their retinues, by visiting embassies and merchants, and by certain of the ministers.[73] But in 649-650, this first great Tibetan emperor died, and the accession to the throne of his young grandson left all real power in the hands of the chief minister, Mgar Stoṅ rtsan, who was to be the de facto ruler for the next two decades.

For some time before his patron died, Mgar Stoṅ rtsan had been consolidating his power. It is more than probable that he was ultimately responsible for the death of his powerful rival, Khyuṅpo Spuṅ-sad Zutse, since he was the minister who discovered Zutse's "plot."[74] Beyond such intrigues, Mgar had apparently gotten more or less complete control over the army, and had developed a favorable international image. He is the only Tibetan from this period whose Chinese portrait survives in believable form[75]—albeit in a later copy—and whose personality and

---

in the same events, and their similar names (both begin with the same character, and the name T'u-yü-hun often appears in the sources in the shorter form T'u-hun). The T'u-yü-hun and the Tibetans both received T'ang princesses almost simultaneously, in early 641 (Molè, 1970:171-172 [n. 470]; *TCTC*, 195:6157, 196:6164). According to the *CTS* and *HTS*, Kao-tsung also gave No-ho-po, the ruler of the 'Aźa, the title Fu-ma tu-wei (Molè, 1970:57). The title could thus have applied to either ruler, and as such would seem already to have been confused by the chroniclers of the early T'ang.

[72] E. Eitel, *Handbook of Chinese Buddhism* (1970) 51; cf. Pelliot, "La théorie des quatre fils du ciel" (1923).

[73] The hat on the statue of Sroṅ btsan sgampo in the Jokhang in Lhasa has an image of Amitâbha on it. It is interesting to speculate if this identification might have been one of the sources for the later identification of this ruler with Amitâbha's emanation, the bodhisattva Avalokiteśvara, who was from later medieval times on considered the "patron" of Tibet.

[74] *OTC*, ii; cf. Satô, 1958, 1:302-303.

[75] See the reproduction in H. Karmay, *Early Sino-Tibetan Art* (1975) 17 (pl. 6).

intelligence were obviously admired by his Chinese adversaries. From 652 to 667, the *Old Tibetan Annals* is full of the doings of the de facto ruler, Prime Minister Mgar. In 655-656, he wrote a code of laws, perhaps the same as the description of administrative organization that is attributed to Sroń btsan sgampo.[76] Then he began work on his greatest accomplishment, the conquest of the ʿAźa.

After their first defeat by the Tibetans, the Tʼu-yü-hun had submitted again to the Chinese. According to the *Annals*, the ʿAźa qaghan, Mu-jung No-ho-po, had made a deal with the Chinese general Su Ting-fang when the latter was in the district of Mtsho Nag ("Black Lake").[77] This was probably during the general's journey through ʿAźa territory on his way back to China from western Central Asia in the early spring of 660. Mgar Stoń rtsan began his long stay in the ʿAźa country by supervising a major defeat of the Tʼu-yü-hun and their Chinese overlords that autumn.[78]

---

[76] *OTA*, Hare year 655-656; *OTC*, viii; see Uray, "The Narrative of Legislation and Organization of the Mkhas-paʼi dgaʼ-ston" (1972). Mgar was thus obviously not illiterate. When the Chinese sources comment that a non-Chinese was illiterate (in modern Chinese, *pu shih tzu*, "does not recognize *tzu*," i.e. Chinese ideographic characters), however, they mean that he did not know literary Chinese. (*HTS*, 216a:6075, which says *pu chih shu*, "does not know writings," is followed by Satô, 1958, 1:300: "*monji no koto wa shiranai ga*.") It is of course possible that, at the time of Mgar's visits to Chʼang-an for the purpose of negotiating the marriage alliance, the Tibetan writing system had still not been developed, or had not yet been learned by him. It is certain, however, that the alphabet had been developed and was becoming widespread during Sroń btsan sgampo's reign (*OTC*, viii). According to traditional Tibetan sources, the emperor and his court all set themselves to the task of becoming literate.

[77] Probably the Khara Nor ("Black Lake"), which is located about 130 miles northwest of the Mtsho Sñon or Koko Nor along a trail going from the Tsaidam to Tun-huang. However, Satô (1958, 1:310, and 1978:32, 236 et seq. and maps), while mentioning this identification, prefers to equate Mtsho Nag with the Wu Hai (Chinese, "Crow Sea"), which was the scene of many later Tibetan battles with the Chinese. L. Petech, "Glosse agli *Annali* di Tun-huang" (1967) 258-259, doubts that Su Ting-fang was there.

[78] *TCTC*, 200:6321. It is unknown where exactly the battle took place. The army was probably led by one of his sons, who is called Chʼi-cheng in

At about the same time, the Chinese conquest of the Western Turks[79] started to have repercussions in the lands of the western Tarim Basin. In 659 Tu-man, the *irkin* of the *Ärski tribe of Western Turks,[80] leading an army composed of his own tribesmen, with contingents from Kashgar and two small western Tarim principalities, attacked and captured Khotan.[81] In response, Su Ting-fang was sent to punish them. He led his army to the River of Šâš (the Jaxartes) and attacked the Turks, forcing the surrender of Tu-man in the later part of the same year.[82] Su then returned to China, where he presented the captives to the emperor in Loyang[83] and was appointed to the Korean campaign.[84] In his absence, however, the *Köngül Turks of the Tien Shan, together with the Yen-mien to their north and the Tibetans to their south, attacked and captured Kashgar.[85] In response, that fall, the Chinese general Cheng Jen-t'ai attacked and defeated the Ssu-chieh, Bayarqu, P'u-ku, and Tongra tribes of the T'ieh-le confederation further to the east of the *Köngül.[86] This was followed by a major uprising of related tribes of the "Nine-surnamed" T'ieh-le,[87] including the Tongra, P'u-ku, Ssu-chieh, and Telengit, in the Tien Shan area. In the winter of 661, three T'ang

---

Chinese. It appears that the *OTA* entry for the Sheep year 659-660 refers to this event; unfortunately, this disrupts the chronology.

[79] See Chavannes (1903), the classic work on the subject.

[80] Ibid., 72-73, 308 (n. 74).

[81] *TCTC*, 200:6319. On one of the principalites, Chu-chü-po, see Moriyasu, 1984:67 (n. 108), and É. Lamotte, "Mañjuśrī" (1960) 65-66 (n. 156).

[82] *TCTC*, 200:6319.

[83] Ibid.; cf. *HTS*, 3:60.

[84] On April 25, 660. (*TCTC*, 200:6320.) *CTS*, 4:79-80, has this one year early. Hsiao Ssu-yeh was appointed to the Korean campaign in the spring of 661 (*HTS*, 3:61; *TCTC*, 200:6323).

[85] *TCTC*, 202:6372. *Köngül seems to be the name behind the Chinese Kung-yüeh. See F. Müller, *Ein Doppelblatt aus einem manichäischen Hymnenbuch (Maḥrnâmag)* (1913) 10, for mention of a Köngül general.

[86] *TCTC*, 200:6322; *HTS*, 3:60.

[87] *TCTC*, 200:6326. The same source also refers to them as "Uyghurs" (Hui-ho), while *CTS* (83:2781) calls them "Nine-surnamed Turks" or just "Nine Surnames," and *HTS* (111:4119) refers to them as the "Nine Surnames of the T'ieh-le."

armies were organized to attack the rebels. Cheng Jen-t'ai was appointed Commander-in-Chief of the T'ieh-le *tao* Expeditionary Army with Liu Shen-li, the Protector General of Yen-jan, and General Hsieh Jen-kuei as his two assistants. General Hsiao Ssu-yeh was named Commander-in-Chief of the Hsien-o *tao* Expeditionary Army along with Assistant General Sun Jen-shih. The third army was headed by the Turkic general *Arśïla Chung, the Commander-in-Chief of the Ch'ang-ts'en *tao* Expeditionary Army.[88] In the following spring, the forces of Cheng Jen-t'ai and Hsieh Jen-kuei[89] defeated the Turks somewhere in the Tien Shan. When the Chinese armies approached the hiding places of the Ssu-chich, Telengit, and other tribes in the Tien Shan, these tribesmen all came out to surrender.[90] The approach of Hsiao Ssu-yeh and his Expeditionary Army to the territories of the *Köngül caused the latter nation, and its subject city of Kashgar, to surrender as well.[91]

It may be in connection with these events that Mgar Ston rtsan, temporarily back from 'Aźa, gathered an army in Źań-źuń.[92] For early in the following year, a Tibetan force was again[93] allied with forces from *Köngül and Kashgar. The combined Tibetan and Turkic armies appeared south of Kashgar, expecting to do battle with the army of the T'ang general Su Hai-cheng, the I-hai *tao* Commander-in-Chief. Su, who was involved in a campaign againt Kucha, had brought about chaos among the Western Turks by killing *Arśïla Mi-she, who was the Hsing-hsi-wang Qaghan, the theoretical ruler of the eastern (*Tarduś) branch of the On oq. He had thus earned the enmity of the qaghan's tribes, the Shu-ni-shih and Barsqân.[94] After having chased these tribes

---

[88] *HTS*, 3:61; *TCTC*, 200:6326. For the name *Arśïla, see Appendix C.

[89] There seem to be no more references in the literary sources to *Arśïla Chung. For his tomb inscription, see the work (unavailable to me at the time of writing) cited by Moriyasu, 1984:63 (n. 57).

[90] *CTS*, 83:2781; *HTS*, 3:62, 111:4141; *TCTC*, 200:6327-6328.

[91] *TCTC*, 202:6372.

[92] *OTA*, Dog year 662-663.

[93] *TCTC*, 201:6333, explicitly says "again" (*fu*).

[94] The Shu-ni-shih was one of the five eastern *Tarduś (Chinese, Tu-lu, To-lu) tribes, and the Barsqân was one of the five western Nu-shih-pi (*Nu

some distance to the area around Kashgar, and having pacified them, Su and his army met the Tibetans and their allies. The Chinese source says that Su's troops were so tired that they did not dare to fight. So Su bought off the Tibetans with his army's military equipment, made peace, and withdrew.[95]

Theoretically, the Tibetans could have rendezvoused with their allies for these campaigns from either the southwestern or the southeastern corner of the Tarim Basin. But, since Kashgar in the northwest was already in the hands of the Tibetans and Western Turks, while Khotan was still under Chinese control and the T'u-yü-hun had yet to be conquered, the Tibetan army must have gone over the high passes north of Gilgit down to the Basin. Thus it is clear that this territory must already have come under Tibetan domination. According to the *Hsin T'ang shu*, sometime during or shortly after the Hsien-ch'ing period (February 1, 656 to February 4, 661), the kingdom of Wakhan was subjugated by Tibet: "Because their land is on the road from the Four Garrisons to Ṭukhâristân, it had to submit to Tibet."[96] It appears therefore that by 663 the Tibetan Empire controlled the far northwestern reaches of the Tibetan Plateau (where the Karakorum range becomes the Pamirs), the kingdom of Balûr,[97] the kingdom of Wakhan in eastern Ṭukhâristân (or the approaches to it from the east), and an area around Kashgar. Tibet had thus gained a strategic advantage that the Chinese obviously did not appreciate until it was too late.

śadpït) tribes. (On these groupings and their names, see Appendix D.) These "tribes" are not necessarily to be considered as distinct ethnic groups. For a recent anthropologically based discussion, see R. Lindner, "What Was a Nomadic Tribe?" (1982). The Barsqân are generally thought to have been based in the southwestern Tien Shan.

[95] *TCTC*, 201-6333; *TFYK*, 449-10r-10v (p. 5324).

[96] *HTS*, 221b:6255. On the Tibetan use of the Pamir route, see also the discussion in Moriyasu, 1984:8.

[97] The correct reading of this country's name, Po-lü in Chinese, was established by Pelliot long ago, but few writers seem to be aware of the fact. (See Pelliot, *Notes on Marco Polo* [1959] 1:91-92.) For example, Moriyasu, (1984:7) transcribes it in Japanese *katakana* as *bororu*, in *romaji* as "Bolor." Chinese transcription rules out either an "e" in the first syllable or an "o" in the second for early medieval pronunciation.

In the summer of 663, the Tibetan war with the ʿAźa at last came to a head. Both sides sent envoys to China asking for Chinese intervention on their side.[98] The Chinese response was to appoint the Governor-General of Liang *chou*, Cheng Jen-t'ai, as Commander-in-Chief of the Ch'ing Hai (Koko Nor) *tao* Expeditionary Army to save the T'u-yü-hun from the Tibetans. But, with the defection of the ʿAźa minister Su-ho-kuei to the Tibetans, the ʿAźa defenses were revealed; the Tibetans attacked and completely crushed the ʿAźa forces.[99] The qaghan, his Chinese princess, and several thousand families—no doubt largely the nobility and their retainers—fled to the Chinese at Liang *chou*.[100] The whole of the once-powerful Mongolic state was now a part of the Tibetan Empire.

But on January 26, 664, Kao Hsien, the Protector-General of *An-hsi*, the "Pacified West" colonial administration then based in Kucha, was appointed Commander-in-Chief of an expeditionary army intended to attack the *Köngül—and possibly the Tibetans—in order to save Khotan.[101] The outcome of this expedition, if it actually was ever mobilized, is unknown.

As for Mgar Stoṅ rtsan, the Tibetan sources only remark that he remained in ʿAźa from 663 to 665.[102] He was doubtlessly con-

---

[98] *TCTC*, 201:6335.

[99] *HTS*, 3:63, 216a:6075; *TCTC*, 201:6336. According to *HTS* (216a:6075), the Chinese army was directed "to encamp at Liang [*chou*] and Shan [*chou*]." The famous Su Ting-fang was sent along as *an chi ta shih*, or "Grand Commissioner for Pacifying and Gathering." (His involvement in this move is not mentioned in either of his biographies, which are model "exemplary accounts.") The army seems actually to have been sent to protect Chinese prefectures from incursions by either Tibetans or T'u-yü-hun. There is no mention of Chinese military interference in the Tibetan-ʿAźa war.

[100] *TCTC*, 201:6336.

[101] *HTS*, 3:63; *TCTC*, 201:6339; cf. *TFYK*, 414:21r (p. 4930). The official title of this expeditionary army is not given in the sources. The Tibetans are not mentioned either, but the *OTA* notes that in the Mouse year 664-665 "the Emperor went to the North," and Khotan is indeed north of Central Tibet. Satô, 1958, 1:312-313, believes the latter entry refers to a campaign against the ʿAźa.

[102] *OTA*, Pig, Mouse, and Ox years 663-664, 664-665, and 665-666.

solidating the Tibetan position there, but he was probably also responsible for the Tibetan embassy which arrived at the Chinese
court on February 14, 665. Their mission was to get the ʿAźa to
restore good relations with the Tibetan ruling house. In addition,
the Tibetans came to "seek the region of Ch'ih Shui for grazing
their animals."[103] Having the ʿAźa as vassals ruling over their own
people would certainly have eased the problems the Tibetans
faced in trying to control a subject people totally un-Tibetan in
language and culture. Moreover, early medieval political ideology did not allow for vassals—in theory, the position of all conquered peoples—to avoid submission to their overlords. (That
such vassals were often referred to with words meaning "slaves"
attests to their subordinate status.) That the Tibetans asked for a
particular area in ʿAźa territory may indicate either that the area
had not yet been completely subjugated—a real possibility—or
that the Tibetans wished to assuage Chinese fears and anger by
requesting T'ang recognition of the new de facto situation. In any
event, although the Chinese denied both requests,[104] the ʿAźa
lands remained under Tibetan control. With this success, Mgar
Stoṅ rtsan returned from ʿAźa in 666 and had an audience with
the Tibetan emperor. He was now an old man, twice prime minister, and his sons were taking over his duties for him. He died in
Ris-pu in the following year.[105]

After *Arśïla Pu-chen, the Chi-wang-chüeh Qaghan—theoretically ruler of the western or Nu-shih-pi branch of the On
oq—plotted against the other qaghan and had him killed, the
Turks "considered Chi-wang-chüeh an oppressor" and pondered
ways of getting rid of him.[106] But when he killed himself, for reasons that are still unknown, the Western Turks found themselves
without a qaghan altogether, according to the Chinese sources,
so in 667 two of their leaders, *Arśïla Tu-chih and Li Che-fu,

---

[103] TCTC, 201:6343; HTS, 216a:6075.
[104] TCTC, 201:6342; HTS, 216a:6075.
[105] OTA, Tiger and Hare years 666-667 and 667-668. The location of Ris-pu is uncertain.
[106] TCTC, 201:6333.

gathered the tribes and together they submitted to Tibet.[107] This remarkable chain of events, unmentioned in Tibetan sources and only very briefly related in the Chinese, marks the first period of Tibetan domination over the Western Turks, and demonstrates the rapidly growing power of Tibet in Central Asia.[108]

In 668, in apparent preparation for an expected Chinese attack, the Tibetans constructed defensive fortifications in the area of the Jima Gol,[109] a river located in ʿAźa territory south of the Koko Nor and called by the T'ang Chinese Ta-fei Ch'uan.[110] In the following year, perhaps as a result of this show of Tibetan strength, a large number of ʿAźa came to the Tibetan court to do obeisance to the emperor.[111] At the same time, the Chinese were debating whether or not to move the T'u-yü-hun to another place south of Liang *chou*. But, because they were afraid that the Tibetans would attack them there too, nothing was done.[112]

---

[107] *TCTC*, 201:6332-6333; *TFYK*, 967:11v (p. 2372). Cf. the discussion on this in Moriyasu, 1984:11-12.

[108] One must doubt the Chinese sources' implication that the Western Turks only submitted to the Tibetans by choice and only because they needed a ruler!

[109] *OTA*, Dragon year 668-669. It may be too easy an equation to make confidently without having a thorough study of the internal historical phonology of Tibetan (including the dialects) at hand, but it would appear that the Tibetan name Jima Gol (the 670 entry has Khol) has been *translated* into Chinese as Ta-fei Ch'uan. This could only have been done through the medium of the Tibetan language because the name is patently an ʿAźa name, and of Mongolic origin. Allowing for the perhaps premature aspiration of the initial consonant *j*, the name is a syllable-for-syllable calque of a Tibetan interpretation of the original name: Ji (= *Che*, "big") + ma ("not") and Gol or Khol (Mongolic and Turkic for "river"), which thus corresponds to the Chinese *Ta* ("big"), *fei* ("not"), *Ch'uan* ("river").

[110] For its identification with the Hoyoyun River, see Satô, 1978:145 and maps. See also the discussion in Molè, 1970:168 (n. 451), which includes a Ta-fei Shan. Petech, 1967:250-251, says that it had to be southwest of the Koko Nor. Hu San-hsing's gloss (*TCTC*, 201:6364) says that the Ta-fei Ch'uan was over 300 *li* west of Shan-ch'eng *hsien*, Shan *chou*. Cf. Moriyasu, 1984:9-10, 63 (n. 47). All agree that the river was somewhere south of the Koko Nor.

[111] *OTA*, Snake year 669-670.

[112] *TCTC*, 201:6359; *TFYK*, 991:13v-14v (p. 11642). That such discus-

Suddenly, in the spring of 670, Tibet launched a major offensive against the remaining Chinese-held countries in the western Tarim Basin. With the assistance of troops from Khotan, which had been captured between 665 and 670, Tibet attacked and took[113] the Kuchean fortified city of Aksu.[114] Only Kucha and Agni,[115] which were located further east, apparently held out against the Tibetans.[116] At this point, however, the Chinese abandoned the Four Garrisons of the Pacified West—the major part of their hard-won colonial empire—with, their historians would have us believe, hardly a whimper. Nonetheless, the same histo-

sions took place would seem to indicate that the T'u-yü-hun had indeed already been conquered (although not yet absorbed) by the Tibetans. But see Moriyasu, 1984:63 (n. 47), 64 (n. 62).

[113] CTS, 5:94, 40:1647; HTS, 3:68, 216a:6076; TCTC, 201-6363; TFYK, 986:10v (p. 11579); cf. Moriyasu, 1984:10-11. The *Köngül Turks, the Kashgaris, and the Tibetans had attacked Khotan, one of the Four Garrisons and the key point on the southern branch of the Silk Road, in the spring of 665. The T'ang Governor-General of Hsi chou, Ts'ui Chih-pien, and a general, Ts'ao Chi-shu, were ordered to its defense. (HTS, 3:64; TCTC, 201:6344; TFYK, 995:15v [p. 11687]; cf. Moriyasu, 1984:8-9.) Previous attacks of the Tibetans and their allies had failed, and the Chinese sources imply the success of their defense in this case as well.

[114] Chinese, Po-huan. Moriyasu, 1984:63 (n. 48), is inexplicably not convinced by Pelliot's arguments for this identification. See Pelliot, "La ville de Bakhouân dans la géographie d'Idrîçî" (1906) 553-556, and "Note sur les anciens noms de Kučā, d'Aqsu et d'Uč-Turfan" (1923) 128-130.

[115] Chinese, Yen-ch'i, present-day Karashahr.

[116] See the discussion in Moriyasu, 1984:10-11. The Tibetans faced the necessity of controlling Kashgar, or at the very least, of placing the fortress-city in friendly hands, in order to attack Aksu from the west. The CTS 5:94, has the Tibetans capturing "Pai chou, etc., 18 prefectures," while the TCTC, 201:6363, has "the 18 prefectures of the Western Regions." It may be significant to note that the capture of cities to the west of Chinese-held territory should not have caused the T'ang to abandon Kucha and Agni. Indeed, the Chinese recaptured the Tarim Basin (between 692 and 694) by defeating the Tibetans and Western Turks in the area of present-day western Kansu, the region that lay west of China but east of Kucha and Agni (see below, Chapter Three). Moreover, the HTS, 217b:6150, refers to the area conquered by Tibet as "the 18 prefectures of Ho[-hsi] Lung[-yu], and the Four Garrisons." Perhaps, then, this expression indicates the area just to the west of ethnic Chinese territories in the Kansu corridor.

rians also record that an ambitious campaign was quickly mounted with the intention of crushing the Tibetans, restoring the ʿAźa to their homelands, and reconquering the Tarim countries.

On May 3, 670,[117] Great Protecting General of the Right Hseih Jen-kuei was appointed Commander-in-Chief of the huge Rasa *tao* Expeditionary Army. His assistant generals were *Arśila Tao-chen and Kuo Tai-feng. In late summer,[118] the army arrived at the Ta-fei Ch'uan. Hsieh first gave orders to Kuo that twenty thousand men should remain behind with the baggage and build two palisades on Ta-fei Shan in order to protect the supplies. Meanwhile, Hsieh would lead his unencumbered forces forward to attack the Tibetans. Hsieh's attack succeeded: he badly defeated a group of Tibetans at the river mouth[119] and captured over 10,000 cattle and sheep.[120] He then camped by the Wu Hai (Crow Lake) to wait for Kuo and his army. Kuo Tai-feng, however, had not built the palisades. As he was slowly proceeding to the rendezvous at Wu Hai, he was attacked by an enormous Tibetan army[121] and severely defeated. Dumping their baggage and military supplies, Kuo's army turned back in full retreat; this necessitated Hsieh Jen-kuei's withdrawal to a camp by the Ta-fei Ch'uan. There the Tibetan general Mgar Khri ʿbriṅ, leading a large army, fell upon the T'ang imperial forces, killing or wounding almost

[117] CTS, 5:94, 196a:5223; HTS, 3:68, 216a:6076; TCTC, 201:6363; TFYK, 986:10v (p. 11579).

[118] On the problem of dating, see Molè, 1970:180-182 (n. 499). TCTC, 201:6364, gives the eighth month (August 21 to September 20), sometime after September 6. TFYK, 443:2r (p. 5254) also gives the eighth month. CTS, 5:94, and HTS, 3:68, both give August 8 as the date of the Battle of Ta-fei Ch'uan. OTA, Horse year 670-671, records that "many Chinese were killed at Jima Khol." See the Note on Chronology.

[119] Or perhaps at a place called Ho-k'ou, as punctuated by the editors of the TCTC (201:6364). Hu San-hsing's gloss says this refers to the mouth of the Chi-shih Ho.

[120] CTS, 83:2783. This "battle" sounds suspiciously like a massacre of shepherds rather than a military engagement. Although there is no explicit evidence, the accounts seem to have been altered from whatever the truth may have been, perhaps to protect Hsieh Jen-kuei from incrimination.

[121] The army supposedly numbered over 200,000 men.

all of them. But the three Chinese generals escaped slaughter; after making peace with Mgar Khri 'briṅ, they returned to China.[122]

This military disaster marked the end of two decades of Chinese domination of the Tarim Basin. A new army was soon organized to be sent west,[123] but this time its destination was more realistically ordered to be Liang *chou*, and its purpose was to defend against an expected Tibetan invasion.[124] The T'ang moved the government of its *An-hsi* Protectorate General back to Hsi *chou* in the Turfan Depression, where it had been originally established. The first period of Tibetan domination over the Tarim states and neighboring regions had begun.

[122] *OTA*, Horse year 670-671; *CTS*, 5:94, 83:2782-2783; *HTS*, 3:68, 111:4142; *TCTC*, 201:6364-6365; *TFYK*, 456:14v-15v (pp. 5405-5406). The number of Tibetans alleged to have attacked the Chinese army is 400,000 this time! The defeated generals were demoted to the rank of commoner on their return to China.

[123] On November 2, 670 (*HTS*, 3:68, 216a:6076; *TCTC*, 201:6365).

[124] *HTS*, 3:69, says this army was to "chastise" or "subjugate" Tibet. Its military destination, however, is here given also as Liang *chou*, thus disproving the above statement.

Chapter 2

THE TIBETAN
EMPIRE
IN THE
WESTERN REGIONS

The Tibetans had now conquered a fairly large expanse of territory in eastern Central Asia. The region straddled the main East-West transcontinental trade routes, and was then a dynamic, integral part of the highly civilized Buddhist heartland of Eurasia.[1] Thus, the loss of this profitable and most strategic part of their colonial empire was a shock to the T'ang Chinese,[2] who for a brief period after the devastating defeat at Ta-fei Ch'uan were unable to devise any serious countermeasure. In 671, the Chinese attempted to reestablish control over the *Tarduś tribes of the Western Turks through the appointment of *Arśïla Tu-chih[3]

[1] On the importance of Central Asian culture for the development of the early Tibetan Buddhist and the Arab Islamic civilizations, see Beckwith, "The Revolt of 755 in Tibet" (1983) and "The Plan of the City of Peace" (1984b).

[2] Cf. Satô, 1958, 1:324.

[3] On May 31, 671. (*HTS*, 215b:6064; *TCTC*, 202:6366.) *TFYK*, 964: 9r (p. 11341), has 670, but this is probably a misprint. Far from demonstrating the submission of his branch of the Western Turks to the Chinese, *Arśïla's appointment indicates rather that he had great need of T'ang help, and may

both as a military general and as Governor-General over the Ch'u-mu-k'un, one of the five ★Tarduś tribes of the On oq. Unfortunately, the sources are silent about the outcome of this scheme. The T'ang did undertake one concrete action in 672, one more revealing of the seriousness of the situation: they moved the T'u-yü-hun farther into China—away from Shan *chou*—because the Chinese believed that their fear of the Tibetans was making them restless.[4]

In view of the various T'ang attempts at dealing with this potent Tibetan threat, the Chinese sources' explanations for the monumental setbacks seem ludicrous. The account in the *Chiu T'ang shu* states: "When Kao-tsung succeeded to the throne, he did not want extensive territories to trouble the people, so he ordered the officials concerned to abandon Kucha and the other [three] of the Four Garrisons, and move the Protector-Generalship of the Pacified West to Hsi *chou*, where it had been of old."[5] This distortion, although not uncommon in Chinese sources, doubtlessly resulted from a desire to conceal the blame for this blow to T'ang imperial prestige by making it seem a voluntary, or even virtuous, action by the emperor. In the meantime, the great defeat of the Chinese imperial army, which had been sent in 670 to the nearby Koko Nor to crush the Tibetans and recover the Four Garrisons, is ample proof of the seriousness and extent of the Chinese loss.

The only other Central Asian power which might have been able to turn back the rising power of Tibet was the Arab caliphate. However, the early Arab conquests did not extend as far as the new Tibetan imperial borders. The furthest east they had reached by 670 was western Ṭukhâristân and Siǵistân.[6] These regions had allegedly been brought under Chinese control as a result of Su Ting-fang's conquest of the Western Turks between

---

have come to court to get it. This is clear from his appointment as Governor-General over only one of the five eastern tribes.

[4] *TCTC*, 202:6368.

[5] *CTS*, 198:5304; cf. *HTS*, 221a:6232.

[6] M. Shaban, *The ʿAbbāsid Revolution* (1970) 32. The Arabs under ʿUbayd Allâh b. Ziyâd first crossed the Oxus in 674 (p. 35).

657 and 659.[7] In fact, this territory passed out of the Chinese sphere of influence directly after the Chinese officially announced its political organization—into T'ang protectorates, prefectures, and so on—in 661.[8] Thanks to Su Hai-cheng's campaign of 662, the region was thrown into civil war, and virtual rebellion ensued as the Western Turks rose against the T'ang.[9] Thus the Chinese attempt to impose a unifying T'ang rule over western Central Asia was a total failure.

For their part, the Arabs still had to contend with many more-or-less independent city-states which tended not to cooperate much with each other. Contrary to the generally accepted view, however, such intransigent independent-mindedness made them much more difficult to subdue than if they had been part of a centralized empire.[10] Moreover, the civil war which followed the death in 683 of Yazîd b. Muʿâwiya, the second Umayyad caliph, was soon to result in the loss of central control over the Arab conquests in Central Asia.[11] In short, the Chinese were at that time Tibet's only potential rivals for the domination of Central Asia from the Pamirs eastward.

[7] *TCTC*, 200:6301-6319, gives the most coherent account.

[8] The best treatment remains that of Chavannes, 1903:67-71. The long glosses in *TCTC*, 200:6324-6325 are also useful.

[9] See Chapter One.

[10] H. Gibb, *The Arab Conquests in Central Asia* (1923) 4 et seq., and Shaban, 1970:3-15, have noted this lack of cooperation and the difficulties the Arabs faced in their conquests. But neither has suggested that the complex political situation, with frequent unpredictable rebellions against Arab authority, was what stymied the caliphate's expansion there for so long. The sudden fall to the Arabs of the Persian Empire and of most of the Eastern Roman Empire would seem to demonstrate the dangers of over-centralization. Despite the fame of these historic collapses, Gibb states: "There is not a hint of united action in the field [by the Central Asians against the Arabs] in *Tabari*'s accounts" (1923:22). One could, however, easily point out many contradictory examples—quite a few of which Gibb himself deals with—in the source he cites. An early example of such cooperation is the account in Ṭabarî (ii:394) of the annual meeting of the "kings of Khurasan" near Khwârizm. Gibb has questioned this account, saying it "possesses little intrinsic probability," among other things. See Gibb, 1923:28 (n. 12).

[11] Shaban, 1970:41 et seq.

Of the former T'ang possessions, Tibet was now theoretically sovereign over at least two of the Four Garrisons—Khotan and Kashgar—as well as Aksu and, probably, the western or Nu-shih-pi branch of the On oq.[12] Nothing is yet known about Tibetan administration of these conquered territories.[13] However, if the contemporary Chinese and Arab conquests can be considered at all comparable in nature, it is most probable that the Tibetans left control in the hands of local dynasts, and merely exacted as much tribute from them as they could. Under such lax control, local rulers of the major Central Asian principalities began to act almost as if they were independent again. Their policy with respect to T'ang China bore great resemblance to that of the rulers of western Central Asian principalities which were coming under Arab domination at the same time. The few major differences were determined in part by the greater proximity of the Tarim Basin to China than of Khurasan to the Arabian homeland.

At the beginning of 674, according to Chinese sources, the kings of *Köngül and Kashgar came in person to the T'ang court, then in Ch'ang-an,[14] to "surrender."[15] The Chiu T'ang shu states

[12] There is no statement concerning the Nu-shih-pi in the Chinese sources at this point, but toward the end of the century Mgar Khri 'brin claimed that they were close to Tibet and of strategic importance to the Tibetan Empire.

[13] The Old Tibetan documents from East Turkistan and Tun-huang have generally been dated to the eighth and ninth centuries, so these copious materials may not reveal much about this early period even after they have been better studied. In addition, extremely little archaeological work has been done in the region. Thus the only usable information available at present on early Tibetan activities in Central Asia comes from literary sources.

[14] TCTC, 202:6371. Moriyasu, 1984:12, has "673" (see Chapter One, note 66).

[15] CTS, 5:98; TCTC, 202:6371. This event could possibly be connected with the appointments of *Arsïla Tu-chih mentioned above. Since *Köngül and Kashgar had both fallen to Tibet with the assistance of *Arsïla's Turks, it would perhaps not have been difficult for these Turks to turn the cities over to the Chinese. Such an interpretation would, however, be erroneous, as shown below. See also Appendix A, where H. Satô's interpretation of the ambiguous data—on further developments with regard to Kashgar—are discussed (Satô, 1958, 1:327-328).

that the T'ang subsequently established a Governor Generalship in Kashgar.[16] Soon afterward, in early 675,[17] Fu-she Hsiung, the king of Khotan, came to China with some seventy followers; later in the same year a Governor Generalship was also created for Khotan. The jurisdiction was named P'i-sha—after the native dynastic name—and had ten prefectures, with Fu-she Hsiung as Governor-General.[18] Coincident with the arrival of Fu-she Hsiung, the pretender to the throne of Persia, Pêrôz, whom the Chinese had appointed Governor-General of Persia a decade before, also came to the Chinese court. The "king of Khotan" and the "king of Persia" are treated in the sources as exact equals, even though the latter had never ruled Persia, and his father, the last ruler of the Sassanid dynasty, had been killed in the course of the Arab conquest forty years before.[19] Since there is no reference to Chinese military activity in the Tarim during this period, and since foreign kings never traveled by choice to the T'ang capital,[20] it seems clear that these kings were refugees rather than victorious rebels who had received Chinese assistance against the Tibetans.[21] If it is true, however, that the Tibetans had let slip their control

---

[16] *CTS* 40:1648; cf. Satô, 1958, 1:327. Since this information occurs at the end of the account in the *CTS*, its remarks on Kashgar's Governor-Generalship could conceivably be taken to apply to the period of the *second* Shang-yüan reign (760-761). There are innumerable references to the second period in the "Treatise on Geography," but no references to the earlier Shang-yüan period, although some probably can be found.

[17] Moriyasu, 1984:12, has "674" (see Chapter One, note 66).

[18] *CTS*, 5:99-100, 40:1648; *HTS*, 221a:6235; *TCTC*, 674:6374. The chronology in *CTS*, 198:5305, is difficult to reconcile with that of the other sources.

[19] In addition to the other embassies to China, it may be noted that, at the beginning of 675, the king of Kucha or his envoy presented the gift of a silver *p'o-lo* (*CTS*, 5:100).

[20] It is highly improbable that the Central Asian rulers who assisted the T'ang in putting down the An Lu-shan rebellion did so of their own free will, despite all the hoopla to the contrary in the Chinese sources. If they had known that the rebellion was destroying T'ang military power, and that the Chinese would therefore not be able to punish them for "rebelling," they would doubtlessly have ignored the T'ang summons.

[21] See further in Appendix A.

over Khotan and Kashgar, in 675 and 676 their dominion was restored.[22]

During these years, Great Minister Mgar Btsan sña ldombu
first mustered Źań-źuń troops,[23] and then led the Tibetan armies
into "Turkistan."[24] The following winter, Mgar again led the armies in Turkistan,[25] this time with the renewed cooperation of
★Arśїla Tu-chih, who had now become qaghan of the Western
Turks, and Li Che-fu.[26] Into the next year, they campaigned together in the area of the former Four Garrisons, from west of
Agni to as far east as Tun-huang.[27] The result, according to Tibetan sources, was victory; the Chinese sources report that "the
Four Garrisons were all lost." Also in 677,[28] the Tibetans raided

[22] Another possible explanation is as follows: After their initial victories,
the Tibetans left the Central Asian states alone, presumably with the understanding that they would pay their tribute. Tibet actually began its second
wave of invasions in 674, and the kings then fled to China. (In this regard, we
should recall that the OTA dating system, or the lack thereof, has not yet
been perfectly elucidated: the source may refer to 674 as well as 675, or it may
simply be off by one year.)

[23] OTA, Pig year 675(-676), summer. The levy was made in Guran, in
Źims, both unknown places. Beginning in the Sheep year 671-672, the OTA
divides each entry by season, usually just "summer" and "winter." See the
Note on Chronology.

[24] OTA, Pig year 675(-676), summer. The Old Tibetan text says he
"went to Turkistan for ltań-yo." The grammatical construction of this sentence does not allow the last word, the meaning of which is unknown, to be
taken as a place name. Nonetheless, every writer on the subject—most recently, Moriyasu (1984:14): "kono Dru-gu (chyuruku) koku no Ltang-yo to wa
. . ."—has hitherto so understood it. I would etymologize the word as a
compound of ltań, "a bale (of goods), and the yo of yobyad, "necessities for
life, provisions, supplies." Perhaps it meant something like "booty" or
"plunder." (The term is somehow reminiscent of the contemporaneous Arabic word athqâl, which was used to refer to valuable caravan goods; see below, Chapter Five.) The clause may thus mean "he went to Turkistan for
plunder."

[25] OTA, Mouse year (676-)677, winter.

[26] HTS, 216b:6077; TCTC, 202:6390. Cf. Chavannes, 1903:74-76, on
this and the subsequent Chinese "campaign" of P'ei Hsing-chien.

[27] HTS, 216a:6079.

[28] OTA, Mouse year (676-)677, winter; HTS, 3:73, 215b:6064,
216a:6077, 221a:6232-6233; CTS, 198:5304. The account in TFYK is chronologically out of order; it refers to the activities of P'ei Hsing-chien in 679.

the fortified Chinese prefectural capitals of Shan *chou*, K'uo *chou*, and Ho *chou*, among others.[29] In response, the T'ang government organized two armies, a T'ao *chou tao* Expeditionary Army and a Liang *chou tao* Expeditionary Army, to punish Tibet. Ultimately, however, the army never went on campaign.[30] In fact, at no time after 670 did any Chinese soldiers or officials enter the new Tibetan sphere of influence. Thus, by the end of 677, Tibet had established control over the whole of the Tarim Basin and the neighboring mountainous lands to the southwest.

The total failure of Chinese attempts to recover the lucrative colonies along the Silk Road apparently stimulated them into direct military action against the nearby northeast flank of Tibet. This came precisely at a time when the Tibetans could least afford it, since in the winter of 677 the Tibetan emperor Khri man slon died, and Źań-źuń revolted.[31] Only the firm governance of the great leaders of the Mgar clan prevented a serious setback for the Tibetan Empire.

Beginning on January 25, 678, the T'ang government mounted a general levy of men from Kuan-tung, Ho-tung, and other prefectures in order to supply the manpower for this new offensive.[32] After some three weeks of bickering among the

[29] *CTS*, 196a:5223; *HTS*, 216a:6076; *TCTC*, 202:6379-6380, 6383. The lists of places attached include a Fang *chou*, located in the same area.

[30] *CTS*, 5:101; *HTS*, 3:72, 216a:6076; *TCTC*, 202:6379-6380.

[31] For the emperor's death see *OTA*, Mouse year (676-)677 winter; *MD*, ja:70r. *TCTC*, 202:6389, appears to record his death in 679; however, the context makes it clear that this is another instance in which the lack of a past perfect tense form in Chinese can create confusion. The beginning of the entry should read: "The Tibetan *btsanpo* having died. . . ." Thus it records the unofficial Chinese knowledge of the Tibetan emperor's death. The next entry in the *TCTC* is that his son, Khri 'dus sroń, succeeded him (Chinese *li*, literally, "was set up [on the throne]"). But this is directly contradicted by the *OTA* account, which states that in the winter of the same year "The emperor, the son Khri 'dus sroń, was born in Lhaluń in Sgregs." The Źań-źuń rebellion is recorded in the *OTA* under the Ox year 677-678. Khri man slon was buried in the Hare year 679-680 (*OTA*). The purpose of the embassy sent to China by Princess Wen-ch'eng late in 679 was to formally announce the death of the ruler. The Chinese then dispatched, on November 24, 679, an envoy to attend the funeral (*TCTC*, 202:6393).

[32] *CTS*, 5:103, 196a:5223; *HTS*, 3:73; *TCTC*, 202:6384.

Chinese generals,[33] Li Ching-hsüan was appointed Commander-in-Chief of the T'ao Ho *tao* Expeditionary Army and Inspector of the Shan *chou* Military-Governorship. Orders were also given to draft troops in Chien-nan and Ho-pei without regard for the social standing of the conscripts.[34]

According to the sources, Li Ching-hsüan's armies reported initial victories over the Tibetans at Lung-chih in Shan *chou* sometime toward the late summer of 678.[35] But on October 3, Li Ching-hsüan's army fought a great battle "across the Koko Nor" with a Tibetan army under the command of Mgar Khri 'brin btsan brod. The Chinese suffered a major defeat. Liu Shen-li, a high-ranking general who was Superior Administrator of the expeditionary army[36] and President of the Board of Works,[37] was captured by the Tibetans.[38] The Assistant Commander-in-Chief, Wang Hsiao-chieh, was also captured.[39] Li Ching-hsüan hastily retreated to Ch'eng-feng Ling (in southwestern K'uo *chou*), but found himself forced into a vulnerable position.[40] Only a nocturnal attack on the Tibetan camp by a suicide squad led by the Ko-

[33] HTS, 3:74; TCTC, 202:6384.

[34] CTS, 196a:5223; HTS, 216a:6077; TCTC, 202:6384.

[35] TCTC, 202:6385. Ssu-ma Kuang only states that Li memorialized his defeat of the Tibetans. CTS (5:103) is more specific; it says that Li memorialized that "the Tibetans entered Lung-chih; Chang Ch'ien-hsü did battle with them—two battles in one day—and beheaded extremely many." According to Satô 1958, 1:329, Lung-chih is to be located in this area of present-day Ch'ing-hai province, 80 *li* (about 28 miles) southeast of Hsi-ning *hsien*.

[36] TFYK, 756:4r-5r (pp. 8993-8994). "Superior Administrator" is my translation of R. des Rotours's translation of the title *Ssu-ma*; see his *Traité des fonctionnaires et traité de l'armée* (1974) 1004.

[37] CTS, 77:2678; TCTC, 202:6385. I suspect that this is a posthumous title, but have been unable to determine this from the sources.

[38] CTS, 5:104, 77:2678; HTS, 3:74; TCTC, 202:6385-6386; TFYK, 443:2v-3r (pp. 5254-5255), 756:4r-5r (pp. 8993-8994).

[39] See note 84, below, for Wang Hsiao-chieh. His name is not mentioned in the accounts that directly pertain to this army.

[40] TCTC, 202:6385, says he "blocked up a canal [to create a moat] to hold his position." But from the other sources it would seem that he had been trapped, with a canal on one side and the Tibetans holding the ridge above him.

rean Hei-ch'ih Ch'ang-chih forced the Tibetan contingent to withdraw; Li was then able to return with the remnants of his army to Shan *chou*.[41]

Although this serious defeat brought about another reevaluation of Chinese policy and strategy toward Tibet, disagreements at the T'ang court prevented any definite actions being taken to change the course already set. One young student from the Imperial Academy remarked at the end of a long analysis of the situation which he delivered at court: "I am afraid that the pacification of Tibet is not something that you can expect to accomplish between dawn and dusk."[42]

In the middle of the following year, P'ei Hsing-chien, who was vice-president of the Board of Civil Office, finally responded to demands from the T'ang emperor and his court that something be done about the continued Tibetan–Western Turkic control of the northern branch of the Silk Road. P'ei proposed to capture the Turks by subterfuge, since direct military action was, in his opinion, impossible. He suggested that Ni-nieh-shih, the son of Pêrôz and therefore the pretender to the Persian throne, be sent back to Persia. While Ni-nieh-shih passed through the land of the Western Turks, P'ei would take advantage of the Persian's diplomatic immunity and catch the Western Turkic qaghan unaware. The plan was approved. P'ei was appointed Envoy for Pacifying the Arabs, and was officially charged with the task of "appointing and setting up [on the throne] the King of Persia."[43]

In the autumn of 679, P'ei Hsing-chien arrived in Qocho under

[41] *CTS*, 5:103, 81:2755, 196a:5224; *HTS*, 3:74, 106:4052-4053, 110:4121, 216a:6077; *TCTC*, 202:6385. The Tibetans were under the command of an otherwise unknown general, Pa-ti-she. Liu Shen-li's son Liu I-ts'ung, a model of filial piety, traveled to the Tibetans to ransom his father. When the younger Liu learned that his father was already dead (*CTS*, 77:2678, reports that he died in captivity in 681), he lamented so grievously that the Tibetans pitied him and gave him the body, which he then brought home.

[42] *TCTC*, 202:6387-6388.

[43] *TCTC*, 202:6390-6391; *CTS*, 84:2802-2803; *HTS*, 108:4086-4087; *TFYK*, 366:9r-10v (p. 4355). Cf. Chavannes, 1903:74-75 (n. 3), where the biography of P'ei in the *HTS* is translated and annotated. The diplomatic immunity is nowhere explicitly mentioned in the Chinese sources.

the guise of escorting Ni-nieh-shih back to Persia. Then, invok-
ing the friendships he had made while he was Governor-General
of the Pacified West,[44] he gathered a group of local youths and
told them he wished to go hunting with them. With this double
disguise covering his true purpose, P'ei was able to capture *Aršïla Tu-chih by treachery and then force Li Che-fu to surrender.
In the process, P'ei captured the commanders of each of the ten
West Turkic tribes as well as the city of Sûyâb in western Central
Asia. P'ei then ordered his second in command, Wang Fang-i, to
stay and build a fortress at Sûyâb while he returned to the T'ang
capital with his prisoners.[45] The Chinese sources laconically report that "the king of Persia was sent to return to his country by
himself."[46]

Although this T'ang victory north of the Tien Shan may have
had repercussions on the countries of the Tarim Basin, which
were nominally under Tibetan control, the Chinese sources make
no mention of them. Indeed, nothing in the sources would lead
one to believe that anything had changed. The whole affair had
taken place outside of the area under Tibetan domination, and no
reliable source records anything with respect to Chinese activity
in the Tarim Basin countries at the time. Moreover, Tibet is ignored in all of the accounts of the P'ei Hsing-chien expedition insofar as it was known to be allied with the Western Turks and appeared invincible at that time. It seems clear that the Chinese
carefully avoided the Tibetans in the Tarim Basin. At the same
time, it is apparent that the Tibetans had not yet involved themselves in the affairs of the region to the north of the Tien Shan.[47]

[44] He had been appointed in 665 (CTS, 84:2802; HTS, 108:4086).
TCTC, 202:6391, states that he had only been chang-shih of Qocho (Chinese,
Kao-ch'ang, Hsi chou). The gloss says he was appointed in 654.

[45] He returned on November 8, 679, according to CTS, 5:105, and HTS,
3:75. On the fortress at Sûyâb, see the comments in my article, "The Plan of
the City of Peace" (1984b).

[46] TCTC, 202:6391-6392. Cf. CTS, 84:2802-2803, 185a:4802; HTS,
108:4086-4087, 215b:6064.

[47] There has been a certain amount of controversy about this episode.
Moriyasu, 1984:15-16, is the most recent to argue that the T'ang recovered
the Four Garrisons in 679. In fact, there is a complete absence of Chinese

But with the capture of the strategic T'ang fortress of An-jung City on Tibet's eastern border, Tibetan control over the whole of China's western frontier to the south of Qocho was secure.[48]

Immediately after P'ei Hsing-chien's return to China, a serious rebellion broke out among the Eastern Turks,[49] and P'ei was appointed to command the armies sent to suppress it. He was victorious in 680 and 681,[50] but these triumphs were soon dampened by the news that the Western Turks, under *Arśïla Ch'e-pu, had rebelled in the spring of 682.[51] When P'ei died before he could lead an army against this revolt, Wang Fang-i, P'ei's former lieutenant and now the Assistant Protector-General of the Pacified West, took command.[52] He attacked the Western Turks as they were besieging *Köngül City, and defeated them by the Ili River. When the "Three-surnamed" Yen-mien Turks, who had allied

---

claims to have reconquered—or even to have recaptured by subterfuge—the Four Garrisons of the Pacified West. The sole source which supposedly would support such a claim is an isolated line in the midst of the general account of the Western Turks in the *TFYK* (967:11v [p. 11372]) which states: "First year of the Tiao-lu [period]: Sûyâb, Kucha, Khotan, and Kashgar were made [or 'were taken to be'] the Four Garrisons." Nothing is said to explain this remark in the source itself, and none of the other Chinese sources support it. It should be further pointed out that the statement in question says nothing about a restoration of Chinese rule over those Garrisons. It merely reports that, henceforth, references to "the Four Garrisons" denote the four cities named and exclude other possibilities, such as Agni. (On the changes of the cities of the Four Garrisons, see Chavannes, 1903:113-114.) What is alone clear from the accounts is that P'ei's mission had succeeded in capturing Sûyâb, which at the time had not been considered one of the Four Garrisons. The Chinese then declared that it was one of the Four Garrisons, no doubt so that they could still claim to rule part of their old colony in Central Asia. Although the Tibetans may have been unable or unwilling to exercise too much control over the Tarim Basin cities, it is clear that the Chinese had at that time no effective influence there.

[48] *CTS*, 196a:5224; *HTS*, 216a:6078; *TCTC*, 202:6396. The compilers of these Chinese histories believed that the Tibetans were then in control of the original Four Garrisons, which the historians specifically list.

[49] In late 679 (*TCTC*, 202:6392).

[50] *TCTC*, 202:6393-6394, 6403-6404.

[51] *HTS*, 3:77, *TCTC*, 203:6407.

[52] *CTS*, 5:109, 84:2804-2805; *HTS*, 3:77, 108:4088; *TCTC*, 203:6407.

themselves with Ch'e-pu, counterattacked by the Issyk Kul, Wang repulsed and then vanquished their combined forces. The leaders of both Turkic groups were captured.[53] Thus, the T'ang managed to maintain their domination over the Western Turks to the north of the Tien Shan. But at the end of 682, the remaining Eastern Turks of the *Arśïla royal clan again rebelled, and this time succeeded. The result was the formation of the Second Eastern Turkic Empire, under Elteriś Qaghan.[54]

The expansionist policies of the three major Asian empires were now for a time hindered by serious internal political difficulties. In the winter of 676-677, Khri maṅ slon had died just as his son, Khri 'dus sroṅ, was being born.[55] A period of uncertainty over the succession lasted until Khri 'dus sroṅ was confirmed as emperor in the winter of 685-686.[56] In China, the later years of Kao-tsung were marked by intrigues surrounding the imminent succession. When he died at the age of 56 on December 27, 683,[57] his consort Wu Chao came to power, first in the name of Chung-tsung, then in the name of Jui-tsung. As already mentioned, the Arab caliphate was wracked at this time by a major civil war that followed the death of the Umayyad Caliph Yazîd in 683. It was only in 691[58] that the dynasty reestablished its control over most of the Arab Empire. For these reasons, and because the expan-

[53] CTS, 5:109; HTS, 3:77, 111:4135 (this source adds the title *cur* to Ch'e-pu's name TCTC, 203:6409.

[54] TCTC, 203:6412.

[55] OTA, Mouse year (676-)677 winter; MD, ja:70r. The name 'dus is also spelled 'du.

[56] OTA, Bird year (685-)686 winter.

[57] TCTC, 203:6416. It is interesting to note that his illness was treated by a court physician who was, according to his name, most probably a Greek. The emperor complained that he could not see, so the doctor suggested that, if he could "lance the head to remove [extra] blood, he could cure [him]." After the operation, which was performed over the objections of the empress, Kao-tsung exclaimed: "My eyes seem to be clear!" (TCTC, 203:6415.) See the discussion of Greek medicine in T'ang China in my paper, "The Introduction of Greek Medicine into Tibet in the Seventh and Eighth Centuries" (1979) 297-302, n. 6.

[58] Shaban, 1970:44.

sionist Mgar clan ministers effectively wielded Tibetan political power, Tibet's grip on eastern Central Asia remained relatively unchallenged until the late 680s, when Wu Chao firmly established herself in power in China.

With the exception of several minor raids on the Chinese border to the east,[59] however, the Tibetans appear to have remained relatively uninvolved in foreign military adventures for several years. Finally, in 685, the T'ang strategists decided to attack Tibet from the north. On December 2, 685, Wei Tai-chia, the President of the Board of Civil Office, was appointed commander-in-chief of an expeditionary army sent to attack Tibet, apparently by way of the Western Turks.[60] This army never left China, however. The only action taken by the Chinese authorities seems to have been the appointment of Yüan Ch'ing, a son of *Aršila Mi-she, the Hsing-hsi-wang Qaghan, as a general and Protector of K'un-ling. Thus he was charged with controlling (on China's behalf) the five *Tarduś tribes which had been under his father.[61] Unfortunately, no more is said about Yüan Ch'ing's activities, if there were any.[62] But it is notable that the geographic area affected by Yüan Ch'ing's appointment was the same—except the cities—as that supposedly recovered six years earlier by P'ei Hsing-chien and three years earlier by Wang Fang-i. Chinese power in Central Asia, even to the north of the Tien Shan, was hardly as firm as the Chinese historians would have us believe.

[59] Their only recorded military action in 680 was a raid on Ho-yüan in which Hei-ch'ih Ch'ang-chih succeeded in driving them off. (*TCTC*, 202:6395; Ssu-ma Kuang shows in his *K'ao-i* that the accounts in the other sources are mistaken.) In the summer of 681, Hei-ch'ih Ch'ang-chih defeated a Tibetan army led by Tsan-p'o and Su-ho-kuei at Liang-fei Ch'uan. (Incidentally, one may suspect this name to be a calque of a Tibetanized one, as was discussed in the case of Ta-fei Ch'uan.) The Chinese captured the Tibetans' supplies and returned. (*CTS*, 196a:5224; *HTS*, 216a:6078; *TCTC*, 202:6401.) The accounts of both the Ho-yüan and the Liang-fei Ch'uan episodes need further examination because of the confusion in the sources between them on the one hand and the accounts of Li Ching-hsüan's defeat on the other.

[60] *TCTC*, 203:6435.

[61] Ibid.

[62] Cf. Chavannes, 1903:281.

Also in 685, the Tibetan Prime Minister, Mgar Btsan sña ldombu, died, apparently from meddling in the imperial succession. His brother, Mgar Khri ʿbriṅ btsan brod, was appointed to replace him, and thus the succession of Khri ʿdus sroṅ as emperor was assured.[63] After eight years of internal strife, Tibet could now address its external problems.

Early in 686, Mgar planned to lead an army into Turkistan,[64] but was delayed until the following year. Meanwhile, the T'ang government went on with its effort to reassert control over the Western Turks. In the autumn of 686, they appointed *Khusraw (also known as the Pu-li *śad*), a son of the Western Turk *Arśila Pu-chen, the Chi-wang-chüeh Qaghan, as the general authorized to inherit the five Nu-shih-pi tribes that his father had ruled.[65]

In early 687, Mgar invaded the "Turkic country of Guzan," in other words, the kingdom of Kucha. It is clear from the Tibetan sources that from this point on he remained outside of Tibet.[66] Wu Chao's reaction to the news of this invasion was to again appoint Wei Tai-chia as a general, this time as Commander-in-Chief of the An-hsi ("Parthia") *tao* Expeditionary Army.[67] This campaign was canceled, however, as was (after trenchant criticism) another she proposed at the end of the year.[68] But in the fol-

---

[63] *OTA*, Bird year 685-686 (no season given). Cf. Satô, 1958:342-344.

[64] *OTA*, Dog year 686(-687) before summer. Cf. Moriyasu, 1984:16-17.

[65] *TCTC*, 203:6441. Cf. Chavannes, 1903:4, 76, 281. The T'ang strategists thus employed the same method they had used in the previous year with Yüan Ch'ing and the Eastern Turks. *Khusraw (Chosroes) apparently lies behind the Chinese transcription Hu-se-lo. The name is Persian, not Turkic.

[66] *OTA*, Pig year 687(-688) before winter; cf. Moriyasu, 1984:17-18. On the equivalence of the name Guzan with one of the many names for Kucha, see P. Pelliot, "À propos des Comans" (1920) 181; cf. Moriyasu, 1984:17, 65 (n. 84).

[67] On January 10, 688 (*HTS*, 4:86; *TCTC*, 204:6446 gloss, *K'ao-i* quotation of a *Shih-lu* passage).

[68] *TCTC*, 204:6456. The famous minister Ch'en Tzu-ang opposed the latter plan in a long argument he presented to the throne. In it, he states: "The nation has recently abandoned the Pacified North, withdrawn from the Shan-yü [Protectorate Generalship], discarded Kucha, and let Kashgar go . . ." (*TCTC*, 204:6456). In other words, Ch'en argues, having just been defeated on the northern and western fronts, and with problems at home—he

lowing year, China finally took action against Tibet. On May 28, 689, Wei Tai-chia was again ordered to be Commander-in-Chief of the An-hsi *tao* Expeditionary Army.[69] The army must have left immediately after it was mustered, for it arrived during the seventh lunar month (July 22 to August 30) of 689 in the vicinity of *Köngül, north of the Tien Shan. In that month, a great battle with the Tibetans took place by the Yin-chih-chia River, southwest of *Köngül, and the T'ang army suffered a severe defeat. The remnants of the army, further diminished by bad weather and supply problems, retreated back to Qocho. Punishment from the T'ang court was swift. Wei was demoted, and Yen Wen-ku, his Assistant Commander-in-Chief and the Great Protector of the Pacified West, was decapitated. T'ang Hsiu-ching, who was the Assistant Protector of the Pacified West and had organized the army's retreat, was rewarded with the appointment as Governor-General of Qocho.[70]

The victorious Tibetan army under the command of Mgar Khri 'brin returned to Tibet in the latter part of the year.[71] It would seem indisputable that the Tibetans had reconfirmed their mastery of the northern Tarim Basin region—at least in the area from *Köngül to Kucha—and had done it without permitting a single Chinese army to penetrate their territories. But not all was well. The T'ang presence in Sûyâb and Qocho continued to pose a serious threat to any real Tibetan expansion into the region north of the Tien Shan. In addition, it is probable that the Tibetans, like the contemporaneous Arabs, had great difficulty in holding on to the new conquests. This was due in part to their inability to keep the same army—made up of independent-minded warriors—mobilized for long without mutinous thoughts arising among the rank and file. Moreover, leaders such as Mgar Khri 'brin had to worry about maintaining their power

---

mentions a famine in Shantung, among other things—it would have been disastrous to mobilize a weak China against the stronger Turks and Tibetans.

[69] *CTS*, 6:120; *HTS*, 196a:5224; *TCTC*, 204:6457.

[70] *CTS*, 6:120, 196a:5224; *HTS*, 4:88, 216a:6078; *TCTC*, 204:6459. *HTS*, 111:4149, states that he was made Governor-General of Ling *chou*.

[71] *OTA*, Ox year 689-690 before the winter assembly.

at court during a prolonged absence on campaign. Such con-
straints were important factors in the subsequent development of
the Tibetan Empire.

Late in the year 690, Wu Chao, who had been the de facto
Chinese ruler since the death of Kao-tsung, officially usurped the
throne. First she was proclaimed by a Buddhist monk to be an incarnation of the "future Buddha" Maitreya and the ruler of the
"Jambudvîpa of the present age," China.[72] Then she changed the
name of the dynasty to Chou, that dynasty of kings who had
reigned during the great age of Classical China.[73] Finally, she was
made *Huang-ti* ("Emperor").[74] With her control over the court
complete, she was now able to turn her attention to the pressing
matter of the state of China's imperium.

Fortunately for the Chinese expansionists, the political situation within Tibet was beginning to show signs of strain. The new
emperor, Khri ʿdus sroṅ, was now old enough to want greater
personal control of the Tibetan government, the administration
of which had rested for decades in the hands of the powerful Mgar
clan. One after another, Khri ʿdus sroṅ began eliminating the less
powerful of these belligerent rivals.[75] Obviously, such internal
discord could only lead to disaster for Tibetan colonialism in
Central Asia.

Thus, towards the end of 690 the political situation in Central
Asia began to favor the Chinese again. The Eastern Turks under
Elteriś Qaghan are said to have repeatedly raided and robbed the
On oq. *Khusraw, the Chi-wang-chüeh Qaghan who was also
the Chinese-appointed Protector-General of Meng-ch'ih (based
apparently in Sûyâb),[76] led sixty or seventy thousand Western

[72] *TCTC*, 204:6466; cf. *CHC*, 3:311.

[73] *TCTC*, 204:6047.

[74] Cf. R. Guisso, *Wu Tse-t'ien and the Politics of Legitimation in T'ang China*
(1978); *CHC*, 3:305 et seq. She had many names and honorific titles. The
sources indicate she was called "Emperor" (Chinese, *ti*) during her reign. Although she is better known by her posthumous name, Empress Wu Tse-
t'ien, I prefer to follow her own intentions and also to give her credit for her
accomplishment; thus I call her "Emperor Wu."

[75] See Satô, 1958:362-372.

[76] See Chavannes, "Notes additionnelles sur les Tou-kiue (Turcs) occidentaux" (1904) 26.

Turks into Chinese-controlled territory. Accordingly, he was rewarded with appointment as Great Protecting General of the Right, and was titled Chieh-chung-shih-chu Qaghan.[77]

In the middle of 691, the T'ang organized an army to attack the Tibetans on their nearer, eastern flank toward Wu-wei. But the army was recalled before it reached Wu-wei,[78] and there matters rested until the beginning of 692. By that time, it was probably obvious that the Tibetans were not prepared to fight off a concerted attack of any kind.[79] Moreover, local rebellions against Tibetan rule made Chinese intervention seem opportune. For these reasons, perhaps, the T'ang now appointed Hsia, the son of Yü-ch'ih Fu-she Hsiung (the former king of Khotan who apparently died in China), as the new king of Khotan. This "Hsia" was evidently the famous King Vijâya Sangrâma "the Lion," although at this point he was but seven years old.[80]

The extent of the turmoil within the Tibetan realm became more obvious when, on Tibet's eastern border with China, a large group of subject Tanguts submitted to the Chinese on February 25, 692.[81] That summer, a Tibetan leader known as Ho-su attempted to defect with a large group of followers from Kuei Ch'uan. Ho-su's plans were discovered and he was arrested. Notwithstanding, another Tibetan, leading eight thousand Ch'iang tribesmen (Tibetan subjects), went over to the Chinese army at the Ta-tu River. It is possible that the subsequent meeting of the Tibetan Mdosmad assembly in Rgyam śigar and the seizure of certain Sumpas was connected with these defections.[82]

[77] TCTC, 204:6469.

[78] CTS, 6:121, 196a:5225; HTS, 4:91; TCTC, 204:6475.

[79] HTS, 111:4148; TCTC, 204:6487.

[80] TCTC, 205:6477; cf. R. Emmerick, Tibetan Texts Concerning Khotan (1967) 52-53. When he reached manhood, he campaigned against "the Turks." Later, in penance for this, he built the vihâra of 'Guźan. One wonders if this means that he was involved in otherwise unknown campaigns against the Turks of the Śâhî dynasty of Kabul in the region of Guṣân, i.e., Kushan.

[81] TCTC, 205:6482; cf. CTS, 198-5292, and HTS, 221a:6216, which both state that 200,000 households submitted.

[82] OTA, Dragon year 692-693 winter assembly of Mdosmad; CTS,

With the news of this Tibetan weakness, T'ang Hsiu-ching, who was the Governor-General of Qocho, urged Wu Chao to re-take the Four Garrisons, which then included Kucha, Khotan, Kashgar, and Sûyâb.[83] She responded by appointing Wang Hsiao-chieh[84] as Commander-in-Chief of the Wu-wei *tao* Expeditionary Army. In this capacity, he led T'ang Hsiu-ching and the Turkic general *Arśïla Chung-chieh against the Tibetans.[85] On December 9, 692, according to the extremely laconic report in the Chinese sources, Wang defeated the Tibetans and recovered the Four Garrisons.[86] The sources are so unexpectedly brief and un-detailed that, in view of the great attention usually afforded to victories, one can seriously doubt that any major battles occurred in 692.

Nonetheless, it is clear that Wang's appointment to the Wu-wei *tao* Expeditionary Army indicates that originally the campaign probably had the very modest but strategically crucial objective of securing the nearer section of the route to the West. Wang's apparent success in this venture then allowed him to re-take virtually unhindered the fortified cities of the Tarim Basin.[87] He moved the Protector Generalship of the Pacified West back to Kucha from Qocho, and stationed an army there to garrison it. Thus ended the first period of Tibet's colonial domination of the countries of the Tarim Basin: through Tibetan internal collapse.

196a-5225; *TCTC*, 205:6482. Cf. *HTS*, 216a-6078, which confuses the account somewhat, and contains numerous variant characters. The *OTA* mentions the seizure of Śochigs or "the *śochigs*" of the Sumpas.

[83] Sûyâb, the only one still under Chinese control, had replaced Agni as one of the official Four in 679. See note 47, above.

[84] Wang was a Chinese general who had been captured and held by the Tibetans in the campaign of 678, in which he served as the Assistant Commander-in-Chief. He is reported to have been treated very well by his captors (*TCTC*, 205:6487). See above, note 39.

[85] *HTS*, 216a:6078; *TCTC*, 205:6487.

[86] *CTS*, 6:123, 196a:5225, *HTS*, 4:93, 216a:6078; *TCTC*, 205:6487-6488; *TFYK*, 358:8r (p. 4243).

[87] It would seem, however, that Khotan was not yet recovered. See below, Chapter Three.

Chapter 3

THE ARABS AND WESTERN TURKS

The Chinese recapture of the Tarim Basin countries came as quite a surprise to both Tibet and China. In China, it was not even agreed that the renewal of military domination in the West was a good thing. Nonetheless, it seems that the logic expressed in a lengthy opinion favoring the retention of the Four Garrisons prevailed. This opinion, which is preserved in the *Hsin T'ang shu*, recalls the long history of Chinese adventurism in the region, and warns about the danger to Ho-hsi, the Circuit "West of the Yellow River," if the Garrisons were abandoned.[1]

It is quite possible that Tibetan unpreparedness was due as much to a policy conflict at court as to the ongoing power struggle between the Mgar clan and the emperor. Nevertheless, far from losing more power as a result of the T'ang victory, the Mgar family seems to have been temporarily strengthened by it. Even the pacifists at court would not have intended to lose such a profitable colonial territory, and perhaps even the emperor saw the advantage of retaining the militarily experienced Mgar clan lead-

[1] *HTS*, 216a:6078-6079.

ers a while longer. In any case, the Mgar family did not intend to allow the T'ang to take over without a struggle.

In the winter of 693-694, Mgar Khri ʿbriṅ assembled an army in Greater Rtsaṅ, and proceeded into the ʿAźa country.[2] In the spring of 694, this Tibetan attempt to maintain control over the Tarim Basin was stopped by the T'ang armies in two key battles along the marches of Chinese Central Asia.[3] At Leng-ch'üan[4] and in the Ta-ling Valley,[5] Wang Hsiao-chieh defeated the Tibetan governor of Khotan, Mgar Btsan ñen guṅ rton,[6] and the allied qaghan of the Western Turks, *Arśïla T'ui-tzu,[7] who had attacked from the north.[8] According to Ssu-ma Kuang, each battle resulted in the loss of over 30,000 Tibetans and Western Turks.[9] Meanwhile, in the far west, Han Ssu-chung, the *shou shih* of the T'ang garrison in Sûyâb, defeated the *Ärski's Niźuk Irkin,[10] who was the allied leader of the fourth arrow of the western branch of the On oq.[11] Han took over 10,000 prisoners, and captured *Bars,[12] the fortified city of the Tibetans and *Ärski.[13] To complete the disaster, the Tibetan leader Mgar Staggu ri zum was taken prisoner by the Sogdians.[14] Thus the T'ang had severely damaged the Tibetans at their two most strategic strongholds: the

[2] OTA, Snake year (693-)694 winter.

[3] HTS, 4:94; TCTC, 205:6493.

[4] Located in the area of present-day Shansi (Morohashi, 1622.90).

[5] Located in the area of the borders of present-day Ch'ing-hai, or Qinghai (CKKCTMTTT, 82).

[6] Emmerick, 1967:58-59.

[7] He was made qaghan in 694 according to HTS, 215b:6065; he is labeled a "false qaghan" in HTS, 216a:6079.

[8] HTS, 216a:6079. *Arśïla T'ui-tzu fled to the Tibetan court in the winter of 694-695 (OTA).

[9] TCTC, 205:6493.

[10] This title is transcribed in Chinese as Ni-shu; see Müller, 1913:10, 39.

[11] Chavannes, 1903:34, 308n. On the *Ärski, see Appendix D.

[12] Chinese, Mo-ssu.

[13] HTS, 216a:6079; TCTC, 205:6493. HTS, 215b:6065, adds that Han also defeated (with Niźuk) "the Turk Shih-chih-han [this can also be interpreted as 'the Türgiś Chih Khan'], (the) Hu-lu, etc."

[14] OTA, Horse year 694(-695) before winter. In view of the Tibetan activity in western Central Asia at this time, it is no longer necessary to assume that he was captured somewhere in eastern Central Asia.

Koko Nor and the regions of the Pamirs and the southwestern
Tien Shan. It may be that by now the Chinese understood that
strong pressure at these points would prevent the Tibetans from
retaking the Tarim Basin.

In the aftermath of this debacle, punishments were meted out
to the responsible Tibetan leaders. Khri zuṅ, the ʿBon Dargyal or
vassal ruler of the ʿAźa, assisted in convoking the Tibetan winter
assembly, as he had done many times before. This time, however,
he was put to death.[15] He had probably been involved in the defeat at Ta-ling, and was in any case a convenient scapegoat. Mgar
Khri ʿbriṅ, who was still Prime Minister, remained in the northeast, safely distant from the emperor in Central Tibet. Another
member of the Mgar clan, Btsan ńen guṅ rton, who was the former governor of Khotan but was now a defeated general, was not
so fortunate. In 695, he was disgraced.[16] Later in the year, he was
tried in Śa tsal and then sentenced to death at Ńenkar by Emperor
Khri ʿdus sroṅ.[17] Meanwhile, Mgar Khri ʿbriṅ plotted Tibetan
retaliation. In response to his raids on Lin-t'ao (T'ao *chou*), the
T'ang organized the Su-pien *tao* Expeditionary Army, with
Wang Hsiao-chieh as Commander-in-Chief and Lou Shih-te as
Assistant Commander-in-Chief.[18] Mgar, in turn, mobilized an
army in ʿAźa, and went out to meet the forces of "the Chinese
general Wang *shang shu*" in battle.[19] The result was a great Tibetan
victory in early 696 at a place on the borders of T'ao *chou* known
to the Chinese by the transcribed foreign name Su-lo-han Mountain. To the Tibetans, however, it was Stag La Rgya Dur ("Tiger
Pass Chinese Graveyard"), after the great numbers of T'ang soldiers killed in the battle.[20]

Mgar Khri ʿbriṅ's prestige at court would thus seem to have

---

[15] *OTA*, Horse year (694-)695 winter. As usual in this source, the account
is imprecise when noting the execution of an important person. It reports
only that he *gum*, "died," rather than *bkum*, was "killed." Incidentally, the
name Khri zuṅ is ambiguous; it means either "conqueror of 10,000" or
"throne-snatcher."

[16] *OTA*, Sheep year 695(-696) summer.

[17] Ibid. The name Śa tsal means "Deer Park."

[18] *HTS*, 4:94, 96; *TCTC*, 205:6503-6504.

[19] *OTA*, Sheep year (695-)696 winter.

[20] *TCTC*, 205:6504; *OTA*, Sheep year (695-)696 winter; *OTC*, 10.

recovered somewhat from the military setbacks of 695. Indeed, soon after the Battle of Stag La Rgya Dur,[21] Tibet was able— from a position of strength—to send an embassy to the T'ang court with a peace proposal—a political marriage.[22] In so doing, the Tibetans were doubtlessly well aware that the recent resurgence of the Eastern Turks made their offer particularly timely. Now under the famous Qapaghan Qaghan (692-716),[23] these Turks had begun regular raids on the Chinese borders. In the autumn of 696, they attacked the fortified city of Liang *chou*, which was very near Tibetan territory, and carried off the Chinese Governor-General.[24] Faced with these troubles, and with a revolt in Khitan further to the east,[25] the Chinese must have welcomed the Tibetan offer of peace.

In reply to the Tibetan embassy, Emperor Wu sent a remarkably astute diplomat-general, Kuo Yüan-chen.[26] When Mgar met with him, he demanded that the Chinese abandon the Four Garrisons, and that the nations of the Tarim and of the Western Turks be freed to live under their own rulers.[27] Kuo objected that the Tibetans were of a different race from the people of the Four Garrisons (in other words, the nations kept under Chinese domina-

---

[21] In the ninth month of 696 according to *TCTC*, 205:6508-6509; cf. the *K'ao-i*, same citation.

[22] *CTS*, 196a:5225; *HTS*, 216a:6079; *TCTC*, 205:6508.

[23] Chavannes, 1903:41-42 (n. 8). His other name is, in Chinese, Mo-ch'o, in Old Tibetan, 'Bug cor. The first syllable of the Chinese transcription, *mo*, does not correspond to *bäg*, as many have thought, because it was used in proper names (including at least one known from Old Tibetan sources), while *fu* was regularly used to transcribe *bäg*. If the word is transcribed according to the system for rendering Old Turkic that is used by L. Ligeti, "À propos du 'Rapport sur les rois demeurant dans le Nord' " (1971), the name should be read Bük cur (p. 179). In light of the Chinese transcription, however, perhaps *Bök or *Bög would be better for the first syllable. Further philological study is needed.

[24] *HTS*, 90:3772; *TCTC*, 205:6507. *CTS*, 6:125, 196a:5225, and *HTS*, 4:96, 216a:6079, mistakenly have "Tibetans" instead of "Turks" here.

[25] Cf. *CHC*, 3:314.

[26] See Chavannes, 1903:179-192.

[27] According to the version in *HTS*, 216a:6079. The other versions all say "divide their [i.e., the Turks'] lands."

tion by the Four Garrisons) and the Turks. He asked Mgar, "How could you not have the intention of annexing them?"[28] One can almost see the innocent look on Mgar's face as he replied, according to the Chinese sources: "If Tibet lusted after territory, we would trouble your borders, and thus invade (your prefectures of) Kan and Liang; why should we wish to scheme for profit over 10,000 *li* away?"[29] Mgar further pointed out that the Western Turks were "extremely far away from China," but that although their eastern five tribes, the *Tarduś, were close to the T'ang's Pacified West, the western five tribes, the Nu-shih-pi, were only separated from Tibet by a desert, and so their raiders could reach Tibet very quickly. Thus, Mgar concluded, the disposition of the Western Turks was a matter of concern for Tibet.[30] Kuo gave no answer, but returned to court along with a Tibetan envoy to report Mgar's proposal to Emperor Wu.[31]

At court, Kuo Yüan-chen disclosed his plans for handling the Tibetan question. He suggested that, as a counterproposal to Mgar, the Chou offer not to abandon the Four Garrisons, but to agree to give up the five Nu-shih-pi tribes in exchange for Tibet's "return" of the Koko Nor lands and T'u-yü-hun people to China. He also suggested pressing the Tibetan peace initiative, since the Tibetans were evidently tired of war. If peace looked promising, the Tibetans would reject Mgar, and inner turmoil—a traditional Chinese foreign policy tactic—would result in the Tibetan Empire. Kuo claimed with good reason that the Tibetans could never

[28] Kuo thus ignored the fact that the Chinese were (and still are) far more different in race and culture from the peoples of Central Asia than were the Tibetans. In the *HTS* version he says: "The various tribes are different from the Tibetans, but have long been registered as people of T'ang." All of this was just posturing. Tibet had dominated the Tarim Basin countries for just as long as the T'ang.

[29] *TCTC*, 205:6508. *HTS*, 216a:6079-6080, has a much longer, more detailed, and substantially different account of this conversation. Note the anachronism that the speakers, as reported by the post-T'ang historians, continued to refer to China as "T'ang" despite Wu Chao's change of the dynastic name.

[30] *HTS*, 216a:6080.

[31] *TCTC*, 205:6508; cf. *TFYK*, 655:15v-17r (pp. 7848-7849).

afford to surrender their northeastern marches to China; the ensuing drawn-out negotiations, he argued, would allow domestic conflicts to erupt in Tibet. The emperor approved his proposals.[32]

Kuo Yüan-chen's estimate of Tibet's strategic prerequisites, as well as of the political situation within Tibet, was remarkably accurate. The Tibetans could not accept Kuo's proposals, and the impasse in the negotiations coupled with China's increasing preoccupation with the Eastern Turks proved disastrous for the remaining members of the Mgar family. Under the pressure of constant Eastern Turkic raids on northernmost China,[33] Wu Chao decided to pursue peace with them via a political marriage with Qapaghan Qaghan's family.[34] This Eastern Turkic rapprochement with China meant that Mgar Khri ʿbriṅ's hands were tied. Too vulnerable at court to undertake foreign military adventures, he and his army were left in the field, but not in action. Mobilized, the army was an expensive but apparently useless burden on the country. The Mgar clan was thus easy prey to Khri ʿdus sroṅ and his supporters led by the minister Maṅ ñen bźi brtsan.[35]

With Khri ʿbriṅ and his armies in the far northeast, the young emperor was able to carry out the first part of his purge without difficulty. Under the pretext of holding an imperial hunting party, he invited the leading members of the Mgar clan—over two thousand people—and had them executed. He then summoned Khri ʿbriṅ and the minister's younger brother, Tsanpʿo,[36] to court. Needless to say, they failed to obey the summons.

---

[32] CTS, 196a:5225; HTS, 216a:6079-6080; TCTC, 205:6508-6509. Cf. Chavannes, 1903:180-182. CHC, 3:315, gives Emperor Wu the credit for all of these ideas.

[33] TCTC, 205 et seq.

[34] Concessions made by the Chinese in the spring of 697 included the handing over to the Eastern Turks of the six prefectures of settled Turks, along with their land, seed-grain, silks, agricultural implements, and iron (TCTC, 206:6516).

[35] Mentioned in OTA, Monkey year (696-)697 winter; CTS, 196a:5225; TCTC, 206:6539. The Chinese version of his name is Lun Yen, i.e., *Blon Ñen.

[36] This is the Chinese rendering of a Tibetan name. Perhaps he can be identified with Phatshab Rgyal tore.

Aside from his natural wariness, Khri ʿbriṅ's refusal may be attributed in part to his military action in Tsoṅka in 698-699. Here, the recalcitrant but still-loyal Mgar Khri ʿbriṅ—he was, after all, responsible for ʿdus sroṅ's enthronement[37]—defeated and captured the Chinese general Thug Pu-śi.[38] Notwithstanding this demonstration of loyalty, ʿdus sroṅ marched north for a showdown.[39] At the beginning of 699,[40] with the approach of the Tibetan emperor, Khri ʿbriṅ's troops scattered and he took his own life.[41] That summer, Khri ʿbriṅ's younger brother Tsan-p'o and over a thousand of his followers, as well as Khri ʿbriṅ's son Kung-jen[42] and 7,000 ʿAźa families, fled to China. There they were received with open arms, and promptly enlisted in the army.[43] The house of Mgar was utterly crushed, and never again played an important role in Tibetan politics.

In 699, the Western Turks also experienced considerable political turmoil. In that year the Eastern Turks' Qapaghan Qaghan formally set up his younger brother as *šad* over their five eastern tribes and his nephew—the son of Elteriš—as *šad*[44] over their five

[37] *TCTC*, 202:6389.

[38] *OTA*, Dog year (698-)699 winter. The identity of the Chinese general is unknown. *Pu-śi* is probably a transcription of his title (as is usual in Old Tibetan renderings of Chinese officials' names); it no doubt represents the common *fu-shih*, "assistant commissioner." (The Fûśîy of the *Maḥrnâmag*—see Müller, 1913:32—is undoubtedly the same Chinese title.)

[39] *OTA*, Dog year (698-)699 winter.

[40] Ibid.; *TCTC*, 206:6539, under the second lunar month.

[41] *OTA*, Dog year (698-)699 winter; *CTS*, 196a:5225-5226; *HTS*, 216a:6080; *TCTC*, 206:6539. Cf. Chavannes, 1903:182. The *Annals* records only that "Mgar having been indicted for great crimes, the emperor went to Phar (in Mdosmad)." (For the location of Phar, see *OTA*, Horse year 706-707.) During the next winter (Pig year [699-]700), those loyal to the emperor were rewarded with *yig-gtsaṅ*, "charters," while "the wealth of those indicted for crimes was counted."

[42] He is apparently to be identified with Mang-pu-chih, or Maṅporje (*CTS*, 196a:5226; *HTS*, 216a:6080), i.e., Mgar Maṅporje Stag rtsaṅ. See *OTC*, 10.

[43] *CTS*, 196a:5226; *HTS*, 216a:6080; *TCTC*, 206:6539-6540.

[44] Qapaghan Qaghan was the brother of Elteriš, whose son—called here Mo-chü in Chinese transcription—would seem to be the same as Mo-chi-lien, better known as Bilgä Qaghan. Since Bilgä's brother, Kül Tegin, led

western tribes. He then appointed his son, Fu-chü, as "Little Qaghan" or "T'o-hsi Qaghan"[45] over the two *šad*s.[46] Yet it would appear that, despite these maneuverings and the pretensions of the Chinese, another Turkic confederation—the Türgiś—had already taken control of the lands of the Western Turks.

Khri ʿdus sroṅ[47] was a man of a seemingly unlimited ambition for power. He was now the indisputable master within Tibet proper.[48] For the neighboring lands, the remainder of his reign was not to be peaceful.

In early 700, Tun Yabghu Qaghan—known to the Chinese as *Arsïla T'ui-tzu—came to the Tibetan court.[49] He was sent to Turkistan in the summer of that year, but his exact destination is unknown.[50] It is possible that his mission was connected with the revolt of "the Tibetan" *Ärski Tegin Po-lu of the Western Turks. He was the Niźuk Irkin of the *Ärski, the leading subtribe of the Nu-shih-pi, who had been allied with Tibet some years previously.[51] In the autumn of 700, he led a rebellion against the

---

several campaigns into the lands of the Western Turks during Qapaghan Qaghan's reign, one would suppose that the "son of Qutlugh" (i.e., the son of Elteriś) could also be identified with him. But, because Bilgä Qaghan was the elder of the two, was in line to succeed to the throne, and has a linguistically similar name, it would seem unlikely that Kül Tegin had the official title.

[45] Cf. Chavannes, 1903:282-283 (n. 5). *T'o-hsi* means "Hold the West" in Chinese.

[46] *TCTC*, 206:6543-6544.

[47] He is often called in Tibetan ʿphrulgyi rgyalpo, an epithet not precisely translatable into English by any one expression.

[48] It was only after his death, in the year of the Snake (705-)706, that a new Prime Minister was appointed.

[49] *OTA*, Pig year (699-)700 winter. This identification was first proposed by Petech, 1967:270. On the name *Arsïla, see Appendix C.

[50] *OTA*, Mouse year 700(-701) summer. See the discussion of Moriyasu's theory below.

[51] Po-lu Tegin is called "the Tibetan" in *TFYK*, 986:15v (p. 11582). Cf. Chavannes, 1904:26. It may be recalled that, in 694, when Tun Yabghu Qaghan (*Arsïla T'ui-tzu) first made his appearance in an army allied with the Tibetans, the T'ang commander in Sûyâb simultaneously defeated the Niźuk Irkin, and captured "the Tibetan" Niźuk's *Bars City. (See above.)

Chinese, who were attempting to augment their control over the Western Turks—then only under nominal Chinese rule—via the Western Turk *Aršïla *Khusraw Qaghan.[52] When attacked, Po-lu holed up in Sûyâb. After a stout resistance, Po-lu lost both the city and his life to the Chinese army, which was aided by *Khusraw and his Turks.[53]

Perhaps in response to the crushing of this rebellion, Tibet launched a series of raids on Chinese territory. In the autumn of 700, Khri ʿdus sroṅ himself led the armies in a raid on Ho *chou*.[54] Meanwhile, the general known as Ch'ü Maṅporje raided Liang *chou* and went on to attack neighboring Ch'ang-sung *hsien*.[55] In 701, the Tibetans joined the Eastern Turks in a large-scale, successful raid on Liang *chou*.[56] That summer, ʿdus sroṅ again led the

Whether or not this was the same Niźuk Irkin, it indicates the same political position (the name is the title of the chief of the fourth arrow of the Nu-shih-pi; see Appendix D) and expresses the same traditional Tibetan-Turkic political alignment. (The concern expressed by Mgar Khri ʿbriṅ about the five Nu-shih-pi tribes indicates the continued Tibetan interest in the area in 696.) On the *Ârski (Chinese, A-hsi-chi or A-hsi-chieh), see Appendix D.

[52] *TCTC*, 206:6545. He was made Commander-in-Chief of the P'ing-hsi *chün* ("Pacify the West Army"), which was garrisoned in Sûyâb, on or shortly after December 27, 699. He had surrendered to China in 690 (*TCTC*, 204:6469) and was still in China in 697 (*TCTC*, 206:6519-6520).

[53] *TCTC*, 207:6550; *TFYK*, 986:15v (p. 11582).

[54] *OTA*, Mouse year 700-701 autumn. Cf. Moriyasu, 1984:22, 67 (n. 109).

[55] *CTS*, 196a:5226; *HTS*, 216a:6080; *TCTC*, 207:6549; *TFYK*, 428:27r-27v (p. 5103). The Chinese subsequently broke Ch'ü Maṅporje's siege of Ch'ang-sung, a county in Wu-wei (*TCTC*, 207:6549). According to *CTS*, 196a:5226, and *HTS* 4:101, 111:4149, four battles were fought in the Hung-yüan Valley by the armies of Lung-yu *tao*, led by T'ang Hsiu-ching.

[56] Moriyasu, 1984:24, suggests that *Aršïla T'ui-tzu might have been used as an envoy to help coordinate the Eastern Turkic–Tibetan venture. This is quite possible. T'ui-tzu's royal *Aršïla blood would probably not have been of much help because he could have been only distantly related to anyone in the Eastern Turkic royal family. But he did speak the same language and that might well have been extremely useful. The major shortcoming in this theory is that the *OTA* says that Tung Yabghu Qaghan was sent to *Drugu yul*, in other words "Turkistan." Later Old Tibetan and classical Tibetan usage employed the word *Drugu* as a generic term for "Turks," including Uyghurs. But in the *Annals*, the single certain reference to the Eastern

armies in raids, this time against Sung *chou* and T'ao *chou*. In the following spring, these raids were repeated, but with unknown results.[57] The raids were the reason for the appointment at the end of 702 of Kuo Yüan-chen to the post of Governor-General of Liang *chou* and Grand Commissioner of the armies of Lung-yu. His task was to defend this strategic city from the Tibetans and Eastern Turks. According to the Chinese sources, he was markedly successful for five years.[58]

Far from having capitulated to the Chinese because of the minor defeats inflicted by T'ang Hsiu-ching,[59] the Tibetans seem not to have been much disturbed. In the winter of 702, the Tibetans in Mdosmad held a great levy of the Sumpas,[60] and then raided Mao *chou* (or Hsi *chou*).[61] They were driven off by the Governor-General, Ch'en Ta-tz'u. In the winter of 703-704, Khri 'dus sron led the armies in a successful campaign to subdue 'Jan, on Tibet's southeastern borders.[62] After spending the summer of 704 on the Yoti River in Rmagrom,[63] he went on a winter cam-

---

Turks uses the name ʿ*Bug cor*, not *Drugu*. Because it appears that the other references to *Drugu* in the *Annals* are all to Western Turks, who according to the Chinese classification included those dominating Jungaria and the neighboring lands in Eastern and Western Central Asia as well as those living further west, this would be the *only* case in the whole of the *Annals* where the source refers to the Eastern Turkic Empire in Mongolia as "Turkistan." Therefore, although Moriyasu's suggestion that T'ui-tzu might have been an envoy for Tibet to the Eastern Turks remains a possibility, it seems rather unlikely given the qaghan's known activity. For a detailed examination of the Old Tibetan names for the Turks, see Moriyasu, 1977a:9, 13-16.

[57] *OTA*, Ox year 701-702 summer and spring.

[58] *TCTC*, 207:6557-6558. Cf. Chavannes, 1903:183.

[59] This is the position maintained by *CHC*, 3:318, where the whole account is generally unreliable. It is certainly true that the Tibetans were then discussing peace with the Chinese via a royal marriage, but these negotiations had been going on for some time; another envoy, sent in the summer of 703, brought official gifts which included 1,000 horses and 2,000 ounces of gold (*CTS*, 196a:5226; *HTS*, 4:103, 216a:6080; *TCTC*, 207:6560, 6562).

[60] *OTA*, Tiger year (702-)703 winter.

[61] *TCTC*, 207:6560, has Mao *chou*; the other sources have Hsi *chou*.

[62] *OTA*, Hare year (703-)704 winter; *OTC*, 7; *CTS*, 196a:5226; *TCTC*, 207:6569; cf. *TCTC*, 207:6626.

[63] *OTA*, Dragon year 704(-705) summer. Rmagrom was the Yellow

paign against the Mywa, a people corresponding in part to the Nan-chao:[64] "He made the White Mywa pay taxes. He subjugated the Black Mywa."[65] But on this campaign, he "went to Heaven,"[66] leaving behind a struggle over the succession.[67]

The years 703 and 704 saw momentous changes in Central Asia. The Western Turks rejected the "cruel and vindictive"[68] Chiehchung-shih-chu Qaghan, *Aršïla *Khusraw, who had been installed by the Chinese in Sûyâb in 700.[69] Instead, they turned to the Bagha Tarqan *Ocïrlïq,[70] a Türgiś who had formerly submitted to *Khusraw. *Ocïrlïq gathered the tribes of the Western Turks in the area around Sûyâb in defiance of the helpless *Khusraw. After setting up an administration of 20 *tutuq*s, each commanding 7,000 men,[71] he finally captured the city of Sûyâb—then

---

River Commandery (cf. *OTAC*, Sheep year [correctly Ape year] 756-757). See G. Uray, "*Khrom*" (1980).

[64] Mywa seems to be an Old Tibetan transcription of the same ethnonym transcribed by the modern Chinese as Miao.

[65] *OTC*, 7, equates the White and Black Mywa, and mentions the (White) Mywa king Kag-la-boṅ, well known from Chinese sources as the Nan-chao king Ko-lo-feng.

[66] *OTA*, Dragon year (704-)705 winter. *CTS*, 196a:5226, records the declaration of court mourning for the Tibetan ruler under the year 705 without specifying the month. *TFYK*, 974:14r (p. 11443), records the same under the seventh lunar month of 705. There is no reason to believe that there was any great recording delay due to his death at a distance from the court. *HTS*, 216a:6080, and *TCTC*, 207:6569, mistakenly place his death in 703. See Note on Chronology.

[67] On this, see my paper, "The Revolt of 755 in Tibet" (1983).

[68] *CTS*, 194b:5190; *TCTC*, 207:6563.

[69] *TCTC*, 207:6563. The account in *HTS*, 215b:6065 (cf. Chavannes, 1903:77), is vague and seems to contradict the account in *TCTC*; *HTS* clearly confuses this event with the account of *Khusraw's earlier surrender "inside" in 690.

[70] His name is given in Chinese transcription as Wu-chih-le, which apparently corresponds to an original *Ocïrlïq. The name is presumably an Old Turkic rendering of the Indian Buddhist name Vajrapâṇi.

[71] This equals 140,000 men, which is fourteen *tümän*. Is this the origin of the subsequent division of the Western Turks into fourteen "tribes"? The Chinese sources use the term *tu-tu*, here translated as "Governor-General."

considered one of the Four Garrisons—and moved his court there in or around 703.[72] His followers having scattered, *Khusraw again fled to safety at the Chinese court.[73] At the beginning of 704, in the hope of quickly replacing *Ocïrlïq, the Chinese appointed *Khusraw's son, *Arsïla Huai-tao, as the qaghan of the On oq.[74] This effort, however, was not successful.

The year 704 also saw Tibetan and Western Turkic cooperation in Tirmidh, a strategic city of Tukhâristân on the Oxus River which controlled the routes south to Balkh and north to the Iron Gate,[75] the mountain pass to Sogdiana. As has already been mentioned, many of the principalities captured by the Arabs in their early conquests in Tukhâristân and Transoxiana had by now regained their indepencence,[76] and so Arab control over these regions was superficial at best. In the turmoil which followed the Arabs' restoration of central control in the 690s, Mûsâ, the son of the displaced governor 'Abd Allâh b. Khâzim of the tribe of Qays,[77] seized the fortress of Tirmidh. Thereafter, he maintained an open rebellion against the Arabs. The local princes and merchants (upon whose business the prosperity of the region de-

---

The Old Turkic borrowing, *tutuq*, is, however, best translated as "military governor." Because Sinological tradition has reserved that translation for the later *chieh-tu-shih*, I have followed most modern historians of the T'ang period in using *tutuq* for the Turkic form of the institution.

[72] It would seem that the appointment of his son to succeed *Khusraw, which follows the remark that he died in Ch'ang-an, indicates *Khusraw's death in 703.

[73] *TCTC*, 207:6562-6563. The dates for all of these events are confused in most of the sources. The general chronology in *TCTC* seems most reliable, and I have followed it. See Chavannes, 1903:41-43, 76-79, and 282-283, for the other sources.

[74] *TCTC*, 207:6569.

[75] Unlike other "Iron Gates" elsewhere, this strategic pass boasted actual iron doors. See the description in *TTHYC*, 872.

[76] Most of these principalities were theoretically still under the suzerainty of the Turkic dynasty of the Yabghus of Tukhâristân. See the discussion of *Arsïla *Boghra below.

[77] Ibn Khâzim, who had governed in the name of the rival caliph 'Abd Allâh b. al-Zubayr, was killed near Marw in 691. See Shaban, 1970:42 et seq., for the most recent and thorough treatment of these events.

pended), however, found him extremely troublesome, and attempted many times to eliminate him. After several years of failure in the direct confrontation of the rebel, these princes and traders decided to try to reach some kind of accommodation with him. Finally, in 704, with the assistance of two Sogdian merchant-princes who had converted to Islam,[78] an alliance was formed between Mûsâ and several princes of Transoxiana and Ṭukhâristân. In the end, however, the two groups could not get along, and the "princes of Transoxiana" turned against Mûsâ. In one of the allied assaults on Tirmidh, Tibetans and Turks are said to have been among the attackers, along with troops of other "princes of Transoxiana" and Ṭukhâristân.[79]

[78] The two Sogdians were the brothers Thâbit and Ḥurayth b. Quṭba. See Shaban, 1970:58-61, for a tantalizing glimpse of the crucial importance of Sogdian traders even in western Khurasan. Especially interesting and worthy of more detailed study are: that Thâbit and Ḥurayth's political connections were on the Marw-to-Sogdiana route; that the two men were clients of the Khuzâʿa tribe of Arabs, which was dominant in Marw (p. 47); that the Sogdian traders in Marw supplied the Arabs with loans for the Transoxanian campaigns of 696 (p. 48); and that the Abbasid revolution of 747 began in Marw, where it had been organized by Arab merchants primarily of the Khuzâʿa tribe (pp. 157-158).

[79] Ṭabarî, ii:1153. The leader of the Tukharistanian contingent was the Nîzak Tarqan, a vassal of the Yabghu (pp. 1152-1153). Cf. E. Esin, "Tarkhan Nîzak or Tarkhan Tirek?" (1977) 327, although her main thesis is improbable. On the well-attested name Nîzak (not *Tirek, as Esin proposes), see Chavannes, 1904:40 (n. 1). Esin has, however, effectively demonstrated one important fact: Nîzak was a title, not a personal name, and was successively applied to several historical rulers (Esin, 1977:323-324). The Nîzak Tarqan was the ruler of the Hephthalite principality of Bâdghîs. Thus Ṭabarî, ii:1153, includes al-Hayâṭila, "Hephthalites," in the army. Shaban (1970:43) on the other hand, introduces Hephthalites where they are not mentioned in the sources. Both Ṭabarî and Balâdhurî, in the places cited in Shaban's note 5 (1970:43), mention only "Turks."

Despite the opinion of Gibb (see below, note 82), there is no reason to doubt the Tibetan participation. *Aršïla *Boghra's petition to the Chinese emperor in 718 specifically states that as of 705—and probably for some time before—Ṭukhâristân was bounded by the Arabs on one side and the Tibetans on the other. Thus the Tibetan leaders were indeed numbered among the "princes of Transoxiana." In fact, the term "Transoxiana" (Arabic, *Mâ warâʾa al-nahr*, "that which is beyond the River") during this period actually

The leader of these Tibetans and Turks was likely as not either the Tibetan ally *Arsïla T'ui-tzu (Tun Yabghu Qaghan), who was the nephew of King *Arsïla Na-tu-ni-li, the Yabghu of Ṭu-khâristân,[80] or the Yabghu's brother, *Boghra, who also was one of the Tibetan-appointed qaghans attempting to rule the Western Turks.[81] (As will be seen, *Arsïla T'ui-tzu fought the Chinese in

referred to everything north and east of the Oxus as far as China. In this respect, it is important to note that Ṭabarî and the accounts he quotes are—unlike other Arab authors—extremely reticent about non-Western peoples. F. Rosenthal, in *A History of Muslim Historiography* (1968) 135, says of Ṭabarî's work: "No notice is taken of the widening of the historical and cultural horizon which had taken place during at-Ṭabarî's lifetime." It is, therefore, significant that Tibetans are mentioned at all in a source as conservative as Ṭabarî; this is strong evidence for their actual involvement in the Mûsâ affair. It is irrelevant that Tibetan involvement is not recorded in the non-Arabic sources, because those sources are quite silent about Mûsâ anyway.

[80] Tun Yabghu Qaghan (Old Tibetan, Ton Yabgo Khagan) was the name or title held by the founder of the dynasty of Yabghus of Ṭukhâristân, who is known from Chinese sources as T'ung Yabghu Qaghan. (See Chavannes, 1903:24 et seq.) T'ui-tzu was the elder brother of *Arsïla Hsien (p. 187), the son of *Arsïla Yüan-ch'ing, and the grandson of *Arsïla Mi-she. He was thus a seventh-generation descendant of Istämi (pp. 3-4). He was also the nephew of *Arsïla Tegin *Boghra (Chinese, P'u-lo; pp. 187, 200 et seq.), who was the younger brother of *Arsïla Na-tu-ni-li (or P'an-tu-ni-li; p. 200 [n. 4]). (The Yabghus of Ṭukhâristân belonged to the royal Turkic clan of *Arsïla [p. 157].) Thus the Yabghu of Ṭukhâristân was T'ui-tzu's uncle.

[81] Nothing more is known about *Boghra's Tibetan connection except that it seems to have been prior to that of T'ui-tzu. The order of appointments given in Kuo Yüan-chen's memorial (*CTS* 97:3046; *HTS*, 122:4364; cf. Chavannes, 1903:188) must be mistaken, since *Boghra had arrived at the Chinese court in 705, and remained there at least until 718 (Chavannes, 1903: 200-202). Of course he was also T'ui-tzu's uncle, and so was no doubt older. Therefore, one can only guess at how long the Tibetans had been involved with the Yabghus of Ṭukhâristân. It is of incidental interest that both versions of Kuo Yüan-chen's memorial list three Tibetan-appointed qaghans of the On oq, the third of whom is called Pa-pu, which elsewhere is a transcription of the Tibetan place-name Balpo. The Chinese transcription, moreover, is the same as that for the Tibetan contender for the throne (apparently the "*btsanpo gcen Lha*"), who was deposed at just this time (*OTA*, Snake year 705[-706] before winter. This hitherto unnoticed fact could force major revisions in my hypothesis on this contender (Beckwith, 1983:5-10). Had the Tibetans at one point attempted to install a half-Tibetan, half-Turkic qaghan

Ferghana only one or two years later; he was thus undoubtedly in Central Asia in 704. *Boghra only arrived at the Chinese court in 705, as his brother's envoy.) Although Ṭabarî unfortunately does not give the names of all of the leaders involved, there is no reason to doubt his evidence.[82] Thus, there can be little question of Tibetan intervention in Ṭukhâristân.

What then were the Tibetans doing so deep inside Ṭukhâristân, when they had problems enough elsewhere? It is difficult to arrive at a precise answer, for here, as elsewhere, the sources are simply too fragmentary to allow definite conclusions.[83] But Tibet's general motivation is quite clear: with the loss of the Tarim region to the Chinese, it was more important than ever to keep open the trade route via the Pamirs and Ṭukhâristân. This trade route passed through the strategic stronghold of Tirmidh. But, despite Tibetan cooperation, the allied attack on Mûsâ again failed. It was only later in 704 that the new Arab governor, al-Mufaḍḍal b. al-Muhallab, sent an expedition which—again in alliance with the "princes of Transoxiana"—finally defeated and killed the tenacious rebel.[84]

Upon the death of the Tibetan emperor Khri ʿdus sroṅ in the winter of 704-705, his son Lha[85] took the throne. Shortly thereafter, however, the powerful dowager empress, Khri ma lod, dethroned Lha in favor of the infant Rgyal Gtsug ru, the future Khri

---

over the On oq? This is apparently the conclusion one must draw from the sources.

[82] Tirmidh is no farther from Tibet than Ferghana. So, with local cooperation, it would have been just as easy for Tibetan troops to fight in Tirmidh as in Ferghana. The comments of Gibb (1923:24) on this subject—"magnified in the legend to huge armies of 'Turks and Hayṭal and Tibetans' "—are not valid. See above, note 79.

[83] See the comments of L. White, Jr. quoted in note 15 of the Epilogue.

[84] Ṭabarî, ii:1162-1163; Balâdhurî, 416-419. Cf. Shaban, 1970:62. The "princes of Transoxiana" may, of course, have included the same Tibetans and Turks.

[85] Or Lha Balpo (in the original, "Balpho"). The Old Tibetan can be interpreted to make Balpo part of his name or, as is usual in the Annals, the name of one of the imperial capitals.

lde gtsug brtsan, popularly known as Mes ag tshoms.[86] Revolts and executions accompanied this virtual coup, but the *Annals* and Chinese sources have little to report on them.[87] It is interesting to note that Lha apparently was not killed, but only forced into semiretirement. It was thus, perhaps, the "Retired Emperor" Lha who actually received and married the Chinese princess Chin-ch'eng in 710.[88] In any event, Tibet experienced more internal unrest, and was conspicuously quiet on its borders with China.

The political situation in China was also rather difficult. On February 23, 705, the former T'ang emperor Chung-tsung was restored to the throne,[89] and on March 3 he changed the dynastic name back to T'ang.[90] Although the struggle for power was by no means yet settled, the tide had definitely turned in favor of Chung-tsung's Li clan. And the death of Wu Chao at the age of 82 in December, 805[91] strengthened their predominance. Needless to say, no new policies were forthcoming from China during this unsettled period.

In the Arab caliphate, unlike the convulsed Tibet and China, a momentous decision was made. In 705, al-Ḥaǧǧâǧ b. Yûsuf, the Arab governor of Iraq and the East,[92] appointed his brilliant young understudy, Qutayba b. Muslim al-Bâhilî, governor of Khurasan.[93] Qutayba began his rule with the reconquest of western Ṭukhâristân in 705.[94] To this early success he added in the fol-

---

[86] *OTA*, Snake year 705(-706) before winter.

[87] Among the revolts was that of the little-known subject country of Serib, which was located on Tibet's southwestern border. (*OTA*, Snake year [705-]706 winter.)

[88] See Beckwith (1983).

[89] *TCTC*, 207:6581.

[90] *CTS*, 7:136; *HTS*, 4:106; *TCTC*, 208:6583.

[91] *CTS*, 7:141; *HTS*, 4:108; *TCTC*, 208:6596. On the end of the Chou, see Guisso, 1978:150-154.

[92] The additional responsibility for Khurasan and Siǧistân had been given to him in 78 A.H./A.D. 697-698 (Ṭabarî, ii:1032). Cf. Shaban, 1970:46, 50, 53 et seq.

[93] Ṭabarî, ii:1178. Cf. Shaban, 1970:61 et seq. Note that there was no titular distinction that indicated the "governor" of Iraq was superior to the "governor" of Khurasan.

[94] Ṭabarî, ii:1180-1181; Balâdhurî, 419-420. Cf. Gibb, 1923:31-32; Shaban, 1970:64.

lowing year the submission of the Nîzak, prince of Bâdghîs, and the capture of Baykand, the vital center of international trade in Sogdiana.[95]

During the same two-year period,[96] a T'ang general, Kuo Ch'ien-kuan, and a Western Turkic general, *Arśïla Kül Cur Chung-chieh,[97] joined forces to invade Ferghana. Chung-chieh was a sometime ally of the T'ang who had submitted to *Ocïrlïq but had left the Türgiś fold after losing a feud with the qaghan's son, *Saqal. Kuo's and Chung-chieh's apparent intention was to raise troops for an attack on *Saqal in order to restore a pro-T'ang *Arśïla Turk to power over the On oq. Their efforts failed, but not until they had caused such damage to Ferghana that its people called on the Tibetans and Arśïla T'ui-tzu to rid them of the forces which were "recklessly invading and robbing as if they were in an uninhabited region."[98] As Kuo Yüan-chen remarked, "they were unable to obtain a single suit of armor or head of horse."[99] T'ui-tzu and the Tibetans made the victory complete by raiding the lands of the Four Garrisons after chasing *Arśïla

[95] Ṭabarî, ii:1184-1189; Balâdhurî, 420. Cf. Gibb, 1923:33-34; Shaban, 1970:65.

[96] These dates are determinable only through the rather circuitous evidence of Kuo Yüan-chen's remarks that he was stationed in Kashgar at the time, and that it was before *Saqal's accession. (The sources only say wang nien "in past year(s)," or just wang, "previously.") Kuo Yüan-chen was Governor-General of Liang chou for five years, from 701 to 705, and was appointed Grand Protector-General of the Pacified West during the Shen-lung period (705-706). *Ocïrlïq, who had been entitled Huai-te chün-wang by the T'ang in the spring of 706 (TCTC 208:6598), died in the winter of 706-707 (TCTC, 208:6608). But, whatever the accuracy of Kuo's comments, they do indicate that *Seqal had not then yet acquired "protector" status with respect to Ferghana.

[97] The title kül cur identifies him as the chief of the Hu-lu-wu, the second subtribe of the eastern (*Tarduś) branch of the On oq. See Appendix D.

[98] CTS, 97:3047; HTS, 122:4364; TCTC, 209:6627. Cf. Chavannes, 1903:188.

[99] TCTC, 209:6627. The versions in CTS, 97:3047, and HTS, 122:4364, are substantially the same. It is nevertheless always surprising how much variation is found among the sources, even when they report an official document. Perhaps the use of quotation marks should be avoided when translating reported speech from the Chinese.

Chung-chieh and Kuo Ch'ien-kuan out of Ferghana and down into the Tarim Basin, presumably via the passes above Kashgar.[100]

After *Ocïrlïq was literally talked to death by Kuo Yüan-chen in the winter of 706-707,[101] the Eastern Turkic ruler Qapaghan Qaghan took advantage of the resultant weakness in the West by invading the Türgis again. On this occasion—according to Ssu-ma Kuang, an all-out attack which left China's northern border undefended—he was unsuccessful.[102] It is possible, however, that the friction between the new Türgis ruler, *Saqal, and his younger brother, Che-nu,[103] was aggravated by this otherwise little-known conflict.

During the same campaign season,[104] Qutayba b. Muslim captured the Bukharan towns of Nûmuśkath and Râmîthan on his way to the siege of the citadel of Bukhara itself. To his surprise, he then found his supply lines cut by a combined army of Turks, Sogdians,[105] and Ferghanians. According to one source, the Turks were led by "Kûr Baghânûn the Turk, son of the sister of the king of China."[106] The presence of a contingent from Fer-

---

[100] CTS, 97:3047; HTS, 122:4364; TCTC, 209:6629. Cf. Moriyasu, 1984:24-25.

[101] CTS, 97:3045; HTS, 122:4362; TCTC, 208:6608. Cf. Chavannes, 1903:283 n. 3. Kuo Yüan-chen and *Ocïrlïq stood outdoors talking for several hours while it was snowing; the qaghan fell ill from exposure and died.

[102] TCTC, 209:6621-6622.

[103] He is first mentioned under the eighth month of 699, when he was sent to the T'ang court. See HTS, 215b:6066; TFYK, 970:18r (p. 11403). Cf. Chavannes, 1903:79, 1904:25.

[104] The campaign season ended before winter, at which point most of the army was dispersed, leaving just garrison troops on duty. See Shaban, 1970:66.

[105] Tabarî ii:1195, has simply "al-Sughd." For a confused and misleading account of this episode, see Gibb, 1923:34-35.

[106] Tabarî, ii:1195. In another manuscript, the name is written kwr . â nw n (ii:1195). The name occurs again, as "Kûrmghânûn" or "Kûr Mʿâbûn" (without "al-Turkî"), in ii:1602 under the year 119 A.H./A.D. 737, but there appears to be some problem with the text at that point. Gibb, 1923:35, throws out both occurrences. It is most probable that the earlier occurrence (at least) has some basis in fact, although it is difficult to identify the Turk in question, the beginning of whose name reflects a *Kül Bagha. See below for possible identifications.

ghana, which seems rather surprising at first, makes sense if it is assumed that their leader was *Arsïla T'ui-tzu, who was fighting in Ferghana in or about this year.[107] In any event, the wily Qutayba managed to extricate himself from this situation and escape back to Arab territory.[108]

*Arsïla T'ui-tzu, who was apparently still alive after the Ferghana incident of 705-706, was clearly dead by 708. This seems to be evidenced by Chinese plans for intervention in Ferghana in that year; these plans presumed that *Arsïla Kül Cur Chung-chieh—not T'ui-tzu—would lead Tibetan troops into Ferghana on China's behalf. It seems most probable that T'ui-tzu died in 707. Moreover, if he died while he was the leader of the combined army that attacked the Arabs at Bukhara in that year, then Qutayba's easy escape is more understandable. Nearly contemporaneous with T'ui-tzu's death was the deposition of the Tibetan Emperor Lha, who was quite possibly a relative (perhaps the son) of the consort known as Qatun, who died in the same or the following year.[109] Perhaps the most significant indication that a new era was at hand was the provisional Chinese decision in the summer of 707 to conclude a new marriage peace with Tibet.[110] It may well be that the prospect of peace with China signaled the demise of *Arsïla T'ui-tzu's clan in Tibet in any event, regardless

[107] It would seem unlikely that Chung-chieh could have been this leader. His depredations, it may be recalled, induced the Ferghanians to call for Tibetan help in the first place.

[108] Ṭabarî, ii:1195.

[109] Qatun is Old Turkic for "Queen." The death of the Qatun (Old Tibetan, *btsanmo Gatun*, "Empress Qatun") is not mentioned in the sources, but *OTA*, Monkey year (708-)709 spring, records her burial. Therefore, she could have died in the Sheep year 707-708. Tibetan practice in those days called for the corpse of an emperor to lie in the embalming house for about two years, but consorts—even the famous Khri ma lod—seem not to have been so treated. See Hoffmann, 1950:12-13. In *HTS*, 216a:6081, she is called *tsu mu k'o-tun* ("the grandmother, the Qatun") and is said to have "again" sent an envoy named Tsung-o, who arrived at the Chinese capital in 709, to request a marriage treaty. The treaty was finalized in 710. It is not explicitly stated anywhere if the Qatun was a Western or Eastern Turk, but, considering the close Tibetan–Western Turkic alliance, it is probable that she was indeed a relative of T'ui-tzu.

[110] *TCTC*, 208:6610.

of his death. The passing of this truly remarkable person marked a hiatus of several years in active Tibetan involvement in Central Asia.

The Türgiś leader *Saqal now succeeded *Arsïla T'ui-tzu as the Turkic protector of Ferghana.[111] He faced the Chinese general Kuo Ch'ien-kuan and *Arsïla Kül Cur Chung-chieh who, despite their previous failures, formed an elaborate plan to attack *Saqal via Ferghana. This time, thanks to the marriage treaty, they expected the assistance of the Tibetans and apparently of soldiers sent by the king of Balûr.[112] According to the plan, another general, Niu Shih-chiang, was to lead Tibetan troops and Chinese levies from Kansu. *Saqal was warned, however, when one of his envoys at the T'ang court discovered the plan. On hearing this news, he immediately sent twenty thousand riders into the Tarim Basin to attack the Chinese.[113] In the winter of 708-709, *Saqal smashed the T'ang forces, trapped Kuo Yüan-chen in a palisade outside Kashgar, captured *Arsïla Kül Cur alive, and killed two Chinese generals.[114] *Saqal then declared himself Qaghan, had his brother Che-nu raid the T'ang borderlands, and defeated and executed Niu Shih-chiang.[115] The T'ang army was lost, Kucha was captured, and "the road to the Four Garrisons was cut."[116] In all of this, however, the Tibetans are nowhere mentioned. It seems that, with the Türgiś envoy's apprehension

[111] See Chavannes, 1903:188-189. *Saqal is transcribed in Chinese as So-ko.

[112] TFYK, 964:13v (p. 11343). Cf. Chavannes, 1903:199, where the folio number for this reference is given as "12r."

[113] The sources say he sent five thousand each to (or "via"; see the discussion of the use of ch'u, which normally means "to go out," in Chapter Six) Kucha, Aksu, Agni, and Kashgar.

[114] CTS, 7:146, 97:3047; HTS, 4:110, 122:4365; TCTC, 209:6627-6628; TFYK, 366:11r-14r (pp. 4356-4357).

[115] The place given for the demise of Niu is in all sources an otherwise unknown city, Huo-shao ch'eng ("Fire-burnt City"). It is my suspicion that this is not a proper name at all, but a defect in the original source, which contained a description of someone—no doubt *Saqal—burning the city he had taken.

[116] CTS, 7:146, 97:3047; HTS, 4:110, 122:4365; TCTC, 209:6628; TFYK, 336:13v (p. 4357).

of the Chinese plans, *Saqal was able to attack the T'ang forces before they had joined the Tibetan troops, who presumably should have been waiting in Ferghana. As for the predicament of Kuo Yüan-chen and the Four Garrisons, *Saqal and Kuo soon managed to come to an agreement. The T'ang recognized *Saqal as "Qaghan of the Fourteen Surnames,"[117] and the Türgiś left the Tarim Basin to the Chinese. Despite this debacle, the T'ang government punished not one of the many culpable and traitorously corrupt high Chinese officials.[118]

The period from 709 to 711 was marked by the absence of aggressive Tibetan, Ferghanian, or Western Turkic military action in Central Asia. The Türgiś in particular were weakened by the conflict between *Saqal and his younger brother, Che-nu, who was not content with the apportionment of tribes he had received on the death of *Ocïrlïq. As for the Arabs, Qutayba b. Muslim was conquering—unhindered by the Turks and Ferghanians—the great Sogdian city-states of Bukhara (in 90 A.H./A.D. 708-709)[119] and Kiśś and Nasaf (in 91 A.H./A.D. 709-710).[120] In that year, he also suppressed a rebellion in Ṭukhâristân, which was led by Nîzak Tarqan. Qutayba executed Nîzak on orders from al-Ḥaǵǵâǵ, and sent the captured Yabghu of Ṭukhâristân to the Arab capital, Damascus.[121] In the following year he led an expedition to Siǵistân but undertook no important action in Khurasan.[122]

---

[117] TCTC, 209:6629. The gloss explains that, in addition to the On oq or "ten surnames," the Yen-mien, Qarluq (Ko-lo-lu), Bagha Tarqan (Chinese, Mo-ho ta-kan—this was *Ocïrlïq's title under *Khusraw, and here apparently refers to *Saqal's own, now-royal tribe), and Tu-mo-chih were now included among the Western Turks.

[118] Tsung Ch'u-k'o and Chi Ch'u-na were the major culprits at court. (Like Ssu-ma Kuang, I find it difficult to accept the favorable—and mistake-filled—account of them he quotes in the K'ao-i; see TCTC, 209:6632.) The two officials were apparently recognized at the time as having taken bribes (from a foreign power, no less), but they were not punished for their crimes.

[119] Ṭabarî, ii:1201 et seq.; Balâdhurî, 420. Cf. Gibb, 1923: 35-36; Shaban, 1970:65.

[120] Ṭabarî, ii:1229; Balâdhurî, 420. Cf. Gibb, 1923:38; Shaban, 1970:67.

[121] See the discussion in Shaban, 1970:66-67; cf. Gibb, 1923:36-38.

[122] Shaban, 1970:67-69.

In 710, only a few months after the arrival in Rasa of the Chinese princess, Chin-ch'eng,[123] the Protector-General of the Pacified West, Chang Hsüan-piao, invaded and plundered "northern Tibet."[124] Although the Tibetans were indignant at such blatantly faithless behavior by the Chinese, with whom they had just concluded a marriage treaty, they did not retaliate. This may have been due to the turmoil at court. Nevertheless, they demanded—and received—as reparations the "gift" of lands in the northeast known as the "Nine Bends West of the Yellow River."[125]

Between 710 and 712, the armies of the Eastern Turks, under the leadership of Elteriš's son, Kül Tegin, and with the assistance of the unsatisfied Che-nu, again invaded the land of the Türgiš. This time they were successful. Qapaghan Qaghan executed both *Saqal and, despite his defection to the Eastern Turks, also Che-nu.[126] Notwithstanding this success, Kül Tegin and his armies

---

[123] See Beckwith, 1983:6 (n. 15), for the details of her journey from China. There I stated that the emperor and princess must have parted before he went to the "villa north of Ma-wei." It now appears to me more likely that the emperor escorted the princess to Ma-wei, where he sent her off, and then returned to Ch'ang-an, where he arrived on March 6. Ma-wei, located on the routes to Tibet and to Szechuan, was the place where in 756 the emperor Hsüan-tsung and his party, who were fleeing from An Lu-shan, met a number of Tibetan envoys. There the imperial party split into two groups, one of which headed south to Szechuan and the other north to Ling-wu. See below, Chapter Six.

[124] TCTC, 210:6661. Although it is known that both sides periodically raided each other's borders, it is interesting that this foray was considered a normal part of the pi ching, or "border struggle," in CTS, 196a:5228. Cf. Moriyasu, 1984:26.

[125] HTS, 4:112; TCTC, 210:6661. It is impossible to believe the story concocted by the Chinese historians to explain away the T'ang acquiescence to the Tibetan demands. Quite probably the Chinese official who is blamed in the histories for suggesting the appeasement of Tibet was simply the scapegoat for an unpleasant policy decision (cf. TCTC, 211:6704). HTS, 216a:6081, gives only evil intentions as the reason for the Tibetan request. On the Chin-ch'eng princess, see especially Uray, 1978:568-570.

[126] The Chinese sources do not give exact dates; they say only "in the Ching-yün period," i.e., the seventh month of 710 to the eighth month of 712. See CTS, 194a:5172; HTS, 215a:6048. The accounts in TT, 199:1079,

had to remain in the West for several years, mercilessly raiding and plundering the Western Turks, in a continuing effort to keep them under control.[127]

In 93 A.H./A.D. 712,[128] Qutayba b. Muslim continued his successful campaigns of conquest by force and trickery. After taking Khwarizmia by treachery, he marched on Samarkand, assisted by Bukhâran and Khwarizmian troops. This caused Ghûrak, the prince of Samarkand, to write to the king of Tashkent for help. In this hour of need, Qapaghan Qaghan responded. Because Qapaghan had become the protector of Ferghana by his conquest of the Türgiś and because he had also become the overlord of the king of Tashkent, major support of Samarkand was in order. He sent Kül Tegin, in command of an Eastern Turkic army with men of Tashkent and Ferghana as well, to attack the besieging Arabs. The Arabs defeated them, however, and although the Eastern Turks profited greatly from this expedition into Sogdiana,[129] Qutayba still managed to enter Samarkand and establish a garrison there.[130]

---

and *CTS*, 194b:5191, mistakenly have the defeat of the Türgiś in the third year of the Ching-lung period (February 15, 709 to February 3, 710). This is clear from their mention of the return of Qapaghan Qaghan's army and the rise of Su-lu as the new leader of the Türgiś. For the Old Turkic texts and translations, see Tekin, *A Grammar of Orkhon Turkic* (1968) 269, 276, 287-289, 294.

[127] The appointment on January 15, 712, of *Arśïla Hsien as Hsing-hsi-wang Qaghan is certainly connected with these attacks, in that he was charged with "calming and pacifying" the On oq (*TCTC*, 210:6669). Unfortunately, this is only described retrospectively in the Chinese sources. The Old Turkic inscriptions mention Kül Tegin's attacks on the Qarluqs, supposedly in 713 (Tekin, 1968:270). The same inscriptions apparently give the preceeding year as the date of his expedition into Transoxiana; there can be little doubt that this was the one to meet the army of Qutayba.

[128] 93 A.H. ran from October 19, 711, to October 7, 712. But, as mentioned above, we know that Qutayba spent the campaign season of 711 on an expedition to Siǧistân.

[129] See Tekin, 1968:289. Since the Turks went as far as the Iron Gate, they certainly passed Samarkand. The text, which is defective at this point, mentions the Täzik (i.e., Arabs), the retreat of the Turkic armies, and the submission of "the Sogdian people." This last may be a reference to Ghûrak.

[130] Ṭabarî, ii:1247-1253; Balâdhurî, 421; Ibn A'tham al-Kûfî, vii:239 et

In Tibet in 712, policy making was given new direction by the accession of the eight-year-old Khri lde gtsug brtsan, better known as Mes ag tshoms, and the death of his powerful grandmother, Khri ma lod.[131] The early enthronement would seem to indicate the victory of an opposition faction at court. This unusual situation may have been influenced by news of a coup mounted by Jui-tsung's third son, Hsüan-tsung, who ascended the Chinese throne on September 8, 712.[132] The very long reign of the new T'ang ruler, who is better known under the epithet *Ming huang* ("Brilliant Emperor") was marked by his supposed patronage of the arts. More significantly, Hsüan-tsung was a partisan of the militaristic, empire-building faction at the Chinese court. And with Tibet in disarray under a youthful monarch, there was nothing in the way of a new T'ang offensive in Central Asia.

To the west, the repeated attacks of armies from Tashkent and Ferghana determined the course of Qutayba b. Muslim's future campaigns. In 713, he gathered a sizeable army, which was composed largely of Transoxanians, and split into two parts. One he sent to Tashkent, where the army captured the city and "burned most of it." Qutayba himself led the other army against "Khuǵanda and Kâsân, the two cities of Ferghana." Nevertheless, even after the army that had taken Tashkent joined him, Qutayba had no luck in his campaign.[133] Unable to take either of the fortified cities, he returned to Marw.

In the lands of the Türgiś, the execution of the qaghan and his brother had brought about the collapse of centralized authority

---

seq.; Ya'qûbî, ii:287. Tashkent had formerly been ruled by the Western Turks (*HTS*, 221b:6246; cf. Chavannes, 1903:141). Qapaghan Qaghan cemented his rule over this city-state by marrying his younger sister to the king of Tashkent; see further below. All of the sources Gibb cites and dismisses as, for example, "exaggeration in opposite interests" (1923:45-47) do in fact support the historicity of the appearance of the Turks at Samarkand at this time. One of the sources quoted by Tabarî specifies that "a son of the qaghan" led the Turkic army.

[131] *OTA*, Mouse year (712-)713 winter.
[132] *HTS*, 5:119, 121; *TCTC*, 210:6674.
[133] Tabarî, ii:1256-1257; Balâdhurî, 422.

among the Western Turks. A revolt broke out, and the rebel leader, Tu-tan, captured Sûyâb by 714.[134] This quickly brought Qapaghan Qaghan and Kül Tegin back to the attack.[135] At the same time, Qapaghan Qaghan also sent an army, which was led by his son, T'ung-o Tegin, and *Qabar Eltäbär, King A-shih-pi of Tashkent, to attack Pei-t'ing in Chinese territory. This expedition met a disastrous end, however, when Protector-General Kuo Ch'ien-kuan crushed them and killed the qaghan's son. Having lost his city to the Arabs,[136] and now fearful of Qapaghan Qaghan after the catastrophe at Pei-t'ing, the Eltäbär of Tashkent submitted to the T'ang.[137] Quickly following up on this Chinese triumph, the T'ang Military Governor of the West of the Desert, *Aršila Hsien, (the Hsing-hsi-wang Qaghan),[138] seized Sûyâb,

---

[134] *TCTC*, 211:6698.

[135] Tekin, 1968:269-270.

[136] Balâdhurî, 422. Ṭabarî, ii:1267-1268, only briefly mentions the Tashkent campaign. Cf. Gibb, 1923:51. In 714, the Arabs seem to have used Tashkent as a base for raids on Isbîgâb. On "Eltäbär," note that after Tun Yabghu Qaghan conquered Transoxiana and other regions of Central Asia, he conferred the title of Eltäbär (Chinese, Hsieh-li-fa) on the kings of all the subdued countries. He then set up *tudun* (Chinese, T'u-t'un) in each to oversee affairs and collect taxes for him (*CTS*, 194b:5181; *HTS*, 215b:6056).

[137] *CTS*, 8:172, 103:3187, 103:3190; *HTS*, 5:123, 133:4543; *TCTC*, 211:6696. Cf. Tekin, 1968:276. Since Kül Tegin is not mentioned in the Chinese sources in connection with the 714 attack, and since T'ung-o Tegin is not mentioned (by that name, at least) in the Old Turkic sources, there is no reason to believe that the campaign led by Kül Tegin in ca. 713 (presumably the one mentioned in *HTS*, 105:4029-4030) was the same as that led by T'ung-o Tegin in 714. Moriyasu, 1984:27, proposes two separate attacks on the city, in 713 and 714. Cf. Chavannes, 1903:24, 52. On the submission of the king of Tashkent (and his wife), see *CTS*, 194a:5172; *HTS*, 215a:6047-6048; *TCTC*, 211:6697. *CTS* includes details on the extent of their enfeoffment. It is interesting to note that the title given his wife, "Chin Shan Princess," was also the title granted in 711 to the daughter of Ch'eng-ch'i (the Prince of Sung) when she was chosen to be the consort of Qapaghan Qaghan in order to seal a marriage pact with the T'ang (*TCTC*, 210:6664). The marriage was called off when Jui-tsung was forced to abdicate in 712 (*CTS*, 194a:5172). Note also in the *CTS* account the lavish bestowal of rewards, including enfeoffment as nobles, upon the victorious generals. This seems to have become a common practice in China during Hsüan-tsung's reign.

[138] He had been appointed qaghan in 711 (*TCTC*, 210:6669).

captured the Western Turkic leader Tu-tan, and forced the submission of thousands of families of Turks.[139] This reestablishment of Chinese power in the heart of Western Turkic territory
sent out shock waves in all directions. Not only had the Chinese
inflicted a tremendous defeat on the Eastern Turks; they had to a
large extent replaced them as the dominant regional power. With
the retreat of Qapaghan Qaghan's armies from the West in 714,[140]
the Western Turks seem to have concluded that Chinese rule had
returned to stay, or was in any case preferable to that of the Eastern Turks. So, beginning with the Qarluqs in the autumn of
714,[141] a flood of Western Turks swept to the T'ang borders submit. This mass exodus impelled Qapaghan Qaghan to attack
again. In response, the T'ang sent the imperial armies to defend
the embattled Turks,[142] and so Qapaghan was subsequently unable to restore Eastern Turkic control.

Simultaneously with the decline of the Eastern Turks and the
reemergence of the Chinese in Central Asia, Arab power reached
its zenith under Qutayba. It was just at this point that the Tibetans
reentered the scene. In the autumn of 714, the Tibetans, led by
Great Minister Khri gzigs and by their ʿAźa vassal, the ʿBon
Dargyal, began a series of raids across the Yellow River. They
plundered from Lin-t'ao and Lan chou to Wei-yüan, the region
around the source of the Wei River. These attacks were blunted
by a series of T'ang holding actions that same winter.[143] But reports in the Chinese sources reveal the extent to which the Tibetans had prepared for military action in the region since 710. They
had built fortresses, had thrown a bridge across the Yellow River,
and had stationed their "Lone Mountain" and "Nine Bends" ar-

[139] HTS, 5:123, TCTC, 211:6698.

[140] Tekin, 1968:270, 276.

[141] TCTC, 211:6705 et seq. The K'ao-i (TCTC, 211:6709 et seq.) quotes
extensively from the Shih-lu at this point, and provides valuable details: the
number of subtribes, the titles of leaders, etc.

[142] TCTC, 211:6710-6712.

[143] OTA, Tiger year 714(-715) summer (levy of "the ʿAźa in ʿO khol in
Silgucin") and winter (they "led an attack on ʿBu śiṅ kun and returned").
CTS, 8:174, 103:3190, 103:3197, 196a:5228; HTS, 5:123, 133:4544-4545,
133:4551-4552, 216a:6081-6082; TCTC, 211:6704-6706.

mies in the area.[144] Notwithstanding this military strengthening, Tibet sent a mission to the Chinese border post at T'ao Shui shortly after the T'ang victories to propose a peace settlement. This was rebuffed, the Chinese sources say, because the Tibetans used "enemy-country protocol." This phrase was to be often repeated over the succeeding decades by Hsüan-tsung and others of the expansionist faction in China as a continuing justification for T'ang hostilities against Tibet. As Ssu-ma Kuang remarks about the Tibetans, "Henceforth they raided the border annually.[145]

As relations with China rapidly deteriorated, Tibet again manifested its longstanding interest in strategically located Ferghana. At the same time, however, Qutayba b. Muslim resumed his campaigns with a full-scale invasion of Ferghana in 715. The Arab conqueror clearly intended to completely subjugate this strong nation, which had long been a thorn in his side. At some point in the campaign, perhaps after Qutayba's initial successes against the citadel of Khuǵanda,[146] the Tibetans entered into a brief, little-known alliance with the Arab forces. *Bâśak, the "king of Ferghana," was defeated, and Qutayba "took possession of his goods, both the trifling and the great."[147] Together, the Arabs and Tibetans installed Aluṭâr, a member of another royal

---

[144] *TCTC*, 211:6705:6706. The memorial quoted by Ssu-ma Kuang states that "they have built a bridge over the Yellow River" and recommends that "we should destroy the bridge." The original Tibetan names of the two armies are unknown; I have given translations of the Chinese names—Tu Shan and Chiu Ch'ü, respectively. Although the Chinese report describes the Tibetan fortresses as symbols of aggressive intentions, it is obvious that they were built (technically speaking) as defensive citadels, intended to hold captured territory. In other words, the Tibetans had constructed counterparts to the string of Chinese fortresses along the Sino-Tibetan frontier.

[145] *TCTC* 211:6706; cf. *CTS*, 196a:5228; *HTS*, 216a:6082. The Tibetan ambassador at T'ao Shui was again Tsung-o.

[146] Ibn A'tham al-Kûfî, vii:250. The name of the citadel is here written *kdh h.* This is undoubtedly a scribal or printing error for Khuǵanda, one of the two great cities of Ferghana that had been unsuccessfully attacked two years before by Qutayba.

[147] Ibn A'tham al-Kûfî, vii:250, has the only detailed account. The name given therein for the king is transcribed *bâ śk*, which would seem to reflect a *Bâśak. Cf. Ṭabarî, ii:1275-1276; Balâdhurî, 422; Ya'qûbî, ii:295.

family of Ferghana, as the new king.[148] The reappearance of effective Chinese power north of the Tien Shan, however, provided an opportunity for the ousted King *Bâśak to seek outside assistance. He fled into T'ang territory, followed closely by an Arab raiding party sent by Qutayba which reached Kashgar and successfully returned shortly thereafter.[149] Qutayba, however, was nearing the end of his remarkable series of conquests. Back in Damascus, the caliph who had patronized him died, and the new caliph regarded him with animosity. Qutayba felt he had no recourse but rebellion. His war-weary army disagreed; they turned on him, and he was killed, defended only by his family and his personal bodyguard of Sogdian archers.[150]

In this time of Arab weakness, Hsüan-tsung's specially appointed censor, Chang Hsiao-sung, urged quick Chinese military action. So Lü Hsiu-ching, the Protector-General of the Pacified West, mustered an army of over 10,000 men—composed of levies of Central Asians under T'ang rule—and made a forced march from Kucha to Ferghana. In December 715, he attacked Aluṭâr in

[148] Dating such events is extremely difficult. The Chinese sources are here, as often, dated retrospectively. (On retrospective entries in the Chinese sources, see the Note on Chronology.) In order to date this series of events, therefore, one must estimate the time necessary for the deposed king to flee to Kucha, rouse the Chinese to action, return with an army, defeat the Arabs, Tibetans, and Ferghanian partisans of Aluṭâr, and return again to Kucha. The *TCTC*, 211:6713, specifically states that the T'ang victory occurred in the eleventh month (December 1-30) of 715. Thus the Chinese dating corresponds very nicely with the Arab dating. (For more on Aluṭâr, see Appendix E.) Note that Gibb, 1923:52 et seq., almost completely ignores Qutayba's last Ferghana campaign. His only reference to the Tibetan alliance with the Arabs, and to the Chinese intervention on the side of *Bâśak, is: "in the following year they restored the deposed king of Farghāna" (p. 60).

[149] Despite Gibb's arguments ("The Arab Invasion of Kashgar in A.D. 715" [1921-1923] and 1923:52 et seq.), there is no reason to reject the historicity of the raid itself. See also the version in Ibn A'tham al-Kûfî, vii:251, which relates that Qutayba sent a force of 7,000 on horse and foot under the command of a certain Kathîr. They raided Kashgar, killed many, and enslaved 100.

[150] Ṭabarî, ii:1283 et seq. Cf. Gibb, 1923:51 et seq. On the archers, see Beckwith, 1984a.

the "connected cities." "From midmorning to late afternoon he slaughtered the inhabitants of the three cities, and captured or decapitated over one thousand people. Aluṭâr fled with some riders into the mountain valleys."[151] Thus, according to the Chinese historians, did the T'ang armies end Arab-Tibetan rule in Ferghana.

The significance of what happened in 715 was not understood at the time. From the T'ang Chinese point of view, the Arabs were still a very distant and therefore relatively unimportant nation. The Arabs seem to have been aware that they had reached the borders of the T'ang Empire, but under the circumstances they did not appreciate what that meant. The fragmentary sources unfortunately do not allow us to even guess how the Tibetans viewed these events. But however much these countries failed to recognize its significance, the events of 715 clearly indicate that a milestone in Eurasian history had been reached. The Arabs from the west, the Chinese from the east, and the Tibetans from the south—the three greatest expansionistic states of early medieval Asia—had converged.

[151] *TCTC*, 211:6713. Cf. Chavannes, 1903:148-149 (n. 3). The "three cities," also called the "connected cities," would appear to be Khuǵanda, Kâsân, and perhaps Akhsîkath (p. 148 [n. 1]).

Chapter 4

THE
TÜRGIŚ
ALLIANCE

It is testimony to the actual weakness of the T'ang, in comparison with their self-portrait in the dynastic histories, that they could not seriously alter the course of events in central Eurasia during the eighth century. In the end, the proud Chinese had to silently accept the fact of equality with their neighbors.[1] On an official plane, of course, none of the great powers of the early Middle Ages publicly accepted equal or subservient status to another great power. All of them seem to have maintained a confident and aggressive stance down to their last days. But it is equally true that a fairly stable balance of power—on a continentwide scale—was finally established in 715. The only problem with this momentous development was that none of the major powers, in particular the Chinese, accepted this state of affairs. Nor did the Türgiś confederation of Western Turks, who were, geographically, in the middle of everything.

Shortly after their defeat of the Türgiś,[2] the Eastern Turks

---

[1] Cf. M. Rossabi, ed., *China among Equals* (1983).
[2] The Qara Türgiś, the "Black Bone" half of the confederation, suffered

withdrew homeward. Very quickly, the scattered tribes of the Türgiś were reorganized and unified by one of the greatest of all the early Turkic leaders. The Chinese transcribed his name "Su-lu," but to the Arabs he was known as Abû Muzâḥim, the "Father of Competition, because he competed with the Arabs."[3] By 715, he had restored stability in his country and felt confident enough to send an embassy to the Chinese emperor, who, in turn, bestowed two titles on him.[4] Apart from these niceties, the embassy had a more serious message: the new Türgiś ruler notified the T'ang that his "hordes amounted to 200,000." "Consequently," the Chinese sources add, "he had taken forcible possession of the West."[5]

In 716, while the Tibetans continued their raids on China's eastern border,[6] Qapaghan Qaghan led the Eastern Turks north on a campaign of devastation into the lands of the Bayarqu tribes; he was completely victorious. On his way back, however, he was so overconfident that he was easily ambushed and killed by some of the very tribesmen he had just beaten.[7] As a result of this un-

---

a particularly devastating loss, according to the Old Turkic inscriptions, which speak of them several times. Theoretically, they constituted only one-half of the tribes, but they were the dominant half for nearly twenty-five years after about 715. It is important to recall that both *Ocïrlïq and *Saqal belonged to the "Yellow Bone" branch. It would seem that the authors of the Old Turkic inscriptions—engraved long after the fact—confused the two branches. Tekin (1968:269-270) has taken Qara to mean "common."

[3] Ṭabarî, ii:1593.

[4] It appears that before 718 he was awarded the fairly ordinary titles of Great General of the Military Guards of the Right and Governor-General. This can be deduced from the sources relating the events of 718, in which he is called by those titles while being presented with more impressive-sounding ones. See TCTC, 211:6714, 212:6733; TFYK, 964:13v (p. 11343); CTS, 194b:5191; HTS, 215b:6067. Cf. Chavannes, 1903:308, 1904:35-37. He also seems to have received the title Shun kuo kung in 718.

[5] TCTC, 211:6714.

[6] HTS, 5:125; TCTC, 211:6716.

[7] CTS, 8:176; HTS, 5:126; TCTC, 211:6719. The Bayarqu presented the qaghan's head to a Chinese then visiting the Eastern Turks. He returned home with it to Ch'ang-an. In true "medieval" fashion, the head was hung up above a broad thoroughfare where everyone could see it.

expected turn of events, the T'ieh-le tribes of Bayarqu, Uyghur, Hsi, and P'u-ku[8] all "surrendered" to the T'ang. The impact on Eastern Turkic dynastic affairs was even more dramatic. Kül Tegin killed Qapaghan Qaghan's son and erstwhile successor, the "Little Qaghan," along with every member of his family except the aged counselor Toñuquq. He then placed on the Eastern Turkic throne his older brother, the "Little Śad," known under the name Bilgä Qaghan, "the Wise Qaghan."[9] The Eastern Turks immediately sent envoys to China requesting peace.[10] Absorbed in their internal affairs, they were relegated to a passive role in the struggle among the great powers for control of Central Asia.

As a consequence of this weakening of their main enemy, the strength and confidence of Su-lu and the Türgiś increased rapidly. In the late summer of 716, according to Ssu-ma Kuang, he declared himself qaghan.[11] Su-lu was well on his way to reestablishing the predominance of the Türgiś in the West.[12] By the summer of 717, the Türgiś had regained much of their former strength. One Chinese report of May 717 claimed that, although the Türgiś were still sending tribute, they were using the tribute missions as a pretext for spying out the border. In June, *Arśila Hsien, the On oq Qaghan, requested permission from the T'ang to lead an army of the subject Qarluq Turks to attack the resurgent Türgiś. The emperor Hsüan-tsung refused his request.[13] The Chinese seemed determined to maintain a posture of neutrality in this intra-Turkic struggle. In July 717, Hsüan-tsung declined to accept presents brought by a Türgiś envoy. This was the early medieval method of refusing to establish diplomatic relations.[14] But if the emperor or his advisers were expecting some

---

[8] Hamilton, Les Ouïghours (1955) 2n, has reconstructed the name as "*Buqut" or "*Buqu."

[9] CTS, 8:176; HTS, 5:125; TCTC, 211:6719.

[10] HTS, 5:126; TCTC, 212:6731.

[11] During the eighth month (August 22–September 20) (TCTC, 211:6720).

[12] See Shaban, 1970:98-99.

[13] TCTC, 211:6727.

[14] TFYK, 971:2v (p. 11405). Cf. Chavannes, 1904:33-34.

Türgiś move, they were as yet unwilling to prepare any offensive military response.

On the Tibetan front, however, Hsüan-tsung's government began a major diplomatic offensive at this time. On July 10, 717, Su-fu-she-li-chih-li-ni, the king of Balûr, was awarded by official decree the title "King of Balûr."[15] Innocuous though it may sound, this indicated formal T'ang acceptance of Balûr as a state within the Chinese *oikoumênê*, and thus deserving of protection. Technically it was not yet considered part of the T'ang empire. But a clear message was sent to Tibet: the Chinese intended to supplant them as the dominant power in the region of the Karakorum, Pamir, and Hindu Kush ranges.[16]

Meanwhile, the Arabs also mounted a diplomatic offensive. In 717, the caliphal seat passed to 'Umar b. 'Abd al-'Azîz. One of his first actions was to send a declaration to the kings of Transoxiana, asking them to embrace Islam as equals of the Arabs.[17] As might have been expected, the response was fairly positive among peoples who had been strongly influenced by the Arabs or who were under their rule. It seems quite likely that the Tibetans, who were included among the princes of Transoxiana, also received the Arab proposal. In the same year, a delegation of Tibetans visited the new governor of Khurasan, al-Ġarrâḥ b. 'Abd Allâh al-Ḥakamî: "Envoys of Tibet called on him, asking him to

[15] *TFYK*, 964:13r-13v (p. 11343). Cf. Chavannes, 1903:199-200, where the folio number is incorrectly given as "12r°." *HTS*, 221b:6251, specifies that he was the king of Great Balûr.

[16] Moriyasu, 1984:28-30, discusses at length the extent of Tibetan influence in the area. But it is difficult to draw any conclusions due to the extreme paucity of material. For instance, whether or not the Chinese had troops in the mountains south of Ferghana is essentially unknown. One thing is clear, however. Although most of the area was not under the direct rule of any major power, Tibetan armies had for years passed freely through it. It was only under Hsüan-tsung, and in fact only after the Arab-Tibetan-Türgiś alliance of 717 failed to capture the Tarim Basin from the T'ang, that the Chinese began to enlarge their influence in the area.

[17] Balâdhurî, 426. Shaban, 1970:86-87, details the concrete benefits which Muslims had but non-Muslims did not, and the general policies of the Arab government which were behind his proposal.

send them someone who would explain Islam to them; so he sent
to them al-Salîṭ b. ʿAbd Allâh al-Ḥanafî,[18] and he sent ʿAbd Allâh b. Maʿmar [b. Samîr] al-Yaśkurî[19] [with an army] to Transoxiana . . ."[20] Al-Yaśkurî led his troops "to Transoxiana, and he
penetrated deeply into the lands of the enemy—and these [lands]
were [located] at the entrance of China."[21]

The Chinese sources confirm the Arabic accounts. On or
about August 15, 717, a Türgiś-led allied army of Tibetans, Arabs, and Türgiś laid siege to Aksu and Üc-Turfan, both on the
northern edge of the Tarim Basin. In response, the Chinese colonial governor, Assistant Grand Protector-General of the Pacified
West T'ang Chia-hui, ordered *Arśïla Hsien, the Western Turkic
qaghan, to lead the "three-surnamed Qarluqs" in an attack on the
besieging forces. The T'ang army, which was composed exclu-
sively of ethnic Turks, drove off the allies.[22] The Arabs under al-

---

[18] He seems to be otherwise unknown, but was obviously a proponent of
the Hanafite school. See D. Dunlop, "Arab Relations with Tibet in the 8th
and Early 9th Centuries A.D." (1973) 306 et seq., on the cultural implications
of this Islamic mission in Tibet.

[19] In spite of Shaban's contention (1970:86), this is not the same person as
the ʿAbd Allâh b. Maʿmar al-Yaśkurî who was killed earlier during a revolt
in Ǵurǵân at the time of the governorship of Yazîd b. al-Muhallab. (A priori,
it would have been rather strange for al-Ǵarrâḥ to entrust such an expedition
to one of Yazîd's men, especially after he had just locked them all up.) Rather,
this was no doubt ʿAbd Allâh b. Maʿmar b. Samîr al-Yaśkurî, one of the
Arab military leaders in Transoxiana. He is also mentioned in Ṭabarî under
82 A.H./A.D. 701-702 and 112 A.H./A.D. 730-731 (ii:1078, 1538).

[20] Yaʿqûbî, ii:302.

[21] Balâdhurî, 426.

[22] TCTC, 211:6728. The information is contained in a memorial to the
throne by T'ang Chia-hui, so the events probably occurred slightly before
the date given here. In his memorial, T'ang claimed that the Türgiś planned
to capture the Four Garrisons, and he gives that reason for mobilizing his
army of subjugated Qarluqs without advance permission from Ch'ang-an.
The Old Tibetan Annals may hint at preparations for this campaign, or for the
simultaneous one in the northeast (see below). In 692, 717, and 721 the
Mdosmad assembly was held in Rgyam śigar. In each of these three years, the
Western Turks conducted major campaigns; in two of them, the Chinese
sources mention Tibetan involvement. Significantly, it would seem, the
third coincided with Tibetan activity in the area of the Pamir and Hindu
Kush mountains.

Yaśkurî escaped back to Islamic territory, and made their way to Tashkent.[23] At exactly the same time, a Tibetan army was severely defeated at the "Bends of the Yellow River" by Kuo Chih-yün, the Military Governor of Lung-yu.[24] So ended what appears to have been a well-coordinated but premature Tibetan effort at the reconquest of the Tarim Basin.

In the following three years, the T'ang diplomatic offensive began to succeed. A host of peoples from Arab-dominated Khurasan sent embassies to China requesting help against the Arabs: in 718, Maimargh and Samarkand; in 719, Kumidh, Samarkand again, and Bukhara, among others.[25] The Yabghu of Ṭukhâristân and the Nîzak, the king of Kâpiśa,[26] also sent embassies in the same year. In 720, other countries, including Wakhan, Udyâna, Khuttal, Chitral, Kashmir, Zâbulistân, and South Hindustan,[27] sent missions to the court at Ch'ang-an.[28]

With regard to the Türgiś, the T'ang resorted to the traditional Chinese ploy of granting official titles; in this way, they could both mollify the Turks and gain some sort of influence at their court. In 718, Su-lu was enfeoffed as the Duke of Shun-kuo ("Duke who obeys the nation" or "Duke of the Obedient Country"), and was appointed Grand Imperial Commissioner over Chin-fang *tao*.[29] As a symbol of having entered into official relations with China on an inferior-to-superior basis, he was given, among other things, a "fish-bag," which contained half of a metal

[23] Balâdhurî, 426; Ya'qûbî, ii:302.

[24] *HTS*, 5:126; *TCTC*, 211:6728; *TFYK*, 434:9v-10r (p. 5158).

[25] *TCTC*, 212:6735. Their petitions are translated in Chavannes, 1903:203-205. The king of Bukhara's petition specifically requests the T'ang emperor to order the Türgiś to come to his aid and destroy the Arabs (p. 203). The same request was made later (in 727) by the Yabghu of Ṭukhâristân (pp. 206-207).

[26] Chinese, Ko-p'i-shih. See Chavannes, 1904:40, and J. Harmatta, "Late Bactrian Inscriptions" (1969) 406 et seq.

[27] *CTS*, 8:181. Chinese, Nan T'ien-chu. Because T'ien-chu referred to what is now northern India, I have rendered it into English as Hindustan.

[28] *TCTC*, 212:6740; Chavannes, 1904:34-45.

[29] Chin-fang *tao* can be loosely translated "Northern Road" or "Northern Circuit."

fish, the other half of which was kept at the T'ang court.[30] Su-lu responded with a "tribute-mission" in 719,[31] and was rewarded at the end of the year with the bestowal of the title of Chung-shun Qaghan, the qaghan "who is loyal and obedient."[32] Nevertheless, the Türgiś still went ahead with their effort to reestablish their rule over the western lands that were not under direct Arab control. Thus, despite their improved relations with China, they took Sûyâb from the T'ang in 719.[33] Simultaneously, they began to pose as the protectors of the lands of Khurasan against the Arabs. The petition of the king of Bukhara, presented at the Chinese court in the same year, requested the Türgiś qaghan to assist the Transoxanians militarily in their struggle with the Arabs.[34] Although the T'ang dynasty was then at its height, and the ambitious Hsüan-tsung had numerous armies at his disposal, the emperor contented himself with awarding the princes various honorary titles and politely encouraging but empty diplomas. A combination of this reluctance to commit troops and, perhaps, anger at the retaking of Sûyâb resulted in no support from Ch'ang-an for a Türgiś alliance. Additional reasons for Hsüan-tsung's inaction may have been the distance involved or even the beginnings of the Arab-Chinese alliance against the Türgiś, which only became openly known in the following decade.

Yet there was at this time some cooperation between the Yabghu of Ṭukhâristân and the T'ang generals of the Four Garrisons, at least according to a petition from the Yabghu's younger brother *Arśila Tegin *Boghra, who was formerly a Tibetan-supported Western Turkic qaghan, to Hsüan-tsung. This petition, which was presented on December 13, 718, reads in part: "Our country's borders adjoin [those of the] Arabs and Tibetans,

[30] *TCTC*, 212:6733; *TFYK*, 964:14r (p. 11343). Cf. Chavannes, 1904:36 (nn. 3-4). On the Tibetans' refusal of the fish-bag, see below.

[31] *TFYK*, 971:3r (p. 11400). Cf. Chavannes, 1904:37.

[32] *TCTC*, 212:6737; *TFYK*, 964:14v (p. 11343). Cf. Chavannes, 1904:42.

[33] Chavannes, 1903:113-114.

[34] *TFYK*, 999:14v-15v (pp. 11721-11722); *TCTC*, 212:6735. Cf. Chavannes, 1903:203-204. The king of Kumidh listed Ṭukhâristân, Bukhara, Tashkent, and Ferghana as under Arab control (p. 204).

and [on] our eastern border are the [T'ang's] western garrisons. Whenever *Boghra's elder brother levies the tribes he sends out military forces to punish [the enemies]. As for discussing striking the [Arab and Tibetan] bandits, he and the Chinese generals are well informed, and they express support and respond to each other. This is the reason that robbery has been prevented on the frontier."[35] Evidently, the Tibetans were passing through Little Balûr, and no doubt Wakhan, on their way to raid the Four Garrisons.[36] In *Boghra's view, in other words, Ṭukhâristân was a strategic country as far as the security and further expansion of China's Central Asian possessions were concerned. It was therefore important for the T'ang to maintain good relations with Ṭukhâristân if the Chinese were serious about breaking Tibetan power in the Pamirs. But, although the Chinese had intervened in Ferghana as recently as 715, and would march into Balûr in 722, they remained militarily quiescent. Apparently intervention in Khurasan proper was not thought by T'ang strategists to be in Chinese interests.

The Tibetan position in the Pamirs was now so compromised by the rash of political defections to the Chinese that a serious conflict between them was practically inevitable. In 720, the T'ang bestowed titles on the kings of Udyâna, Khuttal, and Chitral, supposedly as rewards for preventing the Arabs from invading the Chinese colonial empire in the Tarim region.[37] In the same year, the king of South Hindustan requested Hsüan-tsung to order him to attack the Arabs and Tibetans.[38] Evidently, the threat of the Tibetan-Arab alliance, which was still in effect in 720, was felt even deep in northern India. But even more seriously felt by the Tibetans was the Chinese threat to their one secure route to the West. After Tibetan requests for peace in 716, 718, and 719[39]

---

[35] *TFYK*, 999:14v-15v (pp. 11721-11722). The entire text is translated and discussed in Chavannes, 1903:200-202.

[36] *HTS*, 216a:6083.

[37] *TFYK*, 964:14v (p. 11343). Cf. Chavannes, 1904:42-43.

[38] *TFYK*, 973:13v (p. 11433) et seq. Cf. Chavannes, 1904:44.

[39] On the mission of 718, see Moriyasu, 1984:30-33, especially with regard to the letter of Mes ag tshoms to Hsüan-tsung, which is preserved in

were brushed aside by Hsüan-tsung, the Tibetans ended up at war with China over the lower Pamirs.

In the face of T'ang intransigence, it appears that the Tibetans continued their quiet alliance with the Eastern Turks. In 720, an envoy from Bilgä Qaghan arrived at the Tibetan court.[40] That winter, the Turks foiled a T'ang-inspired plot to overthrow their qaghan. In the process, they besieged Pei-t'ing and defeated and enslaved the Basmïl Turks. They then went on to raid Kan *chou* and Liang *chou*, defeating the Military Governor of Ho-hsi and robbing the Ch'i-pi Turkic tribes which were settled there.[41] It is unknown if Tibetans were involved in this affair, but in the winter of 720-721 they captured a "Chinese fort" called "Sog-soṅ."[42] The outcome of this struggle was a stalemate between the Eastern Turks and the Chinese. In early 721, Bilgä Qaghan sent an envoy to the T'ang court to request peace. Although no formal agreement came out of this embassy, Hsüan-tsung at least admitted in a letter the mutual benefits of trade between the two nations:

TFYK, 981:6v-8r (pp. 11526-11527). In this extremely polite letter, the Tibetan ruler states that he would break ties with the Eastern Turks if the T'ang would resume peaceful relations. The letter was very clearly intended to assuage the ancient Chinese fear of an alliance between Tibet and the nomadic power in Mongolia, which would cut China off from the West. It is difficult, however, to suggest that there was ever much of a relationship between the Tibetans and Eastern Turks when the evidence consists only of this letter and a few other references. On the mission of 719, see *TCTC*, 211:6720, 212:6734, 212:6736. There were at least seven embassies sent to China between the Chin-ch'eng Princess's request to renew the treaty and Hsüan-tsung's eventual grudging acceptance of the Tibetan peace proposal of 730. The long letter from Mes ag tshoms to Hsüan-tsung (see the translation in Pelliot, 1961:98-99) points out that the Sino-Tibetan border conflicts were due to incursions by China, not Tibet.

[40] *OTA*, Monkey year 720(-721) before the summer assembly.

[41] *CTS*, 8:181; *HTS*, 5:128; *TCTC*, 212:6742-6743.

[42] *OTA*, Monkey year (720-)721 winter. Sog-soṅ is otherwise unknown. But, since *Sog* is the Old Tibetan short form (or etymologized singular) of the name Sogdag (Sogdians), it is possible that the Tibetan campaign referred to in the *Annals* was connected with the revolt of the "Six Sogdian Prefectures" that began in 721. It is, however, hard to imagine the Tibetans in the Ordos (see Map I) at this time. See *TCTC*, 212:6745 et seq.

"Our country buys Turkic sheep and horses, Turks receive our country's silks. Both sides are abundantly supplied."[43]

In 720, just as the Tibetans were on the brink of open conflict with the Chinese in the Pamirs, there was a change in Arab colonial policy. In that year, the caliph ʿUmar II was succeeded by Yazîd b. ʿAbd al-Malik, a representative of the expansionist faction among the Umayyads. His new governor for Khurasan, Saʿîd b. ʿAbd al-ʿAzîz, first continued the relatively mild policies of his predecessors. Then, in the spring of 721, a Türgiś army led by Kül Cur entered Sogdiana in support of a rebellion by a group of nobles who had renounced Islam.[44] The Turks had advanced as far as Qaṣr al-Bāhilî, which was located on the route to Samarkand,[45] when Saʿîd finally felt threatened enough to lead an army against them. The result was an Arab victory. But Saʿîd neglected to follow up on this triumph, and his army was soon after easily defeated by the Türgiś in a classic maneuver: "[The Turks] were lying in ambush, and the horses of the Muslims came into their view, so they attacked them; the Turks withdrew, and made [the Arabs] follow them until they passed the ambush; [the Turks] came out against them, and the Muslims were routed."[46] Thenceforth, Saʿîd was impotent in the face of the Turks. He was able only to maintain himself near Samarkand, where he watched and waited until the Turks retired.[47]

When news of the open revolt of such a large number of Sogdian nobles and merchants reached Damascus, the Umayyad government saw no alternative to forceful military action in order to maintain its grip on Transoxiana. A new governor, Saʿîd b. ʿAmr al-Ḥaraśî, was sent to replace Saʿîd b. ʿAbd al-ʿAzîz. The new governor sent on to Khurasan as his temporary surrogate, al-Muġaśśir b. Muzâḥim al-Sulamî, was a military leader who had long complained about Arab softness on the Sogdians. The Arabs now seemed prepared to reassert their authority.

---

[43] *TCTC*, 212:6744.
[44] Ṭabarî, ii:1421, 1428, 1430. Gibb, 1923:61-62; Shaban, 1970:99-101.
[45] Ṭabarî, ii:1421.
[46] Ṭabarî, ii:1428.
[47] Cf. Gibb, 1923:61.

Forewarned, the rebels decided to take immediate action.[48] In the fall of 721, they sent envoys to "the king of Ferghana, Aluṭâr, asking him to help them, and lodge them in his city." Alutâr, who, it may be recalled, had once been enthroned jointly by the Arabs and Tibetans (and later fled from the Chinese), agreed.[49] So, after rejecting all offers of reconciliation from Ghûrak, the king of Samarkand and, by force of circumstance, an Arab ally, the rebels left their countries and fled to Ferghana:[50] "And Kârzang and Ġalang left with the people of Qiyy, and Abâr b. Makhnûn and Thâbit with the people of Iśtîkhan; and the people of Bayârkath left, and the people of Sabaskath, with a thousand men, on them belts of gold, along with the lords of Buzmâgan; and the Dîwâśtîg[51] left with the people of Bungîkath to the castle of Abghar, and Kârzang and the people of al-Sughd entered Khuġanda."[52] The Sogdian rebels now thought they were safe from Arab retaliation.

When al-Ḥaraśî's army arrived at Khuġanda in the spring of 722, however, Alutâr betrayed the Sogdians to the Muslims, and, after a short struggle, Kârzang surrendered.[53] But, having accepted the surrender, the treacherous al-Ḥaraśî then had the captives murdered—between three and seven thousand nobles and commoners. Only the merchants were spared,[54] for "with them was immense wealth which they had brought from China."[55] The savage massacre was a terrifying lesson to the non-Muslims of

---

[48] Cf. Shaban, 1970:101.

[49] Ṭabarî, ii:1440. It is unknown when he regained the throne after the events of December 715. See Appendix E.

[50] Ṭabarî, ii:1139-1140. Cf. Gibb, 1923:62; Shaban, 1970:101.

[51] Ṭabarî (ii:1446, with variants among the manuscripts) spells it Dîwâśtî and notes: "It is said that Dîwâśtî was the *dihqân* of the people of Samarkand, and his name was Dîwâśng [i.e., Dîwâśtig, for Dêvastic], but they Arabicized it Dîwâśnî."

[52] Ṭabarî, ii:1441. Most of the proper names are unknown to me, and not all are pointed in the text. The vowels presumed to be missing are here given as short *a* in all cases.

[53] Ṭabarî, ii:1444.

[54] Ṭabarî, ii:1445.

[55] Ṭabarî, ii:1445-1446.

Transoxiana. "Thâbit Quṭna said, recalling those fallen from among the nobles:"

> The eye delighted in the death of Kârzang,
>   and Kaśśîn, and that which Bayâr suffered,
> And the Dîwâśnî, and that which Galang suffered,
>   at the castle of Khuganda when they were ruined and
>   perished.[56]

Notwithstanding the thoroughness of the massacre, a number of Sogdians somehow escaped the fate of their countrymen. Some even made their way to the Türgiś lands, where they organized a special corps of Sogdian exiles within the Türgiś armies. Thereafter, these expatriates particularly distinguished themselves in the fight against the Muslims.[57]

While the Arabs were completing their subjugation of the rest of Sogdiana, the Tibetans—perhaps in response to requests from "many envoys from the Western Regions"[58]—occupied the region of Little Balûr. Mo-chin-mang, the king, escaped to Chinese territory, where he pleaded with the Military Governor of Pei-t'ing, Chang Hsiao-sung: "Balûr is T'ang's western gate. If Balûr is lost, all of the Western Regions will be Tibetan!"[59] Chang agreed. He sent a combined army of four thousand Chinese and foreign troops under the command of Chang Ssu-li, the Assistant Commissioner of Kashgar, to join the army of Little Balûr in a counterattack to be led by King Mo-chin-mang. On October 29, 722,[60] they attacked and routed the Tibetan army, killing and capturing "several ten-thousands of men" according to the Chinese account.[61] After this setback in Little Balûr, the Tibetans did not undertake military campaigns in the West for several years.[62]

[56] Ṭabarî, ii:1446.
[57] Gibb, 1923:63.
[58] OTA, Bird year 721(-722) summer. On the term "Western Regions" (Old Tibetan, stod-phyogs), see Appendix B.
[59] TCTC, 212:6752.
[60] HTS, 5:129; TCTC, 212:6752.
[61] TCTC, 212:6752.
[62] TFYK, 358:10v-11r (pp. 4244-4245); TCTC, 212:6752. It appears

Within two years the Arabs also suffered a major defeat in Central Asia, in a battle known as "the Day of Thirst."[63] After an unsuccessful campaign in 723, in which Arab armies were pushed back across the Oxus by a Türgiś army, and after a moderately successful campaign in 724,[64] Muslim b. Saʿîd al-Kilâbî, the governor of Khurasan, decided upon a major operation. He led an army into Ferghana, besieged "its capital,"[65] cut down the trees, and otherwise devastated the countryside.[66] But when a Türgiś army led by the qaghan approached,[67] the Arabs fled in headlong

---

from Hui Ch'ao's account (in *WWTCKC*) of his trip to India that the split of Balûr into Greater and Lesser parts was due to Tibetan pressure. This pressure, which is referred to in other accounts, was the Tibetan insistence on using Balûr as a passageway to the Tarim Basin (cf. *HTS*, 221b:6251) and to Ṭukhâristân and Transoxiana. Thus it is not clear that the T'ang victory denied Tibet access to the West. (Cf. Moriyasu, 1984:33-34). An example of this may be drawn from the following incident. In the summer of 723, the Chin-ch'eng Princess wrote to Chandrâpîda, the king of Kashmir, to ask for asylum. Instead of consulting with the king of Little Balûr, who was both a close neighbor and a Chinese ally, Chandrâpîda wrote to the Tegin, the ruler of Zâbulistân (1500 *li* distant from Kashmir), to ask if he would support Kashmir militarily against the Tibetans. The Tegin assented, but then dispatched an envoy to the T'ang court requesting advice. In the tenth month (October 22–November 20) of 724, Hsüan-tsung approved of what they had done. (See *TFYK*, 979:7v-8r [p. 11501], translated in Chavannes, 1903:205-206.) But nothing concrete seems to have come of this. It would thus appear that Tibet was still a power to be reckoned with in the area north of Kashmir, and so Tibetans and their allies continued to move unchecked through the same area after the Chinese victory. (Cf. Moriyasu, 1984:37.)

[63] Arabic, *yawm al-ʿaṭaś*. Ṭabarî, ii:1480.

[64] Ṭabarî, ii:1462 et seq. Cf. Gibb, 1923:64-65.

[65] Presumably, "its capital" (Arabic, *madînatihâ*, lit. "its city") was in a part of Ferghana that was not then under Arab control. According to Ibn Khurdâdhbih, 207-208, "the city of Ferghana" was another name for Akhsî-kath, which was located on the north bank of the Jaxartes (see G. Le Strange, *Lands of the Eastern Caliphate* [1966] 477.) Akhsîkath is said to have been the capital and one of the six or seven major cities of the country (Chavannes, 1903:148). Hui Ch'ao observed that in his day Ferghana was divided into two parts: the north, which was allied with the Türgiś, and the south, which had submitted to the Arabs (*WWTCKC*, 978).

[66] Balâdhurî, 428.

[67] Ṭabarî, ii:1478; Balâdhurî, 428. Gibb, 1923:66, states: "According to

retreat—constantly harried by the Turks—only to find their escape barred by the forces of Tashkent and Ferghana. The Arabs fought frantically. Some managed to cut their way out and escape to Arab-held Khuǵanda.[68] This battle marked a turning point in the conflict over control of Transoxiana. The Türgiš were now unquestionably predominant, and the Arabs were on the defensive.[69]

Further to the East, 724 saw the appointment of a particularly odious T'ang military governor over the Pacified West: Tu Hsien.[70] He had recently proved his resourcefulness by tricking the Türgiš and escaping when pursued by them.[71] Now he was appointed Assistant Grand Protector-General of the Pacified West and Military Governor of the lands West of the Desert.[72] Tu's first action was to discover a purported plot by Yü-ch'ih T'iao, the king of Khotan, to rebel along with "the Turks and various Westerners."[73] He promptly captured and decapitated the king, killed some fifty of his adherents, and installed another king in his place.[74]

the Arab tradition, the Türgesh armies were led on this occasion not by Su-lu himself, but by one of his sons." Gibb's idea that the armies were led by a son of the qaghan apparently derives from a passage in Ṭabarî (ii:1479) which reports "a son of Khâqân followed them." Most likely the qaghan was simply accompanied by his son on the campaign.

[68] Ṭabarî, ii:1478 et seq. Cf. Gibb, 1923:65-66.

[69] Cf. Gibb, 1923:65-66; Shaban, 1970:106-107.

[70] CTS, 98:3076, remarks that Tu "was in An-hsi for four years." This is true only if his year(s) as chien ch'a yü shih, during which he traveled to the Pacified West, are counted.

[71] In 723? TCTC, 212:6758, gives no date. According to CTS, 98:3076, and HTS, 126:4421, this happened much earlier, in 716. All these sources agree, however, that the Turks tried to bribe him, and that, through some deception, he avoided taking the bribe.

[72] On April 2, 724. CTS, 8:190; TCTC, 212:6758. The coappointment is not mentioned in CTS, 98:3076, or HTS, 126:4421.

[73] "Westerners" here translates Chinese, Hu.

[74] CTS, 98:3076; HTS, 126:4421; TCTC, 212:6769. Cf. Chavannes, 1903:82n; Moriyasu, 1984:34. A more precise date than 725 is not given. The origin of this plot, which sounds phony, may have been Tu Hsien himself, who needed a justification for the plundering and subjugation of semi-independent Khotan.

Tu Hsien's arbitrary and oppressive policies were again manifested in the fall of 726 at the T'ang's official international market at Kucha.[75] Türgiš Qaghan Su-lu's T'ang consort, who was of royal Turkic blood, sent an envoy with a thousand horses to trade at the market. The Türgiš envoy is said to have proselytized "the princess's religion"[76] before Tu Hsien, whose anger was aroused: "How dare an *Aršïla woman proselytize me!"[77] He had the envoy severely beaten and locked up; neglected during a snowstorm, the horses died. Unperturbed, Tu then departed for the Eastern Capital, Loyang.[78] Later Chinese historians laud Tu Hsien as one of those few governors of the Pacified West since its reconquest in 692 who "had good administrations and were praised by the people."[79] He was especially favored by Hsüantsung, and when he died the emperor grieved for him.[80] But the consequences of his harsh and high-handed rule were soon to appear.

Not coincidentally, another Chinese official was establishing a similar reputation in the eastern regions of China's colonial empire at about the same time. Wang Chün-ch'o, a native of Ch'ang-lo *hsien* in Kua *chou*, had first made his name as a tough warrior under Kuo Chih-yün, the Military Governor of Ho-hsi and Lung-yu. When Kuo died in 721, Wang succeeded him,[81] and in a short time managed to antagonize the subjugated tribes of

---

[75] Chinese, *hu shih*, lit. "mutual market."

[76] The consort was the Chiao-ho Princess, a daughter of the Chinese-supported On oq qaghan, *Aršïla Huai-tao. Her religion is not mentioned, but was almost certainly Buddhism, the dominant faith of the Western Turks by the early seventh century.

[77] *TCTC*, 213:6775.

[78] *CTS*, 194b:5191; *HTS*, 215b:6067; *TCTC*, 213:6775. Cf. Chavannes, 1903:81-82. Both of Tu's official biographies (*CTS*, 98:3075-3077; *HTS*, 126:4420-4422) omit this outrageous incident. In Loyang, Tu was appointed a chief minister of the Secretariat-Chancellery on October 14, 726 (*CTS*, 8:190; *HTS*, 5:132; *TCTC*, 213:6773). Cf. *CHC*, 3:390 et seq., on Tu's official career. Loyang was the functioning capital from late 724 to late 727 (*CHC*, 3:388-392).

[79] *CTS*, 98:3076; *TCTC*, 213:6773.

[80] *CTS*, 98:3077; *HTS*, 126:4422. He died in 740, when he was over sixty.

[81] *CTS*, 103:3190-3191; *HTS*, 133:4545-4547; *TCTC*, 212:6747.

Uyghur, Ch'i-pi, Ssu-chieh, and Hun which lived in his jurisdiction between Kan *chou* and Liang *chou*.[82] Among other things, he
seems to have slandered Ch'eng-tsung, the leader of the
Uyghurs, and then caused his death.[83] His arrogant and aggressive colonialism could not fail to gain favor for him at Hsüan-
tsung's court.

About this time, the perennial debate over Tibet again surfaced
at the T'ang court. In response to Hsüan-tsung's complaint that
the Tibetans used "enemy-country protocol,"[84] Chang Yüeh, the
President of the Board of War declared: "The Tibetans are dis-
courteous; we really ought to punish the aliens.[85] But our troops
have been deployed for over ten years, and [the mobilized border
prefectures of] Kan, Liang, Ho, and Shan cannot bear their dis-
tress. Although the army sometimes wins victories, what is
gained does not make up for what is lost. I have heard that they
[the Tibetans] have acknowledged their errors and seek peace; I
would hope that we can accept their desire to submit, in order to
relieve our people on the frontiers."[86] When Hsüan-tsung said
that he would discuss the matter with Wang Chün-ch'o, Chang
took leave of the emperor. On his way out, he is said to have remarked to an associate: "Chün-ch'o is brave but does not have
[the ability to] plan; he usually counts on luck. If the two countries were to make peace,[87] how could he [ever] be a success?

---

[82] *CTS*, 103:3192; *HTS*, 133:4547; *TCTC*, 213:6779.

[83] *CTS*, 103:3120; *HTS*, 133:4547, 217a:6114; *TCTC*, 213:6779.

[84] Chinese, *ti kuo li* (*TCTC*, 213:6776). See also earlier, in 714 (*TCTC*,
211:6706). In other words, the Tibetans had referred to China in official dis-
course as the equal, not the superior, of Tibet. In early medieval theory, this
was indeed a diplomatic affront. But the emperor's faction at court seems to
have deliberately pounced on it as the justification for a war against Tibet.
Chang Yüeh was appointed President of the Board of War and "third *ad ho-
minem* chief minister" in 721 (*CTS*, 8:182, 97:3053; *HTS*, 5:128; cf. *CHC*,
3:376 et seq.). Chang was active in Buddhist circles and, by T'ang standards,
can be considered a pacifist.

[85] "Aliens" here translates Chinese, *i*, a generic, slightly pejorative, and
somewhat literary term for foreigners during the T'ang period.

[86] *CTS*, 97:3055, 196a:5229; *TCTC*, 213:6776. Chang seems to be referring to the Tibetan peace initiatives of 716, 718 and 719. See note 39, above.

[87] Chinese, *ho hao* (*CTS*, 196a:5229). *TCTC*, 213:6776, has the expres-

[Therefore,] what I said will certainly not be [accepted and] put into practice!"[88] True to Chang's prediction, Wang advised the emperor to invade Tibet.[89] But, due either to their superior military intelligence[90] or simply to coincidence, the Tibetans attacked first.

In the winter of 726-727, an army led by Stag sgra khoṅ lod raided Ta-tou Valley,[91] attacked Kan *chou*, burned its outlying villages,[92] and retreated. Immediately, Wang Chün-ch'o and his army advanced with the hope of surprising the Tibetan rear. As the Tibetan troops withdrew to the Ta-fei River (Jima Gol) along a road to the west of Wang's Chi-shih Army, however, a heavy snowfall intervened, and great numbers of wounded Tibetans fell victim to the cold. Wang and his assistant generals pursued, but were unable to overtake the Tibetans until they reached the western shores of the Koko Nor. To the Tibetans' dismay, however, Wang had secretly sent men ahead to burn the grass in the area, so many Tibetan horses died. Just as Stag sgra's army had almost completed crossing the Ta-fei River, Wang and his troops, who had traversed the frozen Koko Nor, attacked. Wang captured those Tibetans who were stranded on the near bank of the river, and also took the Tibetan baggage and supply train, which included some ten thousand sheep and horses.[93] For this less-than-heroic victory, Wang Chün-ch'o was personally feted by Hsüan-

---

sion *ho ch'in*, which in T'ang histories normally means "marriage peace." This seems to be an error, since the Tibetan emperor still had a living T'ang consort.

[88] *CTS*, 196a:5229; *TCTC*, 213:6776.

[89] *CTS*, 196a:5229; *HTS*, 216a:6083; *TCTC*, 213:6776.

[90] See the comments of Po Chü-i in a memorial submitted in 810 (*TCTC*, 238:7673): "I have heard that the Uyghurs and Tibetans both have spies. As for Chinese affairs, trifling or great, they know everything."

[91] Chinese, *Ta-tou Ku*, "Big Dipper Valley." *HTS*, 133:4547, has *Ta-tou-pa Ku*.

[92] Chinese, *shih li* in *CTS*, 103:3191, 196a:5229. *HTS*, 216a:6083, has *hsiang chü*. Pelliot, 1961:17, 99, translates both as "villages." *TCTC*, 213:6776, says only "they burned and robbed, and then left."

[93] *CTS*, 8:190, 196a:5229; *HTS*, 5:132, 216a:6083; *TCTC*, 213:6776; *TFYK*, 358:11r-11v (p. 4245), 384:19v (p. 4571).

tsung, who gave him gifts and bestowed titles on him, his wife, and his father. The elated emperor even enfeoffed Wang and his wife, he as Earl of Chin-ch'ang *hsien*, she as Lady of Wu-wei *chün*.[94]

In the autumn of 727, however, the inexorable law of karmic retribution (as the Buddhists might say) manifested itself. At the end of that summer, Mes ag tshoms had himself gone to ʿAźa for the campaign against China.[95] On September 27, Tibetan armies led by the generals Stag sgra khoṅ lod and Cog ro Maṅporje attacked and captured the Chinese fortified city[96] of Kua *chou*. They took Wang Chün-ch'o's father and the prefect T'ien Yüan-hsien prisoner and plundered the city of its food stores and military supplies.[97] Although unmentioned by the Chinese sources, they also took a vast quantity of silk: "The many riches of the Chinese being taken out to the Western Regions, after having been amassed in Kua *chou*, were all confiscated by the Tibetans, who thereby once again found great wealth. Even the ordinary people joined in covering themselves with good Chinese silks."[98]

The Tibetans then turned to attack the Jade Gate[99] Army 200 *li* west of Su *chou*.[100] During this offensive, they captured a number of Buddhist monks,[101] and then released them, sending them back to Liang *chou* to chastise Wang Chün-ch'o. They reportedly said to him: "General, you have always wanted to avenge the na-

---

[94] *CTS*, 103:3191; *HTS*, 133:4547; *TFYK*, 384:19v (p. 4571).

[95] *OTA*, Hare year 727(-728) summer; *OTC*, vii.

[96] *TCTC*, 213:6778. *CTS*, 103:3191, has T'ien Jen-hsien.

[97] The *OTC* account says that the Tibetans "overthrew the Chinese walled city of Kua *chou*." "Walled city" = Tibetan, *mkhar*, the equivalent of Chinese, *ch'eng*, and Arabic, *madîna*. The Old Tibetan verb *phab*, which usually means "conquered" or "subjugated," literally means "threw down," and is translated here as "overthrew." The Chinese sources (*CTS*, 99:3094, 196a:5229; *HTS*, 216a:6083; *TCTC*, 213:6779) attest to the Tibetan destruction of the city walls.

[98] *OTC*, vii.

[99] Chinese, Yü-men *chün*.

[100] *TCTC*, 213:6778 gloss. 200 *li* is about 66 miles. The attack seems to have been unsuccessful (*HTS*, 216a:6083). Cf. P. Demiéville, *Le Concile de Lhasa* (1952) 294-295.

[101] *CTS*, 103:3191; *TCTC*, 213:6778.

tion with your patriotism and courage. Why not go out for just one battle today?"[102] Wang, having heard that his father had been captured, "ascended the city wall, looked westward, and wept: he did not really dare to send out the army."[103]

Meanwhile, Cog ro Mańporje led a detachment to besiege Ch'ang-lo *hsien* in Kua *chou*, but failed to capture it.[104] The combined Tibetan forces then turned west to Kucha,[105] where, together with the Türgiš under Su-lu,[106] they raided throughout the region.[107] Finally, they laid siege to the city of Kucha itself.[108] The siege lasted quite a long time. Chao I-chen, the Assistant Protector-General of the Pacified West, made one attempt to break the siege, but he was easily driven back.[109] Free of concern about more of such attacks, the besiegers took the opportunity to thoroughly plunder the neighboring territories of the Four Garrisons. They opened granary stores, terrorized the local inhabitants, and seized their animals. Only Kucha City, with Chao I-chen's forces bottled up inside, withstood them. As the Chinese chronicles remark, "the Pacified West was barely held."[110]

Before their attack on Kua *chou*, the Tibetans had sent a letter to Bilgä Qaghan of the Eastern Turks, asking if he would like to join the raid. Instead of politely declining the invitation—what one might have expected—Bilgä Qaghan sent the letter to the

[102] *CTS*, 103:3191; *HTS*, 133:4547; *TCTC*, 213:6778; *TFYK*, 453:21r (p. 5374). As usual, the quotations differ from source to source, and there is no way to tell which is more correct.

[103] *CTS*, 103:3191; *HTS*, 133:4547; *TCTC*, 213:6778.

[104] *CTS*, 103:3192–3193; *HTS*, 133:4548; *TCTC*, 213:6778.

[105] *HTS*, 216a:6083.

[106] *CTS*, 8:191; *HTS*, 215b:6067; *TCTC*, 213:6779. Su-lu sought revenge for Tu Hsien's maltreatment of his trade envoy in 726.

[107] *CTS*, 194b:5191; *HTS*, 215b:6067. The correct sequence of events is only made clear from a reading of all the sources; no single account gives the complete story. *TCTC*, 213:6775–6776, misdates Su-lu's campaign by including it in the year-end catchall for 726. Cf. Moriyasu, 1984:34–35.

[108] *TCTC*, 213:6779. The attack is recorded under October 20, 727, but it is uncertain if this date refers to the event itself.

[109] *HTS*, 215b:6067, is the only account that explicitly mentions Chao's attack; it may, however, be inferred from the other sources.

[110] *CTS*, 194b:5191; *HTS*, 215b:6067; *TCTC*, 213:6776. Tu Hsien had left Chao I-chen in charge when he was called to court.

T'ang court, where it arrived on October 6, 727.[111] Hsüan-tsung was of course delighted, and then granted the Turk's request to trade horses—for silk and other commodities, no doubt—at Hsi Shou-hsiang City.[112] So ended Tibetan–Eastern Turkic amity.

While the Tibetans were on campaign at Kucha, the partisans of the murdered Uyghur leader Ch'eng-tsung set out to avenge their fallen chief. They killed Wang Chün-ch'o,[113] and then fled to Tibet.[114] The hatred for Wang among the Uyghurs and Tibetans—and even by the T'ang historians of the day—can still be sensed in the normally dry Chinese chronicles. But when Hsüan-tsung heard about Wang's death, he felt extremely sorry, and bestowed high posthumous honors on him.[115]

Meanwhile, the Tibetan-Türgiś siege of Kucha continued until, with the onset of winter, the Tibetans and Türgiś were forced to withdraw. The campaign and siege had lasted eighty days.[116] This was not, however, an utter disaster. The solidification of the Tibetan-Türgiś alliance on the battlefields of Central Asia was a most important event. The T'ang government remained confused. Expecting further Tibetan attacks, it had mobilized armies in Lung-yu *tao* and Ho-hsi *tao*. Then, when winter arrived without the Tibetans, the Chinese canceled the mobilization. But on January 26, 728, they were surprised by "the spying thralls" sweeping in to raid.[117] No doubt, this foray was prefatory to the Tibetan raid on Kucha, which is reported under February 19, 728. Nothing is known about this raid except that Chao I-chen apparently repulsed the raiders.[118]

---

[111] *CTS*, 8:191; *TCTC*, 213:6779; *TFYK*, 999:25r (p. 11727).

[112] *CTS*, 194a:5177; *HTS*, 215b:6053; *TCTC*, 213:6779.

[113] Dated November 9, 727, in *CTS*, 8:191, and *HTS*, 5:133.

[114] *CTS*, 103:3192; *HTS*, 117a:6114, 133:4547. *TCTC*, 213:6780, has them fleeing to the Turks.

[115] *CTS*, 103:3192; *HTS*, 133:4547-4548.

[116] *CTS*, 196a:5229.

[117] *TCTC*, 213:6781. The term here translated as "thralls" is *lu*, which literally means "captive" or "slave." It was the strongest T'ang pejorative word for "foreigner." The word *fan* in T'ang usage was the ordinary neutral or polite word for "foreigner," "foreign country," "abroad," and so forth.

[118] *CTS*, 8:192; *HTS*, 5:133; *TCTC*, 213:6791.

At this point, a major rebellion broke out in southern China,[119] and for several months the Chinese chroniclers' attention was apparently drawn away from the West.[120] Indeed, the next information that is given is the account of another Tibetan raid on Kua *chou*, which was led by a general Hsi-mo-lang in the autumn of 728.[121] This time, the raid backfired. The raiding party was driven off by the prefect Chang Shou-kuei,[122] and was subsequently attacked in K'o-po Valley by Hsiao Sung, Military Governor of Ho-hsi, and Chang Chung-liang, Military Governor of Lung-yu and Governor-General of Shan *chou*. From there, the victorious Chinese pursued the Tibetans to "their Ta-mo-men City,"[123] which they captured, along with over 1,000 prisoners, 1,000 horses, 500 yaks, and a great quantity of armaments and supplies. After burning Tibet's Camel Bridge,[124] the Chinese forces returned home completely victorious.[125] In the following month, Tibetan misfortunes compounded. While on a raid at Chi-lien City, (near Kan *chou*), they were overwhelmed by an army led by an assistant general of Hsiao Sung.[126] Hsüan-tsung himself claimed credit for planning the strategy which his armies used in this engagement.[127]

In April of 729, the Tibetans suffered two more serious defeats in the northeast. Chang Shou-kuei and Chia Shih-shun, the perfect of Kua *chou*, attacked "the Tibetan Ta-t'ung Army" and

[119] CTS, 8:192; 5:133; TCTC, 213:6781.

[120] TCTC, 213:6781-6782. The rebellion was suppressed with the usual brutality by the end of the year. The executions and tortures are described fairly explicitly in TCTC, 213:6783.

[121] The raid is dated to the seventh lunar month, i.e., August 10–September 7, 728.

[122] CTS, 8:192, 196a:5230; HTS, 5:133, 216a:6084; TCTC, 213:6782.

[123] Literally, "Great Desert-Gate City." For its location, see Satô, 1978:110 et seq.

[124] Chinese, *lo-t'o*, which is identified with the Tibetan place, Rag-tag. See Petech, 1967:253, and Chapter Six, below, under the events of 745.

[125] CTS, 8:192, 99:3094, 196a:5230; HTS, 5:133, 216a:6084; TCTC, 213:6782.

[126] CTS, 99:3094; TCTC, 213:6782-6783; TFYK, 986:22r (p. 11585).

[127] CTS, 196a:5230.

claimed a victory.[128] Then, later in the month, Li Wei, the Prince of Hsin-an and the Military Governor of Shuo-fang, attacked the Tibetan fortress of Shih-pao City,[129] captured it, and established a T'ang garrison there.[130] Upon hearing this news, Hsüan-tsung bestowed the name "Chen-wu Army" on the garrison.[131] Later in 729, the string of Tibetan defeats came to an end. That summer, the *Annals* records a Tibetan victory over the T'ang at a place called Mu le cu le; many Chinese were killed.[132] Nothing more is known about the battle, but it was certainly a great victory, for immediately afterward a T'ang envoy, Li Tson-kan—"Commander-in-Chief Li"[133]—did obeisance at the imperial court at Brag mar in Central Tibet.[134]

Nevertheless, the picture obtained from the official Chinese accounts is of a Tibet reeling from the blows dealt by China. In

[128] In the third month (April 3–May 2). *TFYK*, 986:22r-22v (p. 11585). The Tibetan name for this army is unknown.

[129] Previously a T'ang establishment, according to *TCTC*, 213:6784.

[130] *CTS*, 8:193, 76:2652, 196a:5230; *HTS*, 80:3568, 216a:6084; *TCTC*, 213:6784; *TFYK*, 986:22v-23r (p. 11585-11586), 369:9v-10r (p. 4387).

[131] *TCTC*, 213:6784. *Chen-wu* may be loosely translated as "Awe-inspiring." The name was also used in the Ordos region.

[132] *OTA*, Snake year 729(-730) summer.

[133] Old Tibetan *Tson kan* transcribes Chinese *tsung-kuan*, the well-known title here translated as "Commander-in-Chief."

[134] *OTA*, Snake year (729-)730 winter. That Li is called a "Chinese envoy" means that he was undoubtedly not the defeated general. As Petech (1967:263) has suggested, it would seem that this Li was none other than the Li Wei who had recently captured the fortress of Shih-pao. Li returned to Ch'ang-an before October 21, 729 (*TCTC*, 213:6787). According to *TCTC*, 213:6780, on November 30, 727, "the Grand General of the Chin-wu Guards of the Left, Wei the Prince of Hsin-an, was appointed Assistant Grand Military Governor, etc., of Shuo-fang." (Note that during this period the full [non-Assistant] Grand Military Governorships were held by high-ranking imperial princes who stayed at the capital [*TCTC*, 213:6777]; at this time, the Grand Military Governor of Shuo-fang was Chün, Prince of Chung [*CTS*, 8:191].) Li Wei replaced Hsiao Sung, who was appointed to the corresponding position in Ho-hsi. For Li's other titles, see his biographies (*CTS*, 76:2651-2652; *HTS*, 80:3567-3568). Unfortunately, no mention of a journey to the Tibetan court is made in the Chinese sources dealing with Li's career.

truth, the Chinese armies were quite modest in size, and, despite the number of military clashes, there were no major confrontations between the Chinese and the Tibetans. The only evidence which the Chinese sources adduce to prove a Tibetan decline is the claim that a Chinese spy had been sent to slander Stag sgra khoṅ lod, whom the Tibetans then executed. The loss of this general allegedly "somewhat weakened" Tibet.[135] It is therefore not surprising to read that a Tibetan envoy arrived at the border in the summer of 730 to request peace.[136] After a certain amount of discussion, Hsüan-tsung agreed. Ambassadors shuttled between the capitals, presents were exchanged, grandiose speeches were made, and the affair was settled by the end of the year.[137] The Great Minister Ming-hsi-lieh,[138] the Tibetan envoy dispatched to Ch'ang-àn to complete the formalities, was an experienced diplomat, could speak and read Chinese, and so was not fooled by Hsüan-tsung's attempts to have him accept the symbols of Chinese sovereignty.[139] The two nations remained separate and equal, even in Chinese eyes.[140]

At about the same time, the Türgiś joined the peace process. In 730, they too sent an envoy, Yeh-chih A-pu-ssu,[141] to the

[135] CTS, 196a:5229; HTS, 216a:6083; TCTC, 213:6781. This happened after the Tibetan capture of Kua chou. OTA, Dragon year (728-)729 winter, records Stag sgra khoṅ lod's disgrace.

[136] TCTC, 213:6789, says Tibet sent him "to the border." He is called a nang ku, and his letter is preserved in HTS, 216a:6084, where it is explained that "a nang ku is like an official [with the wealth] of a thousand [head of] cattle."

[137] CTS, 8:196, 196a:5230-5231; HTS, 5:135, 216a:6084-6085; TCTC, 213:6790-6791. A treaty inscription was erected at Ch'ih-ling in about 733 (TCTC, 213:6800).

[138] He is probably the lun (Tibetan, blon, "minister") Mang-je, or *Maṅ bźer, of the envoy's letter. He was not the great minister because, according to the OTA, 'Bro Chuṅ bzaṅ 'or maṅ was appointed to that position in the Dragon year (728-)729 winter, and served until at least the Pig year (747-)748 winter, where a break occurs in the Annals manuscript.

[139] CTS, 8:196, 196a:5230-5231; HTS, 5:135, 216a:6084-6085. TCTC, 213:6791, has an incomplete and inaccurate version.

[140] On these events and their implications, see the important short article by H. Richardson, "Ming-si-lie and the Fish-Bag" (1970).

[141] His name is given only in HTS, 215b:6067, and TFYK, 975:9v (p.

T'ang court. His mission was ostensibly to complain about their treatment at the hands of Tu Hsien. But, since the embassy was given fairly high honors, it is probable that its actual purpose was to mollify the Chinese after the latest Türgiś raids on the Pacified West.[142] Peace was then concluded between the T'ang and the Türgiś.[143] The reason for this apparently sudden Türgiś move, and for the unexpectedly quick and easy peace accord between the T'ang and the Tibetans, is the subject of the next chapter.

11452). Czeglédy has reconstructed this name as *Abuz. See K. Czeglédy, "Gardizi on the History of Central Asia (746-780 A.D.)" (1973) 266 (n 26).

[142] As they had once before (in 718), the Türgiś accepted the fish-bag, the symbol of submission to the T'ang. See *TFYK*, 975:9v (p. 11452), where the aberrant date would seem to be a mistake. This is due, possibly, to the attachment at some time of this entry to the entry on Tu Hsien (also under the sixth month of 729) in the *Shih-lu*.

[143] *CTS*, 194b:5191.

Chapter 5

T'ANG
CHINA
AND THE
ARABS

In 729, the Tibetan army was in Turkistan: not in the Tarim or Jungarian Basins, where the Chinese could hardly have failed to notice them, but in western Central Asia. They were there seemingly at the request of the inhabitants. At that time, the oppressive policies of the Umayyad governor, Aśras al-Sulamî, had provoked open rebellion in Transoxiana among Sogdians and Arabs alike.[1] When the situation became serious, the Khurasanians called in their theoretical overlords of the past, the Western Turks, who now composed the Türgiś confederation under Su-lu. With the aid, apparently, of their Tibetan allies, the Khurasanians and the Türgiś drove the Arab forces almost entirely out of Sogdiana. Only the city of Samarkand and the two fortresses of al-Dabûsiyya and Kamarǵa remained in Arab hands.

Rather than attempt the siege of well-defended Samarkand, Su-lu and the allies turned to nearby Kamarǵa,[2] where they seem

[1] The summary here is largely taken from Gibb's extensive treatment, which is in turn based mainly on Ṭabarî. See Gibb, 1923:69-72. On the Tibetans' Turkistan campaign of 729-730, see note 8 below.

[2] Gibb, 1923:71, (n. 14).

to have expected an easier victory. But the Arab garrison there proved unexpectedly tough, and to Su-lu's discomfort, the siege dragged on. In an unusual attempt to persuade the garrison to surrender, Su-lu brought forth Khusraw, a descendant of the last Sassanid ruler of the Persian Empire, Yazdiġird III. Khusraw's exact relationship to Ni-nieh-shih, the son of Pêrôz who died in China early in the eighth century, is unclear. He is presumed to have lived in Ṭukhâristân.³ Now he called for the restoration of his house, a dynasty which had been defunct for nearly a century. But the past glories of a distant Iran had no appeal for the Transoxanian natives and Arab immigrants in the fortress. Khusraw's attempt to attain a throne he had never seen was a failure.

After further negotiation bogged down, Su-lu ordered an all-out attack on Kamarġa. During the prolonged fighting, the Arab defenders tried repeatedly to kill Su-lu, but to no avail. "They set marksmen behind [the wall the Arabs had erected by the moat]. Among them were Ghâlib b. al-Muhâġir al-Ṭâ'î, uncle of Abû al-ʿAbbâs al-Ṭûsî, and two other men, one of them a Ṣaybânî and the other a Nâġî. They arrived and watched the moat. [When Su-lu appeared,] the Nâġî shot him, and did not miss his nostril; but he had Tibetan armor⁴ on, and the shot did not harm him. And the Ṣaybânî shot him; but none of him was exposed except for his two eyes. Then Ghâlib b. al-Muhâġir shot him, and the arrow penetrated his breast, and he bent over. And that was the worst thing that pierced the qaghan."⁵ The famous Tibetan chain mail⁶

---

³ See Chavannes, 1903:172-173, 258.

⁴ The word for Su-lu's "Tibetan" armor is *kâ śkhw d h*, i.e., **kâśkhûdah*; or *kâ śkhw r h*, i.e., **kâśkhûrah*. The latter part of the word seems to be a scribal error for New Persian, *z r h*, i.e., *zirih*, "armor," "coat of mail."

⁵ Ṭabarî, ii:1521-1522. Gibb omits the incident. It seems likely that this was the injury that caused Su-lu's frailty in one arm, upon which the Chinese historians remarked.

⁶ Tibetan armor in general was famous in the Middle Ages. In my article, "Tibet and the Early Medieval *Florissance* in Eurasia" (1977b) 99, 101, I mistakenly stated that the Tibetans must have imported large quantities of armor. The evidence proves, however, that they undoubtedly manufactured the armor themselves, just as they made the marvelous gold objects, some of them mechanical, which they sent as gifts to the T'ang emperors. On the

that protected Su-lu was well known to the T'ang historians, who described it as follows: "The men and horses all wear chain mail armor. Its workmanship is extremely fine. It envelops them completely, leaving openings only for the two eyes. Thus, strong bows and sharp swords cannot injure them."[7]

The Arabic sources do not mention Tibetans in Su-lu's army, but it appears likely that they did participate in at least part of this campaign.[8] Thus it would seem that the Tibetan army had joined the Türgiś forces for at least the second time in three years. Despite their failure to take Kamarǵa, the Türgiś were now practically unopposed in Transoxiana. The old alliance between Tibet and the Western Turks had been revived, and the Chinese were almost completely unaware of it.

The Tibetan and Türgiś peace initiative of 730—offered to the T'ang suddenly and concluded quickly—is thus easy to understand. With no Chinese threat at their backs, the allies were now able to devote themselves to the struggle for western Central Asia. Tibet began by reasserting itself in the Pamirs. There the Tibetan armies crossed in force over some of the highest passes in the world in order to enter both Khurasan and the Pacified West.

"Tibetan bucklers" frequently encountered in Arabic sources, see Dunlop, 1973:303-304.

[7] *TT*, 190:1023a. The description continues: "When they do battle, they must dismount and array themselves in ranks. When one dies, another takes his place. To the end, they are not willing to retreat. Their lances are longer and thinner than those in China. Their archery is weak but their armor is strong. The men always use swords; when they are not at war they still go about carrying swords." This description appears to reflect that in the *T'ang liu tien*, which was completed in 739; for further references and discussion of the Iranian predecessors of this type of armor and their Chinese developments, see Demiéville, 1952:373-376.

[8] In addition to the *Annals* reference to the return of a Tibetan expedition to Turkistan at the end of the Snake year (729-)730, and beside Ṭabarî's mention of Su-lu's use of Tibetan armor, a T'ang imperial rescript sent to Mes ag tshoms refers to a Tibetan campaign to the West led by Cog ro Maṅporje sometime before 736-737 (*WC*, 12:3v). No other Tibetan campaigns in Turkistan between 729-730 and 736-737 are mentioned in the *Annals*, and the two campaigns that are mentioned are in the same years that the Türgiś had their major campaigns in the West.

At the end of 730, the king of Wakhan traveled to the T'ang court for a lengthy sojourn;[9] it is probable that he left because of this Tibetan and Türgiś pressure.[10] In 732, envoys from both the Arabs and the Türgiś arrived at the Tibetan court;[11] unquestionably, they had come via the Pamirs through Wakhan and Balûr. Thus Tibet seems to have neutralized Chinese influence in this region. Finally, at the end of 734, the Tibetan-Türgiś alliance was formally sealed with the marriage of the Tibetan princess ʿDron ma lod to the Türgiś qaghan.[12]

The Chinese began to be suspicious. In 744, Muktâpîda, the king of Kashmir, dispatched an envoy to China to claim that he and the king of Central Hindustan had defeated the Tibetans and had blocked the "five great Tibetan roads." He offered to provide the necessary supplies for any T'ang army that might come to Balûr.[13] Muktâpîda's offer reflected the growing concern among the Chinese-oriented principalities in the Pamirs over the revived Tibetan activity there. Just how justified their unease was became clear in the following year when Tibet overwhelmed Balûr.[14] Growing Chinese suspicion of the Tibetan-Türgiś alliance was intimated in several undated imperial rescripts of the mid-730s. Chinese suspicions were finally confirmed when they captured a Türgiś mission which, led by an envoy named Kül Inancu, was crossing the Pamirs with gifts and letters for Mes ag tshoms.[15]

Meanwhile, the Türgiś raided the Pacified West in retaliation for the summary execution of their envoy by Liu Huan, the Military Governor of Pei-t'ing.[16] Resistance to the Türgiś was led by

---

[9] TCTC, 213:6791; TFYK, 975:11r (p. 11453).

[10] Cf. J. Chang, Les Musulmans sous la Chine des Tang (1980) 34, who refers to edicts addressed to the kings of Wakhan, Shughnan, Balûr, and Kâpiśa (see WC, 12:7r-9v).

[11] OTA, Monkey year 732(-733) summer.

[12] OTA, Dog year 734(-735) summer; CTS, 194b:5192; HTS, 215b: 6068.

[13] HTS, 221b:6256. Cf. Chavannes, 1903:209; idem, 1904:55.

[14] CTS, 198:5310. Chavannes, 1903:167, appears to have overlooked this.

[15] WC, 11:7r. He seems to have been captured in 735. The letters were in some non-Chinese language or languages.

[16] Liu had accused the envoy of "plotting." Ironically, Liu subsequently

Liu and by Wang Hu-ssu, the T'ang Military Governor of the Pacified West.[17] Kashgar,[18] Qocho,[19] and perhaps Aksu[20] are specifically named as places long-besieged by the Türgiś, although apparently without much success. In reaction to the now-frequent Türgiś raids, the T'ang began to take serious steps. Shortly before 735, Wang Hu-ssu and "the general of the Arab east, the Amîr of Khurasan," concluded an informal alliance, which Hsüan-tsung approved. The objective was joint military action against the Türgiś.[21] Thus, despite all of their statements of support for Khurasanians suffering under Umayyad oppression, the Chinese were after all eager to join their fellow imperialists in Central Asia against the mutually hated Türgiś. Surprisingly, there is no evidence that the Chinese pursued their traditional policy of stirring up internal discord among their enemies. On the contrary, they moved directly to the military option to counter the Türgiś challenge.[22]

In the early winter of 735-736, the Türgiś mounted a major as-

---

revolted, and was executed along with his family (*CTS*, 8:201; *HTS*, 5:138). Their heads were sent to Su-lu, but he was clearly not appeased by this form of reparation. On this, see Chang, 1980:34-36.

[17] *WC*, 10:11r, says "Su-lu . . . throughout the winter [734-735] did not leave Hsi *chou*; recently he again burned the [military-colony] camps, and killed and injured [the people]."

[18] *WC*, 10:8r, says: "From summer up to now [winter], they have besieged Kashgar."

[19] Chang, 1980:34 et seq. Chang has made the most thorough use of Chang Chiu-ling's collection, although unfortunately he has apparently used the versions included in *CTW*. Detailed study of this material in the *WC* would be of great benefit to anyone interested in eighth-century Central Asia, particularly with respect to the military strategy of the Türgiś and the T'ang.

[20] See Chang, 1980:131 (n. 47). I found no reference to Aksu in the places he cites.

[21] *WC*, 5v-6r. Cf. Chang, 1980:38. According to a work cited by Moriyasu, 1984:72 (n. 184), Wang Hu-ssu was appointed to his position in 733.

[22] There is no textual basis for Gibb's oft-quoted theory that the fall of the Türgiś was due to T'ang machinations. Gibb, 1923:85, says, "in his [Su-lu's] own country the dissensions long fomented in secret by the Chinese broke out."

sault against the fortified Chinese cities of Pei-t'ing and Aksu.[23] As the attack turned into a siege at Pei-t'ing, Hsüan-tsung, through his famous minister Chang Chiu-ling, made frantic preparations for a sudden blow that would destroy the enemy.[24] The basic strategy was simple. While huge armies gathered for a coordinated attack on the Türgiś at Pei-t'ing, the forces of Niu Hsien-k'o, Military Governor of Ho-hsi, were ordered to join up with the Arabs and attack the Türgiś homeland around Sûyâb: "You should secretly order [the Military Governor of] the Pacified West to draft 10,000 foreign and Chinese troops; then send someone nonstop to the Arabs to plan with them to take the Yabghu, Bedel,[25] etc. roads to enter Sûyâb. Order Wang Hu-ssu to lead picked cavalry himself to capture their [Türgiś] families."[26] Hsüan-tsung exclaimed excitedly of the opportunity the T'ang had to destroy the Türgiś: "They have led their dogs and sheep to violate our fortresses. This is the day they are going to die!"[27]

At the beginning of 736, Kai Chia-yün, the Protector-General of Pei-t'ing and Army Commissioner[28] of Han-hai, prevailed over the Türgiś.[29] Not long after this, he defeated them again, apparently at Pei-t'ing. An important Türgiś leader, known only as "the Yabghu," was killed.[30] This was a major catastrophe for Su-lu, and he immediately called for peace negotiations. But at first,

[23] *CTS*, 8:203; *HTS*, 5:138; *TCTC*, 214:6812. *WC*, 10:4r, refers to the apparent defeat of the Chinese at Aksu.

[24] Among the many rescripts preserved in Chang's writings which concern this campaign, see especially the one to Niu Hsien-k'o, the Military Governor of Ho-hsi, in *WC*, 8:6r-7r.

[25] Chinese, *Po-ta*. See Chavannes, 1903:143 (nn. 1-2), who makes it clear that the text here means that the army should traverse the Bedel Pass, the main way to Sûyâb from the Tarim Basin. The Yabghu Road remains unidentified.

[26] *WC*, 8:6v.

[27] Ibid. It is not clear whether Hsüan-tsung meant "dogs and sheep" literally, figuratively, or both.

[28] Chinese, *chün shih*. Des Rotours, 1974, 2:729, 913, notes that this is a rare title; perhaps it was more commonly used in border armies.

[29] *WC*, 14:6v; *CTS*, 8:203; *HTS*, 5:139; *TCTC*, 214:6813.

[30] *WC*, 8:7v.

Hsüan-tsung would have none of this.[31] He ordered the continuation of hostilities: "If the Pacified West [Military Governorship] sends out its army to take advantage of this opportunity to attack Sûyâb, all the rogues hiding there can be captured."[32] Eventually, however, reason prevailed. On September 16, 736, the T'ang accepted the Türgiś surrender.[33]

Meanwhile, Cog ro Mańporje and the Tibetan army were on the move. In the autumn or winter of 736, they marched into Turkistan[34] via Little Balûr, which country promptly sent an envoy to the T'ang to complain.[35] It is apparently this campaign to which numerous references are made in Chang Chiu-ling's imperial rescripts. In one letter to Mes ag tshoms, Hsüan-tsung noted that he had heard that "Mańporje" had again been seen going West: "What is the reason? If you are joining with the Türgiś to subvert our West of the Desert [Military Governorship], you will not necessarily succeed."[36] At about the same time, Chang Chiu-ling wrote a "Declaration of Congratulations on the Fleeing of the Bandit Su-lu" to which Hsüan-tsung provied an "Imperial Reply." Chang's Declaration states: "Even if the Tibetans have really gone west, Su-lu will not be able to respond to them, so their [the Tibetans'] defeat is certain."[37] It is thus quite clear that a large Tibetan force entered Central Asia—probably in response to an embassy sent by Su-lu—somewhere west of the Pamirs in late 736.[38]

Reacting to the Tibetan move through Balûr, the Chinese suddenly broke the seven-year-old peace treaty by invading north-

[31] Ibid.

[32] Ibid.

[33] HTS, 5:139; TCTC, 214:6821. It is interesting to note that, despite the joint Sino-Arab planning, the Arabs do not appear in the Chinese sources as participants in this campaign. The Tibetans are similarly absent.

[34] OTA, Mouse year 736(-737) before winter.

[35] TCTC, 214:6827.

[36] WC, 11:13r-13v.

[37] WC, 14:6v-7r. The Imperial Reply (7r-7v) is of little interest.

[38] Hsüan-tsung remarked in a letter to the Türgiś Qaghan (WC, 11:7r) that he had returned to Mes ag tshoms everything captured from Kül Inancu.

eastern Tibet in early 737.[39] Surprise was complete, and the T'ang armies soon reported victory after victory. The sources are unclear about who really instigated this campaign, but it was without doubt Hsüan-tsung himself.[40] This is so even though the sources blame a deputy of one of the border generals, saying that he had forged the orders for the invasion in hopes of winning personal glory. The key evidence for Hsüan-tsung's culpability is that he generously rewarded the victorious generals, while, according to the same sources, these generals were overcome with feelings of guilt and remorse over breaking faith with the Tibetans, and all of them came to bad ends.[41] This would not be understandable unless Hsüan-tsung himself had ordered them to break the formal oaths they had sworn with the Tibetan border generals as a part of the peace treaty.

There can therefore be no doubt that the Chinese invaded Tibet specifically to prevent Tibetan troops from joining up with the Türgiś in the west. The Chinese sources claim that the invasion was undertaken in order to hit the Tibetans in an area that was more accessible to the T'ang armies than was Balûr. In fact, as noted above, there were plenty of T'ang armies available in the Tarim Basin, in close proximity to the Pamirs. Furthermore, the Chinese had tolerated the Tibetans in Balûr for years without doing anything about it.[42] Only now did Hsüan-tsung become angry about the invasion of his vassal-state. It was probably the traditional T'ang fear of the combined power of the Tibetans and Turks—not just the Tibetans alone in the Pamirs—that motivated the Chinese now. In any case, their invasion was so sudden and unexpected that the Tibetans in the northeastern and eastern frontier areas were quickly overwhelmed.[43]

[39] CTS, 9:208; HTS, 5:139; TCTC, 214:6826-6827.

[40] CTS, 196a:5233; TCTC, 214:6827.

[41] CTS, 196a:5233; HTS, 216a:6085-6086; TCTC, 214:6827.

[42] The failed campaigns supposedly undertaken by the predecessors of Kao Hsien-chih (see below under the events of 747) are nowhere described; some doubt must therefore remain about their existence.

[43] The circumstances surrounding China's breach of the treaty indicate that there was very strong opposition at court to the idea of starting a war

Meanwhile, far to the west, Tibetan-Türgiś cooperation proceeded—but against the Arabs, not the Chinese. At the end of 736
or the beginning of 737, the Tibetan army under Cog ro Maṅporje apparently joined the Türgiś army, which was reinforced
by contingents from a great number of petty Central Asian states
that were subject to the Türgiś. Later in 737, another Tibetan
army, led by ʿBal Skyes bzaṅ ldoṅ tsab, entered Little Balûr[44] and
captured its pro-T'ang king.[45] The campaign was clearly undertaken in order to secure Tibetan routes through the Pamirs to the
west, and may have been a preliminary step to the Arab expedition. In any event, due to this success, the whole of the Pamir region northwest of Little Balûr fell into Tibetan hands: "All of its
neighboring countries—over twenty of them—submitted to Tibet. Tribute ceased to arrive [in China]."[46]

At about this time, the Arab governor of Khurasan, Asad b.
ʿAbd Allâh al-Qasrî, launched an invasion of Khuttal.[47] Ibn al-
Sâʾiġî, the lord of Khuttal, wrote to the Türgiś qaghan at
Nawâkath[48] to ask for help. Su-lu made a hasty seventeen-day
march from Sûyâb[49] as the Arabs, forewarned by Ibn al-Sâʾiġî,

---

with Tibet. In order to get around the antiwar faction, Hsüan-tsung seems to
have resorted to trickery. The T'ang historians, who were clearly pacifist in
this instance, reflect this conclusion in their historical accounts.

[44] *OTA*, Ox year 737(-738) before winter. Bruźa, the Tibetan name of
Little Balûr, is certainly related to the modern names for the people of Hunza
and their language, Burusho and Burushaski.

[45] *OTA*, Ox year (737-)738 winter. It states: "The king of Bruźa, having
been overthrown, paid homage [to Mes ag tshoms]. The Chinese envoy Waṅ
ʿDo-śi having paid homage, the Chinese abolished [their] administration [of
Little Balûr?]. . . ."

[46] *TCTC*, 215:6884.

[47] The source material in Ṭabarî on the following section is very extensive. My account derives in part from the summaries in Gibb, 1923:81 et seq.,
and Shaban, 1970:124 et seq.

[48] Ṭabarî, ii:1593.

[49] Ṭabarî, ii:1596. Calculating an approximate distance of 300 miles (as
the crow flies) from Sûyâb to Khuttal, the Türgis averaged over 17½ miles
per day. The distance traveled was actually much greater because they had to
pass through mountainous territory. They were, however, probably
mounted.

were already fleeing. The Turks attacked them as they were crossing the Oxus,[50] and inflicted serious losses on the Arab army. After crossing the river, the Türgiś attacked Asad's camp, and then went on to attack a part of his army that had been sent on ahead. This detachment was escorting what are described as athqâl[51] or amwâl[52]—"heavy loads" of "valuable goods" or "treasures"[53]—probably a consignment which was passing through Khuttal on its way to or from China.[54] On September 30, 737, the Türgiś wiped out the detachment and seized the goods. When Asad finally arrived with the main body of his troops, the Türgiś raiders retired to Ṭukhâristân (instead of to Sûyâb or Nawâkath). Asad returned to Balkh,[55] where, when winter set in, the Arab army was demobilized. The Türgiś, however, remained active. Su-lu gathered troops from Ṭukhâristân, Khuttal, Sogdiana, Uśrûsana, Tashkent, and other nations of Central Asia; then, together with the Arab rebel al-Ḥârith b. Surayǵ and his men,[56] he launched another campaign against Arab Khurasan.

In early December 737, the Türgiś attacked Khulm, but were driven off by the Arab garrison. The invaders then bypassed Balkh, where a surprised Asad was hastily reassembling his

[50] Ṭabarî, ii:1596. There can be no doubt that in the present case the "river of Balkh" is the Oxus. Gibb, 1923:82, says only "the river," and does not mention that Ṭabarî here uses this name for the Oxus. Gibb probably does this because he has earlier argued (p. 77) that the same usage refers to the De-has River.

[51] Ṭabarî, ii:1595.

[52] Ṭabarî, ii:1599.

[53] According to R. Blachère, Dictionnaire Arabe-Français-Anglais (1967) 1198, thiql (plural athqâl) means both "load, burden" and "treasures."

[54] Cf. Shaban, 1970:126-127, who points out that it was definitely not just baggage, as Gibb thought.

[55] Asad had moved the provincial capital to Balkh during his second term as governor. See Beckwith, 1984b.

[56] Ṭabarî, ii:1609: "al-Ḥârith b. Surayǵ and his companions, the king of Sughd, the lord of al-Śâś [Tashkent] Khrâbghrh [*Kharâbughrah, i.e., Qara Boghra] father of Khânâkhrh [*Khânâkharah] grandfather of Kâws ['father of Afśîn'—ii:1613], the lord of al-Khuttal, Ǵabghûyah [the Yabghu of Ṭukhâristân], and the Turks. . . ."

army, and took the capital city of Ġûzġân. Having occupied it, Su-lu sent out his raiding parties. Perhaps he did not realize that Asad might break Arab convention and go to war in winter. This may explain why Su-lu had a small force of only 4,000 with him when he was surprised by the Arabs at Kharîstân; the Türgiś were devastated. Su-lu and al-Ḥârith b. Surayġ escaped and fled to the territory of the Yabghu of Ṭukhâristân,[57] but almost all of their armies were lost. There is no mention in the sources of Tibetan participation in any of these battles, and, unfortunately, the fate of the Tibetan army led by Cog ro Maṅporje to Turkistan is unknown.[58]

Su-lu returned to the Türgiś lands later in the winter of 737-738.[59] There he faced the long-smoldering resentment of the "Yellow Bone" clan chief Bagha Tarqan Kül Cur,[60] who was said to be the descendant of Su-lu's murdered predecessor, *Saqal. According to Ṭabarî's account, "The qaghan [Su-lu] played backgammon one day with Kül Cur, with a pheasant as the stakes. He defeated Kül Cur the Türgiś, and asked of him the pheasant. He [Kül Cur] replied, 'A female one.' And the other said, 'A male!' So they fought, and Kül Cur broke the qaghan's hand. The qaghan swore he would break Kül Cur's hand; Kül Cur retreated and gathered a group of his companions; he attacked the qaghan at night, and killed him."[61] This was not just the death of one

---

[57] Ġabghûyah al-Kharlukhî (Ṭabarî, ii:1612) is a mistake for Ġabghûyah al-Ṭukhârî on the same page.

[58] Of interest as further evidence of Tibetan influence in the area at this time, however, is the account in Ṭabarî (ii:1631) on the Arab campaign in Khuttal of 737. In it, a *câkar* of one of the Sogdians who accompanied Asad possessed a "Tibetan horn" (*qarn tubbatî*) with which he fetched water from the river for Asad and his army chiefs. Cf. Ṭabarî, "Glossarium," p. cxlviii. On the *câkar* system, one closely akin to the *comitatus* system of contemporaneous Western Europe, see Beckwith, 1984a.

[59] Ṭabarî, ii:1613.

[60] He is the Kûr ṣûl of the Arabic sources (Chavannes, 1903:285-286 [n. 3]). Originally the Kül Cur of the Ch'u-mu-k'un tribe of the *Tarduś (eastern) half of the On oq, he was the leader of the Türgiś campaign of 102 A.H./ A.D. 720-721 in Transoxiana (Ṭabarî, ii:1421 et seq.). Su-lu was originally the Cur of the *Cabïś (Chinese, Ch'e-pi-shih) tribe of the "Black Bone" Türgiś.

[61] Ṭabarî (ii:1613) calls the qaghan, as usual, simply "Khâqân"; Kül Cur

man. It was the deathblow to Türgiś unity and, ultimately, to the Türgiś nation: "The Turks scattered, amid raids on one another."[62]

Some of the Sogdian refugee-warriors of al-Iskand fled to Tashkent, whose forces they then joined.[63] Other elements of the Türgiś also took this opportunity to change their political affiliations. Kül Cur attempted to unify the Türgiś under his own command, but was opposed by another chieftain, Tu-mo-tu,[64] who installed one of Su-lu's sons, Ku-ch'o, as T'u-huo-hsien Qaghan[65] in Sûyâb. Another established himself as qaghan in Talas. Kül Cur then sent an envoy to Kai Chia-yün, the Military Governor of West of the Desert, to ask for assistance. As a result, the T'ang government ordered Kai to "gather all the nations from the Türgiś on west."[66] In the autumn of 739, allied with Baghatur Tudun (the king of Tashkent) and al-Iskand (commander of the band of Sogdian refugee-warriors), Kai attacked Sûyâb and captured T'u-huo-hsien Qaghan in the *Qara Range.[67] Simultaneously, he sent Fu-meng Ling-ch'a, guard Commissioner of the Kashgar garrison, and Arsïlan Tarqan, the king of Ferghana, to enter Talas. They did so, captured the other recalcitrant qaghan,[68] and executed both him and his younger brother. They then entered the city of I-chien,[69] where they captured the Princess of

---

is called "Kûr ṣûl" or "Kûr ṣûl al-Turqiśî." It is interesting to note that both the Arabic and Chinese histories report that Su-lu was killed by, respectively, an Arab general and a Chinese general. Thus, one version quoted by Ṭabarî (ii:1593) states "Asad met Khâqân, lord of the Turks, and killed him." The CTS (9:211) records that in the autumn of 739 Kai Chia-yün "broke the Türgiś at Sûyâb and killed Su-lu."

[62] Ṭabarî, ii:1613, 1717.

[63] Ibid. This is confirmed by the Chinese accounts as well; see below.

[64] The name is also written Tu-mo-chih. He is said to have joined Kül Cur in the attack on Su-lu (HTS, 215b:6068). CTS, 194b:5192, and TCTC, 214:6833, claim that he originally supported Kül Cur, but then split with him.

[65] CTS, 194b:5192.

[66] HTS, 215b:6068; TCTC, 214:6834.

[67] Reported under September 22, 739 (HTS, 5:141; TCTC, 214:6838).

[68] CTS, 194b:5192; HTS, 215b:6068; TCTC, 214:6833-6834.

[69] This city has been identified with Akhsîkath in Ferghana, but I am un-

Chiao-ho and Su-lu's consorts.[70] "They [the T'ang forces] gathered all of the scattered people, [to the number of] several tens of thousands, and gave them to the king of Ferghana."[71] Thus, with T'ang help, Kül Cur eliminated his rivals for the position of qaghan. He then wrote a letter to Hsüan-tsung in which he asked permission to submit to China. On November 4, 739, "The Ch'u-mu-k'un, Shu-ni-shih, and *Köngül, among other tribes who had formerly been attached to the Türgiś and had now led their people in [to T'ang territory] to surrender, again requested [permission] to move in to live under the jurisdiction of the Pacified West."[72] Hsüan-tsung granted the request,[73] but he was not yet finished with the Türgiś.

The Tibetans, for their part, had other problems. The situation on their northeastern and eastern frontiers was grim. Although they had sent an envoy to China at the end of 737 to negotiate a restoration of peace,[74] the hostilities continued. In retaliation, the Tibetans raided Ho-hsi in the spring of 738, but Ts'ui Hsi-i, the Assistant Military Governor of Ho-hsi, drove them off. Tu Hsi-wang, the Governor-General of Shan *chou* and Acting Military Governor of Lung-yu, responded by attacking and then capturing the Tibetan city known to the Chinese as "New City." He was ordered to garrison the city and to establish there the Wei-jung Army.[75] Late that summer, the combined armies of Tu Hsi-wang, now full Military Governor of Lung-yu, Wang Yü, the Military Governor of Chien-nan, and Hsiao

---

certain as to why. The first element usually transcribes a Turkic *är* or *ir*. The second element transcribes -*känd* or -*känt*, a common suffix meaning "city," which is equivalent to -*kath*. Could the name refer rather to Uzkand? Another possibility is Su-lu's capital Nawâkath, which is where he undoubtedly left his consorts while on campaign.

[70] *HTS*, 215b:6068, actually has *k'o-tun*, a transcription of the Turkic word *qatun*, "consort."

[71] *HTS*, 215b:6068, *TCTC*, 214:6838.

[72] *HTS*, 215b:6068; *TCTC*, 214:6839.

[73] *HTS*, 215b:6068.

[74] *CTS*, 9:209.

[75] *CTS*, 9:209, 196a:5234; *HTS*, 5:140; *TCTC*, 214:6832. Chinese *wei-jung* means "terrify the westerners."

Chiung, the Acting Military Governor of Ho-hsi invaded Tibet from three directions. One of their first actions was to destroy the Ch'ih-ling stele, which bore the inscriptions of the 730 Sino-Tibetan treaty.[76] That autumn, Tu Hsi-wang continued the Chinese offensive by taking Tibet's Yellow River Bridge and building Yen-ch'üan[77] City on the right bank of the river. When the Tibetans counterattacked, reportedly with a large army, the Chinese commanders withstood them. They then established the Chen-hsi ("Garrison the West") Army at Yen-ch'üan.[78]

Only on the eastern front were the Tibetans victorious. There they defeated a large Chinese force under Wang Yü, who was trying to recapture An-jung.[79] This city, which was located west of Mao *chou* in Chien-nan *tao*,[80] was strategically the most important fortress on Tibet's eastern border. Following up on this success in the autumn of 739, Tibetan troops raided the T'ang garrisons of the Pai-ts'ao Army and the An-jen Army, but were repulsed by Hsiao Chiung, the Military Governor of Ho-hsi and Lung-yu.[81] Tibet suffered another reverse when, in the spring of 740, the Chinese took the city of An-jung through treachery and massacred the Tibetan garrison.[82] Such unprecedented Chinese success brought Tibetan fortunes in the east and northeast to a new low, and now began to shackle the Tibetan capability for campaigns in the far west, which was just what the T'ang strategists had planned.

[76] *HTS*, 216a:6086; *TCTC*, 214:6833.

[77] Literally, "Brine Spring."

[78] *CTS*, 196a:5234; *HTS*, 216a:6086; *TCTC*, 214:6835.

[79] Literally, "pacify the westerners."

[80] *CTS*, 9:210, 196a:5234; *HTS*, 5:140, 216a:6086; *TCTC*, 214:6835. The sources available to Ssu-ma Kuang all say "several ten-thousands" of Chinese soldiers were killed, but for unstated reasons he reduces that figure to "several thousands."

[81] *CTS*, 9:211, 196a:5234; *HTS*, 5:141, 216a:6086; *TCTC*, 214:6838. The Tibetans may have been partially victorious, if a somewhat enigmatic passage in the *Annals* is relevant: "The Great Yellow River (Commandery) was recovered" (*OTA*, Tiger year, [738-]739 spring).

[82] *CTS*, 9:212, 196a:5234; *HTS*, 5:141, 216a:6086; *TCTC*, 214:6840-6841. Tibetan attempts to retake the fortress later in the year all failed.

In April of 740, Hsüan-tsung bestowed awards upon Baghatur
Tudun, the king of Tashkent, and on al-Iskand, the king of Kiśś
and chief of the Sogdian refugee-warriors, for their services in
helping to defeat the Türgiś.[83] Later in the same month, Kai
Chia-yün presented his captives at court in Ch'ang-an. Hsüan-
tsung pardoned T'u-huo-hsien Qaghan and appointed him a general in the imperial guards.[84] Kai then proposed, and Hsüan-
tsung approved, the appointment of *Arśïla Hsin, the son of
*Arśïla Huai-tao, as On oq Qaghan.[85] True to the Chinese tra-
dition of sowing dissension abroad, this appointment inserted
one more discordant element into the Türgiś confederation,
which was just beginning to be reunited by Kül Cur. On May 15,
740, the T'ang position was strengthened by the appointment of
Hsin's wife as the Princess of Chiao-ho,[86] a title which had been
bestowed upon Su-lu's consort decades before. The message was
not lost upon Kül Cur, who protested strongly to the T'ang
court: "To execute Su-lu was, first of all, my plan. How can you
now reward me by setting up *Arśïla Hsin?"[87] To back up his argument, Kül Cur then rebelled along with a certain Wu-su-wan-
lo-shan.[88] Hsüan-tsung was thus forced to temporarily shelve his
plans for annihilating the Türgiś. He ordered Kai Chia-yün to
conciliate Kül Cur with the official appointment as qaghan
charged with unifying the Türgiś people.[89]

[83] *TFYK*, 964:19v-20r (p. 11346).

[84] *TFYK*, 964:20v-21r (pp. 11346-11347); *TCTC*, 214:6841, dates this to
April 28, 740.

[85] *HTS*, 215b:6068; *TCTC*, 214:6841.

[86] *TCTC*, 214:6841. The *Shih-lu* is quoted in the *K'ao-i* as the source for
this.

[87] *TCTC*, 214:6843. *CTS*, 194b:5192, and *HTS*, 215b:6068, also have
versions of the statement; they have different phrasing, but exactly the same
meaning.

[88] *TCTC*, 214:6841 (quotation from the *Shih-lu* in the *K'ao-i* gloss);
TFYK, 977:21r (p. 11482). Wu-su could transcribe a Turkic Oz/Öz, but the
remainder of the name is a mystery to me.

[89] *TCTC*, 214:6843. None of the other sources explain how Kül Cur was
mollified, but *TFYK* (977:21r [p. 11482]) and the *Shih-lu* (quoted in the
K'ao-i gloss in *TCTC*, 214:6841) refer to him at the time of his subsequent
submission as the "Türgiś Qaghan Bagha Tarqan."

It was also apparently in 740 that Naṣr b. Sayyâr, the governor of Khurasan, led a major campaign against Tashkent, where al-Iskand and his men were based[90] with the rebel al-Ḥârith b. Surayǵ. Naṣr failed to take Tashkent after two attempts, even with the 20,000 men he allegedly had. Nonetheless, the ruler of Tashkent agreed to accept an Arab representative in Tashkent and to expel al-Ḥârith to Fârâb.[91] Naṣr then departed for a campaign deep into Ferghana. He penetrated as far as Qubâ, and forced the surrender of the "lord of Ferghana."[92] There were no serious encounters with Turks.[93]

Further to the south, in the Pamirs, the Tibetans maintained their activity in the only military theater where they had enjoyed any recent success. In the fall of 740, they gave the Lady Khri ma lod as a bride to the "Lord of Little Balûr."[94] This secured Tibetan sovereignty over Balûr, and, added to the submission of several other neighboring countries, it indicated a growing Tibetan influence in the Pamirs. Among these territories were Wakhan[95] and Chieh-shih,[96] both of which were then considered part of

[90] Ṭabarî, ii:1613, 1717. TFYK, 971:13r (p. 11411), indicates that al-Iskand had still not submitted to the Arabs by the spring of 741.

[91] The representative was Nîzak b. Ṣâliḥ, mawlâ ("client"; plural, mawâlî) of ʿAmrû b. al-ʿÂṣ. Fârâb was another name for Utrâr.

[92] Ṭabarî, ii:1674-1675.

[93] Ṭabarî, ii:1694-1695. As Gibb (1923:90) points out, Naṣr's campaign could not have taken place in 739, as it seems to be dated in Ṭabarî, but almost certainly in 740. The Arab-Turk encounters mentioned in Ṭabarî are, as Gibb suggests, highly suspect.

[94] OTA, Dragon year 740(-741) summer; TCTC, 215:6885. This was Su-shih-li-chih; he was the successor of Ma-lai-hsi, who was the older brother and successor of Mo-chin-mang's heir, Nan-ni (HTS, 221b:6251). He was called Bruźa rje (Bruźa Lord) whereas the previous, pro-Chinese ruler had been called Bruźa'i rgyalpo (King of Bruźa) by the Tibetans.

[95] King Hsieh-chi-li-fu of Wakhan, "which had previously submitted to Tibet," sent an envoy to the T'ang court in 742 requesting permission to surrender (TCTC, 215:6856; TFYK, 981:8v-9r; HTS, 221b:6255, has Hsieh-chi-fu). Three years later, Fu-meng Ling-ch'a led an apparently successful expedition against the country (CTS, 128:3583; HTS, 153:4847), but it appears to have remained in Tibetan hands until the campaign of Kao Hsien-chih in 747.

[96] See below under the events of 749-750.

Ṭukhâristân. Yet without a strong Western Turkic ally, the Tibetans could hardly face both the Arabs and the Chinese in the
struggle for Central Asia. The once-powerful Türgiś confederation was broken and its elements dispersed. No better evidence of
this exists than the submission to the T'ang at the end of 740, of
Kül Cur, "leading his wives, banner officials, and dignitaries—
over a hundred persons in all."[97]

In 741, Naṣr b. Sayyâr again raided Ferghana.[98] He also came
to an agreement with al-Iskand's Sogdian refugee-warriors in
Tashkent, whereby they were pardoned and allowed to return to
their homes.[99] Naṣr followed up these actions by sending an Arab
embassy to Ch'ang-an. This was apparently quite a high-level affair, since the "Arab leader Ho-sa" was appointed a general in the
palace guards and was presented with a purple robe and a gold fil-
igree belt before being sent home.[100] It is possible that, in this embassy, Naṣr was trying to break the powerful alliance between
Tashkent and Ferghana, an alliance that had become evident—
and potentially threatening to Arab hegemony—during the campaign to suppress the Türgiś successors of Su-lu. The key was
that, as titular vassals of China, both Tashkent and Ferghana
maintained very close relations with Ch'ang-an, and always
pressed to make them closer. In order to maintain the hitherto
friendly Arab-Chinese relationship in spite of his frequent campaigns against these two Chinese vassal states, Naṣr found it necessary to send regular embassies to China.[101] And indeed, these
Central Asian kingdoms were actively trying to convince the
T'ang to do something about the Arabs. In 741, the "assistant
king" of Tashkent, *Inäl Tudun *Külüg, addressed a request to

[97] CTS, 9:213; HTS, 215b:6068; TCTC, 214:6841 gloss, 214:6843;
TFYK, 977:21r (p. 11482).

[98] Ṭabarî, ii:1719. The motivations for and the results of this raid are unfortunately unknown.

[99] Ṭabarî, ii:1717-1718. Cf. Gibb, 1923:90; Shaban, 1970:130-131.

[100] Recorded under Janaury 30, 742, in TFYK, 975:19r (p. 11457).

[101] On the embassies, see Chavannes, 1904:59 et seq. Among other evidence of continued close ties between China and these states, a T'ang princess
was presented to the king of Ferghana.

Hsüan-tsung: "Now that the Turks are subject to the Heavenly Qaghan [the Chinese emperor], it is only the Arabs that are the cause of suffering among the nations. I request that you punish them."[102] Hsüan-tsung, however, preferred to maintain the Sino-Arab alliance: "The Son of Heaven did not consent" to the king's request.[103]

When Naṣr b. Sayyâr returned from his campaigns, he soon found that he had more trouble with his fellow Arabs than with any of the peoples of the East. As a result, he was unable to undertake any further expeditions into Transoxiana during the remainder of his governorship. The Umayyad dynasty was about to collapse, and even his diplomatic skill could not prevent the revolt that ended the dynasty from beginning right under his nose in Marw.[104]

For the T'ang, unlike for the Umayyads, the situation in Central Asia looked good indeed, with the one bothersome exception of the Tibetans in the Pamirs. In 742, Hsüan-tsung again attempted to install *Arśila Hsin as the On oq Qaghan. As might have been expected, Hsin was immediately killed by Kül Cur when he reached Kûlân under escort.[105] Shortly thereafter, the "Great Banner Official" of the "Black Bone" branch of the Türgiś, Tu-mo-tu, surrendered to the T'ang, and was appointed "Yabghu of the Three Surnames"[106] with the title Qutlugh Bilgä Tu-mo-tu Kül Irkin.[107] The T'ang now had a locally supported alternative to Kül Cur. Finally, in the spring of 744, Fu-meng Ling-ch'a, the Military Governor of Ho-hsi, led a "punitive" expedition against Kül Cur and executed him.[108] The T'ang ap-

---

[102] HTS, 221b:6246.

[103] Ibid.

[104] Gibb, 1923:91 et seq.; Shaban, 1970:131 et seq.; E. Daniel, The Political and Social History of Khurasan under Abbasid Rule (1979) 43 et seq. The literature on the Abbasid movement is vast and rapidly growing.

[105] HTS, 215b:6069, has a corrupt form, Mo-ho-tu (Baghatur), for Mo-ho Ta-kan (Bagha Tarqan); TCTC, 215:6854.

[106] On July 28, 742. HTS, 215b:6069; TCTC, 215:6854. This is properly a Qarluq title.

[107] HTS, 215b:6069; TFYK, 965:1v (p. 11348), 975:19v (p. 11457).

[108] HTS, 215b:6069.

pointed Tu-mo-tu, now entitled El-etmiś Qutlugh Bilgä, as the new On oq Qaghan on July 26, 744.[109]

Late in 744, a Türgiś envoy paid homage at the Tibetan court,[110] perhaps in an effort to revive their alliance. But it was too late for the Türgiś. That year, the Eastern Turkic Empire, which had been torn apart by a revolt that began in 742, was succeeded by a coalition of sorts, with a Basmïl qaghan, an Uyghur yabghu in the east, and a Qarluq yabghu in the west.[111] The Basmïl qaghan began his regime by decapitating the last qaghan of the Türk dynasty. The situation changed, however, when the Uyghurs and Qarluqs, along with Wang Chung-ssu, the T'ang Military Governor of Shuo-fang, killed the Basmïl qaghan and enslaved his people toward the end of 744. The Uyghurs then made their own leader qaghan over the Eastern Turks, and began oppressing the Qarluqs.[112] As a result, the "three-surnamed" Qarluq tribes migrated in 745,[113] into the lands of the Western Turks. By 751, they had become the dominant power, in spite of Tu-mo-tu and the other T'ang puppets.[114]

---

[109] *TCTC*, 215:6860; *TFYK*, 965:2v-3r (pp. 11348-11349).

[110] *OTA*, Monkey year 744(-745) summer. This is the last reference to the Tibetan-Türgiś alliance in any contemporaneous source.

[111] *TCTC*, 215:6854-6855.

[112] *TCTC*, 215:6860.

[113] According to the Shine Usu inscription, north side, line 11. See S. Malov, *Pamyatniki drevnetyurkskoy pis'mennosti mongolii i kirgizii* (1959) 31, 35, 39. Cf. P. Golden, "The Migrations of the *Oğuz*" (1972) 50. According to Golden's interpretation, the Three Qarluqs fled west to the lands of the On oq in 745, and, after the subsequent wars with the Uyghurs, the Qarluqs who had remained in the east followed. The recently published Terkhin inscription, south side, lines 3-4, has the Qarluqs fleeing in 746. See S. Klyashtorny, "The Terkhin Inscription" (1982) 343, 345; and Tekin, "The Tariat (Terkhin) Inscription" (1983) 47, 49-50.

[114] For the Chinese synoptic accounts, see I. Ecsedy, "A Contribution to the History of Karluks in the T'ang Period" (1980) 29-37. These accounts state mistakenly that the Qarluq migration took place a decade or two later. But at the time of Kao Hsien-chih's campaigns in the Western Turkic territories—before and after the Battle of Aṭlakh (or "Battle of Talas") in 751— the Qarluqs were already the Turkic military power there. (Cf. Gibb, 1923:96, and below.) In 753, Tun Bilgä, the Qarluq Yabghu, captured the rebel Turk A-pu-ssu alive and delivered him to the T'ang (apparently at Pei-

Meanwhile, the Sino-Tibetan war over northeastern Tibet continued to escalate. At the end of 740, the Tibetans sent an envoy to Ch'ang-an "to report the mourning for the Princess" of Chin-ch'eng, who had died earlier in the year. They took this opportunity to also request peace, but Hsüan-tsung refused.[115] He was so hostile that he even delayed the official court mourning period for his relative the princess for several months, until the spring of 741.[116] It was perhaps due to this rebuff that the Tibetans returned to the fray with new vigor. In the summer of 741, a Tibetan force assaulted Ch'eng-feng Fort, "withstood the Ho-yüan Army," and, turning west, attacked the Ch'ang-ning Bridge and the An-jen Army. In this last engagement, however, the Chinese garrison repulsed them.[117] At the end of the year, Mes ag tshoms himself led a campaign against the T'ang. He destroyed the fortified city of Ta-hua *hsien*[118] and killed the inhab-

---

t'ing). For this feat, he was rewarded with titles, among them Chin Shan *wang* ("Prince of the Altai Mountains"). See *TFYK*, 965:5v (p. 11350). Cf. Chavannes, 1904:87-88. Between December 29, 753, and January 27, 754, the Qarluqs and people of Tashkent sent envoys to Ch'ang-an. See *TFYK*, 971:19r (p. 11414). Cf. Chavannes, 1904:88, where the page reference given is 18v. The famous Old Tibetan geographical document *Byan phyogs na rgyalpo du bźugspa'i rabsgyi yige* (Bacot, 1957) was composed after the establishment of the Uyghur qaghanate and during the struggle for supremacy in the West between the Qarluqs and the Türgiś. (Bacot misunderstands the passage concerned here—lines 85 to 86.) It would seem that the document should be dated to a period before the Tibetans began again to expand into Central Asia, perhaps around the time of the An Lu-shan rebellion in China. Ya'qûbî (ii:436) remarks that the Yabghu of the Qarluqs had converted to Islam in the days of al-Mahdî. Whether or not this is true, he should in any case have converted by 194 A.H./A.D. 809-810, the date of Ya'qûbî's report.

[115] According to *TFYK*, 979:13r (p. 11504), the embassy arrived in the eleventh month (November 24 to December 22, 740); cf. *HTS*, 216a:6086; *TCTC*, 214:6843.

[116] *CTS*, 196a:5235; *TFYK*, 979:13r (p. 11504). The lone reference (*CTS*, 9:213) to a Tibetan embassy in the third month of 741 may be due to a misunderstanding of these events; it probably refers to the date of the declaration of court mourning.

[117] *CTS*, 196a:5235; *HTS*, 216a:6086; *TCTC*, 214:6844.

[118] *OTA*, Snake year 741(-742) summer, calls it *rgya'i mkhar dar khwa hywan*, i.e., "the Chinese fortified-city of Dar-khwa hywan [Ta-hua *hsien*]."

itants.[119] This unusually brutal action was apparently in retaliation for the T'ang massacre of the Tibetans in An-jung City in the previous year. The Tibetans also retook the strategic fortress of Shih-pao City in spite of the capable defense offered by the commander, Kai Chia-yün.[120]

But Hsüan-tsung was not one to give up. In the winter of 742-743, he initiated a series of devastating raids into the northeastern marches of Tibet. Huang-fu Wei-ming, the Military Governor of Lung-yu, defeated "the Tibetans' Ta-ling, etc. armies," and followed this with a victory over the army of "the Maṅporje of the Koko Nor *tao*." In this engagement, five thousand out of thirty thousand encamped Tibetans were killed or captured.[121] A few days later, Wang Ch'ui, the Military Governor of Ho-hsi, defeated "the Tibetans' Yü-hai and Yu-i armies."[122] In the spring of 743, Huang-fu again led a major expedition into Tibet. This time, he chased the Tibetans "over a thousand *li*" until he reached Hung-chi City, which he attacked and captured.[123] This conquest could not, however, have been considered permanent, since the strategic fortress of Shih-pao City remained in Tibetan hands. The Chinese now turned their energies toward it.

In the autumn of 745, Huang-fu Wei-ming attacked Shih-pao. The Tibetan defense was organized by the lord of the vassal ʿAźa and by "the minister Maṅporje." They were successful. The T'ang army was severely beaten, and Huang-fu's assistant general was killed in battle.[124] In the following spring, Huang-fu was

[119] *HTS*, 216a:6086; *TCTC*, 214:6846.

[120] *CTS*, 196a:5235; *HTS*, 216a:6086; *TCTC*, 214:6846.

[121] *HTS*, 216a:6086; *TCTC*, 215:6856; *OTA*, Horse year 742(-743) summer, says: "The minister, the Maṅporje, held a levy of the ʿAźa at Khu ńe moń gańs."

[122] *TCTC*, 215:6856.

[123] *HTS*, 216a:6086; *TCTC*, 215:6858.

[124] *OTAC*, Bird year 745(-746) before winter; *CTS*, 9:219, 196a:5235; *HTS*, 5:145, 216a:6086; *TCTC*, 215:6868. The fragmentary second version of the *Annals* has an important entry on these events, but much of it is problematic. It says: "The Chinese general ʿBá *tsań kun* [Chinese, *chiang-chün*, 'general'] led [in an attack] the Chinese army [? for *byimpo*, probably from Chinese, *ping pu*, 'Board of War'] of Kog *yul*; and both the Maṅporje and the

stripped of his positions and replaced[125] by Wang Chung-ssu as the Military Governor of Ho-hsi and Lung-yu. Wang had enjoyed much success on the Tibetan frontier, and no doubt the T'ang government held great hopes for him. But the situation was more serious than Hsüan-tsung imagined, and Wang warned of the danger of a Pyrrhic victory.[126] For, during the winter, when the Chinese armies were largely immobilized, the Tibetans seem to have had complete control of the area. In the areas of the Chi-shih Army, for example, the Tibetans would wait until the grain grown by the Chinese was ripe; then they would raid and collect it. The T'ang authorities were so helpless to stop this (it happened every year) that the local Chinese nicknamed the area "Tibetan Grain Estates."[127]

Despite the difficulties involved, Hsüan-tsung was determined to retake Shih-pao City. Wang warned him: "Shih-pao is strongly defended. The whole Tibetan nation is guarding it. Now if we array our troops below it, we cannot capture it without several tens of thousands of [our] men being killed. I am afraid that what

---

son-in-law, the ʿAźa lord, fought against Jid-par [or, 'fought [with ʿBá] at Jid-par']; the Chinese forces attacked the great fortified city [*mkharpo che*] of Pud-goṅ at Jid-par, and the Chinese were mostly killed." There is no doubt that the great fortress at Jid-par was what the Chinese called Shih-pao City (Chinese, *shih pao ch'eng*, lit. "Stone Fort [fortified-] City"). Otherwise, the identification of the Tibetan names remains unclear, except that Kog *yul* may be identified with K'uo *chou*. According to Karlgren, 1957: no. 774g, the T'ang pronunciation of K'uo was **k'wâk*. The letter used to write the initial consonant of Old Tibetan *kog* was one of a pair of letters which represented the allophones of one phoneme: in short, the syllable as written could be pronounced either as *kog* or *k'og* (the latter usually transcribed *khog*). Thus Kok *yul* appears to be an excellent Old Tibetan rendering of K'uo *chou*. Moreover, Kog *yul* is later said to be in Rag-tag (*OTAC*, Sheep year 755-756), which was located in Mdosmad (*OTAC*, Pig year 760-761) and included the Rma roṅ ("Yellow River Valley"). Rag-tag, as mentioned above, undoubtedly corresponds to the Chinese Lo-t'o ("Camel"); in 728, it may be recalled, a T'ang force burned Tibet's "Camel Bridge" (Chinese, *Lo-t'o ch'iao*).

[125] *TCTC*, 215:6869-6871 (other reasons are given for his disgrace).

[126] *CTS*, 103:3199-3200; *HTS*, 133:4553-4554; *TCTC*, 215:6878-6879.

[127] In 747. *CTS*, 104:3212; *HTS*, 134:4569; *TCTC*, 215:6878. Qośu Khan was responsible for finally halting the forced grain collections.

would be gained is not comparable to what would be lost."[128] Hsüan-tsung was not pleased. When it became clear that Wang would not help a more unscrupulous general mount the assault, he was imprisoned and nearly executed.[129] It was only through the petition of Qośu Khan, a protégé of Wang who remained in the emperor's favor, that Hsüan-tsung's fury abated, and Wang's sentence was reduced. On December 25, 747, Qośu Khan himself was appointed Military Governor of Lung-yu. Wang's other position, the Military Governorship of Ho-hsi, was given to An Ssu-shun, a cousin of the famous An Lu-shan.[130] Qośu quickly set to work strengthening and expanding T'ang positions in northeastern Tibet.

In 747, T'ang strategists also turned their attention to the other Tibetan flank that was accessible to them, the Pamir-Karakorum region.[131] During the years after the most recent Tibetan conquest of Little Balûr, the Chinese had made three attempts to seize the country from Tibet; all were defeated, however, and the shadowy campaigns are barely mentioned in the Chinese histories.[132] Finally, Kao Hsien-chih, a general of Korean origin, was appointed to the positions of Assistant Protector-General of the Pacified West and Four Garrisons Commissioner-General in Charge of Troops and Horses.[133] Kao set out, apparently in the

[128] *CTS*, 103:3199-3200; *HTS*, 133:4553; *TCTC*, 215:6878.

[129] *CTS*, 103:3200; *HTS*, 133:4554; *TCTC*, 215:6878-6879.

[130] *CTS*, 103:3200, 104:3212; *HTS*, 133:4554, 135:4570; *TCTC*, 215:6879. On An Ssu-shun, who remained loyal to Hsüan-tsung at the time of his cousin's rebellion in 755 but was executed by the emperor anyway, see Des Rotours, *Histoire de Ngan Lou-chan* (1962) 6-7 (n. 2).

[131] Tibet's military commands on the northern border at Tshal-byi (Chinese, Sa-p'i) and Cherchen remained temporarily unmolested. Cf. Uray, "Einige Probleme der tibetischen Herrschaft über das Lop-Nor-Gebiet im 7.-9. Jh." (1979a); Moriyasu, 1984:46-50.

[132] The only sources on these campaigns are the notices in Kao Hsien-chih's biographies that mention the failure of three generals before him (T'ien Jen-wan, Kai Chia-yün, and Fu-meng Ling-ch'a) to recapture Balûr in as many attempts (*CTS*, 104:3203; *HTS*, 135:4576).

[133] Chinese, *Ssu chen tu chih ping ma shih* (*CTS*, 104:3203; *HTS*, 135:4576). This title is not mentioned in Des Rotours, 1974, and appears to be somewhat problematic. First of all, *ping ma* is ambiguous. Des Rotours remarks, ". . . je ne sais pas quelle était exactement la valeur de l'expression *ping-ma*

spring of 747, with an army of about ten thousand men, both Chinese and non-Chinese, all supplied with their own horses.[134] They marched from Kucha to Aksu in fifteen days, then to Gustik[135] in "over ten days," to Kashgar in "over ten days," to the Stronghold[136] of Ts'ung-ling (the "Onion Range" [Pamirs]) in "over twenty days," to the Pamir Valley in "over twenty days," and to the T'e-le-man Valley, "that is, the country of the five Shughnan," in "over twenty days." No doubt many additional days were spent resting at the points mentioned in the itinerary. In T'e-le-man, Kao split his army into three parts, and ordered them to rendezvous at the Tibetan fortress of Lien-yün[137] in the

---

sous la dynastie des T'ang; désigne-t-elle les troupes à pied et les troupes à cheval? Ou bien désigne-t-elle simplement l'armée sans aucune sens précis?" (Des Rotours, 1974, 2:646 [n. 3.) *Ping ma shih* is thus an unknown term to Des Rotours, who translates it "commissaire impérial des soldats et des chevaux" (2:647 [n. 1]). Furthermore, he gives various interpretations of the titles beginning with *tu-* and ending with *-shih*, apparently because of his uncertainty about their meaning. One may note especially his translation (1:397-398 [n. 2]) of the passage from *YHCHTC*, 3:4v (he cites it as "4r"). The *Tu chien mu shih*, which he translates "commissaire impérial à la surveillance général des élevages" (1:398), was simply the official who supervised the *chien mu shih*. Thus *Tu . . . shih* in this text, and generally for the T'ang, clearly means "Supervisory Commissioner" or "Commissioner-General." Des Rotours's translation of *P'ing-lu chieh tu tu chih ping ma shih* as "commissaire impérial au commandement du district de P'ing-lou et chargé entièrement des chevaux et soldats de ce district" (2:822 [n. 4]) should therefore be revised to read "Military Governor, and Commissioner-General of Troops and Horses, of P'ing-lu." It may be significant that both of these *Tu chih ping ma shih* were in frontier or colonial areas. The biographies of Kao Hsien-chih remark that "At this time, foot soldiers all had their own horses" (*CTS*, 104:3203; *HTS*, 135:4576, adds "accompanying them").

[134] The following account is largely derived from Kao Hsien-chih's biography in *CTS*, 104:3203 et seq. The versions in *HTS*, 135:4576 et seq., and *TCTC*, 215:6884 et seq., are abbreviated and less useful. The *CTS* version has been translated in full in Chavannes, 1903:152-154. Cf. *HTS*, 221b:6251-6252.

[135] Chinese, Wo-se-te; Tibetan, Gus-tig. See Saṁghavardhana, 436v-437r (pp. 296-298).

[136] Chinese, *shou cho*, translated by Des Rotours, 1974, 2:785, as "détachements militaires." They were, however, localized; thus my translation.

[137] According to Chavannes, 1903:154 (note d), this place corresponds approximately to present-day Sarhad on the Panj River.

So-le Valley[138] about three days after their departure, that is, on August 11, 747, between seven and nine in the morning. The wing led by the Commissioner of the Stronghold of Kashgar approached from "the northern valley"; that led by the Commissioner of the Stronghold of Aksu from the Red Buddha Hall Road; and Kao himself, with his assistant Pien Ling-ch'eng the eunuch Mediary Commissioner,[139] approached from "the kingdom of Wakhan."[140] The armies crossed the So-le River with difficulty and met at the appointed time. After a battle with the Tibetans that lasted all day, the T'ang forces were victorious. Five thousand Tibetans are said to have perished.[141] The T'ang army captured a thousand men and a thousand horses along with a large quantity of military supplies and equipment.

Kao left Pien with a garrison of three thousand, consisting of the weak and sick among the troops, and then invaded Little Balûr. In the early autumn of 747,[142] Kao captured the capital city, A-nu-yüeh,[143] without a fight. He executed the "five or six" Tibetan-appointed officials there; and, after his troops hurriedly destroyed the cane suspension bridge leading to the east[144]—preventing the Tibetan army from coming to the rescue—he received the surrender of the king of Balûr and his Tibetan queen. Kao garrisoned the city with two thousand men[145] and returned

---

[138] Or So-le-se-ho, in Wakhan (cf. Chavannes, 1903:154 [note d]). That So-le (*Sarïq ?) or So-le-se is the correct name—rather than Chavannes's P'o-le—is clear from *HTS*, 221b:6251, *TCTC*, 215:6885 gloss, and also from the biographies of Li Ssu-yeh (*CTS*, 109:3298; *HTS*, 138:4615). Chavannes identifies it with the Panj (Wakhan) River.

[139] Chinese, *chung shih*. According to Des Rotours, 1974, 2:844, the term refers to a eunuch official.

[140] According to *CTS*, 109:3298, and *HTS*, 138:4615, he had to cross the Hsin-t'u Ho to get there. This can hardly be anything but the Sindhu (Indus) River.

[141] According to Li Ssu-yeh's biographies, some Tibetans drowned while trying to escape across the river (*CTS*, 109:3298; *HTS*, 138:4615).

[142] The eighth month (September 9 to October 8).

[143] *Anavat? It is called Yeh-to City in the account of Little Balûr in *HTS*, 221b:6251.

[144] The bridge was over the unidentified So-i River.

[145] According to the petition of the Yabghu of Ṭukhâristân in *TFYK*,

via the Red Buddha Hall Road to the fortress of Lien-yün later in 747.[146] Around the beginning of November, Kao reached the Pamir Valley, from where he sent his memorial (which apparently arrived at Ch'ang-an at the end of the year) on his victories over Tibet. He continued on to Ch'ang-an, where he was appointed Military Governor of the Four Garrisons of the Pacified West on February 1, 748, and where the king of Balûr and his Tibetan queen were presented to Hsüan-tsung. Hsüan-tsung pardoned the king and gave him a position in the palace guards,[147] but nothing is known about the fate of the Tibetan princess, the Lady Khri ma lod.[148]

In January 749, on the northeastern Sino-Tibetan frontier, Qośu Khan, the Military Governor of Lung-yu, reported that he

---

999:19r-19v (p. 11724). Cf. CTS, 109:3298 (three thousand), and HTS, 221b:6252 (one thousand).

[146] The ninth month (October 9 to November 6).

[147] HTS, 221b:6252. Cf. Chavannes, 1903:152-154.

[148] The whole campaign is recorded most laconically in OTAC, Pig year 747(-748) summer: "The Chinese byimpo having appeared in the land of Gog, Bruźa and Gog were lost." This may be made more intelligible by substituting familiar names for the esoteric ones: "The Chinese army having appeared in the land of Wakhan, Little Balûr and Wakhan were lost." (On byimpo, see above.) The identification of Gog yul has hitherto been confused. See the arguments of Moriyasu, 1984:42, 73-74 (nn. 195, 198), who believes that it ought to correspond to the basin of the Panj (Wakhan) River. Although he correctly points out that F. W. Thomas misread one occurrence of Gog as Kog, Moriyasu also thinks that Gog and Kog should be considered identical. Fortunately, the Annals distinguishes between a Kog in the northeast and a Gog in the northwest. (On Kog, see above, note 124.) Moreover, upon investigation, it develops that gog is simply the Old Tibetan transcription of a native name for Wakhan, which is represented in the first parts of the Chinese transcriptions of two names for Wakhan, Hu-k'an and Hu-mi (HTS, 221b:6255). In the T'ang period, the first "Hu" was pronounced *g'wâk/ɣwâk and the second was *g'wâg/ɣuo (Karlgren, 1957, Nos. 784i and 784k). Both would have been transcribed in Old Tibetan exactly as gog. (The correspondence in phonology between these syllables and those representing the name of the locality in northeastern Tibet is also striking.) Gog yul is thus the Old Tibetan name for the kingdom of Wakhan. On the long period of Tibetan domination in Wakhan, see S. Lévi and É. Chavannes, "L'Itinéraire d'Ou-k'ong (751-790)" (1895) 347-348 (n. 1).

had erected a fortification on the shores of the Koko Nor for the Shen-wei Army. Later that year, however, he was attacked and defeated there.[149] He then built a fortress named Ying-lung City on the island in the Koko Nor; thereafter, the Tibetans hesitated to approach the area.[150] In midsummer of 749, by order of Hsüan-tsung, Qośu Khan led a huge army of 63,000 men against the Tibetan fortress of Shih-pao City.[151] After several days of bitter but unavailing struggle, Qośu threatened to execute his assistant generals. They promised to take the fortress in three days and did, but only at the cost of several tens of thousands of their soldiers, which is what Wang Chung-ssu had originally predicted. They did, however, capture the Tibetan general T'ieh-jen Stag sgra[152] and four hundred of his men. Qośu then sent troops to the west of Ch'ih-ling to establish military-agricultural colonies; he also garrisoned the island fortress in the Koko Nor with 2,000 convicts.[153] On July 21, 749, Shih-pao City was renamed the Shen-wu Army.[154]

For these deeds, Hsúan-tsung bestowed lavish rewards without precedent upon Qośu Khan and his family.[155] The great T'ang poet Tu Fu, who though famous in his lifetime was barely acknowledged by the "Brilliant Emperor," saw things differently. In the "Ballad of the War Wains," a poem written around this time, he poignantly described the results of the relentless campaigns:

[149] The version in *TCTC*, 216:6892, is diametrically opposed to the versions in Qośu Khan's two biographies (*CTS*, 104:3212; *HTS*, 135:4570). Cf. Demiéville, 1952:370.

[150] *CTS*, 104:3212-3213; *HTS*, 135:4570; *TCTC*, 216:6892.

[151] *TCTC*, 216:6896; *TFYK*, 992:16r (p. 11655). On Shih-pao City, cf. Demiéville, 1952:369-370.

[152] *HTS*, 216a:6087, has "their minister Wu-lun-yang-kuo," where *wu-lun* is probably just another transcription of Old Tibetan, *blon* ("minister").

[153] *CTS*, 104:3213; *HTS*, 135:4570; *TCTC*, 216:6896. When winter came, the Koko Nor froze over, thus enabling the Tibetans to attack en masse; Qośu's garrison on the island fortress was wiped out (*TCTC*, 216:6896).

[154] *TCTC*, 216:6896; *TFYK*, 992:16r (p. 11655); *HTS*, 216a:6087. Cf. Demiéville, 1952:369.

[155] *CTS*, 104:3213; *HTS*, 135:4570.

Have you not seen, sir, out by the Koko Nor—
The white bones from ancient times that
    no one has gathered up?
The new ghosts bitterly complaining
    the old ghosts weep;
Under the dark heavens and drenching rains
    they make a mournful sound.[156]

In the autumn of 749, Lo Chen-t'an,[157] the king of Wakhan,
traveled to Ch'ang-an for reasons which are not clear. He requested leave to stay, and accordingly was granted a position in
the palace guards.[158] Wakhan seems to have passed under Chinese
vassalage at this point. A few months later, an envoy of the
Yabghu of Ṭukhâristân presented a petition to Hsüan-tsung concerning the Tibetans in the Pamirs. According to the envoy, it
had been necessary to import supplies from Kashmir because the
T'ang garrison of two thousand men in Little Balûr could not be
supported by the limited local agricultural resources. But this im-
portation was possible only by passing through the little country
of Chieh-shih,[159] which bordered Ṭukhâristân. The yabghu's envoy reported that the king of Chieh-shih had received Tibetan
bribes and had requested the Tibetans to build a fortress or fortresses inside his country. Their intention was to seize the main
road to Little Balûr. Moreover, the envoy complained, the king

[156] *TKPSC*, 1:3r-4v. Note that Li Po, a contemporary of Tu Fu, also received no more than token recognition from Hsüan-tsung and his government. They are together considered to be the two greatest among the many
brilliant poets in Chinese literature.

[157] Mentioned as early as 730 (Chavannes, 1904:51), "Chen-t'an" is almost certainly the word *candan* ("sandalwood") in Chinese transcription.
Chavannes appears to have created several kings out of the passages that refer
to this one king.

[158] *TCTC*, 216:6897; *TFYK*, 975:21v (p. 11458).

[159] *TFYK*, 975:21r (p. 11458) and 965:4v (p. 11349), has Ch'ieh-shuai.
This is the same place—the characters are graphically very close, and the phonology is not too divergent. According to A. Tôdô, *Gakken Kan-Wa daijiten*
(1978), the T'ang-period pronunciation of these names was, for Chieh-shih,
*kıʌt-ṣïi, and for Ch'ieh-shuai, *kʻıɛt-ṣïuĕt (or *ṣïui, an unlikely form); see
pp. 1032, 406. Cf. Karlgren, 1957, No. 499a: *ṣïuĕt.

of Chieh-shih and the Tibetans had been taking advantage of the situation by raiding Ṭukhâristân.[160] The yabghu therefore requested that a T'ang army be dispatched that would arrive in Little Balûr in the early summer[161] of 750 and reach Great Balûr a month later.[162] Hsüan-tsung approved the request.[163] It would appear that the Chinese and their allies had invaded the kingdom of Chieh-shih,[164] no doubt foraging and plundering as they went, so the king saw no recourse but to ally with the Tibetans.

Despite the agreement that the allied invasion would take place in the summer of 750, Kao Hsien-chih seems to have begun the campaign early, sometime between the fall of 749 and the spring of 750. With or without the help of Ṭukhâristân and Kashmir,[165] he again defeated the Tibetans in the Pamirs. On April 22, 750, Su-chia, the elder brother of the deposed king, Po-t'e-mo, was appointed king of Chieh-shih by T'ang imperial decree.[166] Thanks to the latest of his many successful campaigns in the high Pamirs, Kao Hsien-chih became known in the west as "the lord of the mountains of China."[167]

The situation in Central Asia in 750 can be characterized as the

[160] Cf. *HTS*, 221b:6252, and Moriyasu, 1984:42-43.

[161] The fifth month (June 9 to July 7).

[162] The sixth month (July 8 to August 6).

[163] *TFYK*, 999:19r-19v (p. 11724). Cf. Chavannes, 1903:214-215.

[164] What remains unclear, despite the enormous amount of literature on the subject, is the geographic location of the country. All that is certain is that it was located where at least two routes crossed, one running between Little Balûr and Kashmir, the other connecting Great Balûr and the dominions of the Yabghu of Ṭukhâristân. Among the most recent studies, see G. Tucci, "On Swat, the Dards and Connected Problems" (1977) 9-85; K. Enoki, "Appendix I" (1977) 86-91 (an article dealing with Chieh-shih); K. Jettmar, "Bolor—zum Stand des Problems" (1980) 115-132; and Moriyasu, 1984:42. Cf. C. Ts'en, *Hsi T'u-chüeh shih liao pu ch'üeh chi k'ao cheng* (1972) 208-214.

[165] *TCTC*, 216:6898. The gloss from the *K'ao-i* discusses the problem of the paucity of information in the sources.

[166] *TCTC*, 216:6898; *TFYK*, 965:4v (p. 11349). The decree is translated in Chavannes, 1903:215-216.

[167] Arabic, ṣâhib ǧibâl al-Ṣîn (Dhahabî, v:210). Cf. Dunlop, "A New Source of Information on the Battle of Talas or Aṭlakh" (1964) 328. Dunlop translates this phrase "the ruler of the mountains of China."

acme of Chinese military and political power. They had extended
their control to include direct colonial rule over the states of the
Tarim Basin and Jungaria, garrisons in the Pamirian vassal states
of Little Balûr, Chieh-shih, and Wakhan, and a firm alliance with
Ferghana. The fragmented Türgiś peoples, which the T'ang considered to be vassals, were under heavy Chinese political influence. The Tibetans now controlled little more in the west than the
kingdom of Great Balûr. The year 750 represents essentially the
military nadir of the Tibetan Empire. In the north, the Qarluqs
had migrated into the lands of the Western Turks, and were
struggling with the weak Türgiś for mastery over the area. The
Arabs were better off than the Tibetans. The new Abbasid dynasty had recovered some major cities, such as Samarkand,[168] and
the many important cities—including Bukhara[169] and Kiśś[170]—
which had revolted on the fall of the Umayyads were now being
retaken. Other areas, such as eastern Ṭukhâristân and Khuttal,
maintained their virtual independence. And, despite paper submission to China, Tashkent remained independent. In short, the
Chinese and the Arabs were the dominant colonial powers in
Central Asia at the midpoint of the eighth century.

The background of the conflict that now shook Central Asia is
little known, but the major events can be fairly accurately described. Sometime in the early part of 750, the kings of Ferghana
and Tashkent opened hostilities against each other,[171] although to
what extent is unclear. Immediately, the Türgiś revolted against
the T'ang[172] by siding with *Cabïś,[173] the king of Tashkent, who
was their theoretical vassal, against Arsïlan[174] Tarqan, the Ikhśîd
of Ferghana. It is probable that the Ikhśîd had the assistance of al-

[168] But see Gibb, 1923:95.
[169] Ṭabarî, iii:74. Cf. Gibb, 1923:95.
[170] Ṭabarî, iii:79-80.
[171] Ibn al-Athîr, v:449.
[172] *CTS*, 109:3298.
[173] The son of the previous king, *Inäl Tudun Ch'ü-le (mentioned above),
his name (Chinese, Ch'e-pi-shih) is the Old Turkic title *cabïś* (T. Tekin,
1968:322) or, less likely, *cäbïś* (I. Ecsedy, 1980:27 [n. 14]). It is probably significant that the name was also that of Su-lu's subtribe within the Türgiś.
[174] On this name, see Appendix C.

Hanaś, the king of Khuttal, and his *câkars*, since the *câkars* suddenly fled Khuttal—in the face of an Arab force under Abû Da'ûd Khâlid b. Ibrâhîm—and went to Ferghana at precisely this time.[175]

At this point, Kao Hsien-chih entered the picture: "The Ikhśîd asked the king of China for help, so he provided him with a hundred thousand warriors, and they besieged the king of Tashkent. He [*Cabïś] submitted to the king of China, and did not resist him and his companions despite the hurt that they did to them [the Tashkent forces]."[176] Kao, the "king of China,"[177] brutally subjugated the city. After capturing *Cabïś, who had surrendered and accepted peace terms, he sent in his troops. They plundered the city, killed the old and weak, and enslaved the young.[178] At the same time, Kao also defeated and captured the Türgiś qaghan, who was allied with *Cabïś. When he finished, Kao withdrew to the Pacified West, and, in the first month of 751, he presented Hsüan-tsung with the royal captives from his recent campaigns. Among these were the qaghan of the Türgiś, some Tibetan "chiefs,"[179] the king of Tashkent, and the king of Chiehshih.[180] *Cabïś was executed below the K'ai-yüan Gate,[181] and Kao was rewarded with appointment to the highest honorary position on the Board of Civil Office.[182]

But the son of *Cabïś[183] had escaped. He quickly made his way

[175] Ṭabarî, iii:74. Abû Da'ûd went on to raid Kiśś in the next year, 134 A.H. (July 30, 751 to July 17, 752). He killed the king of Kiśś and put the king's brother on the throne. After this victory, Abû Da'ûd acquired much treasure there including things from China (Ṭabarî, iii:79-80).

[176] Ibn al-Athîr, v:449. Cf. Dunlop, 1964:326-327.

[177] Dhahabî, v:210.

[178] *CTS*, 109:3298; *TCTC*, 216:6901.

[179] *HTS*, 216a:6087.

[180] *HTS*, 5:148; *TCTC*, 216:6904.

[181] *CTS*, 109:3298; *HTS*, 135:4578. The K'ai-yüan Gate was "the northernmost of the three gates in the west wall of the outer city" of Ch'ang-an. See H. Wechsler, *Mirror to the Son of Heaven* (1974) 160.

[182] *CTS*, 104:3206; *TCTC*, 216:6904. On the title, see Des Rotours, 1974, 1:35.

[183] Yüan-en, the "son of the king of Tashkent," who had come to court in 749 (*TFYK*, 971:17r [p. 11413]).

to the Arabs at Samarkand, who were under the command of Ziyâd b. Ṣâliḥ al-Khuzâʿî.[184] Ziyâd b. Ṣâliḥ immediately asked Abû
Muslim, the revolutionary leader and governor of Khurasan, for
reinforcements, which were sent partly from Ṭukhâristân[185] and
apparently reached Samarkand in May 751.[186] Hearing that the
Arabs and the native Central Asians were together planning to attack the Four Garrisons, Kao Hsien-chih promptly gathered his
army and marched west, adding Qarluq warriors and Ferghanian
troops along the way.[187] In a preliminary skirmish, the T'ang
forces attacked a position defended by a certain Saʿd b. Ḥamîd.
When they heard of the approach of Ziyâd's army, however, they
withdrew to the town of Aṭlakh,[188] a few miles from the city of
Talas.[189] On the following day, near the end of July 751, the two
armies met.[190] The fierce battle which ensued lasted until the
Qarluqs switched sides; the T'ang forces were routed.[191] On the
night of the defeat, Li Ssu-yeh, Kao Hsien-chih's assistant general, convinced Kao not to rejoin battle in the morning and face a
total disaster, which might have involved their own capture or
death. Unfortunately, the escape route, a narrow path leading
into the White Stone Range,[192] was blocked with retreating Ferghanian troops, camels, and horses. Li eliminated this problem

[184] Ṭabarî, iii:74, has Abû Muslim sending him on campaign to Bukhara
in A.H. 133 (August 9, 750 to July 29, 751).

[185] Dhahabî, v:210; cf. Dunlop, 1964:328.

[186] This dating assumes that Dhahabî's account is off by one year but is
otherwise basically accurate.

[187] TCTC, 216:6907. This source explicitly reports 30,000 "foreign and
Chinese" troops. According to the Arabic sources, Kao had 100,000 men, an
obvious exaggeration; but this figure includes the Turks under his command
(Dhahabî, v:210).

[188] That the battle actually took place at Aṭlakh has been firmly established by D. Dunlop (1964).

[189] Arabic, Ṭarâz. This battle has long been known among Western historians as the "Battle of Talas."

[190] Dhahabî, v:210. HTS, 5:148, agrees with Ibn al-Athîr, v:449, on the
date: the Chinese source places the battle in the seventh month (July 27 to
August 25, 751); thus, the battle occurred between July 27 and July 29, 751.

[191] According to TCTC, 216:6907, the battle lasted five days.

[192] Chinese, Pai-shih Ling.

by clubbing to death those in the way until "the Westerners, etc., hid, and the road was opened."[193] Kao Hsien-chih avoided capture, but thousands of others in the army did not; as captives, they made the long march back to Samarkand.[194] During their captivity, however, the Chinese were not inactive. Some among them taught their captors how to manufacture paper.[195] One even made his way to the capital of the Abbasid caliphate, and then returned to China to write for posterity of the wonders of the West.[196] The Battle of Aṭlakh was the first and last major military confrontation between the Arabs and the Chinese.

Meanwhile, back in the Koko Nor region, the Tibetans were taking a beating at the hands of the T'ang armies. At the end of 750, a Chinese commander attacked Tibet's "Five Bridges" and captured Shu-tun City.[197] Even worse, at some time between 748[198] and 751,[199] Kao Hsien-chih and the Khotanese king Yü-ch'ih Sheng[200] captured the important Tibetan Military Gover-

---

[193] CTS, 109:3299. "Westerners" is my translation here for Chinese, hu. Cf. note 212 below.

[194] CTS, 109:3298-3299; HTS, 138:4616; TCTC, 216:6908. Some of the prisoners, led by Li Ssu-yeh and Tuan Hsiu-shih, escaped back to the Pacified West (CTS, 128:3583; HTS, 153:4847; TCTC, 216:6908; Ibn al-Athîr, v:449).

[195] Tha'âlibî, 543, No. 892 ("The Paper of Samarkand"), specifically states that these teachers had come "from China to Samarkand" because "Ziyâd b. Ṣâliḥ captured them at the Battle of Aṭlakh." Cf. Dunlop, 1964:330, and C. Bosworth, The Book of Curious and Entertaining Information (1968) 140.

[196] This was Tu Huan, author of the Ching hsing chi, "A Record of the Travels," now unfortunately lost. A relative of his, the famous scholar Tu Yu, quoted several long passages from his book in the encyclopedic T'ung tien ("Comprehensive Treasury"). Tu Huan returned to Ch'ang-an in 762. See Pelliot, "Les Artisans chinois à la capitale abbaside en 751-762" (1929) 110-112.

[197] TCTC, 216:6901.

[198] Kao Hsien-chih was appointed Military Governor of the Four Garrisons of the Pacified West on February 1, 748 (CTS, 104:3208; TCTC, 216:6887).

[199] In 751, Kao was replaced as Military Governor of the Pacified West by Wang Cheng-chien, who died shortly thereafter and was replaced by Feng Ch'ang-ch'ing on February 2, 753 (CTS, 104:3208; TCTC, 216:6916).

[200] He was apparently one of the kings named Vijaya Sangrâma in the

norship of Tshal-byi and Cherchen, just south of Lop Nor.[201] The one Tibetan gain at this time was the voluntary submission to Tibet of Nan-chao, a powerful kingdom in Yunnan.[202] For Nanchao, this submission was a matter of self-preservation in the face of massive Chinese attacks.[203] This development was to prove of great importance to Tibet in the prolonged struggle with T'ang China.

At the time, however, Tibet continued to lose on the battlefield. In 753, the Tibetans suffered serious losses to Chinese arms on two fronts. In the summer, Qośu Khan attacked and captured the Tibetan cities of Hung-chi and Ta-mo-men, and, in so doing, "he gathered all the tribes of the Nine Bends [of the Yellow River]."[204] The T'ang promptly established new armies and military commanderies to hold the territory: the Shen-ts'e Army, located 80 *li* west of Lin-t'ao, the Chiao-ho *chün* southwest of K'uo *chou*, and others.[205] Also during 753, Feng Ch'ang-ch'ing, the Military Governor of the Pacified West, invaded Great Balûr. His troops reached the city of P'u-sa-lao, defeated its defenders, and received the submission of the country.[206] Not much is known about the campaign, but it appears that the last Tibetan presence in the Pamir region had been rooted out.[207]

Khotanese *ex eventu* prophecy preserved in Tibetan translation as the *Li yul luṅ bstanpa*. See Emmerick, 1967:100.

[201] *HTS*, 110:4127. See Uray, 1979a. Cf. Moriyasu, 1984:48-50.

[202] In 751 (*TCTC*, 216:6906-6907) or 752 (*CTS*, 197:5281). *TFYK*, 446:17r-17v (p. 5297 top), indicates that Nan-chao had submitted by 754.

[203] *CTS*, 197:5281; *HTS*, 222a:6271; *TCTC*, 216:6906.

[204] *HTS*, 216a:6087; *TCTC*, 216:6918. Recorded under the third month of 754 in *HTS*, 5:150.

[205] *HTS*, 135:4571, 216a:6087; *TCTC*, 217:6927; *TFYK*, 992:16r-16v (p. 11655). The sources do not completely agree on either the dates (753 or 754) or the names of the commanderies.

[206] *CTS*, 128:3583; *HTS*, 153:4847; *TCTC*, 216:6920-6921. The name of the city is P'u-sa-lao in *TCTC*, but Ho-sa-lao in the other sources. P'u-sa is the Chinese transcription of a Prakrit or Central Asian form of the Sanskrit *bodhisattva*.

[207] Nevertheless, it is indicative of Tibet's continued importance in Chinese eyes that, according to the usual interpretation, the Tibetans held the place of honor over the Koreans, Japanese, and Arabs at a formal audience

There were also major internal problems in Tibet, and in 755 they came to the attention of the Chinese. At the very beginning of the year, Stag-sgra, a "prince of the Sumpa,"[208] abandoned Tibet and surrendered to the T'ang.[209] More seriously, the emperor Khri lde gtsug brtsan (Mes ag tshoms) was murdered during a revolt led by the great ministers ʿBal Skyes bzaṅ ldoṅ tsab and Laṅ-myes Gzigs. Sroṅ lde brtsan, the crown prince, was sorely beset, and could not be enthroned. This rebellion had serious implications for the next two decades of internal political development in Tibet.[210] Meanwhile, China seemed nearly invincible.

Then, on December 16, 755,[211] the Turco-Sogdian military governor An Lu-shan rebelled against the T'ang and shook "all under Heaven."[212]

---

with Hsüan-tsung in 753 (Demiéville, 1952:180-181). According to Chang, 1980:76, they were seated in the second highest position, after the Arabs.

[208] Chinese, Su-p'i.

[209] *HTS*, 216a:6087; *TCTC*, 217:6929. Defections such as this were regular occurrences during times of political disturbance in the Tibetan Empire.

[210] For more on this rebellion, see Beckwith, 1983.

[211] *TCTC*, 217:6934. Cf. Des Rotours, 1962:167.

[212] *CTS*, 104:3213; *HTS*, 135:4570; *TCTC*, 216:6916. These three sources quote a conversation between An Lu-shan and his bitter enemy Qośu Khan that took place prior to the rebellion in the presence of Hsüan-tsung. Trying to placate Qośu, An said: "My father was an Indo-European, my mother a Turk; your father was a Turk, your mother an Indo-European." Qośu Khan's father was indeed a Türgiś. (Cf. Des Rotours, 1962:1-2.) In An Lu-shan's case, the word *hu* ("Indo-European, especially Sogdian") almost certainly identifies him as a Sogdian because his surname (An) was commonly used to refer to Sogdians originally from Bukhara. *Hu* did not mean just "Serindian" during the T'ang period, but anyone of Indo-European race (p. 1[n. 3]).

Chapter 6

THE
LATE
EMPIRE

The mighty T'ang Empire, which had made the Western Regions tremble and which had tried to "swallow the peoples of the four directions"[1] was now itself shaken, its powerful armies shattered one by one.[2] The "Brilliant Emperor," Hsüan-tsung, could not control his anger when his attempts to personally direct the campaign against An Lu-shan's rebels led to the slaughter of his troops. For their failures, he executed two of his most experienced generals, Feng Ch'ang-ch'ing and Kao Hsien-chih. Qośu Khan, recalled with his seasoned troops from the Tibetan border, replaced them at the strategic T'ung Pass, just east of Ch'ang-an. Despite overwhelming advice from his generals to the contrary, Hsüan-tsung and his chief minister ordered Qośu to attack. As predicted, the T'ang army was totally crushed; even Qośu Khan was captured.[3] The rebels poured through the pass on the way to

---

[1] TCTC, 216:6889.

[2] For a more detailed account of these events, see CHC, 3:453-461. The description therein is based on the CTS, HTS, and TCTC versions.

[3] CTS, 104:3213-3215; HTS, 135:4571-4574. Cf. CHC, 3:457, 459-460. He was executed by An Ch'ing-hsü late in 757 (TCTC, 220:7041).

Ch'ang-an, and Hsüan-tsung and his coterie fled. On the second day of the flight (July 16, 756), the imperial party encountered a Tibetan embassy of about two dozen men at Ma-wei Station. The emperor's bodyguard slaughtered the hapless Tibetans, and, after accusing Yang Kuo-chung (Hsüan-tsung's chief minister) of collaborating with them, killed him and many of his accompanying family members as well. Even when they demanded the execution of the emperor's consort, Yang Kuei-fei, Hsüan-tsung acquiesced. She was strangled on the spot.[4] After some discussion, it was decided that the emperor would continue his flight to Szechuan, while the heir apparent would go with a small force to Ling-wu in the far northwest to organize resistance against the rebels.[5] Once at Ling-wu, the crown prince usurped the throne. On hearing the news a month later, Hsüan-tsung surrendered the imperial regalia, which he had held for almost forty-five years, to the new emperor, Su-tsung.[6] So ended the reign of the Brilliant Emperor. He had rejuvenated the T'ang dynasty, but he had also brought it to the brink of destruction. He had pressed the Tibetans most mercilessly, but in so doing he had created an enmity that would result in nearly a century of Tibetan aggrandizement at China's expense.

The withdrawal of the most effective elements of the Chinese garrisons in Central Asia to put down the rebellion had an immediate impact on the Tibetan presence there. In 756, a number of envoys from the Western Regions—including the northern Pamir countries of the Black *Ganjak,[7] Wakhan, and Shugh

---

[4] *CTS*, 9:232; *HTS*, 5:153; *TCTC*, 218:6973-6974. Cf. *CHC*, 3:460.

[5] *TCTC*, 218:6975-6976. Cf. *CHC*, 3:460-461. Ling-wu is another name for Ling *chou*.

[6] *TCTC*, 218:6982. Cf. *CHC*, 3:461. Su-tsung is of course his posthumous temple-name.

[7] The name is written *Ban 'jag*, which is a perfectly good transcription of the Middle Persian word for hemp, *banjak*. (See H. Nyberg, *A Manual of Pahlavi, Part II: Glossary* [1974] 44.) This would, however, seem to be a scribal error for *Gan 'jag*, a transcription of *Ganjak* (the country above Kashgar), the language of which was mentioned by the medieval linguist Kâśgharî. In Old Tibetan, the letter *b* is often written with a long tail on the right side, and so may easily be confused with the letter *g*. See Uray, "On the Tibetan Letters

nan[8]—paid homage at the Tibetan court, and Tibetan envoys were sent in return.[9] The reassertion of Tibetan influence in the heart of Central Asia had already begun. The main thrust of the Tibetan military counteroffensive, however, was clearly directed against China, and nothing is known of extensive Tibetan activities in Central Asia for many years after these first contacts with the Pamirs.

After Qośu Khan removed the Chinese garrisons in northeastern Tibet,[10] and when, not long afterward, the T'ang Central Asian garrisons were likewise withdrawn,[11] the Tibetans were freed to reexpand their frontiers into Central Asia and northwestern China. The first place to fall[12] (in the autumn of 756) was Sui *chou*, on Tibet's eastern border. Next were a number of Chinese forts in northeastern Tibet, including those held by the Armies of Wei-jung, Shen-wei, Ting-jung, Hsüan-wei, Chih-sheng, Chin-t'ien, and T'ien-ch'eng, as well as the fortified cities of Pai-ku, Tiao-k'o, and Shih-pao.[13] All of these forts and cities had been established only two years before by Qośu Khan. When

---

Ba and *Wa*" (1955), Table II (Suite), column III, under "VII-Xth century forms" (according to Francke), example "c," which, although not well drawn, does indicate the tail on the letter *b* (*ba*).

[8] Tibetan, *śig nig*. The name is transcribed Shih-ni in Wu-k'ung's itinerary. See Lévi and Chavannes, 1895:346 (n. 3), 347, 362.

[9] *OTAC*, Monkey year 756-757 winter. On chronology problems with this source, see the Note on Chronology.

[10] This was during the last days of 755 (*TCTC*, 217:6943-6944). The *K'ao-i* provides much information on this from various sources.

[11] An account of the activities within China of these forces, which included the king of Khotan and his men, some Ferghanians, and even some Arabs, among many others, lies outside the scope of this book. The Central Asians' influence on China must have been very great, however, and should be investigated in depth. Was their impact on the Chinese as powerful as it was on the Arabs in Iraq after the Abbasid revolution?

[12] In the ninth month, following the *K'ao-i* in *TCTC*, 218:7000. According to this source, Sui *chou* was taken by the joint forces of Tibet and Nan-chao. The *OTAC*, Monkey year (756-)757 winter, reports that the king of Nan-chao led one of the three armies that took Sui *chou*. *OTAC* also dates the capture of Te'u cu mkhar (T'ao *chou* City) first; Se cu (Sui *chou*) followed in the next year.

[13] *TCTC*, 219:7011.

the Tibetans retook the fortified city of T'ao *chou*, the Tibetan "Yellow River" commandery was reestablished, and a minister appointed Military Governor over it.[14] In 757, the Tibetans and their vassals—including the Tanguts, T'u-yü-hun, and others—captured Hsi-p'ing.[15] During the succeeding years, they continued their march through Mdosmad.

By the middle of 763, Tibet had captured the eastern part of Lung-yu *tao*.[16] Later in the year, the Tibetans took Ch'ang-an itself,[17] and, in subsequent years, made further conquests into the ethnically Chinese territories immediately to the north and northwest of the T'ang capital. Hostilities eventually ended with the landmark Sino-Tibetan Treaty of 821.[18] But these events are subjects for another story, one that deserves full treatment elsewhere. Suffice it to say that, with these new conquests, Tibet cut T'ang China off from direct contact with the West. From 763 until the end of the T'ang dynasty, what little news of the West that reached China had to pass through the hostile territory of the Ti-

[14] *OTAC*, (Sheep year 755-756 summer). The parentheses around the dates indicate that the source is defective; they are approximations based on the requirements of the preceding and succeeding passages in the source. As mentioned in the Note on Chronology, the chronology of the *OTAC* is in serious disorder. The animal years simply cannot be made to correspond to the dates, most of them quite certain, in the Chinese sources. Because of the relative uncertainty of the *OTAC* chronology at this point, I have generally followed the Chinese accounts with regard to dating. A serious study of this fragment of the *Annals* is a great desideratum.

[15] *TCTC*, 220:7038.

[16] Lung-yu *tao* corresponded approximately to modern Kansu.

[17] It is odd that the Chinese should have been so hostile to the Tibetans but so friendly to the Uyghurs, considering the striking difference between the apparently mild Tibetan treatment of Ch'ang-an and the shockingly brutal Uyghur treatment of Loyang. One reason may have been northeastern Tibet's location on both sides of the Yellow River, right on China's western frontier. The Uyghurs, on the other hand, were on the opposite side of the river to the north, and were further separated from China by the Gobi Desert. The Tibetans, in short, were dangerously close. Another factor may have been the pro-Turkic inclinations of the powerful Sogdian merchant community in China. The Sogdians were presumably not averse to influencing Chinese politicians with bribes.

[18] On the treaty, see note 158 below.

betans or the not much less hostile realm of the Uyghur Turks. Despite the presence of small T'ang garrisons in the Tarim Basin and Pei-t'ing until late in the eighth century, China was no longer a major factor in Central Asian history; but Central Asia and Central Asians continued to be major factors in Chinese history.

While the Tibetans were engaged on the Chinese front, important changes were taking place to the north. In 758, the Uyghurs, erstwhile allies of the Qarluqs, destroyed an army of some 50,000 Kirghiz, apparently occupied some of their territory, and cut off their communication with the Chinese.[19] In the aftermath of this debacle, the Kirghiz moved into an area from which they could not be seriously threatened by their Uyghur enemies.[20] They also cemented friendships with neighboring peoples by, not long afterward, coming to an agreement with the Qarluqs, Tibetans, and Arabs regarding international trade and communications. This agreement provided for the safety of those traveling between Tibet and the Arab caliphate who had to journey through the lands of the Qarluqs, the new rulers of the Western Turks in Jungaria and west of the Issyk Kul. In Qarluq territory, travelers were joined by Kirghiz escorts, who protected them from Uyghur banditry on their journey.[21] The Arabs com-

---

[19] See C. Mackerras, *The Uighur Empire* (1972) 66-67.

[20] They were, however, nearly constantly at war with the Uyghurs at this time, and were again during the twenty years before A.D. 840 (see below).

[21] This description presumably refers specifically to merchants traveling between Tibet and the caliphate. *HTS*, 217b:6149. Moriyasu, "Zôhô" (1979) 220-224, and in the shorter French version of this article, "Qui des Ouigours ou des Tibétains ont gagné en 789-792 à Beš-balïq?" (1981) 202 (where the reference is misprinted as "le chapitre 215" of the *HTS*), argues cogently for his view that this refers to travelers from Tibet to the Kirghiz in the period after 790. I cannot, however, agree with his interpretation. *HTS* gives no indication of a date, except to note that the defeat by the Uyghurs, which is recorded immediately before this, occurred in the Ch'ien-yüan period (758-760). Furthermore, it nowhere states that the final destination of the Tibetan travelers was the land of the Kirghiz. Since the source reports that Arabs as well as Tibetans and Qarluqs allied together against the Uyghurs, it obviously describes a trade route between Tibet and Arab Central Asia; the Arabs are otherwise inexplicable. In addition, the Kirghiz never (before modern times) dwelt anywhere near western Central Asia, the Pamirs, or the Tarim

pensated the Kirghiz with heavy silk brocades of Arab manufacture. The Kirghiz, in turn, purchased fancy clothing for their women from the Arabs and from the countries of the Tarim Basin and Jungaria.[22] In other words, at the time to which the Chinese report refers, the Uyghurs were raiding the route that was taken by merchants traveling between Tibetan territory and Arab territory. It is also obvious from the same account that the Tibetans were not in control of the Jungarian Basin either; the Qarluqs were, despite Uyghur depredations. There is, however, no mention in the Chinese source of any Tibetan military activity in the Tarim Basin or Jungaria at this time.

After the Tibetans had punished the Chinese in 763 by capturing Ch'ang-an, which the new emperor Tai-tsung had abandoned just in time, and by enthroning a new Chinese emperor (none other than a brother of the Chin-ch'eng Princess), they turned their attention to the northwest.[23] Liang *chou*, raided by

---

Basin. Moreover, they are not mentioned in the Chinese sources on the T'ang period as having appeared any further south than perhaps the northern edge of the Jungarian Basin, and, after 840, the southern edge of the Gobi Desert. After the defect of 758, the Kirghiz had fled to the northwest of the Uyghurs, who were then based in Mongolia. This leaves only one possible location for the trade route described in the Chinese source: It must have run from northern or northeastern Tibet to the eastern edge of Jungaria, then along the northern slopes of the Tien Shan to the Arab dominions in the West. It is true that the Uyghurs were pressuring the people of Pei-t'ing before the Tibetan attack in 789, but the city remained under Chinese rule. The neighboring tribes, in fact, seem to have been fairly independent, although (as the Chinese sources say) they suffered from Uyghur oppression. After the Uyghur capture of the city from the Tibetans and the Uyghur expansion westward, of course, there is no question of a Tibetan presence—even, presumably, of Tibetan merchants—north of the Tien Shan. In short, the text discussed here refers to the period between 758 and 791.

[22] *HTS*, 217b:6148. The name *An hsi* ("the Pacified West") was officially changed to *Chen hsi* ("the Garrisoned West") in 757 (*TCTC*, 220:7051); in 767, it was changed back (*TCTC*, 224:7197).

[23] On the capture of the city, see *OTAC*, end. The dates are missing in the manuscript, but the events it describes should allow the entries to be dated. The dating proposed by F. Thomas (in J. Bacot et al., *Documents de Touen-houang relatifs à l'histoire du Tibet* [1940] 58-59), while logical for the text itself, cannot be accepted. There is also a brief account of the campaign

the Tibetans between 758 and 760,[24] was taken in 764;[25] Kan *chou* and Su *chou* fell in 766.[26] Ten years later, the Tibetans took Kua *chou*.[27] In 781, the town and county of Shou-ch'ang, only 150 *li* south of Tun-huang (which the Tibetans besieged unsuccessfully), was captured.[28] At some time before 781, even Hami[29] was besieged by the Tibetans; it too fell into their hands.[30] The 783 Treaty of Ch'ing Shui finally brought peace between Tibet and China and practically an end to further Tibetan inroads into Central Asia.

Although Tibetan incursions may have ended, Sino-Tibetan hostilities soon broke out again. The Chinese and Tibetans had signed a separate bilateral agreement for Tibetan military assistance against the serious rebellion of Chu Tz'u in 783 and 784. The Uyghurs, putative allies of the T'ang, had joined with Chu in an effort to overthrow the struggling dynasty. But a Tibetan force, guided into battle by a Chinese general, crushed Chu's army and turned the tide firmly in the T'ang's favor.[31] Despite this victory, the Chinese refused to honor their promises as defined in the agreement.[32] The Tibetans were understandably angered.[33] The

---

of this year and of the following thirty years in *OTC*, viii. The Chinese sources contain a vast amount of material awaiting thorough study.

[24] *OTAC* (Dog year 758-759 [?] or 759-760 [?] winter).

[25] *YHCHTC*, 40:2v (p. 557); *CTS*, 196a:5239; *HTS*, 216a:6088.

[26] *YHCHTC*, 40:4v (p. 558), 40:7r (p. 560).

[27] *YHCHTC*, 40:11r (p. 562).

[28] See Demiéville, 1952:172-177, 359-360.

[29] Chinese, I *chou*.

[30] Demiéville, 1952:170-171 (n. 1).

[31] This is a fact admitted by the local reports and by the new emperor, Te-tsung, himself (*TCTC*, 231:7442). Accusations that the Tibetans had been bribed by Chu Tz'u to withdraw are highly doubtful. The charge that Tibetans had indulged in plunder on their way home is meaningless, for it was in no way comparable to the ferocious behavior in China of the T'ang's supposed allies, the Uyghurs, as the same Chinese sources reveal. See especially the glosses from the *K'ao-i* in *TCTC*, 230:7424.

[32] In the seventh month (July 22 to August 20) of 784 (*TCTC*, 231:7442).

[33] Once again, the problem of an anti-Tibetan faction at the Chinese court arises. Li Mi (supported by Lu Chih; see *TCTC*, 231:7429-7431), who advised Te-tsung to renege on his promises (*TCTC*, 231:7442), was the same

main promise had been to give the Tibetans the Military Governorships of the Pacified West and Pei-t'ing upon the success of their mission.[34] Although the Chinese garrisons in this area were not very strong, T'ang governors still dwelt in all of the cities, at least all of those visited by the Chinese monk Wu-k'ung before his departure from Pei-t'ing in 789.[35] As the dynasty had done a century earlier, the T'ang could have recalled its governors and left the local kings to face the Tibetans unaided. But when the Chinese broke the agreement, the Tibetans considered the Treaty of Ch'ing Shui also broken.

T'ang officials immediately began to discuss the danger of a new Tibetan invasion,[36] a possibility made more menacing by the proximity of Ch'ang-an to territories just to the west that remained under Tibetan control. Led by Źań *Rgyal *btsan, the Tibetans began to raid soon enough, and threatened the capital in 786.[37] After a setback, though, they took a new tack.[38] On December 10, 786, they occupied Yen *chou*, in the southern Ordos

---

one who convinced him to make a "grand alliance" with the Uyghurs and others (see below) even though the Uyghurs were allied to Chu Tz'u! (See *TCTC*, 230:7426-7427.)

[34] *TCTC*, 231:7442.

[35] Pei-t'ing was under Chinese rule when Wu-k'ung left it for China on October 6, 789, which was shortly before the Tibetans captured it (*WKJCC*:981). Cf. Lévi and Chavannes (1895). Khotan remained under Chinese rule at least until 790; see É. Chavannes, "Chinese Documents from the Sites of Dandan-Uiliq, Niya and Endere" (1907) 533-536. Cf. Moriyasu, 1984:56.

[36] In 784; see *TCTC*, 231:7446 et seq.

[37] *TCTC*, 232:7470-7473.

[38] This was not all that new, since the Tibetans had raided the same places as early as 778 (*TCTC*, 275:7252-7253), and had occupied Yüan *chou* (in southern Kuan-nei) for some time (*TCTC*, 223:7157) in 763. (*TCTC*, 224:7224, discusses the Tibetan positions in 773.) The Tibetan raids north into Kuan-nei had been preceded by Tangut, and later Nu-la (Tibetan, Lolad) Turk raids, which began shortly after the outbreak of the An Lu-shan rebellion. The Tanguts had supposedly been settled in this area during the early T'ang period in order to keep them away from the Tibetans (*TCTC*, 220:7060 et seq.).

just north of the Great Wall. The Tibetans permitted the local prefect and his troops to leave the city peacefully.[39] In the last few days of December, they also raided and occupied Hsia *chou*,[40] Lin *chou*, and Yin *chou*,[41] all located further east along the Great Wall. The Tibetan occupation of the Ordos was potentially disastrous for the T'ang. It meant that China was now in real danger of being surrounded on land by the Tibetans. This Tibetan campaign was successful enough that the T'ang once again was willing to discuss peace.[42]

The subsequent peace negotiations[43] ended in the abortive Treaty of P'ing-liang of 787. At the treaty ceremony,[44] the Tibetans evened up the diplomatic score by kidnapping many of the T'ang officials and military leaders who were present. Žan *Rgyal *btsan then strategically withdrew the garrisons of Yen *chou* and Hsia *chou*, which were too distant from the Tibetan lines to be easily supplied. To make these cities worthless to the enemy, the Tibetans drove out the inhabitants, burned the buildings, and destroyed the walls before departing.[45] In the following month,[46] the Chinese minister Li Mi developed his famous "Grand Alliance" strategy of containment. That autumn,[47] Li revealed his plan: "I would like His Majesty to make peace with the Uyghurs in the north, come to terms with Nan-chao in the

[39] *CTS*, 12:355, 196b:5249-5250; *HTS*, 7:194, 216b:6095; *TCTC*, 232:7474.

[40] Most of the Tanguts settled in Kuan-nei, the future center of the early Tangut Hsi-hsia state.

[41] *TCTC*, 232:7475, *CTS*, 12:355, and *HTS*, 7:194, state that Hsia and Yin were captured.

[42] *TCTC*, 232:7481-7482 et seq. The Tibetans raided in Kuan-nei again in 788 (*CTS*, 13:365, 196b:5256; *HTS*, 7:196, 216b:6098; *TCTC*, 233:7513).

[43] *TCTC*, 232:7481-7483.

[44] *TCTC*, 232:7486-7487.

[45] *CTS*, 196b:5253; *HTS*, 216b:6096-6097; *TCTC*, 232:7489. Yin *chou* had never been a walled city (see P. Pelliot, 1961:48) and was, with Lin *chou*, apparently not occupied by the Tibetans as long as Hsia and Yen were.

[46] *TCTC*, 232:7495.

[47] *TCTC*, 233:7505.

south, and unite with the Arabs and Hindustan in the West. In this way the Tibetans would themselves be in trouble, and horses would also be easy [for us] to obtain."[48]

The Uyghur-hating Emperor Te-tsung[49] was at first opposed to the inclusion of the Uyghurs in Li's plan. But this was the plan's most crucial element, and Te-tsung was finally convinced. At just about this time—somewhat after the beginning of the reign of the celebrated caliph, Harun al-Rashid[50]—a long war between the Arabs and Tibetans began. It thus appears indisputable that the alliance advocated by Li Mi, whether formal or informal, was indeed concluded.[51] Unfortunately for the Chinese, the T'ang-Uyghur peace[52] came too late to save the T'ang colonies in Central Asia.

In 787, Tibet captured Sha *chou*, or Tun-huang.[53] Having already secured the area of Hami, the farthest outpost of T'ang China's home administration and a city strategically located near the point where the Silk Road forks to the north and south of the Takla Makan Desert, the Tibetan armies were poised for a thrust

---

[48] *TCTC*, 233:7502. The difficulty of obtaining horses, which is understandable considering China's hostile relations with both the Uyghurs and the Tibetans at the time, is mentioned frequently; see, for example, *TCTC*, 133:7501 et seq.

[49] On the reasons for the emperor's reluctance, see *CHC*, 3:567, and C. Backus, *The Nan-chao Kingdom and T'ang China's Southwestern Frontier* (1981) 89.

[50] He reigned from 786 to 809.

[51] There is no record of any treaty being signed with any of the Chinese allies. The T'ang did conclude a matrimonial alliance with the Uyghurs, however, and, somewhat later, pried Nan-chao away from the Tibetans. Wei Kao, the powerful Military Governor responsible for the restoration of diplomatic and military relations with Nan-chao, is recorded as having said in a letter to the king of Nan-chao that China should take advantage of the Uyghurs' offer of help to annihilate Tibet (*TCTC*, 233:7517).

[52] *TCTC*, 233:7505-7506.

[53] See the bibliography in Moriyasu, 1981:193-195 (n. 4). The Tibetans also occupied and rebuilt the walls of Yüan *chou*, in Kuan-nei (*TCTC*, 233:7507). In the early summer (fifth month) of 788, Tibetans raided the prefectures of Ching, Pin, Ning, Ch'ing, and Fu, all of which were in Kuan-nei just north of Ch'ang-an (*TCTC*, 233:7513). In the autumn (ninth month), they raided as far as Fang *chou* (*TCTC*, 233:7515).

into the Lop Nor region[54] and the area of the Two Garrisons, Pei-t'ing and Kucha.[55] At this time, Khotan was still nominally governed by a Chinese resident and the native king.[56] Nothing is known about the status of Kashgar, the fourth of the former Four Garrisons of the Pacified West, but it is presumed that it had already come under Qarluq domination.[57] The Tibetans thus returned to the eastern Tarim region after a long absence, but found ready allies nearby for the next stage of their campaign.

According to the Chinese sources, for some time prior to 789 the Uyghurs had been harassing the people of Pei-t'ing, the Sha-t'o Turks (dependents of the city),[58] and even those neighboring tribes of Qarluq and White-clothed Turks who had submitted to the Uyghurs. The Uyghurs had been expanding into the territory by force, and were extorting exorbitant fees to allow merchants and Chinese officials to pass through Uyghur-controlled lands on journeys between the West and China:[59] "From this point on, although they were able to pass through by this route, the barbarians[60] demanded and took an exorbitant price for the use of it. Six thousand families of different Sha-t'o tribes, who were in dependence on Pei-t'ing, also grew to resent their excessive demands. The three tribes of the Qarluq,[61] and the White-

---

[54] If they had not already recaptured it; see Uray, 1979a.

[55] The Tibetans had appropriated, no doubt with ironic intent, the term "Four Garrisons" for four of their positions in the Kuan-lung region. The first Chinese reference to it that I have noticed is in *TCTC*, 225:7237; it describes the defeat of their Military Governors (Chinese, *chieh-tu-shih*) there in 776. These Four Garrisons are discussed in a gloss in *TCTC*, 247:7999.

[56] See Chavannes, 1907.

[57] This is, however, purely hypothetical. O. Pritsak, "Von den Karluk zu den Karachaniden" (1951), draws numerous conclusions which are not warranted by the Chinese sources.

[58] They were a branch of the *Cigil (Chinese, Ch'u-yüeh); see Hamilton, 1955:135, 151.

[59] Several important studies have been published by T. Moriyasu over the past decade on this period. They have greatly revised the previous interpretation of these events.

[60] Chinese, *lu*; here, the Uyghurs.

[61] Mackerras, 1972:103, "Kharlukh."

clothed Turks,[62] those who were normally subjects of the Uyghurs,[63] were particularly resentful and bitter. They all secretly submitted to the Tibetans, so they and the Tibetans, with the support of the Sha-t'o, together raided[64] Pei-t'ing."[65] In the winter of 789,[66] the Tibetans and their allies attacked the city. When the Uyghurs, under their general the El ügäsi, attacked the besiegers in the early summer of 790, the Tibetans defeated them.[67] The allies then pressed their attack on Pei-t'ing, and, because the people of the city "were bitter about the Uyghurs' insatiable demands, all of them, along with the Sha-t'o chief Chu-hsieh Chin-chung, surrendered to the Tibetans. The Military Governor Yang Hsi-ku fled to Hsi *chou*[68] leading two thousand men who were under his command."[69]

In part due to this defeat and in part due to political turmoil at their court in Ordubalïq, the Uyghurs withdrew. At the Uyghur capital, the El ügäsi came to an immediate understanding with the new qaghan, and, in the autumn of 790, he again turned to the west. This time, however, he led an army composed of "all the troops in the country." Joined by the forces of the Chinese commander Yang Hsi-ku, the objective was to recapture Pei-t'ing. But the campaign was a disaster; more than half their men were

[62] Mackerras, 1972:103, "White-eyed T'u-chüeh." The reading chosen by Mackerras is undoubtedly the result of a textual error due to the similarity of the characters for clothing (*fu*) and eye (*yen*). These Turks may have been Manicheans or, more likely, members of a Muslim sect. Cf. the discussions in W. Barthold, *Turkestan down to the Mongol Invasion* (1958) 198 et seq.; Hamilton, 1955:50; Mackerras, 1972:164 (n. 202).

[63] Mackerras, 1972:103, "Uighurs."

[64] Mackerras, 1972:103, "made trouble in," a strange translation for the Chinese, *k'ou*.

[65] *HTS*, 217a:6125. The translation is by Mackerras, 1972:103, with minor changes as noted above. On the parallels and previous scholarship, see Moriyasu, 1979, and the recent French version of the same article (1981).

[66] *CTS*, 195:5209, *TCTC*, 237:7651, *K'ao-i* gloss. Cf. Moriyasu, 1981:193, 196.

[67] During the fifth month. The El ügäsi had been attacking at least since the fourth month (*TCTC*, 233:7521).

[68] That is, Qocho.

[69] *TCTC*, 233:7521.

killed in battle by the Tibetans and their western allies.[70] Moreover, Yang Hsi-ku, who had intended to return to Qocho, was
murdered by the El ügäsi.[71] This new disaster meant that Kucha,
the one remaining Garrison of the Pacified West, was cut off from
China, where "no one knew if it held out or was lost."[72] Moreover, "[t]he Qarluqs took advantage of the victories to capture the
Uyghurs' Fu-t'u Valley.[73] The Uyghurs were shocked and afraid;
they moved all of their northwestern tribes to the south of their
royal encampment [Ordubalïq] in order to avoid them [the Qar-
luqs]."[74] Qocho, then still in Chinese hands, fell to the Tibetans
in the following year.[75] Sometime before 794 (probably in 791 or
792), the Tibetans finally took Khotan: " 'Bro Khri gzú ram
śags, having invaded the Western Regions, subjugated Khotan
and levied taxes [on the Khotanese]."[76] Thus began the long period of Tibetan rule over Khotan and the neighboring regions of
the southern route through eastern Central Asia.

The respective fortunes of the Uyghurs and the Tibetans in the
Tien Shan region were reversed in the course of 791. In the early
autumn,[77] the Tibetans attacked Ling *chou*, but were driven off by
the Uyghurs, who presented the prisoners and captured cattle to
the Chinese emperor, Te-tsung.[78] That winter, the Tibetans and
Qarluqs suffered a major defeat when the Uyghurs retook part of
Pei-t'ing.[79] The siege of the rest of the city, presumably the fortified part, continued.[80] In December, the Uyghurs presented a

[70] Ibid.
[71] *TCTC*, 233:7522.
[72] Ibid.
[73] This was located to the northwest of the Ötükän Mountains, according
to Hu San-hsing's gloss in *TCTC*, 233:7522.
[74] Ibid.
[75] *YHCHTC*, 40:14v-15r (pp. 563-564): during the seventh year of Chen-
yüan, which was A.D. 791. The common scribal error of Chen-kuan instead
of Chen-yüan is here corrected. (The seventh year of Chen-kuan corresponds
to A.D. 633.)
[76] *OTC*, viii.
[77] Eighth month (September 3 to October 2).
[78] *CTS*, 195:5210; *TCTC*, 233:7524.
[79] *CTS*, 195:5210; *HTS*, 217a:6125. Cf. Mackerras, 1972:106-107.
[80] Karabalgasun inscription (Chinese text), lines 14-15. See the edition in

prize captive, the Tibetan general Źaṅ *Rgyal *sum,[81] to Te-tsung.[82] In 792,[83] the Uyghur crown prince, the later Pao-i Qaghan, led a new assault: "The Heavenly Qaghan, personally leading a great army, annihilated the chief culprits and recovered the city."[84] Many Tibetans, and no doubt Qarluqs and other allies as well, are said to have been killed.[85] The Uyghurs continued on to Qocho, which they captured from the Tibetans later in 792.[86] Probably not long after this (the exact date is unknown), the Uyghurs attacked the Tibetan army which was besieging Kucha, by then the only T'ang outpost remaining from the Four Garrisons of the Pacified West. After a forced retreat, the Tibetans entered Yü-shu,[87] a fortified town located 560 *li* east of Kucha and 70 *li* west of Agni.[88] There they were besieged by the Uyghurs led by Pao-i Qaghan. The Tibetan army was destroyed.[89]

This series of Tibetan defeats had as one of its consequences the defection to the T'ang in 794 of Tibet's long-time vassal, Nan-chao.[90] The immediate cause of this rupture was Tibet's urgent need for soldiers to fight in the northwest and Nan-chao's refusal to supply them.[91] The direct result was a serious weaken-

---

T. Haneda, *Haneda hakushi shigaku rombun shû* (1957) 1:308-309. On the presumed date, see below.

[81] Chinese, Shang Chieh-hsin.

[82] *TCTC*, 233:7524-7525.

[83] This date is a deduction from the fact of the Uyghur capture of Qocho in 792, an improbable occurrence had they not taken Pei-t'ing first. There is no source which gives an explicit date for the Uyghurs' capture of Pei-t'ing.

[84] Haneda, 1957, 1:308 (line 15).

[85] *HTS*, 222a:6274; *TCTC*, 234:7552; *TFYK*, 973:18v (p. 11435).

[86] According to the manuscript Fonds Pelliot chinois 3918. See Moriyasu, "Uiguru to Toban no Hokutei sôdatsu-sen oyobi sono go no Seikki jôsei ni tsuite" (1973) 483-484, and 1979:226-227.

[87] Haneda, 1957, 1:309 (line 16). Cf. É. Chavannes and P. Pelliot, "Un traité manichéen retrouvé en Chine" (1913) 178 (n. 1).

[88] *HTS*, 43b:1151. Cf. Chavannes, 1903:7.

[89] Haneda, 1957, 1:309 (line 16).

[90] *TCTC*, 234:7552-7553. Cf. Backus, 1981:94-98

[91] There were of course other, more fundamental reasons for this reversal. See Backus, 1981:81 et seq. Backus, however, mistakenly finds a breach in Nan-chao vassalage "in the mid-70s" (p. 82). It is clear that the revolt described in the *OTC* is that of 794. The Tibetan source indicates merely that

ing of Tibet's military position along its entire southeastern border, a weakness that lasted through the mid-ninth century. Tibet's overall military posture in Central Asia, however, does not seem to have suffered any further damage. But Tibet had endured a severe setback. From near predominance in the Tarim Basin, the Tibetan forces now apparently settled down to a war of attrition with the Uyghurs around Qocho. Unfortunately, there is doubt about when the Uyghurs established firm control over Qocho,[92] and little else is known about the fate of the city in this period.[93] With the exception of a brief, minor reversal,[94] the border between the Tibetans and Uyghurs in the eastern Tien Shan region appears to have remained around Qocho. Control of the city may have changed hands several times.

Meanwhile, the Tibetans had become intensely involved in a protracted war with the Arabs in western Central Asia. It was no doubt partly due to the support provided by their Qarluq allies that the Tibetans were able to extend themselves so far west. It is also clear, however, that the Tibetans had been able to expand unassisted into the area of the Hindu Kush, via the Pamirs.[95]

The first indication of warfare between Arabs and Tibetans is in a report on a battle that took place in 801 between the Tibetans on one side and the Chinese and Nan-chao on the other. Fought by the Lu Shui on Tibet's eastern border, the Tibetans were defeated in battle: "The Samarkandi and Abbasid Arab troops, and the Tibetan commanders, all surrendered. Twenty thousand suits of armor were captured."[96] It is clear that these soldiers of western

---

the Nan-chao were better at serving two masters than either Tibetan or Chinese historians would like us to believe.

[92] See manuscript Fonds Pelliot chinois 3918, line 9, and the discussion in Moriyasu, 1973:484-487 and 1979:226-229.

[93] There is no information in any source on the Tibetans in this area for the subsequent period up to 851, when the Tibetans were driven from Qocho (Hsi *chou*) and Hami (I *chou*) by the Chinese warlord-prefect of Sha *chou*, Chang I-ch'ao. (On these events, see below.)

[94] In 808; see below.

[95] Cf. K. Jettmar, "Bolor" (1977) 421.

[96] *HTS*, 222a:6277. Chang, (1980:92, translates the whole passage, which gives details about the battle.

Central Asia had been transported east by the Tibetans, perhaps as prisoners of war or hostages.[97]

The next report of Tibetan involvement in the west comes from 193 A.H./A.D. 808-809, when the rebellion of Râfiʿ b. Layth in Samarkand came to a head. Large numbers of Central Asians from many countries, among them "troops of Tibet,"[98] joined the side of Râfiʿ. The situation became so dangerous that Harun al-Rashid himself set out for Khurasan to deal with the rebellion, but he died on the way in Ṭûs on March 24, 809.[99] His older son, al-Amîn, succeeded to the caliphate and to the rule of the provinces west of Rayy; his younger son, al-Maʾmûn, became the heir apparent and ruler of the eastern half of the Arab Empire.[100] Al-Maʾmûn quickly ran into trouble. In 810, he described his problems with the Tibetans, their Qarluq allies, and others in Central Asia in the following way: "I have learned, moreover, of the alienation of Khurasan and the restiveness of its populous and desolate [localities]; of the withdrawal of the yabghu [of the Qarluqs][101] from submission; of the turning away of the qaghan, lord of Tibet;[102] of the mobilization by the king of Kabul for a raid on those places in Khurasan which are near to him; and of the withholding by the Utrârbandah of the tribute which he used to pay. I have no control over any of these things."[103] The prince thought

---

[97] Cf. Chang, 1980:92, who thinks they might have been political refugees. He also notes: "Il se peut qu'ils aient été les premiers Musulmans du Yunnan."

[98] Yaʿqûbî, ii:435. The short notice on this in Ṭabarî, iii:775, refers only to "Turks." The specificity of the expression "troops of Tibet" (none of the other foreign participants are so described) gives Yaʿqûbî's account the ring of authenticity. Daniel, 1979:174, gives a distorted picture of the latter source by omitting, without explanation, selected names, including that of Tibet.

[99] CHI, 4:72.

[100] Ibid.; Shaban, Islamic History (1976) 2:39-40. In 194 A.H./A.D. 809-810, the Arabs raided Qûlân, a city east of Talas, near Mîrkî (Ibn al-Athîr, vi:237). Cf. Barthold, 1958:202.

[101] Arabic, ǧabghûya; as usual, the definite article is omitted.

[102] Arabic, khâqân ṣâhib al-Tubbat; literally, "[of] Qaghan, the lord of Tibet."

[103] Ṭabarî, iii:815. Cf. Dunlop, 1973:310 et seq. Utrârbandah was the title of the ruler of Utrâr, which place was also called Fârâb.

that his best hope lay in fleeing from Khurasan to the Tibetan lines: "I do not think that [there is any other way open to me] except the vacating of the place where I am, joining up with the qaghan, king of Tibet,[104] and seeking refuge with him and his country; for it would behoove me to guarantee my personal security and be in an impregnable position with regard to those who want my betrayal and defeat."[105]

Al-Ma'mûn's problems did not entirely emanate from his eastern front, for civil war over control of the caliphate was nearly at hand. One of his greatest challenges was to stabilize affairs in the east while conserving his resources for the imminent conflict with his brother the caliph. Al-Faḍl b. Sahl, al-Ma'mûn's vizier,[106] advised him: "Write to the yabghu and the qaghan, and appoint the two of them rulers of their two countries, and promise them support in their warfare with the [other] kings. Send some presents and rarities of Khurasan to the king of Kabul and ask him for a truce—you will find him eager to get it. And concede to King Utrârbandah his tribute for this year."[107] Al-Faḍl also proposed that his prince admit into the army the officers and troops who had been heretofore excluded from it. The optimistic

---

[104] The text has *khâqân malik al-Turk*, or "Qaghan, the king of the Turks." The ruler of the Qarluqs, the theoretical successor to the Türgiś qaghan as overlord of the Western Turks, is not intended because in these texts he is always called "Yabghu." The ruler of the Uyghurs is also out of the question, for two reasons: first, the Uyghurs are consistently called Tughuzghuz or Tughuzughuz (for Turkic, Toquzghuz or Toquz Oghuz), and second, al-Ma'mûn would have had to fight his way through enemy Qarluq territory to reach the Uyghurs, whom he could hardly have known much about at that time anyway. Moreover, throughout this section, Ṭabarî refers to the ruler of Tibet as Khâqân, as does Azraqî (cited below), where there is no possibility of confusion with another ruler. The passage in Ṭabarî should therefore be emended to read *khâqân malik al-Tubbat*, or "Qaghan, the king of Tibet."

[105] Ṭabarî, iii:815. I am indebted to my colleague, Professor Wadie Jwaideh, for assisting me in the translation of this and the following two quotations from Ṭabarî.

[106] In office from raǵab, 196 to śa'bân, 202 A.H./A.D. March 18-April 16, 812 to February 12-March 12, 818. See D. Sourdel, *Le vizirat ʿAbbāside* (1960) 2:726.

[107] Ṭabarî, iii:815-816. See note 103.

vizier predicted victory with his plan, indicating that al-Ma'mûn still had an option open to him were he to fail: "you would be able to achieve your aim by joining up with the qaghan."[108]

Al-Ma'mûn "perceived the truth of what he said" and implemented his vizier's proposal.[109] It was just in time to face the invasion of his brother's forces, which left Baghdad for Khurasan in the month of ša'bân, 195 A.H./A.D. April 29–May 27, 811.[110] Despite al-Ma'mûn's doubts, his armies soundly defeated the invaders. After his final victory in 198 A.H./A.D. 813-814, the year of al-Amîn's death, the new caliph did not move to Baghdad as expected, but remained in Marw, which became the capital of a reunited empire.[111] His throne secure, al-Ma'mûn was now able to encourage a jihad against the very Central Asian nations with which he had just concluded peace. He appointed al-Faḍl b. Sahl as his viceroy "over the East from the mountain of Hamadhân to the mountain of Shughnan and Tibet, longitudinally, from the Persian Gulf and India to the Caspian Sea and Ġurġân, latitudinally,"[112] and reopened hostilities in Central Asia.

The campaigns of al-Faḍl were directed against the four states—the kingdom of the Kabul Shah, the kingdom of the Utrârbandah, the realm of the yagbhu of the Qarluqs, and the empire of the Qaghan of Tibet—that had been hostile to or at war with al-Ma'mûn before 194 A.H./A.D. 809-810.[113] The first to capitulate was the king of Kabul, who submitted and became a

[108] Ṭabarî, iii:816.

[109] Ibid.

[110] Ibid.

[111] He finally left Marw in 202 A.H./A.D. 817-818 (Ṭabarî, iii:1025) and entered Baghdad to stay in 204 A.H./A.D. 819-820 (Ṭabarî, iii:1036).

[112] He had already been appointed to this position in April 812, according to Ṭabarî (iii:841), who also reports that he was given the title Dhû al-riyâsatayn, or "Holder of the Two Commands [the army and the fiscal administration]." For two important contemporaneous documents relating to this powerful figure, see W. Madelung, "New Documents Concerning al-Ma'mūn, al-Faḍl b. Sahl and 'Alī al-Riḍā" (1981).

[113] As previously mentioned, the Qarluqs and Tibetans had supported the large-scale revolt of Râfi' b. Layth, who surrendered to al-Ma'mûn in 195 A.H./A.D. 810-811 (CHI, 4:72; Shaban, 1976, 2:40).

Muslim sometime between 197 and 199 A.H.(A.D. 812-813 and 814-815). As a token of his submission and conversion, he sent al-Ma'mūn a golden statue on a silver throne.[114] Saʿīd b. Yaḥyâ of Balkh described it to Azraqî: "A king from among the kings of Tibet became a Muslim. He had an idol of gold that he worshipped, which was in the shape of a man. On the head of the idol was a crown of gold bedecked with chains of jewelry and rubies and green corundum and chrysolite. It was on a square throne, raised above the ground on legs, and the throne was of silver. On the throne was a cushion of brocade; on the fringe of the cushion were tassels of gold and silver hanging down, and the tassels were as . . . draperies on the face of the throne."[115] Al-Ma'mūn sent it to Mecca as a trophy to be stored in the treasury of the Kaʿba. In Mecca, it was first displayed in the Square of ʿUmar b. al-Khaṭṭâb for three days, with a silver tablet on which was written: "In the name of God, the Merciful, the Compassionate. This is the throne of so-and-so, son of so-and-so, king of Tibet. He became a Muslim and sent this throne as a gift to the Kaʿba; so praise God who guided him to Islam."[116] Although it is not surprising that the ruler of Kabul, a Buddhist kingdom, would give a Buddhist

[114] Azraqî, 227, 231, 244 (the date of reception of the statue). Cf. Madelung, 1981:337. The Mecca edition of Azraqî reads both *sbʿ*, i.e., *sabʿ* (pp. 227 and 231), and *tsʿ*, i.e., *tisʿ* (p. 244). Since the dots distinguishing different letters with the same basic shape were seldom written in Azraqî's day, the two words were probably often identical. Perhaps 199 is too late as the date of the king's submission, but one would assume that al-Ma'mūn could not have undertaken any major campaigns until the death of al-Amîn in 198. Unfortunately, there is no explicit reference in Azraqî to fighting with the king of Kabul.

[115] Azraqî, 225. This translation contains several uncertainties due to corruption and other difficulties in the existing manuscripts. I felt, however, that a complete translation, even one with possible errors, would be better than a summary. I am indebted to my colleague, Professor Robert Dankoff, for the assistance he gave me when I first tackled these texts in Azraqî.

[116] Azraqî, 226. This announcement was read aloud to the people morning and night, and praise was offered to God, "who had led the king of Tibet to Islam." The statue and throne were melted down to make coins in 202 A.H./A.D. 817-818, but the crown and tablet were kept in the Kaʿba until the time of Azraqî, who copied the inscriptions on them.

statue to al-Ma'mûn, it is rather unexpected to hear him called a
"king of Tibet." The texts clearly distinguish, however, between
"*a king* from among the *kings* of Tibet" and "the *qaghan* of Tibet,"
who was considered to have the imperial dignity. One may conclude from this that the Tibetans, who were close allies of the
Qarluqs, were at war with the Arabs in the west,[117] and were the
dominant power in the Pamirs,[118] had also made a vassal of the
Kabul Shah.[119] The Shah's submission to al-Ma'mûn at this
point—after little or no resistance, it would seem—was perhaps
his reaction to the danger of being overwhelmed by the increas-
ingly powerful Tibetans.[120] Al-Ma'mûn's posture as a "Khura-
sani" ruler[121] may have been the decisive factor.

Al-Ma'mûn's next move was further to the east. Al-Faḍl b.
Sahl led a campaign "to Kashmir and to the realm of Tibet."[122] He
triumphed in Wakhan and in the country of Balûr, and sent the
captured Tibetan commander and "Tibetan cavalrymen" back to
Baghdad.[123] Al-Faḍl next turned north, where he subdued the
country of Utrâr,[124] and captured the wives and children of the
Qarluq yabghu, who fled to the land of the Kimäk.[125] Al-Faḍl
also recaptured the city of Kâsân and other citadels in Ferghana.[126]

---

[117] The Chinese were aware of this war, which they believed to be responsible for fewer Tibetan raids on China (*CTS*, 198:5316; *HTS*, 221b:6263).

[118] Azraqî, 229. See below.

[119] One may also conclude that a major reason for so many Indian Buddhist sages coming to Central Tibet from Kashmir, and, notably, the famous
Padmasambhava from Udyâna, was the simple fact that Tibet then ruled
much of this region. Cf. Jettmar, 1977:421-422.

[120] Compare the situation of Nan-chao, another of Tibet's vassals, two
decades earlier.

[121] Cf. *CHI*, 4:72; Daniel, 1979:177-178.

[122] Azraqî, 229. For a provisional translation of this difficult section of
Azraqî, see É. Combe et al., *Répertoire chronologique d'épigraphie arabe*, Vol. 1
(1931) 94. The original is unfortunately more than a little corrupt.

[123] Azraqî, 229. Cf. Madelung, 1981:337, "the commander of the cavalry
of al-Tubbat.".

[124] Azraqî, 230. Other places which Azraqî names are al-Trbd, Sâwghar
(north of Utrâr), and Z'wl. On the location of Utrâr and Sâwghar, see Le
Strange, 1966:485.

[125] Azraqî, 230.

[126] Azraqî, 231.

He thus reestablished, and even briefly extended, the Arab Islamic hold on Central Asia. The Tibetans seem shortly thereafter to have recovered, however, and to have held on to some of their positions in the Pamirs until later in the century.[127] Unfortunately, there is no more direct historical source material on their activities—or those of the Arabs—in this region during the rest of the Early Middle Ages.

On Tibet's northeastern frontier, the Uyghurs had continued to press into Tibetan territory. In 808, for example, they attacked and captured the strategic city of Liang *chou*.[128] This defeat resulted in a Tibetan effort at moving the Sha-t'o tribes from that area: as former allies or vassals of the Uyghurs, their loyalty to their new Tibetan masters was suspect, and they could not be trusted in such a sensitive area of the frontier. The Sha-t'o resisted, however, and fled down the Yellow River to the north while fighting off the Tibetans. Finally, in the summer of 808, the remaining 1,300 Sha-t'o tribespeople surrendered to the T'ang at

[127] This follows the accepted view that most of the material in the early Arabic and Persian geographical works dates to this period. See Barthold, "Tibet," in *E.I.1*, 1:742. Note that Barthold mistakenly believed that the Arabs "seem to have generally understood by Tubbat, Little Tibet or Baltistan." All of the early geographers (those writing during and shortly after the period of the Tibetan Empire), however, clearly and accurately described Tibet as bounded by China on the east, India on the south, the Uyghur Turks on the north, and the eastern marches of Khurasan on the west. On this question, see my paper, "The Location and Population of Tibet According to Early Islamic Sources," given at the Csoma de Kőrös Symposium held at Visegrád, Hungary in 1984 and forthcoming in *AOH*.

[128] *TCTC*, 237:7651. It is manifestly clear from these events that the Uyghurs must have come across the desert to the north of Liang *chou* via the Etsin Gol that flows past Kan *chou*. Had they attacked from the Tien Shan region, the Uyghurs would have had to slip past the Tibetan forts in Kansu, which probably extended as far as Hami. Coming from the east would have been just as difficult: there they would have had to face considerable Tibetan strength. This hypothesis is confirmed by the Uyghur attack of 813, which was in the area of Kan *chou*, just west of Liang *chou* (see below). The Uyghurs thus followed a regular route. Indeed, there was an important route that followed the Etsin Gol all the way to the Uyghur court in Mongolia. The route is attested by the location given for the Uyghur capital and the Ötükän Mountains with respect to Kan *chou* in *TCTC*, 237:7651 gloss.

Ling *chou*.[129] In the summer of the following year, the Chinese moved them east of the Yellow River in order to put distance between them and the Tibetans.[130]

Also in 809, the Military Governor of Tibet's Northern *tao*[131] led a punitive expedition against the Uyghurs.[132] That autumn, the Tibetans again attacked the Uyghurs. Fifty thousand Tibetan cavalry rode via P'i-t'i Springs, 300 *li* north of Hsi Shou-hsiang City,[133] to a place called Great Stone Valley.[134] There they plundered an Uyghur embassy that was returning from a mission to the T'ang court in Ch'ang-an.[135] It took four years for the Uyghurs to respond to the Tibetan thrust that had penetrated deep into their territory.

But by the autumn of 813, the Tibetans had finished the construction of a bridge over the Yellow River at Wu-lan.[136] Ssu-ma Kuang comments: "Henceforth, Shuo-fang had no respite from withstanding their raids."[137] In the early winter (tenth month) of that year, an Uyghur army crossed the Gobi Desert to the south and attacked the Tibetans west of Liu Ku,[138] which was located somewhere near Hsi Shou-hsiang City.[139] The Uyghur cavalry,

[129] *TCTC*, 237:7651-7652.

[130] *TCTC*, 237:7660-7661.

[131] The Tibetan term is unknown. This administrative unit was located west of the Yellow River from the Shuo-fang prectures of Ling, Yen, and Feng.

[132] J. Kolmaš, "Four Letters of Po Chü-i to the Tibetan Authorities (808-810 A.D.)" (1966) 404-405.

[133] Located in present-day Inner Mongolia. See Map I. The name Hsi Shou-hsiang *ch'eng* means "West City for Accepting Surrender."

[134] Chinese, Ta-shih Ku.

[135] *HTS*, 216b:6100; *TCTC*, 238:7666.

[136] *TCTC*, 239:7701. Wu-lan was in Hui *chou*, which was about sixty miles downstream (to the north) of Lan *chou* (*CKKCTMTTT*, 735-736).

[137] *TCTC*, 239:7701.

[138] Ibid.

[139] *HTS*, 218:6155, reports that they captured both of these places. The many other localities called Liu Ku ("Willow Valley") seem highly unlikely to be the Liu Ku mentioned here. Hu San-hsing's gloss, which locates this place north of the Tien Shan, must be rejected, as pointed out by Moriyasu, 1981:201 (n. 40).

now several thousand strong, then rode to P'i-t'i Springs, causing the T'ang generals in the area some anxiety.[140] This demonstration, however, was probably intended more for the benefit of the Tibetans than for the Chinese.[141] Notwithstanding, Tibetan raids continued throughout the area northeast of Lan *chou* up to the Gobi. One Tibetan thrust even penetrated "across the desert," to within two or three days' march of "their city walls"—presumably the Uyghur capital, Ordubalïq—in 816.[142] But it was only in 821 that Uyghurs and Tibetans came into full-scale conflict again.

The Uyghur Empire had by now expanded to its greatest east-west extent. In the late spring or early summer of 821, an Uyghur army appeared in Uśrûsana,[143] apparently after attacking a Tibetan and Qarluq force to their west and chasing them across the Jaxartes into Ferghana,[144] where the Uyghurs collected great quantities of plunder from the local people.[145] It was also probably in that year that the Arab envoy, Tamîm b. Baḥr, traveled to Ordubalïq via the Uyghur-controlled lands near Talas, the Issyk Kul, and Jungaria.[146] But these events are deceiving; things were not going so well for the Uyghurs. The Kirghiz, old enemies of

[140] *CTS*, 195:5210; *TCTC*, 239:7701–7702.

[141] Mackerras's puzzlement, 1972:170–171, is thus unwarranted.

[142] *CTS*, 196b:5265. Cf. Mackerras, 1972:172 (n. 250). Moriyasu, 1979:225–226, describes this as a raid across the desert between Lop Nor and Agni. But the Chinese, who apparently believed the Tibetans to be the major power in Central Asia, must have understood the Tibetan raid to have been across the Gobi Desert toward Ordubalïq, for that more closely touched their interests. Moreover, as I have discussed, the historical context heavily favors the Gobi here.

[143] Ṭabarî, iii:1044. For other explanations of this event, see Barthold, 1958:210–211.

[144] Haneda, 1957, 1:310 (line 20). Chinese, Chen-chu Ho.

[145] Haneda, 1957, 1:309 (line 17). The fate of the Tibetan army is unknown. The Karabalgasun inscription does not allow absolute dates to be determined for the events it describes. Such a major Uyghur expedition into Arab-dominated territory should have been noticed by the Arab chroniclers, hence my assumption that the entry in Ṭabarî (see note 143) refers to this event.

[146] For text, translation, and discussion of this material, see V. Minorsky, "Tamīm ibn Baḥr's Journey to the Uyghurs" (1947-1948) 275-305.

the Uyghurs, warred constantly with them and had sworn to destroy them.[147] Moreover, Tibetans in Hami and Lop Nor still kept the Uyghurs out of the southern Tarim and Kansu while Tibetans in Ho-hsi even threatened the Uyghurs' only direct route to China, which passed by P'i-t'i Springs.

By early 821, the Tibetans and Chinese had more or less reached agreement on the terms of a new peace treaty, while the Uyghur qaghan was about to receive a T'ang princess as official reconfirmation of the Sino-Uyghur alliance. On July 1, the Chinese court proclaimed that the new Uyghur qaghan, Chao-li (Pao-i's successor), would receive the Princess of T'ai-ho as his consort.[148] Eight days later, perhaps incensed at the Uyghurs for their diplomatic success while China had still not signed the Tibetan treaty, the Tibetans raided Ch'ing-sai Fort.[149] After a counterattack by the prefect of Yen *chou*, however, they withdrew.[150] The Uyghurs quickly used this Sino-Tibetan clash to their advantage. On July 16, they memorialized Emperor Mu-tsung: "By sending ten thousand cavalrymen via[151] Pei-t'ing and ten thousand via Kucha,[152] we will ward off the Tibetans in order to welcome the T'ai-ho Princess and bring her to our country."[153]

Although this statement might seem to indicate that the

[147] The warfare had begun "over twenty years" before 840 (*TCTC*, 246:7947).

[148] *TCTC*, 241:7791. It is notable that, after the convulsions of the mid-eighth century that shook all of Eurasia (see the Epilogue), the Tibetans began insisting on written treaties with China while the Uyghurs continued to make old-fashioned "marriage-alliances" with the T'ang. The latter type of accords did, however, change in one interesting way: for the first time, natural daughters of the reigning T'ang emperors were married to the Uyghur qaghans.

[149] Unidentified, but obviously located near Yen *chou*.

[150] *CTS*, 195:5211; *TCTC*, 241:7791.

[151] Chinese, *ch'u*. This word has caused much argument among scholars who have discussed this passage. The usage is common in descriptions of military campaigns of the late Ming and early Manchu periods. I am indebted to my colleague, Professor Lynn Struve, for this information.

[152] The text reads *An hsi*, literally "the Pacified West," but by this time the name had become fixed as one of the names of Kucha.

[153] *CTS*, 195:5211; *TCTC*, 241:7791-7792.

Uyghurs intended to attack the Tibetans in the west again,[154] it is obvious that its only purpose could have been to reassure the T'ang that the Uyghurs could protect the princess and the imperial retinue from Tibetan raiders in the Ordos region. This supposition is supported by the memorial of Li Yu, prefect of Feng *chou*, who noted that winter (in the eleventh month) that "three thousand of the Uyghurs welcoming the T'ai-ho Princess had camped at Liu Springs to push back the Tibetans."[155] Since the Military Governor of Ling-wu had in fact just defeated a Tibetan force in the previous month[156] (while the princess was traveling northward nearby), one must conclude that the Uyghurs sent only a fairly small cavalry detachment to the T'ang border at Feng *chou*. There is, moreover, no record of any battle between Tibetans and Uyghurs near Pei-t'ing or Kucha, nor any indication that their relative positions in the area of Qocho changed at this time.

Notwithstanding these Sino-Tibetan troubles, a Chinese delegation had left for Tibet on November 8, 821 to sign the treaty.[157] During 822, Tibet also made peace with the Uyghurs and apparently with Nan-chao as well. By 823, the last Sino-Tibetan treaty—one distinguished, even more than its predecessors, by careful treatment of the two countries as equals—was signed and in effect.[158] This time, both sides observed the treaty stipulations to the letter[159] and peace reigned on the borders of Tibet for the first time in decades; it lasted for over twenty years.

[154] The obvious problem with the passage is that no destination is mentioned for these hypothetical armies. Nevertheless, it would seem to support the supposition that the bulk of Uyghur military strength was now in the west, around the Tien Shan.

[155] *CTS*, 195:5212; *TFYK*, 979:19r-19v (p. 11507). Mackerras, 1972:118, 179 (n. 278), miscontrues this passage.

[156] *TCTC*, 242:7802.

[157] *TCTC*, 242:7800.

[158] See J. Szerb, "A Note on the Tibetan-Uigur Treaty of 822/823 A.D." (1983), for details and a bibliography on the Uyghur treaty. No text of this treaty (or of that with Nan-chao) survives. For the text of the Sino-Tibetan treaty inscription, see F. Li, "The Inscription of the Sino-Tibetan Treaty of 821-822" (1956), and H. Richardson, "The Sino-Tibetan Treaty Inscription of A.D. 821/823 at Lhasa" (1978).

[159] For an example, see *TCTC*, 244:7898.

This new, stable political order in eastern Eurasia was shattered in 840. After considerable turmoil within the Uyghur state, an Uyghur general defected to the Kirghiz and, leading a huge army of Kirghiz cavalry, attacked the Uyghur cities. The victorious Kirghiz not only took the cities; they also captured and killed the qaghan, seized his golden domed tent,[160] and set fire to Ordubalïq, the capital.[161] The Uyghurs fled in all directions. One group escaped into Qarluq territory to the west. *Mänglig Tegin and others, along with fifteen tribes, turned west and south and settled in the area around Pei-t'ing, Kucha, Agni, and Qocho.[162] The dead qaghan's brothers and other members of the royal family and the court—thirteen tribes in all—led their followers to the Chinese border at the T'ien-te Army, and sought to submit to China on their own terms.[163] Another group fled south to the Tibetans.[164] This collapse of the Uyghur Empire thoroughly destabilized Tibet's northern border. Despite their former good relations with the Tibetans, the Kirghiz were in no position to help stem the tide of displaced Uyghurs, even presuming they wished to do so.

To confound matters further, Tibet now had internal troubles as well. In 842, Khri ʿUʾi dum brtsan, better known as Glaṅ

[160] The Kirghiz qaghan had previously sworn to capture it (*HTS*, 217b:6149; *TCTC*, 246:7947). For a description of this tent, see the account of Tamîm b. Baḥr (Minorsky, 1947-1948:283). So far as I can determine, there is no reason to think that it had been "brought from China along with the Princess of T'ai-ho" (Mackerras, 1972:182-183 [n. 296]). Why would the Chinese strengthen their potentially dangerous neighbors by bestowing symbols of imperial legitimacy upon them? It is worth noting that the Tibetan emperor also had such a tent (Demiéville, 1952:202-203) and that the Arab caliph had the equivalent, the "Heaven Dome" in the famous Qaṣr al-Dhahab, or "Palace of Gold" (Beckwith, 1984b).

[161] *CTS*, 195:5213; *HTS*, 217b:6130; *TCTC*, 246:7947. All sources number the Kirghiz force at "100,000 cavalry."

[162] The name *Mänglig Tegin has been reconstructed by Hamilton, 1955:7 et seq. Cf. Moriyasu, 1977b, on the movement of Uyghurs to the T'ien Shan region.

[163] See the unpublished dissertation by M. Drompp, "The Writings of Li Te-yü as Sources for the History of T'ang–Inner Asian Relations" (1986).

[164] *CTS*, 195:5213; *HTS*, 217b:6131; *TCTC*, 246:7947.

Darma,[165] was assassinated by a Buddhist hermit, Lhaluṅ Dpal-gyi rdorje.[166] The succession was disputed, and central authority rapidly disappeared.[167] In Mdosmad, two generals, *Blon* Guṅ bźer[168] and Žaṅ Pei-pei,[169] fought inconclusive engagements for several years.[170] Žaṅ Pei-pei steadfastly refused to submit to his countryman, declaring "How could I serve this dog-rat?"[171] This internecine warfare countinued unabated, with the more cultured Žaṅ Pei-pei more than holding his own against the fairly brutal *Blon* Guṅ bźer. In 849, *Blon* Guṅ bźer inflicted a serious defeat on Žaṅ Pei-pei's forces near a Tibetan bridge over the Yellow River.[172] Perhaps as a result of this internal turmoil, many forti-fied Tibetan cities and other positions in the area of Ho-hsi sur-rendered or fell to the T'ang in that same year.[173] It seems that even lands further inside the Tibetan Empire's borders were also in an unsettled state. In 850, Žaṅ Pei-pei left Shan *chou* in the hands of a lieutenant, T'o-pa Huai-kuang, and marched to the pastures west of Kan *chou*,[174] perhaps to attack the Uyghurs who

[165] See Bacot et al., 1940:82, 89.

[166] Although the story has been somewhat embellished, it appears to be true, due to corroborative traditions about the later life of Dpalgyi rdorje in Mdosmad.

[167] *HTS*, 216b:6105; *TCTC*, 246:7969-7970. The name of Glaṅ Darma's successor in these Chinese sources, i.e., Ch'i-li-hu, corresponds to Tibetan *Khri 'od, i.e., the (Khri) 'Od sruṅs of the traditional Classical Tibetan sources.

[168] Chinese, K'ung-je. *HTS*, 216b:6105, gives his complete name and ex-plains his title. His surname was Mo (i.e., Dbás) and his given name, Nung-li. Je (Tibetan, *bźer*, "steward") is explained as being "like the Chinese title *lang*." His Tibetan name occurs in the Old Tibetan documents from Tun-huang. For example, see M. Lalou, *Inventaire* (1961) 3:159 (no. 1873, "*blon guṅ–bźer*").

[169] Or Pi-pi. His name appears to have been something like *Byi-byi in Tibetan. Of Žaṅ-źuṅ origin, he was Tibet's Military Governor of Shan *chou*. His surname was Mo-lu (i.e., *'Bro), his given name, Tsan-hsin-ya (i.e., *Rtsan *sum *ña). See *HTS*, 216b:6105.

[170] See Demiéville, 1952:26-27.

[171] *TCTC*, 247:7986-7987.

[172] *HTS*, 216b:6106; *TCTC*, 248:8037.

[173] *TCTC*, 248:8038-8039.

[174] *TCTC*, 249:8043. It is interesting to note that one of Guṅ bźer's cap-

were moving into that area (presumably via the Etsin Gol) at the time.[175] Hearing of his adversary's departure, *Blon* Guṅ bźer led a force of 5,000 light cavalry in pursuit. He got as far as Kua *chou*, but gave up the pursuit and turned back. He then went and mercilessly plundered the prefectures of Shan, K'uo, Kua, Su, Hami, and Qocho, among others.[176]

In the spring of 851, Chang I-ch'ao, the prefect of Tibetan Sha *chou* (Tun-huang), sent a memorial to the T'ang court which described how he had driven the Tibetan general of Sha *chou* out of the city. Having given this evidence of good faith, Chang asked permission to submit to the T'ang. His request was of course granted, and he was given the title of Fang-yü-shih of Sha *chou*.[177] *Blon* Guṅ bźer was now in serious trouble: his people were deserting or defecting, and the T'ang rejected his last-ditch request for an official appointment.[178] By this time, Źaṅ Pei-pei had disappeared from the purview of the Chinese chroniclers, but his former deputy, T'o-pa Huai-kuang, was still receiving defectors from Guṅ bźer. Later in the year, Chang I-ch'ao led a sweeping campaign from Sha *chou* into the neighboring prefectures. By the early winter (tenth month), he had captured the prefectures of Kua, Kan, Su, Lan, Shan, Ho, Min, K'uo, Hami, and Qocho from the Tibetans.[179] The T'ang rewarded him by setting up the

---

tains was a monk, Mang-lo-lin-chen (or *Maṅ ra rin-chen). This makes the document studied by Uray, "Notes on a Tibetan Military Document from Tun-huang" (1961), even more important, since it shows actual implementation of the military service requirement. Cf. the discussion in Beckwith, 1983:11 et seq. Note that T'o-pa was a common clan name among the Tanguts; one may assume that T'o-pa Huai-kuang was by origin a Tangut.

[175] CTS, 195:5215; HTS, 217b:6133; TCTC, 248:8032.

[176] HTS, 216b:6106; TCTC, 248:8044.

[177] TCTC, 249:8044-8045.

[178] HTS, 216b:6106-6107; TCTC, 249:8047. One must still credit him for the sheer audacity of going to the T'ang court to ask!

[179] CTS, 18b:629; HTS, 8:249; TCTC, 249:8048-8049; TFYK, 20:9v-11r (pp. 216-217), 170-23r (p. 2057). The *K'ao-i* quotes from the *Shih-lu* and discusses the chronology of these events (TCTC, 249:8049). It makes clear that all sources agree Chang recaptured Hami (I *chou*) from the Tibetans; those sources that have a complete list include, among the other prefectures, Qocho (Hsi *chou*). In the face of such explicit testimony, and in the absence

Return to Allegiance Army[180] in Sha *chou*, with Chang as the Military Governor. His great success and the forces arrayed behind him, however, made him all but independent of the T'ang.[181]

Khotan also appears to have regained its independence from Tibet in 851.[182] Some twelve years later, Chang I-ch'ao described in a memorial to the T'ang court how, leading 7,000 Chinese and foreign troops, he had recaptured Liang *chou* from the Tibetans.[183] By now, little was left of Tibet's once vast colonial empire. In 866, at about the same time as an upheaval that shook the new Uyghur state in the Tien Shan region,[184] the Tibetan general T'o-pa Huai-kuang entered K'uo *chou*, which apparently had returned to Tibetan control. He captured *Blon* Guṅ bźer alive, executed

---

of any clear evidence that the Uyghurs had been in control of Hami or Qocho in 851, I cannot accept the arguments of Moriyasu, 1981:203–204. Even though Qocho was doubtlessly under strong Uyghur cultural influence at the time, it was located at the Tibetan-Uyghur frontier, and must have changed hands many times. It is hard to believe that it remained in unchallenged Uyghur possession during the half century from 792 to 851 (or 866; see below). Since, as has been shown, disaster struck the Uyghur state two years before the political collapse of Tibet in 842, the Tibetans had a good chance to retake Qocho then, if they had not done so long before. Chinese sources indicate that *Blon* Guṅ bźer raided Hami and Qocho in 850, seemingly because Źaṅ Pei-pei was unable to defend the two prefectures from his depredations. The presence of Uyghurs in Qocho in 851 can indicate any number of things, but the one source that refers to them makes no reference as to how or when they got there. The Chinese sources clearly show that Qocho was captured by Chang I-ch'ao from the Tibetans in 851, and then taken by the Uyghur chief P'u-ku Chün in 866, but from whom is unknown. It may be that P'u-ku Chün did not capture Qocho from the Tibetans, but that does not necessarily mean that he did capture it from Chang I-ch'ao. Indeed, it is quite possible that the Tibetans of Qocho revolted against Chang after his victory. In the final analysis, the sources are so sparse as to leave too much room for speculation on many points.

[180] Chinese, Kuei-i *chün*.

[181] Cf. the discussion in L. Čuguevskiĭ, "Touen-houang du VIIIᵉ au Xᵉ siècle" (1981).

[182] J. Hamilton, "Les règnes khotanais entre 851 et 1001" (1979) 49–50.

[183] *TCTC*, 250:8104, dates this to 863, but *HTS*, 216b:6108, has 861. Liang *chou* generally remained under local Tibetan control, however, until the Tanguts captured it in the eleventh century.

[184] See Moriyasu, 1977b, for details.

him, and then sent the head of his enemy—the last known high-ranking representative of Tibetan imperial power in Central Asia—to Ch'ang-an.[185] Guṅ bźer's remaining followers fled to the city of Ch'in *chou* in China, where they were easily subdued.[186] Of all the Central Asian territory conquered by the once powerful Tibetan Empire, only bits and pieces, such as the Lop Nor region,[187] Liang *chou*, and parts of the Pamirs, remained under local Tibetan control. Soon, they too passed out of the historian's ken, and one epoch of world history gave way to another.

[185] *TCTC*, 250:8115. The other Chinese sources (quoted in Moriyasu, 1977b:119) have condensed the account of these events and, in so doing, have introduced serious errors. It is not possible to accept the story that P'u-ku Chün executed Guṅ bźer, as does Moriyasu, 1981:203.

[186] *TCTC*, 250:8115. They were captured by the Tibetan chief Shang Yen-hsin (i.e., Żaṅ *Yan *sum), who had previously surrendered to the T'ang and received an appointment (*TCTC*, 249:8064-8065).

[187] Uray, 1979a.

TIBET AND
EARLY MEDIEVAL
EURASIA
___ TODAY ___

The Tibetan Empire of the Early Middle Ages was located far
from Western Europe, which was then dominated by the Frankish Carolingians, and it does not appear that either nation knew
of the other's existence.[1] Yet the strange turnings of fate have in-
tertwined the history of early medieval Tibet with that of medi-

---

[1] This chapter is a brief essay rather than a detailed and well-documented
treatise, as it perhaps should be. It assumes general familiarity, which is the
most that I myself can claim, with the broad issues of early medieval European history. Many of the ideas and arguments that I express are derived
from or are parallel to those of other scholars, but it has not been possible to
record my debt to them at every point. My intention has not been to assert a
bold, new theory, but only to debunk some of the more tenacious misconceptions by viewing them from a new perspective. I only hope that I have not
introduced new ones. Many topics have been, unfortunately, left out. One of
them, which is alone worthy of a powerful book, is the subject of "the barbarian." Even today, some of the most respected scholars continue to use the
term "barbarian" when discussing non-"Roman" Western Europeans and
non-Chinese Asians from antiquity through the "High" Middle Ages or the
Renaissance (in East Asia, down to the twentieth century!). In addition, as
will be seen, I prefer to emphasize the unity of, and continuity within, the
early medieval period. (See note 5.)

eval Europe. Much like the Frankish Empire, the Tibetan Empire is not generally considered to have been highly cultured, as certain other Eurasian states of the time supposedly were. If these two empires are ever credited with achieving anything remarkable—even by A.D. 800—it is the political unification of vast regions, the kind of accomplishment expected of militarily oriented "barbarians."[2] This view, which the Belgian historian Henri Pirenne developed theoretically, has long been deeply embedded in the European historiographical tradition. In this century, it has received encouragement from the political propaganda which continues to describe the social system of Tibet as it was before the Chinese invasion of 1950 as "feudal" or "medieval." By logical extension, therefore, early medieval Tibet is supposed to have been "primitive," or at least as backward as contemporaneous Western Europe allegedly was.[3]

[2] For a comparison of Franks and Tibetans, see Snellgrove and Richardson (1968) 16. For one view of the Franks, see J. Wallace-Hadrill, "Frankish Gaul" (1970) 44: "The significant domestic achievement of the early Carolingians was the reduction of the Roman Midi, a world of which the Frank had hitherto had only occasional direct experience." The traditional Tibetan historians' conceit of viewing early Tibetan history negatively has, with few exceptions, been taken literally by most modern historians of Tibet.

[3] For a convenient summary of Pirenne's theory, see his *Medieval Cities* (1956) passim. According to him the unified urban culture of the Roman "Mediterranean Commonwealth" was the most admirable development—in his *Mohammed and Charlemagne* (1954) 17, he calls it "that wonderful human structure, the Roman Empire"—in human history up to that time. He argues that it continued to exist, despite the Germanic migrations, until the Islamic conquest of the Middle East, North Africa, and Spain. This event effectively blocked commerce between Western Europe and the rest of the civilized world, and, as a result, it reverted to a marginal, rural, illiterate existence. The coronation of Charlemagne as Holy Roman Emperor in A.D. 800 formally signalled the beginning of the feudal Middle Ages in Western Europe (Pirenne, 1954:232-235). The view of early medieval Europe as backward relative to the rest of the world—by no means original with Pirenne, of course—is ultimately based on the idea that Europe had declined since the golden age of Rome. It is so firmly entrenched that it constantly affects medievalists' comparative views of other areas, including Tibet.

Another important result of Pirenne's thesis has been its impact on contemporary historiography, most importantly through the works of Fernand

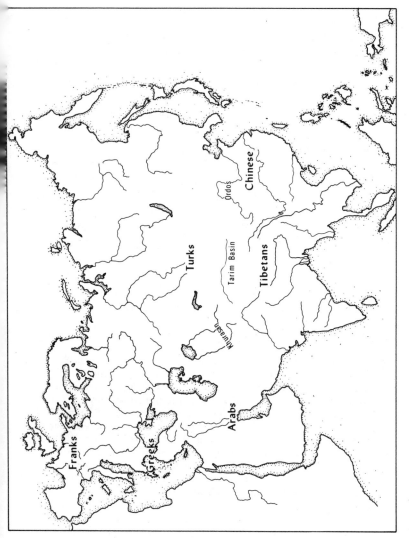

II. Early Medieval Eurasia

A result of this peculiar attitude has been the imposition of rather unexpected interpretations on early medieval Tibetan, Islamic, Turkic, and Chinese history. These are all vast fields of study in their own right, and there are certainly enough problems in each of them to keep historians busy for centuries, but it would seem desirable to search for a view of the Early Middle Ages that dispels the gloom currently pervading the field. What, if anything, did the great states of early medieval Eurasia have in common, and why? How can we justify the rejection of a centuries-old view about perhaps the most crucial period of Western European history?

It has long ago been noted that the classical age in the West was contemporaneous, and in many ways comparable, with the classical age in the East; moreover, both ended in a similar fashion during the age of the great *Völkerwanderung*.[4] The following period should be viewed from a similar perspective. Thus, in the early seventh century, Eurasia became divided among several great empires, all of which collapsed politically—or, in the case of the Byzantine Empire, underwent revolutionary change—in the middle of the ninth century.[5] This period of about two

---

Braudel, author of the famous *La Méditerranée et le Monde Méditerranéen à l'époque de Philippe II* and cofounder of the influential *Annales* school of historiography. In this book, Braudel takes Pirenne's theories about the unity imparted by and the importance of the Mediterranean and applies them to the period immediately following the end of the Middle Ages. For a critique, see S. Kinser, "*Annaliste* Paradigm? The Geohistorical Structuralism of Fernand Braudel" (1981) 77. Despite this and other recent criticism (p. 64 [n. 5]), the prestige of the *Annales* school has given new life and influence to the Pirenne Thesis, which consequently is less and less criticized. As a result, many scholars who have not taken part in the controversy, or are even unaware of its existence, have subscribed to Pirenne's views or have accepted his premises without questioning them.

[4] For a recent statement of this theory, see R. Lopez, *The Birth of Europe* (1967) 26-30.

[5] Ibid., p. 108 et seq. The Greeks, who finally rejected iconoclasm in 843, soon recovered from two centuries of internal heterodox-orthodox strife, economic difficulties, and military losses. (See G. Ostrogorsky, *History of the Byzantine State* [1957] 195 et seq.) On the critically important shift of the

hundred years is what has been called the Early Middle Ages in this book.[6]

The human network which extended itself over the Eurasian continent (and neighboring areas such as North Africa) during the Early Middle Ages, and which brought about a civilization

---

trade routes between northern Europe and the Middle East in the 830s, see A. Lewis, *The Northern Seas* (1958) 216-218, 249-250, and especially T. Noonan, "What Does Historical Numismatics Suggest about the History of Khazaria in the Tenth Century?" (1983). As I discuss below, the middle of the eighth century also constituted a great watershed in world history, a change which in some respects was already recognized at the time. The great revolutions which wracked these early medieval empires were strangely similar: they were in all cases (except perhaps that of the Khazars) both political and cultural; they happened within the short period of thirteen years; and they were all connected with international trade or traders. Notwithstanding these revolutions, the newer empires of the Franks, Arabs, and Tibetans continued to expand into Central Eurasia until the end of the eighth century.

[6] Periodization must be of some importance to all historians, for without this tool they cannot practice their profession. To medievalists, however, it is of fundamental importance, for even the name of medieval studies could hardly exist without it. The current, nearly universal disdain for serious periodization is the means by which those who would avoid the great issues of medieval history are sheltered; imprecision thus flourishes unabated. The sixth-century descriptions of Gregory of Tours, for example, are nonchalantly applied to the eighth or ninth century, while Emperor Yang-ti of the Sui dynasty is compared to Charlemagne, who lived two centuries later (see A. Wright, *The Sui Dynasty* [1980] 9-12). The postwar boom of social-scientific theories and methods has had an overwhelming effect on historiography; old problems, such as issues of periodization, have been buried alive. Ironically, this has occurred just as the rapid growth of Oriental studies has rendered the solution of the old problems even more important and the quest for the solutions even more vital than ever before. The richness of Oriental source material that has emerged is one of the brightest spots in recent historical scholarship. It is particularly unfortunate that, with most of the important surviving sources for early medieval Islamic, Tibetan, and Chinese history now fairly easily available, Western scholars have abandoned the ideal of writing a synoptic history of the Old World. It is as if a paleontologist discovered a fossil that was the long-sought "missing link" in the evolution of a species only to find that other paleontologists were not interested in evolution any more. One would like to think that the controversy aroused by the Pirenne Thesis represents a flicker of hope in the field, but it is not very promising. Despite the vast and detailed criticism of the Thesis in the fifty

with many common features, depended upon a complex system of trade routes. By the mid-sixth century, there had been a perceptible increase in international trade,[7] which was solidly based on routes in use since the late classical period. In addition, a degree of political centralization unknown since classical times, perhaps, was responsible for the number of new routes which were pioneered at this time. The momentous changes of the mid-seventh through the mid-ninth centuries, however, most likely resulted from another factor.

In the middle of the sixth century, the steppe—the barometer of Eurasia—forecast the future. The revolt of a people who called themselves *Türk bodun*, "the Turk people," overthrew the obscure qaghanate of the Jou-jan, a Mongolic people identified with or related to the Avars, who had controlled the eastern steppe for nearly a hundred years. With terrible swiftness, these Turks chased their surviving former overlords across the length and breadth of Inner Asia—as far, in fact, as the borders of the Chinese, Persian, and Graeco-Roman worlds. In the space of a single generation, the Turks built a vast empire of their own, which covered nearly the entire Eurasian steppe and impinged on the borders of all of the great Old World civilizations, including the Central Asian city-states and India. The Turks made it their first order of business to inform their neighbors to the east and west that they were vitally interested in trade.[8] When the Turks

years since Pirenne's death, no one has ever seriously questioned its basic premises or those of most other historians of the Early Middle Ages. In his book, *The Origins of the Middle Ages* (1972), Bryce Lyon conscientiously reviews all of the critical literature dealing with the theory. After this examination of criticism that makes one wonder how anyone could take Pirenne seriously any more, Lyon concludes that "Pirenne's theory has by no means been completely discredited. His grand tableau of the early Middle Ages has actually been little changed. . . . Some historians have found Pirenne deficient in his analysis of the evidence, but most, except perhaps classical historians, admit that his large picture or synthesis has credibility" (pp. 82-83).

[7] Lewis, 1958:110 et seq.

[8] See D. Sinor, *Inner Asia* (1971) 102, 104-106. The sources are explicit: "[Under T'u-men/Bumïn Qaghan,] they began to come to the border to trade in silk fabrics and remnants, and wanted to open relations with China" (*CS*, 50:908).

annexed most of the Central Asian city-states—great centers for the east-west and north-south caravan trade—in the second half of the sixth century, they also removed the political obstacles to relatively high-volume transcontinental trade.

The scanty historical records do no provide much explicit information on significant results of the Turkish expansion, but there is no doubt that it directly stimulated international trade. Although both the Greek and the Chinese sources remark on the Turks' interest in trade from the outset, modern historians have not paid this much serious attention. Medieval chroniclers recognized that the Turks opened relations with the Persians in order to participate more fully in the Silk Road trade,[9] from which they wanted a bigger share of the profits. Like the Northmen of Europe, the Turks valued commerce enough to risk warfare to defend or expand their interests. The Turkic Empire split almost immediately between the Eastern Turks, who were centered in the area of present-day Mongolia, and the Western Turks, who were centered in the area of present-day Kirgizia west of the Issyk Kul. Other important Turkic peoples were the Khazars of the Pontic Steppe and the Bulgars of the eastern Balkans. However divided the Turks were, that the silk routes remained in the hands of a people interested as much in trade as in warfare was of great import to the countries at the extremities of the trade routes as well as to those in between.

The Turks' great interest in commerce did not mean that they dominated it; they were its patrons. Most of the international trade during the Early Middle Ages was in the hands of others. These were generally not Greeks, Chinese, or, as European medievalists are fond of pointing out, Franks. Individual merchants from the peripheral Eurasian states rarely traveled far on the Silk Road since direct transcontinental trade was almost totally monopolized by two or three great trading peoples: the Jews, the Norsemen, and the Sogdians. In the West, Jewish and Nordic merchants apparently operated, respectively, from western Cen-

[9] Sinor, 1971:104-105.

tral Asia (Khazaria and northern Persia) to the Atlantic[10] and from the Black and Caspian Seas to the Baltic and North Seas. The Sogdians seem to have worked the routes from eastern Central Asia (Sogdiana and the northeastern marches of Persia) to the Pacific.[11] These peoples kept their trade secrets to themselves, so little direct information on transcontinental trade is available. Enough is known, however, to allow scholars to paint a reasonably accurate picture of it. Edward Schafer's *Golden Peaches of Samarkand*, Guy Le Strange's *Lands of the Eastern Caliphate*, and Archibald Lewis's *Northern Seas*[12] together provide a fascinating glimpse of commercial life in China, Central Eurasia, and the West during the Early Middle Ages.

The profits from this trade in silk, spices, perfumes, war materiel, horses, and other products stimulated not only imperialism, but also local industry and local trade.[13] Consonant with the spread of commerce, which was nurtured by the locus of the transaction, the city, was the spread of literacy and "civilization," the culture of cities. By the end of the seventh century, nearly all of settled Eurasia had become literate. Not everyone was a reader, of course, but writing systems had been adopted in every nation-state: those who needed to do so could read and write. Ironically, one of the major proofs most commonly adduced for the supposed decline of civilization in Frankish Western Europe is that, under the Merovingians and early Carolingians, Latin was written in a corrupted form. What was written, however, was simply

[10] Jewish merchants also traded by sea to India and, perhaps, to southern China. See M. Gil, "The Rādhānite Merchants and the Land of Rādhān" (1974), and, on the period from the eleventh century on, S. Goitein, *Letters of Medieval Jewish Traders* (1973).

[11] The Sogdians also traded at least as far south as Kashmir and Ladakh. Since many of the Sogdians were Nestorian Christians, one wonders if they did not trade much further to the West as well. (See Uray, "Tibet's Connections with Nestorianism and Manicheism in the 8th-10th Centuries" [1983].) I have unfortunately had to leave southern Asia largely out of the discussion due to my only rudimentary knowledge of the region.

[12] See the important article by Noonan (1983) on trade in southeastern Europe, with special attention to Khazaria. Le Strange (1966) deals with the later medieval period as well.

[13] See especially Lewis, 1958:110 et seq.

the modern literary language of the day, which was related to the language that would soon become Old French. As may be inferred from the remarks of Gregory of Tours,[14] this language had its own standards of correctness just as modern literary English has a standard different from Old English or Middle English. No one would argue nowadays that French is merely a corrupt and debased form of Old French or Vulgar Latin. No one would assert that Classical Arabic, which is based on the Old Arabic of the Koran, is merely a corrupt form of Ancient Arabic or Babylonian. It therefore seems untenable to suggest that the kind of language written in the early medieval Frankish kingdom is any indication of the country's cultural "decay" from some imaginary classical literary age of Western (as opposed to Mediterranean) Europe.[15] On the contrary, that so much was written in "Current Latin" as well as in Classical Latin in northwestern Europe at the time is proof of the cultural advances then being made among a people that had been, not long before, quite illiterate. Comparable to the presumption of early medieval Frankish illiteracy is the frequent use of the term "pre-classical Tibetan" for the written form of early medieval Tibetan instead of the unbiased and more significant term "Old Tibetan." Conversely, it is widely assumed, though without much justification, that a majority of the inhabitants of the contemporaneous Muslim world were highly literate. The prevalent scholarly view is truly perverse: one of the

[14] See L. Thorpe, trans., *Gregory of Tours: The History of the Franks* (1974) 38-40, 63.

[15] On Western Europe's "decay," see below. Another important justification for this theory is the relative paucity of primary sources concerned with history from this period. Because the ancients wrote more about history than the writers of the Middle Ages, who preferred religious subjects, it seems to have been concluded that early medieval Europeans were basically unable to write history or that the few medieval histories that have survived do not deserve serious consideration. In his *Medieval Technology and Social Change* (1976), Lynn White, Jr., aptly observes "If historians are to attempt to write the history of mankind, and not simply the history of mankind as it was viewed by the small and specialized segments of our race which have had the habit of scribbling, they must take a fresh view of the records, ask new questions of them, and use all the resources of archaeology, iconography, and etymology to find answers when no answers can be discovered in contemporary writings" (p. v).

most remarkable things about the age was precisely its achievement in the field of literacy.

A new characterization of the Early Middle Ages should be based on the accomplishments of the period rather than just its shortcomings. Antiquity, for example, has long been admired for its Aristotle, Buddha, and Confucius, not for its slave economy, institutionalized public brutality, and other negative features, which should of course be studied as well. It is time for similar treatment of the early medieval period. Historians' negative preconceptions about the Early Middle Ages are not limited to the topics adopted from Pirenne and his successors. Such views pervade every major subdivision of medieval studies, from musicology and the history of technology to Insular art and literature. Ironically, specialists usually see in the period the revolutionary developments in their own subfield, but no other. This contrast between the specialized works and the synoptic accounts remains one of the great paradoxes of medieval studies.

The composition of a balanced, synthetic history of culture in early medieval Europe is naturally best left to a "Europeanist." It may, however, be a long time before such a work is written. For the present, an outsider's view will have to serve; it may indeed provide some new or, at least, entertaining insights. In what follows, several major topics of early medieval studies are examined from an internationalist point of view in order to demonstrate the essential international unity—in particular, the inseparability of Western Europe and Tibet from the rest of Eurasia—of that epoch.

Learning and Literary Activity

During the reign of Charlemagne (768-814), there began a literary movement which encouraged the transmission of the Latin literary heritage to the Frankish kingdom. This literary renaissance peaked about 850 and passed by the end of the century. Among the many respectable thinkers involved in this movement, perhaps the most famous was the philosopher-theologian John Scotus Eriugena. The legacy of this movement was not only the basis for much of subsequent medieval European literature, but also the preservation of a great deal of the Classical Latin literature that has survived to the present day.

Harun al-Rashid, Charlemagne's Arab contemporary and ally, also presided over a literary efflorescence, different only in that it necessarily included translation into Arabic. In the beginning, translators concentrated on works in Syriac, a closely related tongue, and some in Sanskrit. Later, during the reign of Harun's son al-Ma'mûn, a large number of works were translated directly from the Greek. This movement also peaked during the mid-ninth century, and produced one great Arab philosopher, al-Kindî, a contemporary of Eriugena and, one might add, his equal in the depth and breadth of his learning.[16]

A great literary movement also began under the Buddhist emperor Khri sroṅ lde brtsan, the Tibetan contemporary and adversary of Harun and Charlemagne. During his reign, a huge number of Sanskrit works (and some Central Asian and Chinese texts) entered Tibetan culture. Translated into Tibetan, these works formed the foundation of Tibetan Buddhist civilization. Much more work obviously needs to be done in this field before wide-ranging assessments can be made, but it seems clear that, by 840, Franks, Arabs, and Tibetans had embarked upon intellectual movements with similar values and objectives. In terms of level and extent of scholastic learning, it seems that they roughly equaled both each other and the early medieval Greeks and Chinese.

Architecture

It is often said that Aachen, the Frankish capital under Charlemagne and his son Louis the Pious, was pitifully insignificant[17]

---

[16] It is incorrect to assume that most of the translation was done by 840, when the great translators were actually just beginning their work. (For precise dating, see F. Sezgin's monumental *Geschichte des arabischen Schrifttums* [1967–].) In fact, almost every one of the great thinkers (the greatest of whom were nearly all Central Asians) who emerged from the Muslim world—including Avicenna, Alfraganus, Algazel, and others—lived long after this period. Al-Khwârizmî (Algorismus, d. 850) was the sole exception.

[17] Even R. Sullivan's synoptic *Aix-la-Chapelle in the Age of Charlemagne* (1963) takes this position.

compared to Baghdad, the splendid Abbasid capital, which was
built at about the same time. Although practically nothing is yet
known about its early medieval form, the Tibetan capital, Rasa,[18]
is similarly denigrated. It seems generally acepted that, because
the caliphate and, even more so, T'ang China were more populous (and thus their cities were larger[19]) they were therefore more
advanced than Western Europe and Tibet. It would be, perhaps,
far more relevant to compare the important politico-religious
monuments erected by these nations rather than the sheer bulk of
their populations. It is in such structures that the achievements of
a culture are given physical expression. The beautiful palace
chapel in Aachen, which was finished about 798 and is the most
famous surviving example of Carolingian architecture, is considered puny in comparison to the Late Classical Hagia Sophia in
Constantinople or the wonderful architecture of Baghdad in the
days of Harun al-Rashid. (One may assume that the *vihâra* of Sa-
mye, which was built at the same time near the Tibetan imperial
precinct at Brag-mar, has been similarly disparaged.) This comparison might seem impossible to disprove since the original City
of Peace, which was finished in 763, disappeared long ago. The
Mosque of Ibn Ṭūlūn in Cairo, however, was most probably
modeled directly on the congregational mosque that once stood
in the center of the City of Peace.[20] Built in the mid-ninth century
of stone rather than Mesopotamian brick, the Cairo mosque is indeed beautiful—as was, by all reports, its prototype. But significantly, neither this nor any other early Abbasid structure, including famous caliphal palaces such as the Qaṣr al-Dhahab (Palace of
Gold) in the City of Peace, possessed nearly as much unob-
structed interior space as the chapel at Aachen. Also, none seem
to have been significantly taller. Contemporary reports about
Baghdad remark on the great height of the Qaṣr al-Dhahab's cen-

[18] The usual Old Tibetan name was Rasa, but there was an earlier name
which is unknown. It could conceivably have been Lhasa, the later medieval
and modern name.

[19] See J. Lassner, *The Topography of Baghdad in the Early Middle Ages* (1970)
155-168, 178-183.

[20] Beckwith (1984b).

tral dome, but it was apparently no more than 130 feet tall. Ironically, the great City of Peace itself was constructed almost entirely of mud.[21]

Technology

Since the publication of Lynn White's *Medieval Technology and Social Change*, medievalists have become aware of the rapid technological[22] progress in Western Europe during the eighth and ninth centuries. The Arabs at that time are not known to have yet made any striking technological advances, but they appear to have been at least on an equal level with the Byzantine Greeks, who were probably on a par with the T'ang Chinese. Despite an article by White,[23] the astonishingly high level of Tibetan technology during this period remains little known. In addition to Chinese reports about amazing golden automata and other Tibetan manufactured items, both Arabic and Chinese sources remark on the workmanship of Tibetan armor, which is said to have been so fine that it was impenetrable.[24] There is hardly any basis for criticizing either the level or the quality of technology in

[21] Ibid. Cf. Lassner, 1970:52-53. The apex of the dome, which spanned 20 cubits (about 30 feet), was eighty cubits (about 130 feet) from the ground. (On the cubit in Islam, see W. Hinz, "Dhirāʿ," *E.I.2*, 2:231-232.) The height of the chapel tower seems to have been approximately the same as the Qaṣr al-Dhahab, but the main dome of the octagon is nearly twice as broad; it now stands about 118 feet high. See F. Kreusch, "Kirche, Atrium und Portikus der Aachener Pfalz" (1965) and L. Hugot, "Die Pfalz Karls des Grossen in Aachen" (1965) 562.

[22] Distinguished from "technology," "science" is a word that by etymology and intention includes metaphysics, history, and many other areas of intellectual endeavor, not just "hard sciences" like physics and chemistry. (The Italian cognate still has this meaning, as does the German calque, *Wissenschaft*.) The normal, unqualified usage of "science" in modern English, however, makes it inappropriate for the present discussion.

[23] Lynn White, Jr., "Tibet, India and Malaya as Sources of Western Mediaeval Technology" (1960).

[24] See above, Chapter Six. Even more astonishing is the quantity of armor manufactured, since it is said that soldiers were clothed in it from head to foot, with only two openings for the eyes, and war horses were also covered.

the young empires of Eurasia during the two centuries before A.D. 840.

Economy

One of Pirenne's most crucial points, that Western Europe reverted to a primitive, rural, subsistence economy with little use for money, has been frequently disproven. Strangely, many medievalists continue to believe in this theory and attempt to carry it further. More specifically, it is still nearly universally agreed that the cessation of the minting of gold coins in the eighth century and the loss of the state minting monopoly (while the Islamic caliphate supposedly kept both) unequivocally demonstrate that Western Europe was economically more backward than the East. The rise of European feudalism, this theory continues, was therefore the result of the decline of commercial life.[25] Today there are

[25] Whatever decline of urban life occurred in northwestern Europe, it took place during the late classical period, long before the coming of Islam. It was thus a function of the problems of late classical civilization. By early medieval times, these changes were ancient history. It would be difficult, in any event, to demonstrate that classical Roman cities, in which a large percentage of the land was devoted to ceremonial edifices, government buildings, and palaces, were any more viable commercially than early medieval cities. The ancient Roman cities may appear to have been like the ceremonial-governmental centers of our own modern cities, and their citizens may have enjoyed urban luxuries such as theaters and public baths, but one must ask if these ancient cities were really centers of commercial life. In fact, most were creations of the Roman government, just like the military camps and the military roads that connected them all to Rome. It would thus appear to be no coincidence that many of them disappeared when the Roman government collapsed and the subsidies ended.

It is also misleading to compare arbitary figures from the total area of an urban complex like Baghdad with the contemporary walled Chinese capital Ch'ang-an, or with Constantinople or Aachen. It is almost impossible to determine precisely where early medieval Baghdad was, not to speak of what it was. (See Lassner, 1970:155-168, 178-183.) Even a cursory glance at a plan of Ch'ang-an will reveal the extent to which its vast area—much of it totally deserted—was occupied by palaces and religious establishments. (See the discussion by Arthur Wright in CHC, 3:79-80.) The main reason for the differences in gross size (a quantitative, not a qualitative, difference) was the great

few medievalists who would argue that Western Europe was not economically backward at this time.[26]

But, far from having abandoned coinage, the Carolingians were quite interested in it. Their new silver deniers, which they struck in great quantities, were a departure from past Western coinage and became models for future coinage throughout northwestern Europe. In fact, already in the seventh century silver was becoming the dominant medium of exchange.[27] It is, moreover, well known that the great hoards of Islamic coins of this period that have been found in Russia, Finland, and Scandinavia are of silver pieces.[28] Although the distinguished British numismatist Philip Grierson thinks that the presence of coin hoards and literary references to coinage and commerce do not prove the existence of commerce using such coinage,[29] it is common knowledge among economic historians of Islam that silver, not gold, was the standard coinage of the caliphate during this period. Gold dinars were indeed struck and circulated in the old Roman provinces of the Levant, where trade with the Byzantine Empire (including parts of Italy) was still relatively active. In Muslim Spain and North Africa, however, the coinage was silver, as it was in Persia, Central Asia, and India.[30] Moreover, although silver and gold were almost never coined in Tibet and China before modern times, standardized silver bullion was widely used for commer-

---

disparity between the population of North China and the populations of the Arab caliphate, the shrunken Byzantine Empire, and the rapidly expanding but sparsely populated Frankish and Tibetan empires.

[26] Archibald Lewis is the notable exception among the synoptic historians, although even he does not really argue against this dogma. See Lewis, 1958:179 et seq.

[27] Lewis, 1958:131-134, 179-180; P. Grierson, "Money and Coinage under Charlemagne" (1966).

[28] Lewis, 1958:214 et seq. Gold pieces are extremely rare. The Rus merchants insisted on payment in silver dirhams. Cf. Noonan, 1983:266 et seq.

[29] In his "Commerce in the Dark Ages" (1959), Grierson attempts to explain away the evidence and to use select elements of it to support the theory of an economically moribund "Dark Ages."

[30] E. Ashtor, *A Social and Economic History of the Near East in the Middle Ages* (1976) 83; cf. Beckwith 1977b:103.

cial purposes in these states during the Early Middle Ages.[31] According to Grierson, the reason for this predominance of silver coinage in Western Europe, gold coinage in the Byzantine Empire, and both among the Islamic states, was the value of gold relative to silver in each of these areas. This difference of valuation caused gold to flow east and silver west. Grierson concludes that the adoption of the silver denier by the Franks was a sign of economic recovery.[32]

But Grierson merely creates an answer to solve a created problem—that Western Europe was economically depressed. A more cogent explanation is that the Franks simply adopted the coinage which was most useful for *international* commerce, for the entire civilized world of the Early Middle Ages was in fact on a silver standard. Gold was a valuable commodity, but unimportant as coinage. The rapid economic growth of northern Gaul and the Baltic and North Sea areas, the early hoards of silver dirhams discovered among the trade route from the Islamic world via the Caucausus, Russia, and the Gulf of Bothnia to Scandinavia (and the shift northeastward of this route during the 830s), together with source references to Scandinavian Rus merchants using the route during this period, indicate that northwestern Europeans actively participated in money-based international trade.[33]

In contrast, the Byzantine Empire, hurt by religious controversy, civil war, and the loss of much territory, had *at that time* far less economic power than most historians ascribe to it. Indeed, contrary to the usual glowing picture, one should characterize the economic conditions of early medieval Byzantium as profoundly depressed.[34] The early medieval Greeks are the ones who should

[31] This was so despite an apparent abundance of gold, especially in Tibet. D. Twitchett, *Financial Administration under the T'ang Dynasty* (1970) 71; Beckwith, 1977b:99. On the nonmonetary nature of gold in the Frankish kingdom, see Lewis, 1958:227.

[32] Grierson, "The Monetary Reforms of 'Abd al-Malik" (1960) 242-264. Silver coins had, of course, been minted in Gaul for centuries. The Carolingian denier was only a new *type* of silver coin.

[33] Noonan, 1983:266.

[34] Lewis, 1958:226-227, misses this point and so reaches incorrect conclusions.

be suspected of economic backwardness, not the Franks. That the Frankish government was unable to completely suppress widespread private minting and counterfeiting only shows that, like T'ang China in the same period, the economy was growing faster than coins could be produced by the state.[35] And although payment in kind was doubtlessly common in the Frankish kingdom, it is known to have been extremely common—to the point of being institutionalized by the state—in both the Islamic[36] and Chinese[37] empires as well. Insofar as money is concerned, then, early medieval Western Europe was in no way economically backward for its day.

One of the most problematic conclusions drawn by Pirenne and other historians of his school about the economy of the Early Middle Ages in Western Europe is that its international trade, although not completely nonexistent, was overwhelmingly concerned with such economically irrelevant luxury goods as slaves, armor and armaments, silks and other expensive fabrics, and spices and perfumes. In other words, they say, the major trade was in items that were valuable individually or in relatively small quantities rather than in items that were valuable only in huge quantities, such as wheat or lumber. Therefore, they conclude, this trade was an unimportant stimulus to local economic development. This is a specious argument.[38] The relative importance

[35] Twitchett, 1970:66, 70, 74-76, 79.

[36] Ashtor, 1976:38-42. See also his remarks on the condition of the serfs, as the land-bound "peasants" he refers to could be called (p. 67 et seq.). Nothing, however, should mislead one into thinking that the Middle East was then anything but overwhelmingly agricultural.

[37] Twitchett, 1970:70-71, 78, 80-81.

[38] Grierson, 1959:126-127, quotes R. Southern, *The Making of the Middle Ages* (1953), in support of this view: ". . . it was to satisfy this taste that merchants travelled, sailors perished, bankers created credit and peasants raised the numbers of their sheep. As so often happens, the secondary effects are of more interest than the primary ones: . . . the activities and organization which existed to satisfy the demands of the relatively few coloured the whole history of the Middle Ages, and are the foundation of modern commerce and industry" (1959 ed., p. 42). What is most surprising is that, although this quotation might support the argument of the paragraph in Grierson in which it appears (about distinguishing between "the mutual buying and selling of

of any commerce must be judged by its total value, as measured by money exchanged, not by some moralistic idea of what that commerce should consist of, such as simple items for the good peasantry, but weapons and other extravagances for the bad nobility. Unfortunately, it is impossible to determine the dollar value of early medieval commerce anywhere in the world, since practically no reliable statistics survive. The related *a priori* argument—that, because "true" commerce did not exist, the *mercatores* of Aachen could only have been servants who ministered to the subsistence needs of the Carolingian court—is therefore difficult to justify.[39]

Finally, the apparent decline of southwestern Gaul from the end of the seventh century, about which Pirenne and his followers have argued at length, was paralleled by the rapid economic and cultural growth of northern Europe. The strange economic self-isolation of the Byzantine Empire, which it caused by practicing late-Roman, authoritarian policies of controlling or eliminating Mediterranean trade, would seem to indicate the solution of the

surplus farm produce or peasant handicrafts . . . from . . . the activities of the *mercatores*"), it is clearly a strong statement against Grierson's main point, the supposed backwardness of Western Europe's economy. His subsequent argument, that what has been called early medieval economic activity was merely theft, extortion, or gift-giving, is nonsense. (Would the Norse have turned up their noses at gold coins had they obtained them solely by such methods?) No age has had a monopoly on such activities, which are always of greater interest to chroniclers than is ordinary commerce. Grierson fails to discredit the careful work of generations of medievalists from Alfons Dopsch to A. R. Lewis (Grierson, 1959:124, 130). On his theory that the Vikings—which must include the Rus, although he does not mention them—were only thieves, and that the Scandinavian coin hoards were simply the product of Viking raids or exploitation, see T. Noonan, "Did the Khazars Possess a Monetary Economy?" (1982).

[39] See also B. Bachrach, *Early Medieval Jewish Policy in Western Europe* (1977) 166 [n. 22]. The argument that new trading centers such as Quentovic and Duurstede were not "true" cities because they were constructed largely of impermanent wooden buildings is simply nonsense. Acceptance of such an argument means denying that the T'ang Chinese had cities, since, as in Japan until the present century, almost all of their buildings were constructed of wood. Likewise, most Islamic cities were built rapidly and almost entirely out of mud.

problem. In response to this Byzantine restrictiveness, east-west trade routes had shifted to the north, and partly to the south, of the Mediterranean basin, which remained almost entirely under Byzantine control until the middle of the ninth century.[40] Pirenne's discovery of the mysterious "shift of Europe's focus" northward thus itself disproves his economic theory about European isolation and, by extension, his conclusion about the origins of medieval civilization in the West.

Political Activity

One condition often adduced to demonstrate the backwardness of Europe during the Early Middle Ages was the apparent inability of the central government to exercise its authority in the provinces without frequent rebellions that required the constant attention of the sovereign himself. Thus the Frankish king continually traveled about his domain, presumably just to hold it together, and personally led his army on campaigns against both external and internal enemies. Charlemagne's restless peregrinations are contrasted with the supposedly untroubled reign of Harun al-Rashid. Islamicists, however, are aware that the Arabs campaigned annually against "the tyrant"—the Byzantine emperor—and that these campaigns, as well as the annual pilgrimage to Mecca, were often led by the caliph. Harun had to move around for other reasons as well, including the pacification of problem areas and the struggle against foes both outside and inside of his empire.[41] Indeed, most other early medieval rulers—Tibetans,

[40] Notably, trade in the Byzantine Empire did not begin to recover until the blockage and subsequent shift to the northeast of the Baltic-Caspian trade routes in the mid-ninth century. International trade had long been bypassing the troublesome Byzantine Greeks (see Lewis, 1958:226-229, 249-250), and this in itself would have contributed to the shrinkage of the Mediterranean trade. The insignificant economic development of the southerly parts of the Frankish Empire in comparison to the north would seem to indicate that trade with the Byzantine Empire was far less important to the Frankish economy than was the northern trade, which had largely bypassed the Greeks.

[41] As described above, he died on a campaign to quell a rebellion in Central Asia.

Turks, Byzantine Greeks, as well as Chinese—had to do the same, especially early in their careers when they were energetic but not so firmly on the throne.[42]

The establishment of the Carolingian dynasty by Pippin the Short in 751 can be considered most significant with respect to Western European isolation, or the absence thereof. Although commonly accepted to have occurred during an economic depression in Europe, this event is thought to have been unrelated to contemporary Eurasian affairs. But it is a curious fact that, unlike the preceding and following centuries, the middle of the eighth century—specifically the period from 742 to 755—saw fundamental changes, usually signaled by successful political revolts, in every Eurasian empire. Most famous among them are the Carolingian, Abbasid, Uyghur Turkic, and anti-T'ang rebellions, each of which is rightly considered to have been a major watershed in the respective national histories. Significantly, all seem to have been intimately connected with Central Eurasia.[43] The Abbasid revolution, for example, began in 747 in Marw, a Central Asian trading city with a large Sogdian population; it resulted in the caliphate coming under strong Central Asian influence.[44] The Uyghur Turks, who rebelled against their *Arśīla Turk masters in 742, were completely dominated by the Sogdians, to the point of being converted to Sogdian Manicheism in 763 and eventually adopting the Sogdian writing system. And An Lu-shan, the Inner Asian leader of the great rebellion that nearly

---

[42] Significantly, unlike many of the Byzantine and Chinese emperors, none of the Carolingian monarchs until after Louis the Pious (d. 840) suffered violent deaths or were fatally poisoned. Moreover, despite frequent uprisings, the horrendous purges and internal rebellions that shook the Byzantine world throughout the Early Middle Ages and the cataclysmic rebellions in China (particularly from 755 on) have no parallel in the unified Frankish kingdom under the Carolingians.

[43] The Tibetan revolt, as previously mentioned, was ultimately tied to a Central Asian source. (See Beckwith, 1983.) That the Carolingian revolt occurred during an economic depression and a worldwide political crisis would seem to support the idea that international relations were of fundamental importance to early medieval Western Europe.

[44] See the discussion in Beckwith, 1984a.

overthrew the T'ang dynasty—and totally changed T'ang China—was half-Sogdian and half-Turkic in origin. The much-discussed conversion of the Khazars to Judaism in the 740s and the important role of Jews (as examined by Bernard Bachrach[45] and others[46]) and of the Nordic-Slavic trade for the Carolingians are significant trends in themselves. But when combined with what is well known about the other great states of the Early Middle Ages, they impel one to believe that the occurrence of the revolution—"the Carolingian Renaissance"—in mid-eighth-century Western Europe was not coincidental.

The importance of the international trade routes through Central Eurasia cannot be overemphasized. All of the great early medieval powers bordered on and had intimate political and military involvement in that vast region, and the newer powers, the Frankish, Arab, and Tibetan empires, expanded deep into it. Indeed, in the opinion of Charlemagne's biographer Einhard, the emperor's greatest military accomplishment after his conquest of the Saxons[47] was his triumph over the Avars, a once-powerful Inner Asian people that had lived in Pannonia for centuries.[48] Similarly, even a cursory examination of the major Arabic and Chinese sources for the period (Ṭabarî and Ssu-ma Kuang, respectively) reveals that Central Eurasia was the overwhelming focus of Arab and Chinese foreign policy and the source of strong cultural influences on them. There should be little doubt that Central Eurasia was a most influential factor in the history of the early medieval empires.[49] Scholars of earlier generations had

[45] Bachrach, 1977.

[46] On the importance of Old Testament Jewish concepts to the Carolingians, see especially W. Ullmann, *The Carolingian Renaissance and the Idea of Kingship* (1969).

[47] That the Saxons lived between the Franks and the important Nordic-Inner Asian trade routes, a fact thus far overlooked, presumably had much to do with the eagerness of Pippin and Charlemagne to conquer them.

[48] See also J. Déer, "Karl der Grosse und der Untergang des Awarenreiches" (1966).

[49] W. Bark is one of the few scholars of the medieval West who notice the importance of the steppe peoples and Central Asia for European development. See his *Origins of the Medieval World* (1960) 137. Some of the most in-

good reason to look to that region for their "missing link" in world history.

It now seems evident that the view of the early medieval world held by Pirenne, his followers, and many other medievalists is based upon several fundamental conceptual errors. Unfortunately, the current nation-centered trend in historiography is doing nothing to correct these fallacies. Fields such as early medieval Tibetan and Frankish history have thus been linked by unsound historiographical premises. Meanwhile, those few modern scholars who specialize in medieval Central Eurasia have essentially given up on the internationalist approach, and are unaware of the problem just described.[50] Pirenne's great contribution to early medieval studies was his discovery that something very important happened during the eighth century: a change in the trend of Old World development. All of the criticism of his thesis derives from his misinterpretation of that great change. Even his detractors credit Pirenne with having called attention to what he termed "the shift in Europe's focus" from the Roman South, facing the Mediterranean Sea, to the Germanic North, facing the Baltic and North Seas. But this presumes, among other things, that all of what is now Western Europe had previously constituted a homogeneous civilization and that the center of it had merely shifted its location northwards. Pirenne and most of those who have since written on the subject also claim that, although the areas of Europe occupied in antiquity by the Romans were not totally devastated by the Germanic and Inner Asian migrants, they still were "barbarized" to greater or lesser degrees. But, it

teresting arguments against the Pirenne Thesis have come from Bark, who proposes instead that the backwardness of early medieval Europe—note that Pirenne defined "early medieval" as c. A.D. 800 on—was beneficial because it was the necessary preliminary, a clearing away of entangled undergrowth so to speak, for the great developments in Europe during the later Middle Ages. (See p. 39.)

[50] The widespread and frequently deliberate use of the pejorative term "barbarians" for the peoples of Central Eurasia, in contrast to neutral or glowingly positive terms for other ancient peoples (primarily the Greeks and Chinese), attests to the seriousness of the problem.

should be asked, was northern Europe "civilized" to begin with? The supposedly highly cultured northern regions of the Roman Empire, including most of the territory north of the Mediterranean provinces, were almost totally devoid of important literary[51] figures during the classical and late classical periods. From the seventh century onward, however, there were—suddenly, it seems—many writers in those places, and Italy and Spain were no less literate in the seventh century than they were in the sixth.[52] In other words, literate civilization *expanded* into what had been essentially preliterate territory.[53]

If one looks beyond Europe, one is impressed by the same sudden expansion of literate civilization across the length and breadth of Asia during the seventh century: from the Arabian peninsula to Turkic Mongolia and from the Tibetan Plateau to Japan. The inhabitants of Central Asia began to use literary Sogdian, Khotanese, and Tokharian (along with Arabic, Tibetan, Turkic, and Chinese) for the production of more ambitious and extensive writings. By the end of the early medieval period, almost all areas of Eurasia that were to be literate before our own century had become literate.

Except possibly for some classicists, people nowadays take it for granted that cultural stagnation is undesirable. Dynamic new growth is the sign of a vital civilization, not of a dying one. But even classicists will not maintain that late Roman literature or art was as new, and therefore as dynamic or intellectually stimulating, as the achievements of early Rome or Greece.[54] The Western

[51] The following argument also applies to other fields of endeavor, such as the arts, music, technology, scholasticism, and so forth.

[52] Pirenne, 1956:7, himself stresses the predominance into the seventh century of Mediterranean literary figures.

[53] That the educational system and the subjects treated by literature changed during the eighth century, as pointed out by P. Riché (*Les Écoles et l'enseignement dans l'Occident chrétien* [1979]), does not mean that the later literature is less important, no matter how uninteresting it may seem to the twentieth-century scholar.

[54] Bark, 1960:138, citing Michael Rostovtzeff's *Social and Economic History of the Roman Empire* (1926) 166, makes this point with regard to technology.

European, Tibetan, Islamic, and Inner Asian realms were not declining; they were progressing, and very rapidly at that. Furthermore, there is no reason to consider the Tibetan and Frankish empires as backward when contemporary Eurasian standards are taken into account. In like manner, there are no grounds for supposing the culture of Harun al-Rashid's caliphate to have been already as sophisticated as it is portrayed in the *late* medieval *Thousand and One Nights*.

The evidence shows that, during the Early Middle Ages, the Tibetan Empire and Frankish Western Europe were integral parts of a civilized world which included the Islamic caliphate and T'ang China and was "focused" (to adapt Pirenne's usage) on Central Eurasia. It may be suggested that the great disparities in level of civilization which apparently developed between Tibet and Western Europe on the one hand and the Islamic and Chinese worlds on the other seem to have arisen during the period immediately following the final collapse, around 840, of most of the large centralized states of the early medieval world. Others will hopefully pursue this subject, but they should do so stripped of the illusion of a "barbarian" Europe or Tibet and of the equally imaginary fairy-tale-like conceptions of the early Arab caliphate, the Byzantine Empire, and T'ang China.

ON THE
DEGREE OF
TIBETAN
—— DOMINATION ————

The duration and extent of Tibetan rule in the Tarim region has been the subject of a certain amount of muted debate. Since the publication of Hisashi Satô's pioneering work on the Tibetan Empire, his contention—that the Tibetan domination of the region was soon weakened by the loss of several of the Four Garrisons to China and was not reestablished until 689—has been accepted by nearly all scholars. Most recently, it has received support from the authors of the volume on the Sui-T'ang period in the *Cambridge History of China* and from Takao Moriyasu, author of the hitherto most extensive work dealing specifically with the Tibetans in Central Asia.[1] But although Satô's theory is also seemingly supported by several rather obscure references in the scanty Chinese sources on Central Asia for this period, it cannot be maintained in view of the full evidence.

According to Satô, in "674-675 Kashgar and Khotan were recovered," by China, and soon after, Tibet, "joining forces with A-shih-na-tu-chih in Turkestan . . . met the T'ang force. P'ei

[1] Moriyasu, 1984.

Hsing-chien took the A-shih-na-tu-chih groups by a strategem [*sic*], built the Sui-yeh fortress . . . and secured the road to Sogdiana, in 679."[2] It was only later, in 687-689, that Mgar Khri 'brin undertook "military operations in the direction of Eastern Turkestan, and reduced Kucha."[3] This was just in time for Wang Hsiao-chieh to recover the Four Garrisons in 692, "and the An-hsi Commandery was once more established in Kucha."[4] These points are buttressed in the text by numerous quotations from various Chinese sources, most importantly from the *Ts'e fu yüan kuei*, to which Satô has apparently attached overriding credence. There are, however, numerous difficulties facing his argument.

First of all, it is important to remember that the Chinese did not abandon the Pacified West Protector Generalship. Satô states that "for the 22-year period down to 692 the An-hsi Commandery was unable to function."[5] This contention is not supported by the sources and is apparently due to the common confusion of *An hsi*, (the "Pacified West"), a Chinese administrative unit, with Kucha, a city in eastern Central Asia. The sources specifically state that, after the Tibetan capture of Aksu and the T'ang retreat from the Four Garrisons in 670, the Pacified West Protector Generalship was moved back to Hsi *chou* (Qocho), where it had been before the first T'ang conquest of what became the Four Garrisons.[6] Not only was *An hsi* not the same as Kucha, but it would have been highly unusual for the T'ang Chinese to abolish what seems to have been an integral part of their governmental ideology without a word in its defense. For, like the *tu-hu-fu* (Protector Generalship) of *An hsi*, the Chinese had Protector Generalships of *An nan* (Annam), *An pei*, and *An tung*, representing the three other directions of the four quarters of the world in which the T'ang were expanding their conquests. (It is perhaps not irrelevant to

[2] Satô, 1958:327, 332-333; 1959:12. These and the following quotations from Satô are taken from the English "Summary of the Contents," translated by R. A. Miller, at the end of the second volume (1959).

[3] Satô, 1958:346-348; 1959:13.

[4] Satô, 1958:352 et seq.; 1959:13.

[5] Satô, 1958:324 et seq.; 1959:12.

[6] For example, see *CTS*, 198:5304.

note that the fifth direction—*à la chinoise*, the center—was graced with the presence of the capital city of Ch'ang-an, "Eternal Peace.") It should therefore be noted that, until the late T'ang, mentions of *An hsi* (including attacks on it) refer either to the place where the Pacified West Protector Generalship was then located or to the area of the Pacified West in general, whether or not it was still under T'ang control.

The second point is that records of embassies to China that appear in the Chinese sources by themselves mean only one thing with respect to the political status of the sending country: these nations were independent of China. (Regions under direct Chinese rule did not send missions to the Chinese capital to *ch'ao kung* or pay tribute. They paid taxes, of course.) Of the actual meaning of *ch'ao kung* there can be no doubt, since the paying of tribute was commonplace even from powerful to weaker nations. It is well known that Tibet sent many missions to China to "pay tribute," as did the Arabs, Japanese, Indians, and many other nations. The independent and contemporary Old Tibetan historical sources, however, record frequent Chinese (as well as Arab, Turk, and other) embassies to Tibet to *phyag-tshal* ("pay tribute") at the same time. Furthermore, it has long been accepted by Sinologists that many of the so-called "embassies" to China were nothing more than officially sanctioned trade missions. With the overriding commercial concerns of the Tarim Basin cities, three or four of which constituted the Four Garrisons, one can readily appreciate that any missions which they might have sent to China during this period were most likely trade missions.

As pointed out in Chapter Three, kings only traveled in person to China when they had lost their thrones, had been defeated by the Chinese, or—already under Chinese rule—when the Chinese needed them and their armies for military campaigns. During the An Lu-shan rebellion, for example, some of these vassal kings "volunteered" to assist the T'ang. The only exceptions were the foreign rulers who came to China with their armies as mercenaries. These were normally hired to assist in the suppression of a rebellion, as were some who fought An Lu-shan. When the non-mercenary kings who traveled to Ch'ang-an were not executed or retained at the imperial court, they were usually sent home (these events are regularly mentioned in the T'ang histories). But in the cases adduced by Satô, despite the announcement of the reorganization of their countries into Chinese administrative units with the kings as their heads of state, none of the kings who surrendered are mentioned as having been sent home. In fact, the accounts in the Chinese sources of these kings coming to court are identical to the contemporaneous ones relating to Pêrôz, the "King of Persia," who had never ruled his country, despite his appointment by the Chinese. In short, the kings who came to China in the 670s had been deposed and were refugees, not victors over the Tibetans. As refugees often do, these kings (and their families) soon became émigrés. The Khotanese sources translated into Tibetan, for example, apparently report that the king of Khotan died at the Chinese court and that his son was still there in 691 when he was appointed king by the Emperor Wu.

The third point is that the Chinese designation of a given region as a Chinese administrative unit (for example, a *tu tu fu*) without the appointment and dispatching of Chinese administrative officials was as meaningless as the frequent "appointment" of a reigning king as the T'ang government's officially approved king. In such cases, no discernible change occurred in the given country. The Chinese sources would lead us to believe (and many Sinologists have so believed), however, that the T'ang Empire stretched into western Central Asia as far as eastern Persia. This is ridiculous and is not only dismissible on the basis of Chinese sources; it is also disproved by the copious and well-known Arabic histories of the period. One must be careful, therefore, not to accept at face value the grandiose statements of T'ang historians about Chinese conquests, particularly in view of their reluctant admission of defeat by a foreign power. Most Chinese sources on the T'ang period omit any mention of events—in particular, the loss of territory—which occurred after the first conquests or, at the latest, after the second reconquest. (In any case, there is so little information on the period after the mid-eighth century in geographical works that one might easily assume that the T'ang dynasty was overthrown by An Lu-shan.) One must be equally

suspicious of unprovable claims about the establishment of bu-
reaucratic administrative units, particularly when the major
sources on the period ignore them or deny their existence.

The fourth and final point is that the Chinese sources never explicitly mention the reconquest, recovery, or return to submission of a single one of their former Four Garrisons between 670
and 692. All that is reported is the "surrender" of individual rulers
of some of those countries, the arrival of "tribute" missions (i.e.,
embassies or trade delegations), or other such events. It cannot be
imagined that the Chinese historians would have failed to trum-
pet any reconquests as loudly as possible. Since such victories are
not mentioned, one must therefore assume that they did not take
place. The same sources not only never deny Tibetan domination
over the Tarim Basin during the period; on the contrary, they repeatedly stress this fact. In addition, it must be emphasized that
at no time between 670 and 692 did any Chinese army penetrate
the Tarim Basin west of Turfan, into the area once held for the
T'ang by the Four Garrisons. Any suppositions of Chinese authority in the area can thus only be considered fictitious, extra-
neous (e.g., local rebellions against Tibetan authority), or irrelevant (e.g., trade missions to China cloaked in the early medieval
guise of "tribute missions"). None of the references adduced by
Satô record Chinese military or civil action in the Tarim Basin region. (Jungaria is another matter, but no one has yet argued that
the Tibetans were involved there. One could perhaps theorize
that the reason the Chinese proclaimed victory so loudly after the
successful mission of P'ei Hsing-chien in 679 was that they felt
they had defeated the Turkic allies of the Tibetans and had captured Sûyâb, which had been in Tibetan [or Tibetan-allied
Turkic] hands. Tibet, however, is not even mentioned in the accounts of this mission.) No Chinese officials were dispatched to
the Tarim region, no Chinese reports returned from it, and, consequently, the Chinese sources are almost totally silent on hap-
penings there during this period.

In conclusion, it is impossible to concur with Satô's theory about
the reestablishment of Chinese power in the Tarim Basin between

670 and 692. At most, his sources can be understood to indicate that the cities of the Tarim region were lightly governed by Tibet or, at some point, managed to free themselves for a year or two from absolute Tibetan control. It appears, however, that these sources show the loss of independence of the native Central Asian rulers to Tibet.

ON THE WESTERN REGIONS IN OLD TIBETAN SOURCES

Scholars of early Tibetan history have hitherto understood the term *stod-phyogs*, frequently found in Old Tibetan sources, to be synonymous with the word *stod*, which literally means "upper" but in Old Tibetan is the usual word for "west." *Stod-phyogs* is thus commonly translated as "the upper direction" or "the west." Although perfectly logical and sometimes accurate, this interpretation does not always accord well with the contexts in which the word occurs. These contextual problems can be divided into three groups:

1. Those for which no other specific (or known) locality is mentioned: *OTA*, Bird year 721(-722) summer; *OTAC*, (Mouse year 760-761); *OTC*, viii; Saṃghavardhana, 300c. Compare the Chinese translation, published by Pelliot and Haneda,[1] which translates the term as *hsi* ("west"). It is clear from the context, however, that it should have been translated as *hsi yü*, a T'ang word for the lands of the West,

---

[1] P. Pelliot and T. Haneda, *Manuscrits de Touen-houang* (1926), "Shih chia mu ni ju lai hsiang fa mieh chin chih chi," line 33.

which meant generally all of Eurasia directly to the west of China and south of Afghanistan, including even India. Commonly, it was used to mean the countries of the Tarim Basin and its vicinity. Now, *hsi yü* is usually rendered as "the Western Regions."

2. Those which correspond to an area in or near the Pamirs, an area of course more or less to the west of Central Tibet. It is also higher than Tibet and is to the west of the region of Tibet traditionally known as *stod*. I have noted one example, from *OTAC*, Monkey year (756-)757: "the envoys of the *stod-phyogs* [countries] of Black *Ganjak, Wakhan, and Shughnan paid homage [at the Tibetan court]."

3. Those which correspond to the area of the Tarim Basin:

   a. *OTC*, vii: In capturing the city of Kua *chou* in 727, the Tibetans seized great stores of Chinese silk goods, which were to have been sent out to *stod-phyogs*. This can only mean the Chinese *hsi yü* (Western Regions), which were mostly north and northwest of Tibet.

   b. *OTC*, viii: During the reign of Khri sroṅ lde brtsan, the Tibetans "invaded *stod-phyogs*, and, having subjugated Khotan, levied taxes [on the country]." Khotan is, of course, north of Tibet and much lower in elevation.

   c. *Li-yul luṅ bstanpa* (R. Emmerick, 1967:40): A Khotanese monk searched "throughout *stod-phyogs*." Again, this can hardly be anywhere else but the Chinese *hsi yü*.

   d. *Li-yul choskyi lorgyus* (R. Emmerick, 1967:40): "the monks of the four fortified cities [Tibetan, *mkhar bźi*] of *stod*." Although this example omits the *-phyogs*, it definitely refers to what the T'ang Chinese called "the Four Garrisons of the Pacified West" (*an hsi ssu chen*), i.e., the four most strategic fortified and garrisoned T'ang cities in the Tarim Basin and its vicinity. In other words, *stod* is here used to mean "west of China."

The conclusion is transparent, for all instances in which the geographic location of *stod-phyogs* may be positively identified refer to areas within the scope of the T'ang term *hsi yü*. Both words have the same literal meaning and are used to describe the same areas, even though it does not always make geographic sense for the Tibetans to have used *stod-phyogs* in this way.

Appendix C

ON THE ROYAL CLAN OF THE TURKS

It is well known from Chinese sources that the royal clan of the Turks was named "A-shih-na." The name, in its modern Mandarin guise, has not so far been satisfactorily explained. An examination of all the sources, however, allows an identification to be made. In the *Chou shu*, the royal clan of the Turks is identified with a nomadic nation of the classical period:

> As for the Turks, indeed they are a separate race of the Hsiung-nu, with the clan name A-shih-na.[1]

The *Chou shu* then goes on to relate the story of the origin of the Turks and of the name A-shih-na, in two versions:

> . . . The [pregnant] wolf fled to the mountains north of the Kingdom of Qocho. The mountains had a cavern. Inside the cavern there was level ground and luxuriant vegetation for several hundred *li* around; on all four sides there were mountains. The wolf hid therein, and subsequently gave

---

[1] *CS*, 50:907. On the origin myths of the Turks, see D. Sinor, "The Legendary Origin of the Türks" (1982).

birth to ten boys. When the ten boys grew up, the wives they [had procured] outside became pregnant, and afterward each had one clan name—A-shih-na was one of them.[2] [First version]

. . . Na-tu-liu had ten wives; all of the sons which they bore took the mother's tribe as [their] clan name. A-shih-na was the son of his youngest wife [or concubine: literally, "little wife" (*hsiao ch'i*)]. When Na-tu-liu died, the ten sons of the mothers wished to select one man from among them to establish [as the ruler]; so they came together under a large tree, and they made an agreement that they would elect and establish whoever could jump the highest toward the tree['s limbs]. The son of A-shih-na was young in years, and as he was the one who jumped the highest, the sons all accepted him as the ruler.[3] [Second version]

Related to this material is a statement found in the account of the Turks by the Byzantine Greek writer Menander Protector (fl. 558-582):

As for Arsílas, it is a name for the most ancient monarch of the Turks.[4]

The Chinese sources make it abundantly clear that A-shih-na was the name of "the most ancient monarch of the Turks." The name is therefore undoubtedly the Chinese transcription of the name transcribed by the Greeks as "Arsílas."[5]

---

[2] *CS*, 50:907.

[3] *CS*, 50:908.

[4] *FHG*, 4:245b.

[5] I have assumed that the final *s* is a Greek ending, and have thus given the name in the reconstructed Turkic form *Arsïla. The normal T'ang reading of the first character as *ar* (at least in foreign names) is clear from many examples, including the name Arsïlan/Arslan. Although the latter is not attested in early ("Runic") Old Turkic, it is attested as the personal name A-hsi-lan (*Arsïlan/Arslan) in at least three instances in T'ang Chinese sources: (1) Name of a Turkic subtribe in the Ho-ch'ü (Bends of the Yellow River) area, in A.D. 716 (*TCTC*, 211:6720-6721). (2) Name or title of a brother of the king of Bukhara in 726 (Chavannes, 1903:138). (3) Name or

According to the aforementioned myths, the early Turks lived in the mountains north of Qocho and had to acquire their wives from outside their territory. It is therefore logical to assume that some of them came from Qocho. The name A-shih-na was, according to the *Chou shu*, the name of the foreign mother of the first ruler of the Turks. The Chinese first heard of the Turks from precisely the region of the Kingdom of Qocho, into the mountains to the north of which the first Turk or Turks fled.[6] Thus the possibility exists that the royal clan name of the Turks was due to a marriage between an early Turk ruler and a princess of Qocho. In Tokharian (the language of Qocho), one finds the title Ârśilâñci, which is assumed to be a form of the title of the kingdom's rulers.[7] This title is thus perhaps the source of A-shih-na/Arsílas,[8] the name of the royal clan of the Turks.

---

title of the king (Arsïlan Tarqan) of Ferghana, in 739 (Chavannes, 1903:147). One of his Turkic forebears was named A-se-na, i.e. *Arsïlna, *Arsïrna, *Arsïdna, etc. (*HTS*, 221b:6250). So far as I am aware, the earliest usage of the word *arsïlan* in a Turkic text also is as a personal name. If this is another form of the A-shih-na of the *Chou shu*, one would naturally assume that it is not a native Turkic word, and indeed may have originally meant something quite different from its later meaning, "lion." This later meaning may actually prove the word's foreign origin, since the habitat of the lion did not extend as far north as Central Asia, let alone Siberia, in historical times. See also note 8 below.

[6] *CS*, 50:907.

[7] See P. Poucha, *Thesaurus Linguae Tocharicae Dialecti A* (1955) 25, and the literature cited there.

[8] The borrowed title or name seems to have taken several forms or to have become connected to other words. It may thus be the result of a concatenation involving a loanword from the Khotanese for lion. (The lion is mostly known in Asia only as a mythical beast. Consequently, the word for lion in most Asian languages is borrowed from elsewhere.) E. Hovdhaugen, "Turkish Words in Khotanese Texts" (1971) 180 (n. 6), cites the word "*aślañye* 'lion country?'." I think it highly doubtful that the name Aśnâs, which appears in Arabic sources (see Ṭabarî, iii:1017) as the name of a famous Turk in the service of the caliphs, is a transcription of the name transcribed by the Chinese A-shih-na.

ON THE
ON OQ

According to Chinese sources, the Western Turks were organized into ten divisions (*pu*):

> Each division had one man over it. The man received one arrow. They were called the ten *šad* [Chinese, *she*]; they were also called the ten arrows. . . . They call an arrow a tribe, [thus] they are called the Ten Clan tribes.[1]

This description fully explains the Old Turkic name for the Western Turks—On oq, or "Ten Arrows."

The On oq were further subdivided into an eastern and a western branch, each with five tribes.[2]

Eastern
The To-lu, or *Tarduš,[3] tribes, each headed by a *cur* (Chinese, *ch'o*):

[1] *HTS*, 215b:6058; cf. *CTS*, 194b:5184.
[2] *CTS*, 194b:5186; *HTS*, 215b:6061.
[3] *Tardu[š] Qaghan Niźuk (Chinese, To-lu K'o-han Ni-shu) was also

1. Ch'u-mu-k'un [ch'üeh]-lü *ch'o*
2. Hu-lu-wu ch'üeh *ch'o*
3. She-she-t'i tun *ch'o*
4. T'u-ch'i-shih[4] ho-lo-shih *ch'o*
5. Shu-ni-shih ch'u-pan *ch'o*

Western

The Nu-shih-pi, or Nu(?) *šadpït,[5] tribes, each headed by an *irkin* (Chinese, *i-chin*):

1. A-hsi-chieh ch'üeh *i-chin*, or *Ärski kül *irkin*
2. Ko-shu ch'üeh *i-chin*, or Qośu kül *irkin*
3. Pa-sai-kan tun sha-po-[lo] *i-chin*, or Barsqan Tun Iśbara *irkin*
4. A-hsi-chieh ni-shu *i-chin*, or *Ärski Niźuk *irkin*
5. Ko-shu ch'u-pan *i-chin*, or Qośu ch'u-pan *irkin*

Note that the western branch had two *Ärski arrows and two Qośu arrows. There were, in addition, tribes which either overlapped or did not form a part of the On oq system.

---

called Ta-tu Qaghan (i.e., Tardu, which Menander Protector wrote as Tárdou [*FHG*, 4:247a]). See *CTS*, 194b:5183. The Chinese transcribed the name Tardu in at least six different ways (see the index to Chavannes, 1903). Three of these may be reconstructed to read Tardu and three to read Tarduk or Tarduγ. According to C. Ts'en, *T'u-chüeh chi shih*, 1958b:860, at least one form, Ta-t'ou, is to be identified with Tarduś. The title *cur* (or possibly *cor*: there is no way to determine the precise quality of the vowel on the basis of native Turkic transcriptions, but the Old Tibetan form *cor*, representing a Turkic *cur*, and the Arabic form *ṣûl* together indicate the form I have adopted) is clearly associated with the Tarduś chiefs in at least three instances in the Old Turkic inscriptions: (1) "westwards the Tarduš lords—Kül čor at the head[;] and the šadpït lords" (translation by T. Tekin, 1968:280, of the Bilgä Qaghan inscription). (2) "Iśbara Bilgä Küli Čor reigned ruling and governing the Tardus people" (translation by T. Tekin, 1968:294, of the Küli Cur inscription). (3) "from the Kirgiz kaghan, Tarduš İnanču čor came" (translation by T. Tekin, 1968:273, of the Kül Tegin inscription).

[4] This is assumed to be a variant transcription of Türgiś.

[5] C. Ts'en, 1958b:878, identifies the *shih-pi* of Nu-shih-pi with a "*šada-pyt.*"

ON ALUṬÂR, KING OF FERGHANA

The name Aluṭâr (Chinese, A-liao Ta) is mentioned in Ṭabarî, ii:1440. He was apparently a descendant of King A-liao Ts'an, who had been set up as the ruler of Hu-men *ch'eng* in the early seventh century ("during the Chen-kuan period" [627-649]) by O-po-chih, the son of the Turkic conqueror of the country, ★Arsïlna (Chinese, A-se-na) Shu-ni. O-po-chih himself ruled in Kâsân (Chinese, K'o-sai *ch'eng*). A-liao Ts'an, in turn, was the nephew of the former king, the Turkic-named Ch'i-pi, who had been killed by the Western Turk K'an Baghatur (*HTS*, 221b:6250; see Chavannes, 1903:148-149). On ★Arsïlna and on ★Arsïlân, a later ruler of Ferghana, see Appendix C. The name Aluṭâr (or perhaps ★Aloṭâr) seems from the Chinese evidence to be composed of two parts, the first of which is ★Alu or ★Alo. Thus, this is not a personal name, but rather a dynastic name or, as is normal for almost all the rulers named in the sources of this period, a title that presumably means "king." If this is so, the word is strikingly reminiscent of the Kuchean ("Tokharian B") word for king, *walo*. (See W. Thomas, *Tocharisches Elementarbuch* [1964] 239.) Aluṭâr and A-liao Ts'an would then translate as

"King Târ" and "King *Tsan (*Chan?)." Based on the comments of medieval Chinese travelers, it is presumed that the language of Ferghana was different from the neighboring tongues, which were all Iranic. In light of the foregoing conclusion about "Aluṭâr," could the mystery language of Ferghana have belonged to the Tokharian branch of Indo-European?

AFTERWORD

It is gratifying to see this book given a second lease on life with a new paperback edition. Although I myself have gradually drifted away from the subject since finishing the manuscript in 1983–1984, I have published in recent years two articles that are directly relevant to it, namely, "The Tibetans in the Ordos and North China: Considerations on the Role of the Tibetan Empire in World History" (1987) and "The Impact of the Horse and Silk Trade on the Economies of T'ang China and the Uighur Empire: On the Importance of International Commerce in the Early Middle Ages" (1991).

The fact that so very few contemporary scholars have published substantial primary-source-based work on the Tibetan Empire in Central Asia (I know of only two besides myself: the late Géza Uray of Hungary and Takao Moriyasu of Japan[1]) has narrowed the chances of this book's creating much of a stir among specialists.[2] Even when it includes those who have writ-

---

[1] The late Professor Uray was unable to review the book because of his poor health and preoccupation with completing his own projects on the subject. Professor Moriyasu was one of the readers of the manuscript for the publisher; his detailed comments have been incorporated into the book, as can be seen in many of its footnotes.

[2] The summary at the head of Leonard Van der Kuijp's review article

ten on the subject somewhat marginally, but who have relied on personal knowledge of the original written sources, the total number of "specialists" in early medieval Central Asian history probably does not exceed a dozen worldwide. Nevertheless, this book does deal to some extent with the histories of all the great empires of the Early Middle Ages; accordingly, it has received attention from several quarters, including general interest readers, "world systems" historians,[3] and scholars specializing in Persia, Tibet, and China.[4]

Substantial questions that deserve special attention have been brought up in the reviews of this book by the Tibetologists Luciano Petech (1989) and Leonard Van der Kuijp (1991).[5] I will not address all of the issues they have raised. When a point in question has been passed over in silence, it is either because the matter is trivial or because I do not agree with the reviewer and think

---

(1991) on this book states: "Several works and numerous articles have been devoted to the history of imperial Tibet. The fine study of Ch. Beckwith is the only one of its kind in the [sic] Western language." This is somewhat inaccurate, insofar as it asserts that this book is a history of "imperial Tibet," and that it is the only history of this subject in a Western language. It is not, of course, a history of imperial-period Tibet, nor even of the Tibetan Empire as a whole—in fact, there are in Western languages many studies, including a few books, on imperial Tibet, though it is true that there are no books on the Tibetan Empire as a whole in any Western language. This book's uniqueness stems simply from its being the first book in any language on the Tibetan Empire in Central Asia.

    [3] One of the moving forces in this new branch of history, Andre Gunder Frank, has quoted extensively from the present work in his new book, *The Centrality of Central Asia* (1992).

    [4] A few minor errors noted in reviews not discussed in this Afterword have been corrected silently in the text; the reprinting process unfortunately did not allow for the correction of insignificant typographical or other technical errors.

    [5] I would like to thank both reviewers for having taken the time to read this book and write conscientious, honest reviews. Any disagreement I may have with them does not diminish my deep respect for their learning or my gratitude for their generosity. Their criticisms have been rendered in the spirit of scientific debate; it is in exactly the same spirit that my comments here are written.

(in the absence of new data) that it does not call for further discussion at present. With regard to questions involving citations of the publications of others, I have passed over certain instances because I have a low opinion of the works in question and believe that citing them will lend potentially harmful validation and support.[6] As Petech remarks, I condemn such publications with silence, *more sinico*.[7]

With respect to citation of secondary literature, I should state further that in no ordinary field of study is it necessary, customary, possible, or even desirable to cite every publication, in every language and discipline, that may be relevant to a research topic, for the very good reasons that there are far too many publications, no one can know all the languages and disciplines in which scholarship is published, and—most important of all—

[6] This last consideration is much more serious than it may seem to nonspecialists, who are unaware of the harm Central Eurasian studies as a whole has suffered and continues to suffer from the publications of academic dilettantes and charlatans. The well-known fact that quotations can take on new, independent life in scholarly literature is particularly true, it would seem, when they are quotations of incorrect statements and bibliographic citations of worthless publications.

[7] Both Petech and Van der Kuijp note my failure to cite the works of Zuihô Yamaguchi, particularly his book *Toban ôkoku seiritsu shi kenkyû* (1983). Yamaguchi's numerous articles, mostly on early Tibetan ethnonyms, do not pertain to the subjects covered here. As for the book, I learned of it too late to consult it: I made my last revisions to the manuscript in the spring and summer of 1984, after which I submitted it to the publisher. It was at the end of the summer of 1984 that I first met Professor Yamaguchi, at the conference of the Csoma de Körös Soceity held in Visegrád, Hungary. He described his new book to me, and I described mine to him. He told me that the two books had practically nothing in common, and that I should not delay publication of my book in order to take his work into consideration. (I could not have done so anyway if I wished to be awarded tenure at my university!) When it came time to write the preface, I still had not yet seen Yamaguchi's book and simply overlooked it. Nevertheless, I should emphasize that the two books indeed have practically nothing in common with regard to period, subject matter, approach, and methodology. Yamaguchi's book is interesting in itself, however, and I recommend it to anyone looking for different approaches to the early history of the Tibetan Empire.

most of the publications are not worthy of serious attention. Central Eurasian studies,[8] a branch of "Oriental studies," is no exception to this rule, despite what book reviewers may say. Of course, I have never intentionally passed over a work—no matter how flawed—that makes a significant contribution to the history of the Tibetan Empire in Central Asia, but I did omit, due to oversight or ignorance, a few useful secondary studies, and I was unable to utilize a number of recent works because they were unknown or unavailable to me until after I had sent the manuscript to the publisher. I am fairly confident that none of these works would have changed the text beyond expansion of the footnotes and bibliography.[9]

Petech and others call attention to my criticism (in the prologue) of the "Sino-Tibetan hypothesis." More a conjecture than a scientific hypothesis, this theory posits that Chinese (representing the Chinese family of languages) and Tibetan (representing the Tibeto-Burman family of languages) are "genetically" related. Petech says, "Sometimes the Author defends with great determination ideas which, though not always novel, are still highly debatable" (1989:155). Most readers would not be aware that my criticism could hardly be regarded as a position that is taken for granted among orientalists or linguists. In fact, the op-

---

[8] The term *Central Eurasia* is rapidly replacing the term *Inner Asia* (in the broad sense, as contrasted to Inner Asia in the narrow sense, which has meant, in practice, Tibet, East Turkistan, and Mongolia), because it is more accurate and also more relevant to recent political changes in that part of the world. Central Eurasia *includes* Central Asia, as well as Mongolia, Tibet, Siberia, and easternmost Europe.

[9] I received rather sudden notice that this book was to be reprinted and accordingly had very little time to make corrections and write this Afterword. Under such circumstances it was, regrettably, impossible to track down and examine the numerous works mentioned by Petech and Van der Kuijp. It is also still true, unfortunately, that many scholarly works in Chinese and Japanese are extremely difficult to obtain. (This is particularly the case for Japanese publications.) There would be little point in padding this Afterword with such titles, and so they have been omitted. One work I would like to have seen is the full Tibetan translation of the chapters on the Tibetan Empire in the T'ang histories (Don-grub-rgyal and Ch'en, 1983), mentioned by Van der Kuijp 1991:105).

posite view—that Chinese and Tibetan are "genetically" related language families—is almost universally unquestioned, to the point where many believers treat any criticism of the idea as blasphemy. Few scholars have so much as suggested that there might be something wrong with the idea,[10] while the "Sino-Tibetanists" almost always ignore what little criticism they receive. Open debate by informed linguists—that is, trained historical linguists who know both Old Tibetan and Classical Chinese, at the very least[11]—is needed to improve what is at present a sorry situation.

Van der Kuijp takes umbrage at my transcription of Old Tibetan: In a note, he states, "[Beckwith's] argument (p. xiii) that this enables him to write 'Tibetan words as words' seems to prejudge the nature of the 'Tibetan word,' something that is not all that transparent when reading what Tibetan linguists themselves have said about the subject. . . . I have for convenience standardized the Tibetan . . ." (1991:94). The reviewer makes several errors here. First, there is no exact equivalent *in Tibetan* of the English word *word*, so it is hardly possible for traditional Tibetan linguists to have written on the subject. Nevertheless, the Tibetans have been able to make excellent dictionaries of their language—organized by headword and excluding grammatical formatives (prefixes, suffixes, etc.), much as in English or German

[10] For a thoroughgoing criticism of the "Sino-Tibetan hypothesis," see Miller (1988); for a recent article on the current state of "Sino-Tibetan" from the point of view of a practitioner, see Matisoff (1991). Because Matisoff makes no mention of Miller's article, it may be worthwhile to give a brief quotation from the latter here: "In S[ino-]T[ibetan] studies even the possibility of loans between Chinese and Tibetan has scarcely ever been entertained. The merest similarity in sound and sense between one word in Tibetan and another word in Chinese has typically been seized upon as evidence for genetic relationship, while the possibility of borrowing has remained virtually unexplored. Yet surely their long history of geographical proximity, along with the centuries of social, religious and political contacts between the Chinese and the Tibetans, would imply the existence of a considerable stock of lexical borrowings in both directions" (1988:518).

[11] For further comments on the parameters and methodology that should be involved in a scientific study of the relationship between Tibetan and other languages, see Beckwith (1992).

dictionaries—without the benefit of a clear and unambiguous word for *word*. If suddenly we are to base everything we do on the way medieval Tibetans did it—or for that matter, on how modern Tibetans do it—we will be forced to accept other problematic aspects, too, such as the fuzziness among grammatical categories[12] that apparently permeates all traditional Tibetan grammars. The concept of the word is a serious matter in linguistics. Because the reviewer implicitly accepts *some* definition of what is a word in Tibetan—he uses the term *word* himself to refer to Tibetan lexical items such as *grobo* (1991:103)—it would be interesting to know what that definition is and the criteria, if any, he has used to arrive at it.

Second, it is impossible to "standardize" any transcription of Tibetan, because no standard exists. All Tibetologists regularly bemoan this fact, and Van der Kuijp himself implies it in his note. In this regard I would comment only that my transcription of Old Tibetan is actually more "standard" than Van der Kuijp's, since it at least follows the transliteration practices of most Old Tibetanists, with one exception: I write words as words in an attempt to treat Tibetan as a language rather than as a string of unconnected or haphazardly semi-connected syllables (as I explain on pp. xiii–xiv).

With respect to the word *btsanpo*, translated regularly here as "emperor," Van der Kuijp argues that this meaning is not clear for early Old Tibetan (1991:101), even though I cite several Chinese-Old Tibetan glosses that make it unquestionable that the title should be so *translated* (at least, as long as we translate the Chinese equivalents as "emperor"). Obviously, as I explain in Chapter 1, most of the early rulers (before Khri Slon mtshan, at least) would hardly be characterized as emperors in the "usual"

---

[12] Consider, for example, the lumping together of the Classical Tibetan "postjunction" *la* and the dative-locative case endings in the category called *la don*. Because the postpositions in Old and Classical Tibetan are also conjunctions (whence my neologism *postjunction*), and the dative-locative case has numerous functions that are restricted to it alone, it is clear that the *la don* category, which is appropriate for modern spoken Tibetan, is inappropriate for earlier forms of the language.

sense of the term. But if we are going to be picky here, it must be remarked that English usage of the term "emperor" for the rulers of Japan (translating the Japanese word *tennô*, a title specifically restricted to the ruler of that country), Ethiopia, and probably many other places also does not fit the"usual" sense of the term. The real problem here is one of worldview rather than of lexicography, as hinted at in the discussion on pp. 14–15 (n. 10). In this connection, Van der Kuijp's discussion of the use of the word *rgyalpo* is in error as well, because whatever this word meant in later periods (the reviewer mentions the Yuan, Ming, and Ch'ing dynasties of *China*) is completely irrelevant for the Old Tibetan period.

The same problem of methodology crops up in Van der Kuijp's discussion of the name of the early ruler Dri gum btsanpo. In his view, the name should be analyzed and spelled differently, in accord with a large number of late Tibetan literary sources he cites: "Suffice it to stress that Beckwith's reading of the name is far from certain and that, in my opinion, the 'learned etymologies' of the names of the hazy epoch of pre-imperial Tibet need to be taken more seriously than is usually done (1991:98)." The problem here is that the name is well attested in Old Tibetan (there is even a dated inscription, as Van der Kuijp himself points out on p. 97), and there is no question that *in the Old Tibetan period* the name was spelled as I have given it. Whatever the original etymology of the name, a history of the Tibetan Empire in Central Asia based on contemporaneous sources must of necessity accept the spelling given in Old Tibetan texts. It would appear that the reviewer has been led astray by his overreliance on the rich corpus of late (post-Imperial) Tibetan sources, which—though fascinating and important in themselves—present a radically different picture of the Imperial period than do the contemporaneous Old Tibetan sources. I cannot emphasize enough the necessity of distinguishing carefully between Old Tibetan and Classical Tibetan, as well as between Old Tibetan sources and later Tibetan sources.[13]

[13] The reviewer spends a great deal of energy trying to demonstrate that

An additional point with regard to later Tibetan sources deals with their coverage. Certainly, there is much interesting material pertaining to the history of the Imperial period of *Tibet* in these sources, though it is often impossible to do more than make conjectures about this material. If the many interesting-sounding sources Van der Kuijp cites had been available to me at the time (most of them were not even published yet, as he himself points out), I would of course have examined them. Nevertheless, these sources do not have anything to contribute on the history of the Tibetan Empire *in Central Asia* and the international power struggle that took place there in the Early Middle Ages—that is, on the declared subject of this book.

The empire's prehistory, a topic I summarily cover in the first few pages of this book, constitutes virtually the sole subject of Van der Kuijp's review. Yet I am not convinced by his attempts to redo my translations of the extremely difficult Old Tibetan verse texts dealing with this period. In general, I believe my translations are as sound as any translations of Old Tibetan verse can be, and they do in any case make much better sense than the reviewer's. Nearly all of his arguments hinge on lexical definitions, a thorny problem when dealing with Old Tibetan, a language for which no dictionaries, by either native or foreign scholars, exist.[14] In one instance, however, he has justly criticized my translation. This is in connection with two lines of a song, wherein I translated the word *grobo* as "wheat" (p. 13, n. 7). I agree that my translation is probably incorrect. The correct translation is surely "roan horse(s)," which is well attested in Classical Tibetan dictionaries and is perfectly parallel with the

the verb *phab* means "overthrew" not only in Old Tibetan but also in later texts and even in Modern Tibetan (Van der Kuijp, 1991:104). Actually, I did not intend to imply that the word has the meaning only in Old Tibetan, but rather that the literal meaning of the word, which occurs in Old Tibetan texts and is usually best translated as "conquered" or "subjugated," is in fact "threw down" or "overthrew." See the present book, p. 101 (n. 97).

[14] Here I would like to note the publication of an invaluable tool for Old Tibetan studies, which should figure in any discussion of the Old Tibetan lexicon: the concordance to *Choix de documents tibétains*, by Imaeda and Takeuchi (1990).

"yaks" of the following line. Although the new translation (simply substituting "roan horses" for "wheat") may be more difficult to explain in the historical context, it is surely correct. It is a mystery to me why Van der Kuijp mentions this possibility but rejects it.

Petech (1989:155) and Van der Kuijp (1991:105) both justly take me to task for failing to give any explanation of why I accept the equation of Fu-kuo with T'u-fan (i.e., Fu-kuo = Tibet or a part of it, not some otherwise completely unknown locality in between China and Tibet), and for failing to give any citations of works where this is explained. Although Petech's sharp eyes seem to have caught the allusion to my implied equation of Chin. *Fu* with Tib. *(S)pu* (pp. 14–20), the latter apparently being the original ethnonym of the people who conquered Bod and became "Tibetans," he did not follow up the accompanying reference to my doctoral dissertation (Beckwith, 1977),[15] where this very question is treated extensively and in excruciating detail. I consider the latter work (in consort with the other historical evidence given in the present book) to have settled the matter beyond serious doubt.

Petech says I erroneously equate "the Chinese general Su Ting-fang . . . with Se'u Den-pan of the *Annals*; but the fact remains that anc. Tib. *se'u* always transcribes Chin. *hsiao* (anc. *sieu*) and not Su." However, the Chinese character for the man's surname had more than one reading, as any historical dictionary of Chinese will confirm (e.g., Morohashi No. 29225). It may also be read *hsiao* (this is the modern Mandarin equivalent of the alternative pronunciation *sieu*), and in fact the character is used as the phonetic in a good number of other common characters read *hsiao*. It is obvious that the Tibetans' T'ang informant did indeed pronounce it *se'u* (i.e., *sieu*, the ancestor of the modern pronunciation *hsiao*). The confusion could have been avoided if I had simply accepted the testimony of the Old Tibetan source and

---

[15] Essentially the same material, somewhat rearranged, appears in Beckwith (1978). This citation was omitted from the bibliography of the present book.

transcribed the name Hsiao Ting-fang, but the fact remains that the character for the general's surname is (today, at least) always read *su*. In any case, there is no error in my identification of the individual concerned (p. 27) and his involvement in the events of A.D. 670.

Van der Kuijp (1991:105–6) takes issue with my treatment of the events of 678 in northeastern Tibet, disagreeing with my translation of the Chinese phrase *yü Ch'ing Hai chih shang*, "across the Koko Nor," which I enclosed in quotation marks to indicate uncertainty as to what exactly it meant (p. 44). To begin with, it is absolutely impossible that it took place "*in* Qinghai" (my emphasis), or "[in] the upper [region] of Qinghai," as the reviewer suggests, since at the time in question the name Ch'ing Hai (= "Qinghai") meant only the Koko Nor, a lake. If it had been winter, one could assume it meant that the armies fought *on* ice, but without a more detailed context it simply remains unclear exactly what area—presumably somewhere in the vicinity of the lake—is meant by the text (which assumes the reader has knowledge of the physical perspective of the original Chinese report). Van der Kuijp's comments on the name of the Tibetan commander, and on the capture of the Chinese general Liu Shen-li, also may be safely dismissed. It is well known that the special chapters of the T'ang histories dealing with foreigners often suppress details that may be found in biographies. While the reverse is also, but less frequently, true, the fact remains that the long biographies tend to be more accurate, and far more detailed, than the laconic summaries found in the chapters on foreigners. As a rule, in T'ang historiography on foreign affairs, the more detailed account is to be preferred. Certainly the modern Tibetan writer Dge'dun chos'phel, who had little (if any) knowledge of either Classical Chinese or Central Asia, is not a reliable guide for details concerning the history of the Tibetan Empire in Central Asia.

On p. 91, my remarks on the offer of the king of South Hindustan to attack the Arabs and Tibetans are in error. To quote Petech: "This king, whose Chinese name can be easily reconstructed as Srî Narasiṃha Poṭavarman, is to be identified with

Narasiṃhavarman II (c. 695–722) of the Pallava dynasty of Tamil Nadu. His quite gratuitous offer of help, which could not possibly materialize for obvious geographic reasons, was evidently prompted by reasons of prestige and/or maritime trade" (1989:156).

On pp. 94–95, I unaccountably left out any clarification of the name and city of the Sogdian ruler "Dîwâśtîġ of Bunġîkath." He is vaguely identified in note 51 via my provision of the more familiar spelling Dêvastic, but in any case there should have been fuller annotation. As Petech points out, "Dîvastič was the Sogdian prince of Pyandžikent [i.e., Panjikent, given in my text in its Arabic guise as Bunġîkath], whose rich archives were unearthed half a century ago on Mount Mugh." This is one regrettable example of how my determination to set reasonable limits to the source materials for this book, thereby (as explained in the preface) restricting myself to narrative sources except when absolutely unavoidable, led me to the extreme position of not referring to the Mount Mugh materials (though these do not contain narrative sources relevant to the subject of this book).

Finally, I note that many of the reviewers would have liked me to write another sort of book. Whether it was the topic as a whole that was not exactly right, or the period, or the nation, or the locale, or the angle (traditional political-military history), few reviewers were satisfied with my choices. I do not apologize. Indeed I am grateful that so many people are able to envision the possibilities for other books. Certainly the long and erudite review article by Van der Kuijp demonstrates how much can be done with a tiny fraction of the material in this book. However, what even Van der Kuijp fails to realize, I think, is how vast the subject really is. Similarly, Petech's criticism of my willingness to attempt to draw "generalizations starting from . . . somewhat scanty materials" (1989:155) is unwarranted for the period in question. Anyone familiar with the enormous body of historiography on Western Europe's early medieval period, for which the skimpy narrative sources available for major rulers such as Charles Martel and Charlemagne are no better than the Old Tibetan sources for their contemporaries in Tibet, could not fail to be astounded at the wealth of data on both internal and foreign affairs—especially those of Central Asia—that can be found in the Arabic and Chinese histories. The problem is surely not the lack of source material but its vastness and the difficulties we face in grappling with it. Many books could and should be written about early medieval Central Asia—from many points of view, including the same point of view as mine. The political, economic, and cultural relationships between Central Asia and the rest of the world are without question of fundamental importance to an understanding of the history of any of the early medieval empires; they hold the key to a unified history of Eurasia during the Early Middle Ages.

REFERENCES

Beckwith, Christopher I. "On Fu-kuo and T'u-fan." In *Chao T'ieh-han hsien-sheng chi-nien lun-wen chi*, 1–19. Taipei, 1978.

———. "The Tibetans in the Ordos and North China: Considerations on the Role of the Tibetan Empire in World History." In Christopher I. Beckwith, ed., *Silver on Lapis*, 3–11. Bloomington, 1987.

———. "The Impact of the Horse and Silk Trade on the Economies of T'ang China and the Uighur Empire: On the Importance of International Commerce in the Early Middle Ages." *Journal of the Economic and Social History of the Orient*, 34 (1991) 183–198.

———. "Deictic Class Marking in Tibetan and Burmese." In Martha Ratliff and Eric Schiller, eds., *Papers from the First Annual Meeting of the Southeast Asian Linguistics Society (1991)*, 1–14. Tempe, 1992.

Don-grub-rgyal and Ch'ing-ying Ch'en. *Thaṅ-yig gsar-rñiṅ las byuṅba'i bod chenpo'i srid-lugs*. Hsining, 1983.

Imaeda, Yoshiro, and Tsuguhito Takeuchi. *Choix de documents tibétains conservés à la Bibliothèque Nationale, complété par quelques manuscrits de l'India Office et du British Museum. Tome III. Corpus syllabique*. Paris, 1990.

Matisoff, James A. "Sino-Tibetan Linguistics: Present State and Future Prospects." *Annual Review of Anthropology*, 20 (1991) 469–504.

Miller, Roy A. "The Sino-Tibetan Hypothesis." *Li-shih yü-yen yen-chiu-so chi-k'an*, 59 (1988) 509–540.

Petech, Luciano. Review. *Central Asiatic Journal*, 33 (1989) 154–156.

Van der Kuijp, Leonard. "A Recent Contribution on the History of the Tibetan Empire." *Journal of the American Oriental Society*, 111 (1991) 94–107,

Yamaguchi, Zuihô. *Toban ôkoku seiritsu shi kenkyû*. Tokyo, 1983.

TABLE OF RULERS

Frankish	Byzantine	Arab[a]
CAROLINGIANS[e]	HERAKLEIANS[f]	ORTHODOX CALIPHS
	Herakleios (610-641)	
		Abû Bakr (632-634)
Pippin I (d. 639)		
		'Umar b. al-Khaṭṭâb (634-644)
	Constantine III (641)	
	Heraklonas (641)	
		'Uthmân b. 'Affân (644-656)
Grimoald I (d. 662)	Constans II (641-668)	'Alî b. Abî Ṭâlib (656-661)
		UMAYYADS
		Mu'âwiya I (661-680)
	Constantine IV (668-685)	Yazîd I (680-683)
		Mu'âwiya II (683-684)
		Marwân I b. al-Ḥakam (684-685)
	Justinian II (685-695)	'Abd al-Malik (685-705)
Pippin II (679-714)	Leontios (695-698)	
	Tiberius III (Apsimaros) (698-705)	Al-Walîd I (705-715)
	★Justinian II (705-711)[g]	
	Philippikos (711-713)	
	Anastasios II (713-715)	Sulaymân (715-717)
	Theodosios III (715-717)	'Umar b. 'Abd al-'Azîz (717-720)
Carl (714-741) (Charles Martel)	ISAURIANS Leo III (717-741)	Yazîd II (720-724)
		Hiśâm (724-743)
		Al-Walîd II (743-744)
		Yazîd III (744)
		Ibrâhîm (744)
		Marwân II al-Ḥimâr (744-750)

Tibetan[b]	Eastern Turkic[c]	Chinese[d]	
	TURKS	**T'ANG**	
Khri sroṅ brtsan (618-641) (Sroṅ btsan sgampo)	Ch'u-lo Qaghan (d. 620)	Kao-tsu (618-626)	620
	Ellig Qaghan (d. 634)		630
Guṅ sroṅ guṅ brtsan (641-646)	Szu-li-pi Qaghan (d. 645)	T'ai-tsung (626-649)	640
*Khri sroṅ brtsan (646-649)			
	Chü-pi (c. 650)		650
		Kao-tsung (649-683)	
	[Interregnum c. 650-679]		660
Maṅ sroṅ maṅ brtsan (649-677)			
			670
	Ni-shu-fu Qaghan (d. 680)	Chung-tsung (684)	680
	Fu-nien Qaghan (d. 681)	Jui-tsung (684-690)	
Khri 'Dus sroṅ (677-704)	Elteriś Qaghan (d. 692)	**CHOU**	690
		Wu (690-705)	
Lha (704-705)		*T'ANG	700
Khri ma lod (705-712)		*Chung-tsung (705-710)	
			710
	Qapaghan Qaghan (692-716)	*Jui-tsung (710-712)	
	Bilgä Qaghan (716-734)		
			720
Khri lde gtsug brtsan (712-755)	I-jan Qaghan (734)	Hsüan-tsung (712-756)	730
(Mes ag tshoms)	Tengri Qaghan (d. 741)		740
	Ku-to Yabghu Qaghan (d. 742)		
	Ozmïś Qaghan (d. 744)		
	Hu-lung-fu Po-mei Qaghan (d. 745)		
	UYGHURS		
	Ku-li P'ei-lo (744-747)		

TABLE OF RULERS (cont.)

	Frankish	Byzantine	Arab[a]
750	Pippin III (741-768) (Pippin the Short)	Constantine V (741-775)	
760			**ABBASIDS** Al-Saffāḥ (750-754) Al-Manṣūr (754-775)
770		Leo IV (775-780)	Al-Mahdî (775-785) Al-Ḥâdî (785-786)
780	Karol (768-814) (Charlemagne)	Constantine VI (780-797)	
790			Harun al-Rashid (786-809)
		Irene (797-802)[h]	
800		Nikephoros I (802-811)	
810		Staurakios (811) Michael I Rhangabe (811-813) Leo V (813-820)	Al-Amîn (809-813)
820	Hludowic (814-840) (Louis the Pious)	**AMORIANS** Michael II (820-829) Theophilos II (829-842)	Al-Ma'mûn (813-833)
830			
840			Al-Muʿtaṣim (833-842)

NOTES: Dynasty names are in SMALL CAPITALS. An asterisk indicates a restored ruler or dynasty. Dates are drawn mostly from secondary sources and are, generally speaking, as accurate as they can be, considering the frequent disagreements among these sources. Dates are dates of rule; the date of death often, but not always, coincides. Joint or competing rulers are not included.

[a] Chronology from C. Bosworth, *The Islamic Dynasties* (1967) 3-7.

[b] Chronology based on the *Old Tibetan Annals* and other sources. Since the time of year is not given very precisely in Old Tibetan sources, dates follow the traditional conversion to the Western calendar. Dates for the period after 765 are traditional ones.

[c] Chronology from M. Liu, *Die chinesischen Nachrichten zur Geschichte der Ost-Türken (T'u-küe)* (1958) table entitled "Stammbaum der Herrscher der Ost-T'u-küe"; and Hamilton (1955) 139-141.

Tibetan[b]	Eastern Turkic[c]	Chinese[d]	
	Mo-yen Cur (747-759)		750
		Su-tsung (756-762)	760
Khri sroṅ lde brtsan (756-797)	Bögü (759-779)	Tai-tsung (762-779)	
			770
			780
	Tun Bagha Tarqan (779-789)	Te-tsung (779-805)	
	Talas (789-790)		790
	Qutlugh Bilgä (790-795)		
Ṁu ne btsanpo (797-799)			800
	Huai-hsin (795-805)		
		Shun-tsung (805)	
Khri lde sroṅ brtsan (799-815)	Külüg bilgä (805-808)		810
	Alp bilgä Pao-i (808-821)	Hsien-tsung (805-820)	
Khri gtsug lde brtsan (815-838)			820
	Küclüg bilgä Ch'ung-te (821-824)	Mu-tsung (820-824)	
		Ching-tsung (824-827)	
	Qazar Chao-li (824-832)		
	Alp külüg bilgä Chang-hsin (832-839)	Wen-tsung (827-840)	830
Khri 'U'i dum brtsan (838-842)	Wu-tu Kung (839-840)		
		Wu-tsung (840-846)	840

[d] Chronology from *CHC*, 3:xviii-xix.

[e] Chronology from J. Wallace-Hadrill, *The Fourth Book of the Chronicle of Fredegar* (1960), and B. Scholz, *Carolingian Chronicles* (1970). Before 751, the leaders of the Austrasian house of the Carolingians controlled Frankish affairs through the position of *major domus* ("mayor of the palace"), which they held (with only short interruptions) under the Merovingian kings. They had the title *dux* ("duke"). In 751, Pippin III, popularly known as "Pippin the Short," became the first Carolingian king, and held the title *rex* ("king"). Karol, better known as Charlemagne, was crowned Emperor "of the Romans" on Christmas Day, 800.

[f] Chronology from H. Turtledove, trans., *The Chronicle of Theophanes* (1982) xxi.

[g] Last of the Herakleians.

[h] Last of the Isaurians.

GLOSSARY

T'ang Chinese Titles

Commander-in-Chief (military), *tsung kuan*[1] 總管
Expeditionary Army, *hsing chün* 行軍
General, *chiang chün* 將軍
Governor-General, *tu tu* 都督
Military Governor, *chieh tu shih* 節度使
Prefect, *ts'e shih* 刺史
Prince, *wang* 王
Protector-General, *tu hu* 都護

Common T'ang Geographical Terms

ch'eng 城 Walled City[2]
chou 州 Prefecture
chün 郡 Commandery (alternate name for a Prefecture)
chün 軍 Army[3]
hsien 縣 County
tao 道 Circuit (administrative term); Road (direction of attack)

---

[1] This has been left untranslated when it refers to nonmilitary officials.
[2] This has generally been translated "City."
[3] This has generally been translated "Army."

Chinese Characters

This is a complete list of the Chinese characters transcribed in this book. Names of dynasties, book titles, names that only appear in the Table of Rulers, and modern names are omitted. Alphabetization is according to the *CHC* style.

A-ch'ai 阿豺
A-hsi-chi 阿悉吉
A-hsi-chieh 阿悉結
A-hsi-chieh ch'üeh *i-chin*
　阿悉結闕俟斤
A-hsi-chieh ni-shu *i-chin*
　阿悉結泥孰俟斤
A-hsi-lan 阿悉爛
A-liao Ta 阿了達
A-liao Ts'an 阿了參
A-nu-yüeh 阿弩越
A-pu-ssu 阿布思
A-se-na 阿瑟那
A-se-na Shu-ni 阿瑟那鼠匿
A-shih-na 阿史那
A-shih-pi 阿失畢
an chi ta shih 安集大使
An hsi 安西
An-hsi 安息
An hsi ssu chen 安西四鎮
An-jen 安人
An-jung 安戎
An Lu-shan 安祿山
An nan 安南
An pei 安北
An Ssu-shun 安思順
An tung 安東

Chang Ch'ien-hsü 張虔勗
Chang Chiu-ling 張九齡
Chang Chung-liang 張忠亮
Chang Hsiao-sung 張孝嵩
Chang Hsüan-piao 張玄表
Chang I-ch'ao 張義潮
chang shih 長史
Chang Shou-kuei 張守珪
Chang Ssu-li 張思禮
Chang-sun Wu-chi 長孫無忌
Chang Yüeh 張說
Ch'ang-an 長安
Ch'ang-lo *hsien* 常樂縣
Ch'ang-ning 長寧
Ch'ang-sung *hsien* 昌松縣
Ch'ang-ts'en *tao* 長岑道
Chao I-chen 趙頤貞
Chao-li 昭禮
ch'ao kung 朝貢
Che-nu 遮弩
Ch'e-pi-shih 車鼻施
Ch'e-pu 車薄
Chen hsi 鎮西
Chen-hsi 鎮西
Chen-kuan 貞觀
Chen-wu 振武
Chen-yüan 貞元

Ch'en Ta-tz'u 陳大慈

Ch'en Tzu-ang 陳子昂

Cheng Jen-T'ai 鄭仁泰

ch'eng 城

Ch'eng-ch'i 成器

Ch'eng-feng 承風

Ch'eng-feng Ling 承風嶺

Ch'eng-tsung 承宗

Chi Ch'u-na 紀處訥

Chi-lien 祁連

Chi-shih 積石

Chi-shih Ho 積石河

Chi-wang-chüeh 繼往絶

Ch'i-cheng 起政

Ch'i-li-hu 乞離胡

Ch'i-pi 契苾

Chia-liang i 嘉良夷

Chia Shih-shun 賈師順

Chiang 姜

Chiang-hsia 江夏

Ch'iang 羌

Chiao-ho 交河

Chiao-ho chün 澆河郡

Chieh-chung-shih-chu
   竭忠事主

Chieh-shih 羯師

Ch'ieh-shuai 揭帥

chien ch'a yü shih 監察御史

Chien-nan 劍南

Ch'ien-yüan 乾元

Chih-sheng 制勝

Ch'ih-ling 赤嶺

Ch'ih Shui 赤水

Ch'ih-shui ch'eng 赤水城

Chin-ch'ang hsien 晉昌縣

Chin-ch'eng 金城

Chin-fang tao 金方道

Chin Shan 金山

Chin Shan wang 金山王

Chin-t'ien 金天

Chin-wu 金吾

Ch'in chou 秦州

Ching chou 涇州

Ching-lung 景龍

Ching-yün 景雲

Ch'ing chou 慶州

Ch'ing-hai tao 青海道

Ch'ing-sai 青塞

Ch'ing Shui 清水

Chiu Ch'ü 九曲

Chu-chü-po 朱俱波

Chu-hsieh Chin-chung 朱邪盡忠

chu tao tsung kuan 諸道總管

Chu Tz'u 朱泚

ch'u 出

Ch'u-mu-k'un 處木昆

Ch'u-mu-k'un [ch'üeh-] lü ch'o
   處木昆[闕]律啜

Ch'u-yüeh 處月

Chung 忠

Chung-chieh 忠節

chung shih 中使

Chung-shun 忠順

Chung-tsung 中宗

Ch'ü 麯

Ch'ü-le 屈勒

Chün 浚

chün shih 軍使

Fa Ch'iang 發羌
fan 蕃
Fang *chou* [near Ho *chou*] 芳州
Fang *chou* [near Ch'ang-an]
　坊州
Fang-yü-shih 防禦使
Feng Ch'ang-ch'ing 封常清
Feng *chou* 豐州
Feng Te-hsia 馮德遐
fu ["again"] 復
fu ["clothing"] 服
fu [bäg] 匐
Fu *chou* 鄜州
Fu-chü 匐俱
Fu-ma tu-wei 駙馬都尉
Fu-meng Ling-ch'a 夫蒙靈詧
Fu-she Hsiung 伏闍雄
fu shih 副使
Fu-t'u 浮圖

Han-hai 瀚海
Han Ssu-chung 韓思忠
Hei-ch'ih Ch'ang-chih
　黑齒常之
ho ch'in 和親
Ho *chou* 河州
ho hao 和好
Ho-hsi 河西
Ho-k'ou 河口
Ho-sa 和薩
Ho-sa-lao 賀薩勞
Ho-su 曷蘇
Ho-tung 河東
Ho-yüan 河源

hsi 西
Hsi *chou* [Qocho] 西州
Hsi *chou* [near eastern Tibet]
　悉州
Hsi Hai 西海
Hsi-hai chün-wang 西海郡王
Hsi-mo-lang 悉末朗
Hsi-p'ing 西平
Hsi Shou-hsiang *ch'eng*
　西受降城
Hsi yü 西域
Hsia 瑕
Hsia *chou* 夏州
hsiang chü 鄉聚
hsiao ch'i 小妻
Hsiao Chiung 蕭炅
Hsiao Ssu-yeh 蕭嗣業
Hsiao Sung 蕭嵩
Hsiao-Yüeh-chih 小月氏
Hsieh-chi-li-fu 頡吉里匐
Hsieh Jen-kuei 薛仁貴
Hsieh-li-fa 頡利發
Hsien 獻
Hsien-ch'ing 顯慶
Hsien-o *tao* 仙萼道
Hsin 昕
Hsin-an 信安
Hsin-t'u Ho 信圖河
Hsing-hsi-wang 興昔亡
Hsiung-nu 匈奴
Hsüan-tsung 玄宗
Hsüan-wei 宣威
Hu 胡
Hu-k'an 鑊侃

Hu-lu 胡祿

Hu-lu-wu 胡祿屋

Hu-lu-wu ch'üeh *ch'o*
　胡祿屋闕啜

Hu-mi 護蜜

Hu-se-lo 斛瑟羅

hu shih 互市

Huai-tao 懷道

Huai-te chün-wang 懷德郡王

Huang-fu Wei-ming 皇甫惟明

Huang-ti 黃帝

Hui Ch'ao 慧超

Hui *chou* 會州

Hui-ho 回紇

Hun 渾

Hung-chi 洪濟

Hung-yüan 洪源

Huo-shao *ch'eng* 火燒城

i 夷

I-chien 曳建

I *chou* 伊州

I-hai *tao* 颶海道

I-lin 宜林

Jui-tsung 睿宗

Kai Chia-yün 蓋嘉運

K'ai-yüan 開遠

Kan *chou* 甘州

K'an 瞰

Kao-ch'ang 高昌

Kao Hsien 高賢

Kao Hsien-chih 高仙芝

Kao-tsung 高宗

K'ao-i 考異

Ko-lo-feng 閤羅鳳

Ko-lo-lu 葛邏祿

Ko-shu ch'u-pan *i-chin*
　哥舒處半俟斤

Ko-shu ch'üeh *i-chin*
　哥舒闕俟斤

K'o-p'i-shih 訶吡施

K'o-po 渴波

K'o-sai *ch'eng* 渴塞城

k'o-tun 可敦

k'ou 寇

Ku-ch'o 骨啜

K'u Shan 庫山

Kua *chou* 瓜州

Kuan-lung 關隴

Kuan-nei 關內

Kuan-tung 關東

Kuei-ch'uan 貴川

Kuei-i *chün* 歸義軍

K'un-ling 崑陵

Kung-jen 弓仁

Kung-yüeh 弓月

K'ung-je 恐熱

Kuo Ch'ien-kuan 郭虔瓘

Kuo Chih-yün 郭知運

Kuo Tai-feng 郭待封

Kuo Yüan-chen 郭元振

K'uo *chou* 廓州

Lan *chou* 蘭州

lang 郎

Leng-ch'üan 冷泉

li 里

Li Che-fu 李遮匐

Li Ching 李靖

Li Ching-hsüan 李敬玄

Li Mi 李密

Li Ssu-yeh 李嗣業

Li Te-yü 李德裕

Li Wei 李禕

Li Yu 李祐

Liang *chou* 涼州

Liang-fei Ch'uan 良非川

Lien-yün 連雲

Lin *chou* 麟州

Lin-t'ao 臨洮

Ling *chou* 靈州

Ling-wu 靈武

Liu Huan 劉渙

Liu I-ts'ung 劉易從

Liu Ku 柳谷

Liu Shen-li 劉審禮

Lo Chen-t'an 羅真檀

lo-t'o 駱駝

Lou Shih-te 婁師德

lu 虜

Lu Chih 陸贄

Lu Shui 瀘水

lun 論

Lun Yen 論巖

Lung-chih 龍支

Lung-hsi 隴西

Lung-yu 隴右

Lü Hsiu-ching 呂休璟

Ma-lai-hsi 馬來兮

Ma-wei 馬嵬

Mang-je 莽熱

Mang-lo-lin-chen 莽羅藺真

Mang-pu-chih 莽布支

Mao *chou* 茂州

Meng-ch'ih 濛池

Mi-she 彌射

Min *chou* 岷州

Ming-hsi-lieh 名悉獵

Ming-huang 明皇

Mo 末

Mo-chi-lien 默棘連

Mo-chin-mang 沒謹忙

Mo-ch'o 默啜

Mo-chü 默矩

Mo-ho ta-kan 莫賀達干

Mo-lu 沒盧

Mo-ssu 沒斯

Mu-jung No-ho-po 慕容諾賀鉢

Na-tu-liu 訥都六

Na-tu-ni-li 那都泥利

Nan-chao 南詔

Nan-ni 難泥

Nan Shan 南山

Nan T'ien-chu 南天竺

nang-ku 囊骨

Ni-nieh-shih 泥涅師

Ni-shu 泥孰

Ning *chou* 寧州

Niu Hsien-k'o 牛仙客

Niu Shih-chiang 牛師獎

Nu-la 奴剌

Nu-shih-pi 弩失畢

Nung-li 農力

Pa-sai-kan tun sha-po[-lo] *i-chin*
拔塞幹暾沙鉢[羅]俟斤
Pa-ti-she 跛地設
Pai *chou* 白州
Pai-ku 百谷
Pai-shih Ling 白石嶺
Pai-ts'ao 白草
P'an-tu-ni-li 般都泥利
Pao-i 保義
Pao-wang 寶王
Pei-t'ing 北庭
P'ei Chü 裴矩
P'ei Hsing-chien 裴行儉
pen chi 本紀
pi ching 比境
Pi-pi 婢婢
P'i-sha 毗沙
P'i-t'i 鸊鵜
Pien Ling-ch'eng 邊令誠
Pin *chou* 邠州
Pin-wang 賓王
P'ing-hsi *chün* 平西軍
P'ing-liang 平涼
*P'ing-lu chieh tu tu chih ping ma
    shih* 平盧節度都知兵馬使
Po Chü-i 白居易
Po-huan [Aksu] 撥換
Po-lan 白蘭
Po-lu 薄露
Po-lü [Balur] 勃律
Po-ta 勃達
Po-t'e-mo 勃特沒

P'o-le 婆勒
p'o-lo 頗羅
pu [division] 部
Pu-chen 步真
pu chih shu 不知書
Pu-li 步利
pu shih tzu 不識字
P'u-ku 僕骨
P'u-ku Chün 僕固俊
P'u-lo 僕羅
P'u-sa-lao 菩薩勞

Sa-p'i 薩毗
Sha *chou* 沙州
Sha-t'o 沙陀
Shan-ch'eng *hsien* 鄯城縣
Shan *chou* 鄯州
Shan-yü 單于
Shang Chieh-hsin 尚結心
Shang-mi 商彌
Shang shu 上書
Shang Yen-hsin 尚延心
Shang-yüan 上元
she 設
She-she-t'i tun *ch'o* 攝舍提暾啜
Shen-lung 神龍
Shen-ts'e 神策
Shen-wei [Army] 神威
Shen-wu 神武
shih 氏
Shih-chih-han 施質汗
shih li 市里
shih lu 實錄
Shih-ni 識匿

Shih-pao 石堡
Shou-ch'ang 壽昌
shou cho 守捉
Shou-hsiang 受降
Shou shih 守使
Shu 蜀
Shu-ni-shih 鼠尼施
Shu-ni-shih ch'u-pan *ch'o*
　　鼠尼施處半啜
Shu-tun 樹敦
Shun-kuo *kung* 順國公
Shuo-fang 朔方
So-i 娑夷
So-ko 娑葛
So-le 娑勒
So-le-se-ho 娑勒色訶
Ssu chen tu chih ping ma shih
　　四鎮都知兵馬使
Ssu-chieh 思結
Ssu ma 司馬
Su-chia 素迦
Su *chou* 肅州
Su-fu 素福
Su-fu-she-li-chih-li-ni
　　蘇弗舍利支離尼
Su Hai-cheng 蘇海政
Su-ho-kuei 素和貴
Su-lo-han 素羅汗
Su-lu 蘇祿
Su-p'i 蘇毗
Su-pien 肅邊
Su-shih-li-chih 蘇失利之
Su Ting-fang 蘇定方
Su-tsung 肅宗

Sui *chou* 巂州
Sun Jen-shih 孫仁師
Sung 宋
Sung *chou* 松州

Ta-fei Ch'uan 大非川
Ta-fei Shan 大非山
Ta-hsing 大興
Ta-hua *hsien* 達化縣
Ta-ling 大嶺
Ta-mo-men 大莫門
Ta-shih Ku 大石谷
Ta-tou Ku 大斗谷
Ta-tou-pa Ku 大斗拔谷
Ta-t'ou 達頭
Ta-tu 大渡
Ta-t'ung 大同
Ta-yeh 大業
Ta-Yüeh-chih 大月氏
Tai-tsung 代宗
T'ai-ho 太和
T'ai-tsung 太宗
Tang-hsiang 黨項
T'ang Chia-hui 湯嘉惠
T'ang Hsiu-ching 唐休璟
T'ang-mao 唐旄
Tao-chen 道真
Tao-tsung 道宗
T'ao *chou* 洮州
T'ao Ho 洮河
T'ao Shui 洮水
Te-tsung 德宗
T'e-le-man 特勒滿
ti 帝

ti kuo li 敵國禮

Tiao-k'o 雕窠

Tiao-lu 調露

T'ieh-jen 鐵刃

T'ieh-le 鐵勒

T'ien-ch'eng 天成

T'ien-chu 天竺

T'ien Jen-hsien 田仁獻

T'ien Jen-wan 田仁琬

T'ien tzu chia ch'en 天子家臣

T'ien Yüan-hsien 田元獻

Ting-jung 定戎

To-lu 咄陸

To-lu K'o-han Ni-shu
    咄陸可汗泥孰

T'o-hsi 拓西

T'o-pa Huai-kuang 拓跋懷光

Tsan-hsin-ya 贊心牙

Tsan-p'o 贊婆

Ts'ao Chi-shu 曹繼叔

tsu mu k'o-tun 祖母可敦

Ts'ui Chih-pien 崔知辯

Ts'ui Hsi-i 崔希逸

Tsung Ch'u-k'o 宗楚客

tsung kuan 總管

Tsung-o 宗俄

Tsung-wang 賓王

Ts'ung-ling 蔥嶺

Tu-chih 都支

Tu Fu 杜甫

Tu Hsi-wang 杜希望

Tu Hsien 杜暹

tu hu fu 都護府

Tu Huan 杜環

Tu-lu 都陸

Tu-man 都曼

Tu-mo-chih 都摩支

Tu-mo-tu 都摩度

Tu Shan 獨山

Tu-tan 都擔

tu tu fu 都督府

T'u-ch'i-shih ho-lo-shih *ch'o*
    突騎施賀邏施啜

T'u-chüeh 突厥

T'u-fan 吐蕃

T'u-fan t'ien tzu 吐蕃天子

T'u-hun 吐渾

T'u-huo-hsien 吐火仙

T'u-yü-hun 吐谷渾

Tuan Chih-hsüan 段志玄

Tuan Hsiu-shih 段秀實

T'ui-hun 退渾

T'ui-tzu 俀子

T'ung-o 同俄

Wan-t'ou *ch'eng* 曼頭城

wang 王

Wang Cheng-chien 王正見

Wang Ch'ui 王倕

Wang Chün-ch'o 王君㚟

Wang Chung-ssu 王忠嗣

Wang Fang-i 王方翼

Wang Hsiao-chieh 王孝傑

Wang Hsüan-ts'e 王玄策

Wang Hu-ssu 王斛斯

wang nien 往年

Wang Yü 王昱

wei jung 威戎

Wei-jung 威戎

Wei Kao 韋臯

Wei Tai-chia 韋待價

Wei-yüan 渭源

Wen-ch'eng 文成

Wo-se-te 握瑟德

Wu Chao 武曌

Wu-chih-le 烏質勒

Wu Hai 烏海

Wu-k'ung 悟空

Wu-lan 烏蘭

Wu-lun-yang-kuo 兀論樣郭

Wu-su-wan-lo-shan 烏蘇萬洛扇

Wu Tse-t'ien 武則天

Wu-wei 武威

Wu-wei *chün* 武威郡

Yang Hsi-ku 楊襲古

Yang Kuei-fei 楊貴妃

Yang Kuo-chung 楊國忠

Yang-ti 煬帝

Yang-t'ung 羊同

Yeh-chih A-pu-ssu 葉支阿布思

Yeh-to 孼多

yen 眼

Yen-ch'i 焉耆

Yen *chou* 鹽州

Yen-ch'üan 鹽泉

Yen-jan 燕然

Yen-mien 咽麪

Yen Wen-ku 閻溫古

Yin-chih-chia 寅識迦

Yin *chou* 銀州

Ying-lung 應龍

Yu-i 遊奕

Yü-ch'ih Sheng 尉遲勝

Yü-ch'ih T'iao 尉遲眺

Yü-hai 漁海

Yü-men 玉門

Yü-shu 于術

Yüan-ch'ing 元慶

Yüan *chou* 原州

Yüan-en 遠恩

BIBLIOGRAPHICAL ESSAY

The history of Central Asia is of fundamental importance for an understanding of Eurasian history. The region that linked the great civilizations of the Old World and that was the focus of political, military, and economic activity for all bordering states during the Early Middle Ages—when the shape of the early modern world was determined—is of the greatest relevance to the histories (even in the narrow nationalistic sense) of China, the Middle East, and Europe. This must have been the view of an earlier generation of Orientalists, among the greatest of whom were F. W. K. Müller, Édouard Chavannes, W. Barthold, and Paul Pelliot. The works of that generation remain the standard references for nonspecialists and, in many cases, for specialists as well on selected topics of Central Asian studies. This generation of scholars produced no synoptic history of the Tibetan Empire in Central Asia, but it would not be an exaggeration to say that the received opinion on this subject was largely formulated during those early days of Central Asian studies. It is, then, necessary to briefly examine the development of the current image of imperial Tibet, an image much revised in this book, and to comment on the primary

241

sources, which reveal the early medieval writers' conception of that image.

With the exception of a few pioneering studies largely devoted to the translation of important Chinese or Tibetan sources, the historiography of the Tibetan Empire has been until recently a matter marginal to the historiography of neighboring lands. But the publication of the first book-length study in the field, the two volumes in Japanese by Hisashi Satô,[1] marked the beginning of a boom in ground-breaking research on the history of the early Tibetan state. Soon after, articles by Géza Uray on various problems of Old Tibetan historiography began to appear, and several handbooks and historical surveys devoted considerable space to treatment of the imperial period. In 1979, a brief, preliminary survey by the present writer and a paper by Géza Uray appeared.[2] In the following year, Jih-ming Chang's dissertation in French was published, although it has unfortunately remained unknown to historians of Tibet.[3] Finally, in 1984, Takao Moriyasu published his superb study, in which he discusses most of the major philological problems of the central period of the Tibetan Empire.[4] None of these studies, however, was intended to be a synthetic, narrative history of the Tibetan Empire (or of the various empires of the day, including the Tibetan) in Central Asia. It is hoped that the present work remedies this deficiency.[5]

Unfortunately, as a result of contemporary historians' increasing preoccupation with "national" history—instead of the "international" history that attracted their predecessors—the record of Tibetan involvement in Central Asia during the Early Middle

[1] Satô, 1958-1959.
[2] Beckwith, "The Tibetan Empire in the West" (1980); Uray, 1979a.
[3] Chang, 1980.
[4] Moriyasu, 1984.
[5] In this connection, the remark of Paul Pelliot may be recalled: "Il faut espérer qu'un jour prochain quelqu'un reprendra en un examen d'ensemble tous les textes d'origine tibétaine ou chinoise que permettent de reconstituer l'histoire brillante, mais éphémère, de l'ancien empire tibétain." (Pelliot, 1915:26.) I do not pretend to claim that this book is the long-delayed fulfillment of the great Pelliot's wish, but I hope that it will serve until such a work can be written.

Ages is seemingly only of marginal interest to specialists in medieval Inner Asia. With few exceptions, Sinologists, for example, are now simply uninterested in the history of medieval international relations, if they are even aware of its existence. The same may be said of Arabists. Even Tibetologists are no longer as involved in the field of Old Tibetan studies. This has mainly been due to the availability of a vast corpus of Classical Tibetan material which refugees have brought out of Tibet since 1950. In the case of overall Tibetan studies, this development has not been undesirable. But research on the Tibetan Empire in general and on the Tibetan colonial enterprise in particular has not made as much progress in the past thirty years as has general Tibetan history. In addition, what has been done—above all, the superb scholarship of Géza Uray—has not drawn the attention of historians of neighboring lands that it would have in the past. As a consequence, recent writers on Central Asia seem to be less aware of Tibetan activity there than were those who wrote during the early part of this century. Despite the coverage of recent events in Afghanistan, Central Asian history as a whole is not currently a flourishing field.

Strangely enough, probably the greatest attention paid to the Tibetans in early medieval Central Asia is in the work of Sinologically trained Turkologists who deal with the period. The most important single work on the history of the Turks in Central Asia, in fact, was written by the Sinologist Chavannes and published in 1903. This work remains the fundamental study of T'ang Chinese sources not only on the Turks, but also on many other peoples of Central and Inner Asia, including the Tibetans. Chavannes's perception of the revolutionary effects on Eurasia of the establishment of the Western Turkic empire in Central Asia, together with his extensive coverage of the Chinese source material available to him, constitute a remarkable monument of Orientalist scholarship. James Hamilton's fairly recent study of the Uyghurs is another work—perhaps the most important since Chavannes—in which the Tibetans are discussed to some extent.[6]

---

[6] Hamilton, 1955.

This work seems to have set off an explosion of Uyghurological studies, which have been published fairly constantly ever since. Among these is the useful book by Colin Mackerras,[7] which provides a general translation of some of the Chinese material available on the Uyghur Turks in Mongolia. Most recently, the studies of Takao Moriyasu have provided a much-needed critical reexamination of problems in the history of the Uyghurs and Tibetans during this period. In addition to the Uyghur specialists, the articles of I. Ecsedy on the Uyghur-Tibetan conflict and on the Qarluqs have drawn attention to previously neglected subjects. Sinologists specializing in the T'ang period could have been expected to be interested (as were the T'ang Chinese themselves) in the history of contemporary Tibet, but this has not been the case. There are, however, several important studies of Chinese sources on general Tibetan history of the period. Among these are the translations by S. Bushell,[8] P. Pelliot,[9] H. Satô,[10] and P. Takla[11] of the chapters on Tibet in the two *T'ang shu* and the excellent study by Paul Demiéville[12] on the so-called debates between the Chinese and Indian schools of Buddhism in Tibet.[13] But much more needs to be done, especially on the Tibetan occupation of most of western China in the eighth and ninth centuries, a subject which this book does not cover in detail.

Although Sinologists never seem to have been terribly interested in the fortunes of the T'ang Chinese in Central Asia, the exploits of the early Arabs in that part of the world have long fascinated Arabists. The first important work on the subject was Hamilton Gibb's famous short book, which was published in

---

[7] Mackerras, 1972.

[8] S. W. Bushell's translation appeared in the *Journal of the Royal Asiatic Society*, new ser., 12 (1880) 435-541, but has remained inaccessible to me.

[9] Pelliot, 1961.

[10] Satô, "Toban den" (1973).

[11] P. Takla, *Rgya'i yig-tshaṅ naṅ gsalba'i Bodkyi rgyal-rabs gsalba'i meloṅ* (1973). This is an abridged translation.

[12] Demiéville, 1952.

[13] On this subject, see the important article by Yoshiro Imaeda, "Documents tibétains de Touen-houang concernant le concile du Tibet" (1975).

1923.[14] This pioneering treatise brought much attention to bear on early medieval Islam in Central Asia, but it did so largely as the result of the controversial thesis to which it was directed. Gibb's theory supposed that the Hâsimiyya revolt of 747, which ended in the overthrow of the Umayyad dynasty and the establishment of the Abbasids in 749, was rooted in a pan-Iranian nationalism that arose in the face of foreign invaders, the Arabs. Despite periodic pronouncements that it has been settled, this thesis is still rather hotly debated. At the end of this work, Gibb states that the Abbasid revolt, the terminus of his account, led ultimately to the restoration of "Iranian" independence.

Gibb's student, M. A. Shaban, has respectfully and extensively quoted and cited his teacher in his first and most important work,[15] which deals with the background of the Abbasid revolt in Central Asia. His conclusions, however, are markedly different. Shaban argues that economic factors were responsible for what was primarily an Arab revolt against Arab rulers. The book's most important contributions, usually overlooked by its many critics, are the introduction of primary source material not used by Gibb and the provision of source citations (generally absent in Gibb's work). Among recent studies, the one attempt at a synoptic account, including information from a wide variety of sources, is Elton Daniel's book on the Abbasids in Khurasan.[16] Unfortunately for the purposes of this book, Daniel applies an ahistorical definition to the term Khurasan, which during the early medieval period referred to all Arab possessions east of the Great Iranian Desert. He also edited out at least one reference to Tibet in his account.[17] It is long past time for an Islamicist to rewrite the history of the Arab conquests in Central Asia, and of Arab relations with non-Arabs there, from an internationalist's point of view.

Regarding Central Asia itself, unfortunately almost nothing has been done with the native sources and with the results of ar-

[14] Gibb, 1923.
[15] Shaban, 1970.
[16] Daniel, 1979.
[17] Ibid., p. 174.

chaeological exploration since the early part of this century. That work, while still valuable, could certainly be greatly improved upon and expanded. Despite the existence of general surveys and of articles and books on specialized subjects relating to the region, there is still not one synoptic account of Sogdiana,[18] of Ṭukhâristân, or any of the other early medieval lands of Central Aisa. Perhaps Soviet scholars, who have published valuable archaeological studies in this field, will begin to remedy this deficiency for western Central Asia.

There are numerous works of a more general nature dealing with Central Asia or Inner Asia as a whole. Although only a few are based on primary sources, they are often valuable for their conceptualizations (whether correct or not) that, in any case, bring attention to Central Asian history. Foremost among such works, and the only one to be demonstrably based on primary sources, is Barthold's famous book on western Central Asia down to the Mongol conquest.[19] Nothing has yet been written to replace it. For eastern Central Asia, the brief survey by W. Samolin[20] provides what is essentially a summary of previous scholarship supplemented by a few source references. For the early medieval period, it is no longer useful. The often-quoted work of the popular historian R. Grousset,[21] who depended totally on secondary sources, is to a large extent irrelevant to the present subject. L. Kwanten's recent book,[22] which was apparently intended as a scholarly updating of Grousset, is instead also based completely on secondary sources, but is far more inaccurate than Grousset. The mystical theories Kwanten has developed on the supposed existence of a continuous Inner Asian "historiographical tradition" among such nomadic peoples as the Huns,

[18] Among the several useful recent books on aspects of the history of Sogdiana and other areas of Central Asia, one may note in particular G. Azarpay, *Sogdian Painting* (1981), and B. Litvinsky, *Adžina-Tepa* (1971).

[19] Barthold, 1958.

[20] W. Samolin, *East Turkistan to the Twelfth Century* (1964).

[21] R. Grousset, *The Empire of the Steppes* (1970).

[22] L. Kwanten, *Imperial Nomads* (1979). Cf. the incisive comments in C. Hung, "China and the Nomads: Misconceptions in Western Historiography on Inner Asia" (1981) 600.

Turks, and Mongols are not based on any known sources and must be rejected as pure speculation.[23]

The famous work of Owen Lattimore on the Inner Asian nations in relationship to China[24] and the equally well-known work of Wittfogel and Fêng[25] on the impact of Inner Asian conquerors on later medieval China are so full of theories that it would take another book to discuss even a few of them. It must be pointed out, however, that the one theory directly relevant to this book, Lattimore's explanation for Tibetan imperial expansion,[26] is not based on primary sources and should be viewed with more than a little skepticism. Suffice it to say that these authors were primarily preoccupied with Inner Asia's relationship to China, not with the history of Central Asia and its relations with neighboring countries, only one of which was China.

Finally, there are several general works on the history of the foreign powers that were involved in early medieval Central Asia; these often include valuable discussion of our subject. Most important among these are the encyclopedic works, especially the *Encyclopaedia of Islam* (both editions), which is unparalleled in early medieval Asian studies. Also of fairly high quality are the *Cambridge History of Iran* and the *Cambridge History of China*. The one complete survey history of Tibet, by W. D. Shakabpa,[27] although excellent for recent Tibetan history, is not sufficiently informed on the imperial period. In a popular work coauthored with D. Snellgrove,[28] Hugh Richardson gives a fair account of early Tibetan history, but the book is now useful largely for its excellent photographs of imperial-period monuments located within Tibet. Other Tibetological handbooks and historical treatises, such as those by L. Petech,[29] G. Tucci,[30] E. Haarh,[31] and

---

[23] Kwanten, 1979:4 et seq.
[24] O. Lattimore, *Inner Asian Frontiers of China* (1940).
[25] K. Wittfogel and C. Fêng, *History of Chinese Society* (1949).
[26] Lattimore, 1940:209 et seq.
[27] Shakabpa, 1967.
[28] Snellgrove and Richardson, 1968.
[29] L. Petech, *A Study on Chronicles of Ladakh* (1939).
[30] G. Tucci, *Tibetan Painted Scrolls* (1949).
[31] E. Haarh, *The Yar-luṅ Dynasty* (1969).

H. Hoffmann,[32] although useful contributions in one way or another, are only marginally concerned with the Tibetan colonial
empire. An exception to this is the handbook by R. A. Stein[33]
which notes the importance of the Tibetan colonial enterprise for
the development of Tibetan civilization.

As discussed at length in the Epilogue, the modern academic
view of imperial Tibet is essentially a clone of the modern academic view of early medieval Western Europe. Despite many dis-
claimers, generally to the effect that modern medievalists are interested in the Middle Ages for what it was and have no negative
opinions about its civilization, the image of the "Dark Ages" lives
on in the groves of academe, casting its shadow over the historiography of lands as distant as Tibet. This bias is particularly evident in the works of the older generation of Tibetologists of both
East and West.[34] Ignoring for a moment the extremely powerful
influence of modern political and radical prejudices, one should
note the continuing distortion of perspective experienced by
most individuals who have taken it upon themselves to write anything about Tibet for any reason. It is probably no exaggeration
to say that all of the general books (and most of the specialized
books) about Tibet assume, and stress constantly throughout,
that the country and its people were and are abnormal. Biases unfortunately die hard, and, along with many other misleading foreign ideas about Tibet, they may outlive their modern perpetua-
tors. In any case, it is obvious that much of the current output of
books on Tibet—scholarly and otherwise—is feeding upon itself.
Few writers bother to glance at the vast amount of primary
source material available today.

The early medieval world held quite a different view of Tibet
from that held today. Although none of the Arabic or Chinese,
sources that mention Tibet describe it as a paradise, it cannot be
denied that nearly everything they do say is positive. The Chinese,

[32] Hoffmann, 1975.
[33] R. Stein, *Tibetan Civilization* (1972).
[34] See the Epilogue.

for instance, constantly remark on the evil habits of various foreign peoples—and, sometimes, of their own people as well. But such remarks are almost never made about the Tibetans, who were acknowledged to be China's most powerful rival and were usually at war with the T'ang. The products of Tibet—especially marvellous things, often mechanical, made of metal (most memorably, of solid gold)—were considered so wondrous as to deserve public display in the imperial palace. The Arabs also had a high opinion of Tibetan craft, sometimes extolling the same things as the Chinese. Throughout the classical period of Islamic civilization, for example, the expression "bucklers of Tibet" was a byword for both excellent armor and a distinctive round design. Due to its high quality and worldwide demand, the musk of Tibet was universally considered one of the most valuable items in existence. And of course one can not forget the flattering picture of Tibetan culture painted by the Arabs in their famous account of the inexplicable joy experienced by visitors to Tibet. Such is the rather different view of the Tibetan Empire that one finds in contemporaneous sources.

The most important of these sources are, due to the vicissitudes of history, not in Tibetan but in Chinese. Nevertheless, the recently discovered Old Tibetan sources are of immense importance for Tibetan history as a whole and the imperial period in particular. It would not be possible, for example, to determine the correct names of many of the key actors in Tibetan history without these sources, and many important events would remain unknown. By far the most valuable of these sources for the history of the Tibetan colonial empire is the text from Tun-huang now known as the *Old Tibetan Annals*.[35] Although it is generally considered to have been an official compilation, and unpleasant events seem to have been played down or omitted (as in the Old Tibetan inscriptions), its chronology is fairly accurate. It has been the main Tibetan source used in the writing of this book, but it unfortunately breaks off about the year 765. Another Old Tibetan work from Tun-huang, the so-called *Old Tibetan Chroni-*

[35] Reproduced in *CDT*. See the Preface.

cle,[36] is a literary narrative covering the same period; it often supplements the material in the *Annals*. A geographical text from Tun-huang contains a small amount of historical information along with extremely important geographical data on early medieval Inner Asia.[37] Despite their great value for economic, institutional, intellectual, and other approaches to Tibetan and Central Asian history, other Old Tibetan documents, of which precious few have yet been studied, are unfortunately of little use for the present work. The Classical Tibetan histories are, with few exceptions, generally unreliable for the early medieval period. Outstanding among the exceptions is the *Mkhaspa'i dgáston* ("Festival of the Learned"), a brilliant historical work by Gtsuglag 'phreṅba (the second Dpábo incarnation of Gnas-naṅ) which makes an occasional and very general reference to Tibetan political successes in Central Asia. These are so vague, however, that they were of little use in the preparation of the present book.

Arabic sources for the history of the Tibetan Empire are few, widely scattered, and even more difficult to interpret than the Old Tibetan ones. They have been studied, although not too carefully, by many famous scholars, almost all of whom were ignorant of Tibetan. The single most important source is the great history of Ṭabarî, *Ta'rîkh al-rusul wa al-mulûk* ("History of the Prophets and the Kings"), the index references to which Barthold briefly examined in his *Encyclopaedia of Islam* article on Tibet. The well-known reliability of Ṭabarî's work, which is mostly a compendium of often conflicting narrative accounts, is somewhat offset by his extreme conservatism, so that he probably omitted much relating to Tibet and other foreign nations. The histories of

---

[36] Reproduced in *CDT*. See the Preface. I have retained the paragraph divisions of the manuscript in its present state, as used by Bacot. It is important to realize, however, that the manuscript consists of pieces that were wrongly attached long ago, as has been pointed out by several scholars. These problems are discussed in detail in *CDT*.

[37] Pelliot tibétain 1283, reproduced in *CDT*. For the most recent study of this important document and for a bibliography of earlier studies on it, see Moriyasu, "La Nouvelle interprétation des mots *Hor* et *Ho-Yo-Hor*" (1980), and his more detailed study in Japanese (1977a).

Ibn A'tham al-Kûfî, Balâdhurî, and Ya'qûbî, three near-con-
temporaries of Ṭabarî, are valuable for their more coherent nar-
ratives, which include much material absent from Ṭabarî's compilation. Azraqî's *Akhbâr Makka* ("Account of Mecca") contains
additional valuable information. These historical works are the
main Arabic sources for this book. Unfortunately, although the
medieval Arabic geographies include much that is interesting and
useful for relatively early Tibetan history, their early medieval
dating is unreliable and they have little which is relevant to the Tibetan Empire's political history. Almost all of these early geographical works are now available in critical editions with indices,
and most have been translated into French or another Western
European language.[38] Arabic compendia, such as the works of
Yâqût, Qazwînî, and others, have much of interest to say about
Tibet, but they are all much later in date and do not contain reliable information on the history of the Tibetan Empire.

Despite their relative paucity, unequal coverage, and often
fragmentary condition, the Old Turkic primary sources—all epigraphical—are of unusual importance.[39] They are the only surviving records of an Inner Asian steppe people of the early medieval period. Speaking with their own voices, in their own
language and script, the Turkic texts are sometimes nearly as
moving as the poetry of *Beowulf.* Beside their cultural importance, the Old Turkic inscriptions[40] provide precise information
about important historical characters and events in Central Asia.
The scholarship on these inscriptions is still rather uneven, and
clear rubbings or photographs are quite unobtainable, but the

[38] For the most recent study of this material, see my paper, "The Location
and Population of Tibet According to Early Islamic Sources," to appear in
the proceedings of the Csoma de Kőrös Memorial Symposium held in Visegrád, Hungary in 1984.

[39] It seems fairly clear that the Turkic manuscripts and inscriptions in
Sogdian ("Uyghur") script were all (or nearly all) written after the destruction of the Uyghur Empire in Mongolia in 840. Although some speak of
events which might be datable to the Early Middle Ages, it is practically impossible to prove such dates, let alone to test the documents' reliability.

[40] These include the "Uyghur" Turkic inscriptions of this period, which
were Old Turkic runic inscriptions produced under Uyghur rule.

most important of them are by now well-enough edited that they can be used fairly readily.

Without doubt, the Classical Chinese sources are the most extensive and detailed body of material relating to the subject of this book. The epigraphical materials seem of little importance for the history of Central Asia, and there are no manuscript narrative histories from the period. But several great traditional compilations have survived, and these constitute the most important body of source material for the history of early medieval Central and Inner Asia. Foremost among these sources is the chronicle by Ssu-ma Kuang called the *Tzu chih t'ung chien* ("Comprehensive Mirror for Aid in Governing"). Written when the primary sources of two of the other major chronicles of the period were still available, this work reflects Ssu-ma Kuang's ability to make historiographical judgments on the wisdom of his predecessors' decisions. More importantly, he was able to include much that had been omitted by previous Chinese historians, in particular material on Central Eurasia. As many modern historians have noted, his work forms the necessary starting point for any investigation of the T'ang period.

Also of great importance are the two official dynastic histories of the T'ang, the Five Dynasties period *Chiu T'ang shu* ("Old T'ang History") and the Sung period *Hsin T'ang shu* ("New T'ang History"). These are particularly valuable for their specialized treatment of various foreign nations and their biographies of famous people of the day. The treatises on foreign nations have, however, been greatly overrated as sources for Central Eurasian history, especially in comparison to materials that can be found elsewhere. These chronicles were written with a particular didactic point in mind, and their contents were often selected in what today seems a rather peculiar manner. There are, in addition, numerous other Chinese sources which contain materials used in the preparation of this book.[41]

---

[41] Of particular importance is the Sung encyclopedia, *Ts'e fu yüan kuei*, a huge work which contains some material not in the other sources and variant versions of much that is. Unfortunately, this work is cursed with an unusually large number of serious textual errors, to the point where its reliability

The only contemporaneous literary sources from Central Asia itself are several religious histories, *ex eventu* prophecies, and similar texts, all related to Khotan. These sources survived by being translated into Old Tibetan—one of them subsequently into Chinese—and preserved in either the Tibetan Tanjur or the Tunhuang literary cache or both. Some pioneering work has been done on these texts, but most need critical editions, and all deserve a much more thorough examination. Despite their great intrinsic value, their usefulness for this book has proved to be rather limited.

There are of course many other types of sources beside literary histories for early medieval Central Asian history. Among them are, most importantly, the large number of religious texts that contain evidence bearing on certain historical problems. There is some numismatic evidence, but it has received little attention. Since I lack the technical expertise in numismatics necessary to investigate such evidence properly, and since numismatics bears only indirectly on the political history I deal with in this book, I have regrettably had to ignore the numismatic evidence. The archaeological evidence, which might well prove a treasure trove for historians of Central Asia, is practically nonexistent. Work on this has barely begun. In most areas, the knowledge of city plans and the location and construction of major fortresses is a goal for the future.[42]

The political history of the Tibetan Empire in Central Asia should be read with the understanding that the view of history presented in the sources, and thus what can be reconstructed at

must often be seriously questioned. The confidence many scholars place in it is unfounded. Among other sources, potentially the most useful are the little-studied collections of official documents written by various T'ang officials. Preserved at the time for their literary merit, several—particularly those of Chang Chiu-ling, Lu Chih, Po Chü-i, and Li Te-yü—contain a vast amount of information on Inner Asian history. They deserve to be thoroughly investigated by students of China and Inner Asia.

[42] A beginning has been made in the archaeological study of western Central Asia, particularly the area of Khwârizm. For an excellent survey of the results, see A. Belenitskiy, *Srednevekovïy gorod sredney azii* (1973).

the present, is radically different from the view of a twentieth-century observer from the West. The interest of the chroniclers, whether governmental functionaries or monks, was above all in the morality of powerful individuals, the emperors and kings and leaders of the day. Thus it is no wonder that the pages of early medieval chronicles are full of gruesome events amid ostentatiously pious deeds. Modern readers (and writers) are often justifiably frustrated by the gaps that seem to appear just where information is most needed. It may be suggested that one way to understand the Early Middle Ages would be to try to follow the interests of those early medieval men who wrote, whatever their supposed limitations. Political disorder, violence, war—none of these have ever been the monopoly of a single age. Nor have they ever totally dominated one. But if any epoch of world history comes to mind when comparisons with the Early Middle Ages are made, none would be more apt than our own. Perhaps in the sometimes heroic, oftentimes tragic history of early medieval Central Asia there are lessons for leaders of the present day.

BIBLIOGRAPHY

Classical and Medieval Sources

Azraqî, Abû al-Walîd Muḥammad b. ʿAbd Allâh al-. *Akhbâr Makka.* Mecca, 1965.

Balâdhurî, Abû al-ʿAbbâs Aḥmad b. Yaḥyá b. Ǧâbir al-. *Kitâb futûḥ al-buldân.* Leiden, 1866; repr. Leiden, 1968.

Chang Chiu-ling. *Ch'ü chiang Chang hsien sheng wen chi.* 4 vols. [Ssu-pu ts'ung-k'an, chi-pu, Vols. 616-623.] Shanghai, n.d. [*WC*]

Ch'in ting ch'üan T'ang wen. 21 vols. Kyoto, 1976. [*CTW*]

Dhahabî, Muḥammad b. Aḥmad al-. *Ta'rîkh al-Islâm wa ṭabaqât al-maśâhir wa al-aʿlâm.* Cairo, 1947–.

Dpábo Gtsug-lag ʿphreṅba. *Chos-byuṅ Mkhaspaʿi dgáston.* 2 vols. Delhi, n.d. [1980]. [*MD*]

Fan Yeh. *Hou Han shu chu.* 5 vols. Peking, 1965; repr. Taipei, 1973. [*HHS*]

Hsüan Tsang. *Ta T'ang hsi yü chi.* In *Taishô,* Vol. 51 (No. 2087) 867-947. [*TTHYC*]

Hui Ch'ao. *Wang wu T'ien-chu kuo chuan.* In *Taishô,* Vol. 51 (No. 2089), 975-979. [*WWTCKC*]

255

Ibn al-Athîr, 'Izz al-Dîn Abû al-Ḥasan 'Alî. *Al-kâmil fî al-ta'rîkh*. 13 vols. Beirut, 1965-1967.

Ibn A'tham al-Kûfî, Abû Muḥammad Aḥmad. *Kitâb al-futûḥ*. 8 vols. Hyderabad, 1968-1975.

Ibn Khurdâdhbih, 'Ubayd Allâh b. 'Abd Allâh. *Kitâb al-masâlik wa al-mamâlik*. Leiden, 1889; repr. Leiden, 1967.

Li Chi-fu. *Yüan ho chün hsien t'u chih*. Taipei, 1973; repr. Taipei, 1979. [*YHCHTC*]

Li Tsung-t'ung, ed. *Ch'un ch'iu tso chuan chin chu chin i*. 3 vols. Taipei, 1971. [*CCTC*]

Li Yen-shou. *Pei shih*. 10 vols. Peking, 1974. [*PS*]

Ling-hu Te-fen. *Chou shu*. 3 vols. Peking, 1971; repr. Taipei, 1974. [*CS*]

Liu Hsü. *Chiu T'ang shu*. 16 vols. Peking, 1975. [*CTS*]

Müllerus, Carolus, ed. *Fragmenta Historicorum Graecorum*. Vol. 4. Paris, 1868. [*FHG*]

Ptolemaios, Klaudios. *Geographie 6, 9-12: Ostiran und Zentralasien*. Part 1. Ed. and trans. Italo Ronca. Rome, 1971.

Saṁghavardhana, *Dgra bcompa Dge'dun 'phelgyi luṅ-bstanpa*. In Daisetz T. Suzuki, ed. *The Tibetan Tripitaka: Peking Edition*. Vol. 129 (Tokyo, 1957), 296b-299e [Bstan-hgyur mdo-hgrel skyes-rabs II gtam-yig ṅe: 435r-444r.]

Spanien, Ariane and Yoshiro Imaeda, eds. *Choix de documents Tibétains*. Vol. 2. Paris, 1979. [*CDT*]

Ssu-ma Kuang. *Tzu chih t'ung chien*. 10 vols. Peking, 1956; repr. Taipei, 1979. [*TCTC*]

Sung Ch'i and Ou-yang Hsiu. *Hsin T'ang shu*. 20 vols. Peking, 1975. [*HTS*]

Ṭabarî, Abû Ǵa'far Muḥammad b. Ǵarîr al-. *Ta'rîkh al-rusul wa al-mulûk*. 15 vols. Leiden, 1879-1901; repr. Leiden, 1964-1965.

Tha'âlibî, 'Abd al-Malik b. Muhammad al-. *Thimâr al-qulûb*. Cairo, 1965.

Tu Fu. *Tu Kung-pu shih chi*. 2 vols. Taipei, 1966. [*TKPSC*]

Tu Yu. *T'ung tien*. Shanghai, 1935. [*TT*]

Wang Ch'in-jo. *Ts'e fu yüan kuei*. 20 vols. Hong Kong, 1960. [*TFYK*]

Wei Cheng. *Sui shu*. 3 vols. Peking, 1973; repr. Taipei, 1974. [*SS*]

Ya'qûbî, Aḥmad b. Abî Ya'qûb al-. *Ta'rîkh al-Ya'qûbî*. 2 vols. Beirut, 1960.

Yüan Chao. *Wu K'ung ju Chu chi*. In *Taishô*, Vol. 51 (No. 2089) 979-981. [*WKJCC*]

Journals and Collective Publications

Acta Orientalia Academiae Scientiarum Hungaricae. [*AOH*]

American Historical Review. [*AHR*]

Archivum Eurasiae Medii Aevi. [*AEMA*]

Aris, Michael, and Aung San Suu Kyi, eds. *Tibetan Studies in Honour of Hugh Richardson*. Warminster, 1980. [*TSHHR*]

Braunfels, Wolfgang, ed. *Karl der Grosse: Lebenswerk und Nachleben*. 5 vols. Düsseldorf, 1965-1968. [*KDG*]

Bulletin of the School of Oriental (and African) Studies. [*BSO(A)S*]

The Cambridge History of China. Vol. 3. Cambridge, 1979; repr. Taipei, 1979. [*CHC*]

The Cambridge History of Iran. Vol. 4. Cambridge, 1975. [*CHI*]

Chung-kuo ku chin ti-ming ta tz'u-tien. Shanghai, 1930; repr. Taipei, 1979. [*CKKCTMTTT*]

East and West. [*EW*]

Encyclopaedia of Islam. 1st ed. Leiden, 1913-1934. [*E.I.1*]

Encyclopaedia of Islam. 2d ed. Leiden, 1960–. [*E.I.2*]

Journal Asiatique. [*JA*]

Journal of the American Oriental Society. [*JAOS*]

Journal of the Economic and Social History of the Orient. [*JESHO*]

Sitzungsberichte der Preussischen Akademie der Wissenschaften. Philologisch-historische Klasse. [*SPAW*]

Taishô shinshû daizôkyô. 85 vols. Tokyo, 1924-1932; repr. Tokyo, 1960-1978. [*Taishô*]

T'oung Pao. [*TP*]

Tôyô Gakuhô. [*TG*]

Wiener Studien zur Tibetologie und Buddhismuskunde. Nos. 10-11. [Ernst Steinkellner and Helmut Tauscher, eds. *Proceedings of the Csoma de Kőrös Symposium Held at Velm-Vienna, Austria, 13-19 September 1981*. Vols. 1-2.] Vienna, 1983. [*WSTB*]

Zeitschrift der Deutschen Morgenländischen Gesellschaft. [*ZDMG*]

Zentralasiatische Studien. [*ZAS*]

Secondary Studies

Ashtor, E. *A Social and Economic History of the Near East in the Middle Ages*. Berkeley, 1976.

Azarpay, Guitty. *Sogdian Painting: The Pictorial Epic in Oriental Art*. Berkeley, 1981.

Bachrach, Bernard. *Early Medieval Jewish Policy in Western Europe.* Minneapolis, 1977.

Backus, Charles. *The Nan-chao Kingdom and T'ang China's Southwestern Frontier.* Cambridge, 1981.

Bacot, Jacques. "Reconnaissance en haute Asie septentrionale par cinq envoyés ouigours au VIIIᵉ siècle." *Manuscrits de Haute Asie conservés à la Bibliothèque Nationale de Paris (Fonds Pelliot)*, Vol. 4. Paris, 1957.

Bacot, Jacques et al. *Documents de Touen-houang relatifs à l'histoire du Tibet.* Paris, 1940.

Bark, William C. *Origins of the Medieval World.* New York, 1960.

Barthold, W. "Tibet." *E.I.1,* 1:741-743.

———. *Turkestan down to the Mongol Invasion.* 2d ed., London, 1958.

Beckwith, Christopher I. "Aspects of the Early History of the Central Asian Guard Corps in Islam." *AEMA,* 4 (1984a) 29-43.

———. "The Introduction of Greek Medicine into Tibet in the Seventh and Eighth Centuries." *JAOS,* 99 (1979) 279-313.

———. "The Location and Population of Tibet According to Early Islamic Sources." Paper presented at the Csoma de Kőrös Symposium held at Visegrád, Hungary in 1984. Forthcoming in *AOH.*

———. "The Plan of the City of Peace: Central Asian Iranian Factors in Early ʿAbbâsid Design." *AOH,* 38 (1984b) 143-164.

———. "The Revolt of 755 in Tibet." *WSTB,* 10 (1983) 1-16.

———. "A Study of the Early Medieval Chinese, Latin, and Tibetan Historical Sources on Pre-Imperial Tibet." Ph.D. Dissertation, Indiana University, 1977.

———. "Tibet and the Early Medieval *Florissance* in Eurasia: A Preliminary Note on the Economic History of the Tibetan Empire." *Central Asiatic Journal,* 21 (1977b) 89-104.

———. "The Tibetan Empire in the West." *TSHHR:*30-38.

Belenitskiy, A. M. et al. *Srednevekovïy gorod sredney azii.* Leningrad, 1973.

Blachère, Régis et al., eds. *Dictionnaire Arabe-Français-Anglais (Langue classique et moderne).* Paris, 1967–.

Bosworth, C. E. *The Book of Curious and Entertaining Information: The "Laṭāʾif al-maʿārif" of Thaʿālibī.* Edinburgh, 1968.

———. *The Islamic Dynasties.* Edinburgh, 1967.

Chang, Jih-ming. *Les Musulmans sous la Chine des Tang (618-905).* Taipei, 1980.

Chao, Lin. *Yin hua lu.* Shanghai, 1958.

Chavannes, Édouard. "Chinese Documents from the Sites of Dandan-Uiliq, Niya and Endere." In M. Aurel Stein, *Ancient Khotan: Detailed Report of Archaeological Explorations in Chinese Turkestan*. 2 vols. (Oxford, 1907) 1:521-547.

──────. *Documents sur les Tou-kiue (Turcs) occidentaux*. St. Petersburg, 1903; repr. Taipei, 1969.

──────. "Notes additionnelles sur les Tou-kiue (Turcs) occidentaux." *TP*, 2d ser., 5 (1904) 1-110.

Chavannes, Édouard, and Paul Pelliot. "Un Traité manichéen retrouvé en Chine." *JA*, 11th ser., 1 (1913) 99-199, 261-394.

Ch'en, Yüan. *Chung hsi hui shih jih li*. 2d ed., Taipei, 1972.

Combe, É. et al. *Répertoire chronologique d'épigraphie arabe*. Vol. 1. Cairo, 1931.

Conrady, August. *Eine indo-chinesische Causativ-Denominativ-Bildung und ihr Zusammenhang mit den Tonaccenten*. Leipzig, 1896.

Čuguevskiĭ, L. I. "Touen-houang du VIIIᵉ au Xᵉ siècle." In Michel Soymié, ed. *Nouvelles contributions aux études de Touen-houang* (Geneva, 1981) 1-56.

Czeglédy, K. "Gardizi on the History of Central Asia (746-780 A.D.)." *AOH*, 27 (1973) 257-267.

Daniel, Elton L. *The Political and Social History of Khurasan under Abbasid Rule*. Minneapolis, 1979.

Déer, Josef. "Karl der Grosse und der Untergang des Awarenreiches." *KDG*, 1:719-791.

Demiéville, Paul. *Le Concile de Lhasa: Une controverse sur le quiétisme entre bouddhistes de l'Inde et de la Chine au VIIIᵉ siècle de l'ère chrétienne*. Paris, 1952.

Des Rotours, Robert. *Histoire de Ngan Lou-chan*. Paris, 1962.

──────. *Traité des fonctionnaires et traité de l'armé*. 2 vols. Leiden, 1948; repr. San Francisco, 1974.

Dopsch, Alfons. *The Economic and Social Foundations of European Civilization*. New York, 1937; repr. New York, 1969.

Drompp, Michael. "The Writings of Li Te-yü as Sources for the History of T'ang–Inner Asian Relations." Ph.D. Dissertation, Indiana University, 1986.

Dunlop, D. M. "Arab Relations with Tibet in the 8th and Early 9th Centuries A.D." *Islâm Tetkikleri Enstitüsü Dergisi*, Vol. 5 (1973) 301-318.

──────. "A New Source of Information on the Battle of Talas or Aṭlakh." *Ural-Altaische Jahrbücher*, 36 (1964) 326-330.

Ecsedy, Ildikó. "A Contribution to the History of Karluks in the T'ang Period." *AOH*, 34 (1980) 23-37.

———. "Uigurs and Tibetans in Pei-t'ing (790-791 A.D.)." *AOH*, 17 (1964) 83-104.

Eitel, Ernest J. *Handbook of Chinese Buddhism*. 2d ed., Tokyo, 1904; repr. Amsterdam, 1970.

Emmerick, R. E. *Tibetan Texts Concerning Khotan*. London, 1967.

Enoki, K. "Appendix I" *EW*, 27 (1977) 86-91.

Esin, Emel. "Tarkhan Nīzak or Tarkhan Tirek? An Enquiry Concerning the Prince of Bādhghīs Who in A.H. 91/A.D. 709-710 Opposed the ʿOmayyad Conquest of Central Asia." *JAOS*, 97 (1977) 323-332.

Fuchs, Walter. "Hui-ch'ao's Pilgerreise durch Nordwest-Indien und Zentral-Asien um 726." *SPAW*, 30 (1938) 426-469.

Gibb, H.A.R. *The Arab Conquests in Central Asia*. New York, 1923; repr. New York, 1970.

———. "The Arab Invasion of Kashgar in A.D. 715." *BSO(A)S*, 2 (1921-1923) 467-474.

Gil, Moshe. "The Rādhānite Merchants and the Land of Rādhān." *JESHO*, 17 (1974) 299-328.

Goitein, S. D. *Letters of Medieval Jewish Traders*. Princeton, 1973.

Golden, Peter. "The Migrations of the *Oğuz*." *Archivum Ottomanicum*, 4 (1972) 45-84.

Grierson, Philip. "Commerce in the Dark Ages: A Critique of the Evidence." *Transactions of the Royal Historical Society*, 5th ser. 9 (1959) 123-140.

———. "The Monetary Reforms of ʿAbd al-Malik." *JESHO*, 3 (1960) 241-264.

———. "Money and Coinage under Charlemagne." *KDG*, 1:501-536.

Grousset, René. *The Empire of the Steppes: A History of Central Asia*. New Brunswick, 1970.

Guisso, R. *Wu Tse-t'ien and the Politics of Legitimation in T'ang China*. Bellingham, Wash., 1978.

Haarh, Erik. *The Yar-luṅ Dynasty*. Copenhagen, 1969.

Hamilton, James R. *Les Ouïghours: À l'époque des cinq dynasties, d'après les documents chinois*. Paris, 1955.

———. "Les Règnes khotanais entre 851 et 1001." In Michel Soymié, ed. *Contributions aux études sur Touen-houang* (Geneva, 1979) 49-54.

Haneda, Tôru. *Haneda hakushi shigaku rombun shû*. 2 vols. Kyoto, 1957-1958.

Harmatta, J. "Late Bactrian Inscriptions." *Acta Antiqua Academiae Scientiarum Hungaricae*, 17 (1969) 297-432.

Hinz, W. "Dhirā'." *E.I.2*, 2:231-232.

Hoffmann, Helmut. "Die Gräber der tibetischen Könige im Distrikt 'P'yoṅs-rgyas." *Nachrichten der Akademie der Wissenschaften in Göttingen, Philologisch-historische Klasse* (1950) 1-14.

————. *The Religions of Tibet*. London, 1961.

————. *Tibet: A Handbook*. Bloomington, n.d. [1975].

Hovdhaugen, Even. "Turkish Words in Khotanese Texts. A Linguistic Analysis." *Norsk Tidsskrift for Sprogvidenskap*, 24 (1971) 163-209.

Hugot, Leo. "Die Pfalz Karls des Grossen in Aachen." *KDG*, 3:534-572.

Hung, Chin-fu. "China and the Nomads: Misconceptions in Western Historiography on Inner Asia." *Harvard Journal of Asiatic Studies*, 41 (1981) 597-628.

Imaeda, Yoshiro. "Documents tibétains de Touen-houang concernant le concile du Tibet." *JA*, 263 (1975) 125-146.

Jettmar, Karl. "Bolor—A Contribution to the Political and Ethnic Geography of North Pakistan." *ZAS*, 11 (1977) 411-448.

————. "Bolor—zum Stand des Problems." *ZAS*, 14 (1980) 115-132.

Karlgren, Bernhard. *Grammata Serica Recensa*. Göteborg, 1957.

Karmay, Heather. *Early Sino-Tibetan Art*. Warminster, 1975.

Kinser, Samuel. "*Annaliste* Paradigm? The Geohistorical Structuralism of Fernand Braudel." *AHR*, 86 (1981) 63-105.

Klyashtorny, S. G. "The Terkhin Inscription." *AOH*, 36 (1982) 335-366.

Kolmaš, Josef. "Four Letters of Po Chü-i to the Tibetan Authorities (808-810 A.D.)." *Archiv Orientální*, 34 (1966) 375-410.

Kreusch, Felix. "Kirche, Atrium und Portikus der Aachener Pfalz." *KDG*, 3:463-533.

Kuan, Tung-kuei. "Han-tai ch'u-li Ch'iang-tsu wen-t'i ti pan-fa ti chien-t'ao." *Shih-huo*, 2 (1972) 129-154.

Kwanten, Luc. *Imperial Nomads: A History of Central Asia, 500-1500*. Philadelphia, 1979.

Lalou, Marcelle. *Inventaire des manuscrits tibétains de Touen-houang conservés à la Bibliothèque Nationale (Fonds Pelliot Tibétain) Nᵒˢ 1283-2216*. Vol. 3. Paris, 1961.

Lamotte, Étienne. "Mañjuśrī." *TP*, 48 (1960) 1-96.

Lassner, Jacob. *The Topography of Baghdad in the Early Middle Ages: Text and Studies*. Detroit, 1970.

Lattimore, Owen. *Inner Asian Frontiers of China*. New York, 1940.

Le Strange, Guy. *The Lands of the Eastern Caliphate.* Cambridge, 1905; repr. London, 1966.

Lévi, Sylvain. "Les Missions de Wang Hiuen-ts'e dans l'Inde." *JA,* 9th ser., 15 (1900) 297-341, 401-468.

Lévi, Sylvain, and É. Chavannes. "L'Itinéraire d'Ou-k'ong (751-790)." *JA,* 8th ser., 6 (1895) 341-384.

Lewis, Archibald R. *Naval Power and Trade in the Mediterranean A.D. 500 to 1100.* Princeton, 1951; repr. New York, 1970.

———. *The Northern Seas: Shipping and Commerce in Northern Europe, A.D. 300-1100.* Princeton, 1958.

Li, Fang-kuei. "The Inscription of the Sino-Tibetan Treaty of 821-822." *TP,* 44 (1956) 1-99.

Ligeti, L. "À propos du 'Rapport sur les rois demeurant dans le Nord.' " In *Études Tibétaines, dédiées à la mémoire de Marcelle Lalou* (Paris, 1971) 166-189.

———. "Le Tabghatch, un dialecte de la langue Sien-pi." In L. Ligeti, ed. *Mongolian Studies* (Amsterdam, 1970) 265-308.

Lindner, Rudi. "What Was a Nomadic Tribe?" *Comparative Studies in Society and History,* 24 (1982) 689-711.

Litvinsky, Boris. *Adžina-Tepa: Arkhitektura, živopis', skul'ptura.* Moscow, 1971.

———. "Central Asia." *Encyclopaedia of Buddhism.* Vol. 4. (n.p. [Colombo], 1979) 21-52.

Liu, Mau-ts'ai. *Die chinesischen Nachrichten zur Geschichte der Ost-Türken (T'u-küe).* 2 vols. Wiesbaden, 1958.

Lopez, Robert S. *The Birth of Europe.* New York, 1967.

Lyon, Bryce. *The Origins of the Middle Ages: Pirenne's Challenge to Gibbon.* New York, 1972.

Mackerras, Colin, trans. and ed. *The Uighur Empire according to the T'ang Dynastic Histories: A Study in Sino-Uighur Relations, 744-840.* Columbia, S.C., 1972.

Madelung, Wilferd. "New Documents Concerning al-Ma'mūn, al-Faḍl b. Sahl and ʿAlī al-Riḍā." In Wadād al-Qāḍī, ed. *Studia Arabica et Islamica: Festschrift for Iḥsān ʿAbbās on His Sixtieth Birthday* (Beirut, 1981) 333-346.

Malov, S. E. *Pamyatniki drevnetyurkskoy pis'mennosti mongolii i kirgizii.* Moscow, 1959.

Martinez, A. P. "Gardīzī's Two Chapters on the Turks." *AEMA,* 2 (1982) 109-217.

Miller, Roy Andrew. Review of *Introduction to Sino-Tibetan. Parts 1 and 2*

(Wiesbaden, 1966-1967), by Robert Shafer. *Monumenta Serica*, 27 (1968) 398-435.

Minorsky, V. "Tamīm ibn Baḥr's Journey to the Uyghurs." *BSO(A)S*, 12 (1947-1948) 275-305.

Molè, Gabriella. *The T'u-yü-hun from the Northern Wei to the Time of the Five Dynasties.* Rome, 1970.

Moriyasu, Takao. "Chibetto-go shiryô chû ni arawareru Hoppô min-zoku——Dru-gu to Hor——." *Ajia Afurika Gengo Bunka Kenkyû* [Journal of Asian and African Studies], 14 (1977a) 1-48.

——. "La Nouvelle interprétation des mots Hor et Ho-Yo-Hor dans le manuscrit Pelliot tibétain 1283." *AOH*, 34 (1980) 171-184.

——. "Qui des Ouigours ou des Tibétains ont gagné en 789-792 à Beš-balïq?" *JA*, 269 (1981) 193-205.

——. "Toban no Chûô Ajia shinshutsu." *Kanazawa Daigaku Bunga-kubu Ronshû, Shigakuka-hen*, 4 (1984) 1-85.

——. "Uiguru no seisen ni tsuite." *TG*, 59 (1977b) 105-130.

——. "Uiguru to Toban no Hokutei sôdatsu-sen oyobi sono go no Seiiki jôsei ni tsuite." *TG*, 55 (1973) 466-493.

——. "Zôhô: Uiguru to Toban no Hokutei sôdatsu-sen oyobi sono go no Seiiki jôsei ni tsuite." *Ajia Bunka-shi Ronsô*, 3 (1979) 200-238.

Morohashi, Tetsuji. *Dai Kan-Wa jiten.* 13 vols. Tokyo, 1955-1968.

Müller, F.W.K. *Ein Doppelblatt aus einem manichäischen Hymnenbuch (Maḥrnâmag).* [*Abhandlungen der Preussischen Akademie der Wissen-schaften*, Philologisch-historische Klasse, 1912.] Berlin, 1913.

Nakamura, Hajime. *Bukkyôgo daijiten.* Vol. 2 (1975).

Noonan, T. S. "Did the Khazars Possess a Monetary Economy? An Analysis of the Numismatic Evidence." *AEMA*, 2 (1982) 219-267.

——. "What Does Historical Numismatics Suggest about the History of Khazaria in the Tenth Century?" *AEMA*, 3 (1983) 265-281.

Nyberg, Henrik S. *A Manual of Pahlavi, Part II: Glossary.* Wiesbaden, 1974.

Ostrogorsky, George. *History of the Byzantine State.* New Brunswick, 1957.

Pelliot, Paul. "À propos des Comans." *JA*, 11th ser., 15 (1920) 125-185.

——. "Les Artisans chinois à la capitale abbasside en 751-762." *TP*, 2d ser., 26 (1929) 110-112.

——. *Histoire ancienne du Tibet.* Paris, 1961.

——. "Neuf notes sur des questions d'Asie centrale." *TP*, 2d ser., 26 (1929) 201-266.

Pelliot, Paul. "Note sur les anciens noms de Kučā, d'Aqsu et d'Uč-Turfan." *TP*, 2d ser., 22 (1923) 126-132.

———. *Notes on Marco Polo*. 3 vols. Paris, 1959-1973.

———. "Quelques transcriptions chinoises de noms tibétains." *TP*, 2d ser., 16 (1915) 1-26.

———. "La Théorie des quatre fils du ciel." *TP*, 2d ser., 22 (1923) 97-125.

———. "La Ville de Bakhouân dans la géographie d'Idrîçî." *TP*, 2d ser., 7 (1906) 553-556.

Pelliot, Paul, and Tôru Haneda. *Manuscrits de Touen-houang*. Vol. 1 Kyoto, 1926.

Petech, Luciano. "Glosse agli *Annali* di Tun-huang." *Rivista degli studi orientali*, 42 (1967) 241-279.

———. *A Study on the Chronicles of Ladakh*. Calcutta, 1939.

Pirenne, Henri. *Medieval Cities: Their Origins and the Revival of Trade*. Princeton, 1925; repr. New York, 1956.

———. *Mohammed and Charlemagne*. London, 1939; repr. London, 1954.

Popper, Karl. *Conjectures and Refutations: The Growth of Scientific Knowledge*. New York, 1962; repr. New York, 1965.

Poucha, P. *Thesaurus Linguae Tocharicae Dialecti A*. Prague, 1955.

Pritsak, Omeljan. "Von den Karluk zu den Karachaniden." *ZDMG*, 101 (1951) 270-300.

Richardson, Hugh E. "Ming-si-lie and the Fish-Bag." *Bulletin of Tibetology*, 7 (1970) 5-6.

———. "The Sino-Tibetan Treaty Inscription of A.D. 821/823 at Lhasa." *Journal of the Royal Asiatic Society* (1978) 137-162.

Riché, Pierre. *Les Écoles et l'enseignement dans l'Occident chrétien de la fin du Ve siècle au milieu du XIe siècle*. Paris, 1979.

Rosenthal, Franz. *A History of Muslim Historiography*. 2d ed., Leiden, 1968.

Rossabi, Morris, ed. *China among Equals*. Berkeley, 1983.

Samolin, W. *East Turkistan to the Twelfth Century: A Brief Political Survey*. The Hague, 1964.

Satô, Hisashi. *Chibetto rekishi chiri kenkyû*. Tokyo, 1978.

———. *Kodai Chibetto shi kenkyû*. 2 vols. Kyoto, 1958-1959.

———. "Toban den." In Akira Haneda, et al. *Kiba Minzoku shi*. Vol. 3 (Tokyo, 1973) 103-291.

Schafer, Edward H. *The Golden Peaches of Samarkand*. Berkeley, 1963; repr. Berkeley, 1981.

Scholz, Bernhard W., trans. *Carolingian Chronicles*. Ann Arbor, 1970.

Sezgin, Fuat. *Geschichte des arabischen Schrifttums*. Leiden, 1967–.

Shaban, M. A. *The ʿAbbāsid Revolution*. Cambridge, 1970.

———. *Islamic History: A New Interpretation*. 2 vols. Cambridge, 1971, 1976.

Shakabpa, W. D. *Tibet: A Political History*. New Haven, 1967.

Shirakawa, Shizuka. *Kōkotsubun no seikai*. Tokyo, 1972.

Sinor, Denis. *Inner Asia: History, Civilization, Languages*. 2d ed., Bloomington, 1971.

———. "The Legendary Origin of the Türks." In E. V. Žygas and P. Voorheis, eds. *Folklorica: Festschrift for Felix J. Oinas* (Bloomington, 1982) 223 257.

Snellgrove, D., and H. Richardson. *A Cultural History of Tibet*. New York, 1968.

Sourdel, Dominique. *Le Vizirat ʿAbbāside, de 749 à 936 (132 à 324 de l'Hégire)*. 2 vols. Damascus, 1959-1960.

Sperling, Elliot. "A Captivity in Ninth Century Tibet." *The Tibet Journal*, 4 (1979) 17-67.

Stein, R. A. *Tibetan Civilization*. Stanford, 1972.

Su, Chin-jen, and Lien-tzu Hsiao. *"Ts'e fu yüan kuei" T'u-fan shih liao chiao cheng*. Chengtu, 1982.

Sullivan, Richard. *Aix-la-Chapelle in the Age of Charlemagne*. Norman, 1963.

Suzuki, Chusei. "China's Relations with Inner Asia: The Hsiung-nu and Tibet." In John K. Fairbank, ed. *The Chinese World Order: Traditional China's Foreign Relations* (Cambridge, Mass., 1968) 180-197.

Szerb, János. "A Note on the Tibetan-Uigur Treaty of 822/823 A.D." *WSTB*, 10 (1983) 375-387.

Takla, P. T. *Rgyaʿi.yig-tshan nan gsalbaʿi Bodkyi rgyal-rabs gsalbaʿi melon*. Dharamsala, 1973.

Tekin, Talat. *A Grammar of Orkhon Turkic*. Bloomington, 1968.

———. "The Tariat (Terkhin) Inscription." *AOH*, 37 (1983) 43-68.

Thomas, Werner. *Tocharisches Elementarbuch*. Vol. 2. Heidelberg, 1964.

Thorpe, Lewis, trans. *Gregory of Tours: The History of the Franks*. Harmondsworth, 1974; repr. Harmondsworth, 1977.

Tôdô, Akiyasu. *Gakken Kan-Wa daijiten*. Tokyo, 1978.

Ts'en, Chung-mien. *Hsi T'u-chüeh shih liao pu ch'üeh chi k'ao cheng*. Peking, 1958a; repr. Kyoto, 1972.

———. *T'u-chüeh chi shih*. Peking, 1958b.

Tucci, Giuseppe. "La regalità sacra nell'antico Tibet." In *The Sacral Kingship* (Leiden, 1959) 189-203.

———. "On Swat, the Dards and Connected Problems." *EW*, 27 (1977) 9-85.

———. *Tibetan Painted Scrolls*. 3 vols. Rome, 1949.

———. *The Tombs of the Tibetan Kings*. Rome, 1950.

Turtledove, Harry, trans. *The Chronicle of Theophanes*. Philadelphia, 1982.

Twitchett, D. *Financial Administration under the T'ang Dynasty*. 2d ed., Cambridge, 1970.

Ullmann, Walter. *The Carolingian Renaissance and the Idea of Kingship*. London, 1969.

Uray, Géza. "The Annals of the ʿA-ža Principality: The Problems of Chronology and Genre of the Stein Document, Tun-huang, Vol. 69, fol. 84." In L. Ligeti, ed. *Proceedings of the Csoma de Kőrös Memorial Symposium, Held at Mátrafüred, Hungary 24-30 September 1976* (Budapest, 1978) 541-578.

———. "Einige Probleme der tibetischen Herrschaft über das Lop-Nor-Gebiet im 7.-9. Jh." Paper read at the Csoma de Kőrös Symposium in Csopak, Hungary on September 24, 1979. [1979a]

———. "The Four Horns of Tibet. According to the Royal Annals." *AOH*, 10 (1960) 31-57.

———. "*Khrom*: Administrative Units of the Tibetan Empire in the 7th-9th Centuries." *TSHHR*: 310-318.

———. "The Narrative of Legislation and Organization of the Mkhas-pa'i dga'-ston." *AOH*, 26 (1972) 11-68.

———. "Notes on a Tibetan Military Document from Tun-huang." *AOH*, 12 (1961) 223-230.

———. "The Old Tibetan Sources of the History of Central Asia up to 751 A.D.: A Survey." In J. Harmatta, ed., *Prolegomena to the Sources on the History of Pre-Islamic Central Asia* (Budapest, 1979b) 275-304.

———. "On the Tibetan Letters *Ba* and *Wa*: Contribution to the Origin and History of the Tibetan Alphabet." *AOH*, 5 (1955) 101-121.

———. "Queen Sad-mar-kar's Songs in the Old Tibetan Chronicle." *AOH*, 25 (1972) 5-38.

———. "Tibet's Connections with Nestorianism and Manicheism in the 8th-10th Centuries." *WSTB*, 10 (1983) 399-429.

Wallace-Hadrill, J. M. *The Barbarian West, 400-1100*. 3d. ed., London, 1967; repr. London, 1969.

————, trans. *The Fourth Book of the Chronicle of Fredegar, with Its Continuations*. Edinburgh, 1960.

————. "Frankish Gaul." In J. M. Wallace-Hadrill and J. M. Manners, eds. *France: Government and Society. An Historical Survey.* (2d ed., London, 1970) 36-60.

Watson, Burton. *Records of the Grand Historian of China, Translated from the Shih Chi of Ssu-ma Ch'ien*, 2 vols. New York, 1961.

Wechsler, Howard J. *Mirror to the Son of Heaven: Wei Cheng at the Court of T'ang T'ai-tsung*. New Haven, 1974.

White, Lynn, Jr. *Medieval Technology and Social Change*. Oxford, 1962; repr. London, 1976.

————. "Tibet, India and Malaya as Sources of Western Mediaeval Technology." *AHR*, 54 (1960) 515-526.

Wittfogel, Karl A., and Chia-Shêng Fêng. *History of Chinese Society: Liao (907-1125)*. [*Transactions of the American Philosophical Society*, new ser., 36 (1946).] Philadelphia, 1949.

Wright, Arthur E. *The Sui Dynasty*. New York, 1978; repr. Taipei, 1980.

————. "The Sui Dynasty (581-617)." *CHC*, 3:48-149.

Wylie, Turrell V. *The Geography of Tibet According to the 'Dzam-gling-rgyas-bshad*. Rome, 1962.

Zürcher, Erik. *The Buddhist Conquest of China*. 2 vols. Leiden, 1972.

INDEX